W9-CIM-840

Teaching Young Children to Read

Dolores Durkin
UNIVERSITY OF ILLINOIS

Teaching Young Children to Read

ALLYN AND BACON, INC., BOSTON

470 Atlantic Avenue, Boston, Mass. 02210

Library of Congress Catalog Card Number: 71–169521

Printed in the United States of America

Third printing . . . July, 1973

To the memory of my father

Contents

Preface

At one time, school instruction in reading for children younger than six was unheard of—or, if the possibility was mentioned, responses were anything but supportive. In recent years, however, it has become a fairly widespread practice. Now, for instance, kindergarten reading is common. Even directors of nursery schools and day care centers are beginning to wonder if their children might be ready to start.

Why earlier reading has become a reality can be explained by reasons that are both sound and questionable. The thesis of this book is that it *is* a reality and because it is, educators must be concerned about ways to teach reading which are suitable for younger children. The underlying philosophy thus moves away from the position that *no* child should be taught to read before first grade, but it departs equally fast from those who seem to feel that earlier instruction requires no new thoughts about methods and materials.

Essentially, then, this book has been written for those who work with beginners in reading. More specifically, its purpose is to help nursery school, kindergarten, and first grade teachers provide instruction that is both appropriate and productive. Because it dwells on interesting, highly personal ways to teach reading, its many suggestions for both methodology and materials should also have relevance for those whose responsibility is slightly older children who, because they have experienced failure, are badly in need of more interesting opportunities to be successful. The repeated attention given to the basic importance of spoken language should also make its content relevant for those whose primary concern is to help children become more proficient in that.

In writing the various chapters, I kept several audiences in mind. Aware that those preparing to teach have difficulty visualizing instruction, I have included countless numbers of illustrations taken directly from classrooms. Coupled with those are descriptions of sample lessons and homemade materials. Reproductions of commercially available materials are included, too. Sometimes, dialogues between teacher and children are presented.

Experienced teachers were not forgotten. For example, nursery school and kindergarten teachers who believe that traditional programs no longer are suitable will find a great deal of help for transforming traditional activities into opportunities for teaching reading. On the other hand, those who fear that the national move toward earlier instruction will lead to unfortunate pressures will be relieved to find that I share their concern. In fact, this is why I have given a large amount of space to descriptions of instruction that will neither frustrate the slow child nor bore the bright one.

To be sure that the bright ones are taught as much as they can comfortably learn, the content of this book covers much more material than will ever be taught even to the most advanced first grader. This is to insure that first grade teachers are ready to teach all that can be learned by the most able of children. In addition, the "extra" is included to make sure that teachers of the young have a broad picture of where their children have been and where they are going insofar as reading ability is concerned.

Providing perspective also is the reason for some historical material in two of the chapters. One gives a brief history of the nursery school and kindergarten in America; the other outlines how the reading readiness concept has been shaped and altered over a period of several decades. I believe such material to be important because, as has been said many times before, those who do not know the past are bound to repeat its errors.

One final word. While both experienced and inexperienced teachers have been kept in mind as the various chapters were prepared, the children themselves were never forgotten. How to take advantage of their great interest in themselves, how to turn practice into game-like activities —these are some of the topics that get attention because the children were not left out. Hopefully, at least bits and pieces of this book will help their teachers turn learning to read into a successful but also enjoyable venture. That is why it was written.

DOLORES DURKIN

I

Background Information

1

Introduction

Age, as the passing years teach us all, is a relative thing. Consequently a book entitled, *Teaching Young Children to Read,* has an immediate obligation to define "young." In this and the following chapters it refers to children in nursery schools, kindergartens, and first grades.

This combined grouping is not meant to suggest that two years make no difference in the abilities and behavior of a child. Obviously they do. Rather, the combination seems justified because nursery school, kindergarten, and first grade classes all have some children who are ready to learn to read. Because this book deals with beginning instruction, it thus pertains to and includes all three groups. Because of its focus, it should also be helpful to those who work with children having problems with reading since they, very often, require beginning instruction, too.

While the content of this book does have special relevance for nursery school, kindergarten, and first grade, it is not an identical kind. The meaning the various chapters will have for first grade teachers, for instance, is different from the contributions they might make to a kindergarten or nursery school teacher's program. The difference could be accounted for in a variety of ways, but one of the more encompassing explanations is that our society *expects* all first graders to be reading. Because of this expectation, a first grade teacher is not likely to begin a new school year wondering, "Will I be teaching any of these children to read?" Instead, her thoughts are more apt to be, "I hope I'll do a good job teaching reading this year, even with the children for whom learning to read turns out to be a difficult task."

In contrast with this posture, kindergarten teachers and those who teach nursery school are more likely to start a year thinking, "I wonder whether any of these children are or will be ready for some reading this year." As was pointed out earlier, the assumption of this book is that some of these younger children will be ready. As will be pointed out later, another assumption is that whether or not they will be ready is partially dependent upon a teacher's program. But, this latter assumption will be made clearer in subsequent chapters.

Meanwhile, it can be predicted that at least a few of you are already objecting to the contention that kindergarteners and even some children of nursery school age are ready for reading. In addition, others of you might have recently visited kindergarten classrooms or perhaps nursery schools that have become cluttered with workbooks and noisy with drill; and so you are objecting also and even in a mood to do away with all reading instruction for all children until they are at least in first grade. Actually, the two reasons for my wanting to write this book deal with both of these reactions, so let me discuss them now.

REASONS FOR THIS BOOK

For over ten years I have been doing a series of studies concerned with the focus of this book: young children and reading. The initial research studied preschoolers who learned to read at home (1). Exactly how they learned was examined through home interviews. Later, how their reading ability compared with that of classmates who did not begin early was analyzed through annual testing done over a six-year period. From the first set of data I found that young children can become readers in ways that are playful and interesting for them. From the second set it was shown that, as a group, the early readers maintained their lead over classmates who did not begin to read until the first grade.

Combined, both sets of data led to another study: The development and evaluation of a pre-first grade curriculum based on what had been learned about the ways children can begin to read at home (2). Because the age of four was the most common time for the preschoolers to display interest in reading, the school program began with a group of four year olds and continued with them for two years.

Once again, results of the research demonstrated that children younger than six—and they need not be especially bright—can learn to read in ways that are devoid of pressure and full of interest. These findings, coupled with those from the earlier studies of home readers, became one reason for wanting to write a book that would help teachers of young children introduce them to reading in ways that would be productive, but also of interest.

And then another motivating factor developed. This was the awareness that a growing number of kindergartens—for both good and questionable reasons—were beginning to teach reading using procedures that did not seem to take into account the age of the children, the possibility that not all five year olds are ready for reading, or the strong likelihood that not all have yet developed an interest in it. The result for these kindergartens is a preponderance of whole class instruction depending mostly on basal readers, workbooks, and drill, with little or no attention being given to the obvious fact of great differences among any group of five year olds. Another end result, therefore, is still another reason for wanting to write a book that will help teachers provide interesting and appropriate opportunities for young children to learn to read, if and when they are ready.

CONTENT OF THE BOOK

Just as the motivation for writing this book derived from a variety of sources, so too has its content. Admittedly, one of the sources for the latter is this writer's opinions. Because decisions about reading instruction at all grade levels still depend more on opinion than carefully documented research findings, an apology for this particular source does not seem warranted. Nonetheless, opinions have obvious shortcomings.

Another of the sources contributing to the content is my research. In fact, it has been the richest source of help. In this case it has not just been the studies. They, to be sure, were fruitful; but, in addition to their own contributions, they have also resulted in a rich variety of contacts with teachers, children, administrators, and parents. Not all these groups were directly connected with the research. All, however, have been effective instructors and, therefore, other sources of help in preparing this book.

Still other kinds of assistance—and I am less consciously aware of their specific influence—came from the usual experiences in the life of a professor: attendance at professional meetings; the reading of books, articles, and reports written by other professors and researchers; contacts with students; and planned and unplanned conversations with colleagues. With these it is probably true to say that some of the most productive sources were the individuals and groups that reacted negatively to my particular opinions and ideas about teaching young children to read. In fact, what can be learned from contrary points of view is what makes them palatable, if not inviting.

ORGANIZATION OF THE BOOK

Generally, the sources that contributed to this book's content also provided guidelines when decisions were made about specific foci for chapters. For example, as I observed pre-first grade children who were learning to read with ease and even enjoyment, I could not help but wonder why the notion that success with beginning reading requires a mental age of about 6.5 years became so entrenched, and for so long, in both our thinking and our educational practices. As I talked to kindergarten teachers and early childhood education specialists and heard them denounce the possibility of introducing reading instruction into the kindergarten curriculum, I could not help but wonder why the function of kindergarten and the function of first grade have been defined so differently over the years and, further, why for so long there has been a separation—even a chasm—between the kindergarten program and the first grade curriculum.

This and other wondering ceased as I began to study the professional literature of the twentieth century that deals with topics like nursery school, kindergarten, and reading readiness. What I learned not only did away with much of my puzzlement, but also impressed me with the importance of knowing about the history and development of an educational idea or practice. That he who does not know the past is bound to repeat its mistakes also became clearly apparent as excesses of earlier decades were compared with the different but equal excesses which are visible now.

It is because of these conclusions about the importance of a historical perspective that this chapter is immediately followed by two others that deal with the development of ideas over time. The content of Chapter 2 is described in its title, "History of Nursery Schools and Kindergartens in America." Some of the purposes of the chapter are to contrast the emergence of nursery schools and kindergartens and to explain why kindergartens—even those that are a part of publicly supported elementary schools—have traditionally had the goal of "social and emotional development"; why there has been a cleavage between the kindergarten and the rest of the elementary school; and why some kindergarten and nursery school teachers now use workbooks and drill in an attempt to make their programs look academically respectable.

The next chapter, "Readiness for Reading," also treats its topic within a historical framework. Essentially the purpose of Chapter 3 is to explain why there have been different answers to the question, "When is a child ready to begin to read?" However, as it develops the explanation it also considers matters like readiness assessment and readiness tests. Concluding that different children are ready for reading at different ages, Chapter 3 then shows with examples how teachers of young children can provide the ready ones with opportunities to begin.

While the content for the next chapter does not depend exclusively on my research with pre-first grade reading ability, the chapter itself, "Language Arts Approach for Beginning Reading," probably would not be singled out in this book were it not for that research.* For example, when I myself was a first grade teacher I taught reading by concentrating on reading. It is likely that an earlier preservice methods course had given some attention to interrelationships among the language arts; nonetheless I believe I was convinced at that time that one taught children to read by concentrating on reading.

Later, when I had the opportunity to study how preschool children can learn to read at home—and here I refer to children who learn because they are interested, not because of pressure from overly eager parents—the interrelationships became clear in a way that no course ever succeeded in explaining. For instance, I learned from the children that beginning reading ability can be the product of an interest in learning to print. Or, to put it differently, some preschoolers in the research began their academic life at home by scribbling. In time this changed to an interest in copying objects and, later, letters of the alphabet. Then, almost inevitably, the child who could form letters was also asking, "Mommy, how do you make my name?" And soon the children who were writing and spelling were also reading. At first they read the few words they themselves could write. Later they were reading what others had written in books and also on highway signs, menus, television commercials, food packages, and so on. As they learned, of course, they were also teaching about a language arts approach for beginning reading, the topic developed in Chapter 4.

Chapter 5, "Behavioral Characteristics of Young Children in Classrooms," also has its roots in my research. In this case the need for educators to take a special look at young children in a school setting became very clear when I was developing the two-year pre-first grade program. As I observed with great frequency in the classrooms of the four and five year olds involved in the project, I noticed that I was always ending up with two quite different conclusions: what a delight to teach young chil-

* The term "language arts" encompasses listening, speaking, reading, and writing.

dren—but how difficult! To maximize the meaning these two persistent conclusions might have for others, in particular those who teach young children, I made copious and detailed notes about the happenings that filled my head with the two conflicting thoughts. These notes, combined with others I took while visiting in other nursery school, kindergarten, and first grade classes, are the basis for Chapter 5. Essentially its message is this: There are characteristics of young children that make it difficult to teach them in a school setting but, too, there are other characteristics that make this assignment one of the most refreshing and rewarding experiences a teacher will ever have.

The next chapter, "Classroom Behavior of Teachers of Young Children," is closely related to Chapter 5. Again, the content is based on what I have observed in classrooms in many different parts of the country where I found teachers whose instruction ranged from what I would call "excellent" to "unbelievably poor." Fortunately, one can learn from both and so descriptions of both are included in Chapter 6. Hopefully its contents will not only help you think about teaching, but also have a positive effect on your own behavior in the classroom.

On the assumption that the first six chapters provide a framework for thinking about teaching, the next four move on to the specifics of instruction in the language arts. The first of these chapters, as it considers, "Extending Listening-Speaking Vocabularies," deals with a major responsibility of those who work with young children. In fact, it focuses on a goal that ought to be at the core of all school programs for these children, whether or not they include reading. As the chapter does this, the guiding assumption is that young children are able to pick up many language skills in a somewhat incidental fashion; but, secondly, that planned instruction for enhancing oral language ability is mandatory.

Chapter 8, "Teaching Writing," also makes several assumptions.* Its inclusion in this book, for instance, is based on the assumption that ability to write can result in ability to read, or, to put it somewhat differently, that ability in writing goes hand in hand with ability in reading. Another and more basic assumption of Chapter 8 is that many children younger than six are ready for writing and, in fact, want to learn if only because they consider this to be a "big kid" skill.

The next two chapters are both concerned with reading per se. Chapter 9 deals with instruction comprised of whole word identification. It thus deals with the kind of help a parent gives by answering "walk," when his young child asks, "What does that word say?" Whether such help merits being called a "method" of teaching is certainly debatable. None-

* In this book "writing" refers to printing or, as it is sometimes called, "manuscript writing." The latter term contrasts with "cursive writing," a skill usually introduced during the second or third grade.

theless, the point of Chapter 9 is that one way to instruct a child is to identify written words for him. Which words should be identified, how should such identification proceed, how can it be made maximally productive—these are some of the practical questions Chapter 9 answers for those of you who are or will be teaching young children in school.

Recognizing that there is neither the time nor the need to identify every word a child will eventually have to read, the next chapter is designed to teach you how to teach phonics viewed as a way of helping children learn to figure out words themselves. Written on the assumption that some of you might also be beginners as far as phonics is concerned, Chapter 10 starts at the beginning. It goes over fundamental terminology, discusses the two major ways to teach the content of phonics, and then shows how both are useful. Because the question, "Are these children ready?" is a common one among teachers of young children, Chapter 10 gives attention to readiness for phonics. This same chapter also deals with structural analysis, of immediate importance because of the immediate need to deal with both singular and plural nouns and the various tenses of verbs.

The next chapter, Chapter 11, attempts to put the pieces together by considering "Language Arts Programs." Following this, the final chapter shifts the focus from the school to the home, and from the child to his parents. Such a shift is natural for a book that is partially based on research findings about children who learned to read at home. But the need for the shift has been made apparent through other sources, too. For example, to work with young children in a school setting and, in addition, to know something about their families, is to become keenly aware that each child is a mirror of life at home. This is not to deny that older children also reflect their home life. Rather, it is to point out that parents exert a unique influence on young children. This makes a chapter about parents of special relevance in a book dealing with the education of children enrolled in nursery school, kindergarten, and first grade.

REFERENCES

1. Durkin, Dolores. *Children Who Read Early.* New York: Teachers College Press, Columbia University, 1966.
2. ———. "A Language Arts Program for Pre-First Grade Children: Two-Year Achievement Report," *Reading Research Quarterly,* V (Summer, 1970), 534–565.

2

History of Nursery Schools and Kindergartens in America

A problem inherent in any discussion of nursery schools and kindergartens is the lack of a single referent for each. What "nursery school" brings to mind, for example, might be five different things for five different people. In doing home interviews for various studies, I also learned that even the act of enrolling a child in nursery school has different meanings in different communities (10). In some, attendance has status value and not to enroll a child is to suggest the possibility of an inadequate family income. In other communities, quite to the contrary, a child's attendance signifies his mother *has* to work and thus needs baby-sitting service. In still other neighborhoods, mothers who enroll their young children in school are viewed as being eager to get rid of them for at least part of each day. And still other mothers make sure their children get to nursery school so that they will be just as ready for kindergarten as are the children of their friends.

But notions about kindergarten vary, too. For instance, if you attended kindergarten as a child but have not visited one since, then for you the term probably elicits recollections of play activities involving blocks, dolls—and, yes, bead stringing. On the other hand, if you have had fairly recent opportunities to observe in many kindergartens, then it is safe to predict that what you saw varied greatly even though each program bore the label "kindergarten." In some communities what you yourself experienced as a child still makes up the program. In others you might have been surprised to find that the kindergarten has changed to a close copy of a highly structured first grade program; and so in these you saw workbooks and basal readers and heard children drill on letter names and even letter sounds.

Some of the reasons why both nursery schools and kindergartens vary can be found in their histories. Consequently, to know those histories is to have a better understanding of current school programs for pre-first grade children.

NURSERY SCHOOLS

Right now I can think quickly of five friends and acquaintances who have children in nursery schools. One of these children attends a school in which the program is comprised of what now seems like a customary combination: free and organized play, storytelling, music, art, and crafts. Another is enrolled in a school that has a similar program, but also the goal of having four year olds available to psychometrists who are revising some tests and constructing others. Consequently the children are tested regularly at two-week intervals. The third child in the group of five attends a school which emphasizes—and advertises—the "academics." In practice this means the children learn to print their names and to know the alphabet. Another of the schools has a different specialty—the "arts." In this case much of each morning is spent on music and art projects. The remaining child goes to school because both parents work. As a result, he is enrolled in a nursery school which opens at seven in the morning and closes at six in the evening. At this particular school, the child has two snacks each day plus lunch—also a morning and afternoon nap. In between the eating and the resting he plays with other children, paints pictures, sings songs, and listens to stories.

Besides knowing about these five nursery schools through the eyes of parents, I have visited others. Because they also show some diversity in matters like goals, programs, and length of day, I find it difficult to respond when someone asks, "What *is* nursery school?"

Diversity has not always been characteristic. In fact, when nursery schools came into existence in this country more than fifty years ago there was great uniformity about them. Because the earliest ones had some connection with what was happening in Europe, a few comments about education on the Continent but especially in England need to be made before the first of the American schools are discussed.

European Provisions for the Young

It seems likely that people have always been concerned about the education of young children. Descriptions of some of the initial European efforts to provide for it characterize them as being dominated by Puritanical doctrines (39). And so, when children were brought together to be taught, it was for moral and religious training. On the assumption that nobody is too little to go to hell, the groups often included quite young children (30).

Under this Puritan influence, there were not only restrictive programs but also very restrictive discipline. Typically there was a reaction, too. In this case the reaction of dissatisfaction, coupled with problems growing out of the Industrial Revolution, led to a new definition of society's obligations toward the young. Essentially it represented a move away from care of the soul to care for the body—and understandably so. Let me explain.

Among the changes in Europe that went along with the Industrial Revolution of the nineteenth century was the creation of many factories. Owners soon learned that women were not only more adept than men at many factory jobs but could also be hired for less money (14, 39). The result? Many working mothers plus many uncared for children who were joined by still more as families began moving from rural areas to urban centers. Such conditions prompted the beginnings of philanthropic involvements with what came to be called "infant schools." Pioneering in a movement that spread throughout Europe was Robert Owen, a Scottish cotton mill owner who, in 1816, started a school for young children whose parents were factory workers. One author has noted that it came at a time when "there was greater interest in child labor than in child education" (6, p. 2).

In planning his school, Owen is said to have believed in "training and education without punishment" and felt that young children "should not be annoyed with books" (14, p. 56). In fact, his intention was simply to provide a substitute for home care. Other individuals working with and in the infant schools had different reasons for "not annoying the children with books." For example, one is supposed to have commented: "I allow for no writing for the poor. My object is not to make fanatics, but to train up the lower classes in habits of industry and obedience" (35, p. 330). Another concern about the children of the poor—and it was they, for the most part, who attended infant schools—was to avoid making them "discontented with their lot" (14, p. 78). Whatever the motivations, infant schools were custodial rather than academic in nature.

According to all accounts of these schools, they also became more and more like the earlier Puritanical classes with their strict discipline and even harsh punishment (39). Predictably there was another reaction. This time—at least in England—it resulted in the establishment of what came to be called "nursery schools." According to one author, the goals of these schools were to improve physical health and to provide a "suitable environment for growing minds" (14). According to another, the major purpose was to "meet the health and special needs of young children in the slums of London" (6).

One leader in the nursery school movement was Margaret McMillan who, in a 1919 publication called *The Nursery School,* described with great detail not only a curriculum but also a program for training teachers (27). Among those trained by Miss McMillan were teachers who later came to America to help educators establish nursery schools here.

Nursery School Movement in America

Although the influence of educators like McMillan was clearly apparent in the development of nursery schools in America, not all their ideas were put into practice. For instance in *The Nursery School,* a book frequently quoted by early twentieth-century American educators, McMillan provided detailed descriptions of how she and her colleagues in England taught young children the alphabet and introduced them to reading and writing. Yet none of these goals or procedures was given much attention as nursery schools began to develop in this country. One reason is that their emergence came at a time when professional education in America was permeated by ideas connected with the Progressive Education Movement. As a result, educators—and certainly educators interested in the young child—tended not to think in terms of academic goals and structured programs. This helps to explain why goals like social and emotional development were both suggested and accepted, and why some of the proposals made by individuals like Margaret McMillan and Maria Montessori were bypassed.

Other factors that explain why the earliest American nursery schools followed nonacademic patterns are rooted in some of the more individual reasons for their coming into existence. Therefore let me mention and describe a few.

Reasons for the Early Nursery Schools

Essentially, the development of nursery schools in America was a phenomenon of the 1920s. However some did exist earlier. In 1916, for instance, faculty wives at the University of Chicago organized the first of the cooperative type in which parents play active roles. As described by its founders, this school was designed to provide "group training" for their children, but also to help them become more knowledgeable parents (14). As one author put it, this was an attempt to make parenthood a profession (6).

Other more organized and widespread attempts to make motherhood a profession were connected with undergraduate college programs. A notable example is the Merrill-Palmer School in Detroit, established under the will of Mrs. Lizzie Merrill Palmer. In part that will read:

> I hold profoundly the conviction that the welfare of any community is divinely, and hence inseparably, dependent upon the quality of its motherhood and the spirit and character of its home, and moved by this conviction, I hereby bequeath the remainder of my Estate for the founding of a school to be known as the Merrill-Palmer Motherhood and Home Training School, at which young women shall be educated and trained with special reference to fitting them for the discharge of the functions and service of wifehood and motherhood (39, p. 193).

Recognizing the importance of practical experience, educators at Merrill-Palmer had opened a nursery school by 1922. Its primary purpose was to give college students the opportunity to learn about children from children. Other nursery schools with the same goal were soon organized on other campuses, most often in connection with Departments of Home Economics at Land Grant Colleges. The first of this type was started at Iowa State College in 1924.

During the same decade, researchers began to see in the nursery school great possibilities for studying children. As a result, classes which eventually became well known as centers of research were established at such places as Yale; Teachers College, Columbia University; and the Universities of Iowa, California, and Minnesota. In these and other institutions, researchers were interested to learn more about the development of children before they entered elementary school. Such an interest fostered the use of "preschool" as a description of the children even though they were, in fact, enrolled in a school. The same interest also gave support to nonstructured, nonacademic programs because researchers wanted to study their subjects in "natural surroundings" (6). In such surroundings, researchers seem to have been especially interested in physical development. This was of concern to professional educators connected with the schools, although they also spoke and frequently wrote about the importance of a child's behavior. As one educator emphasized in a 1926 publication: "The satisfactory social and emotional adjustment of the child is one of the main considerations in the minds of people who are directing the nursery school movement" (14, p. 306).

The Depression and Day Care Nurseries

While educators of the 1920s typically made distinctions between a nursery school and a day care nursery, available descriptions of the two fail to identify essential differences in programs. In fact, on the basis of a variety of written accounts of these earlier times, it seems accurate to say that if the reason for a program was to take care of young children whose parents worked or were simply too poor to provide adequately for their children, it was referred to as "day care" and was often day-long in length. On the other hand, if a program came into existence because of the interests and concerns of well-educated parents, or professional educators, or researchers, it was more likely to be referred to as a "nursery school" (14, 19, 39).

If such a distinction has some validity, then it can be said that while the 1920s saw the emergence of the nursery school, a plentiful supply of day care centers characterized the 1930s. This is not to suggest that custodial care for pre-elementary school children was a new development in the United States at this time. Rather, it is to point out that the decade of the 1930s, with its Great Depression, were years in which day care nurseries became uncommonly numerous.

Why did a Depression lead to the establishment of day care nurseries? One reason was stated very effectively by Gesell when he wrote in a 1924 article that "poverty, ignorance, and neglect press with exceptional weight upon children of preschool age" (16, p. 644). While the poverty of the Depression was one reason why the federal government stepped in and allotted funds for nursery schools during the 1930s, another equally significant reason was its interest in providing employment for the many adults who were now without jobs. This led to the establishment of day care nurseries directed and taught by adults employed under an emergency relief program and, as a consequence, to a staff that was separate from the elementary school structure. Within such a framework, "more than 1,900 emergency nursery schools were reported by the Works Progress Administration in 1934–35, enrolling approximately 75,000 children" (17, p. 45). Apparently by 1942 the federal government judged the great emergency to be over because, in that year, the federally supported programs were ordered closed.

World War II and Day Care Nurseries

Quickly following the crisis of the Depression came another: World War II. In fact it was in 1942, the year schools of the Depression era closed, that a Selective Service Act was passed. Subsequently, because of the need for massive war production, many women took jobs in factories and were even highlighted in a popular song of the times called, "Rosie the Riveter." While Rosie riveted someone had to care for her preschool children. Again the government stepped in, allotting funds once more for day care nurseries.

Like the earlier "emergency" schools, these were custodial in nature. Growing out of troubled times, they were also viewed as opportunities to make a positive contribution to the emotional and social development of the children. The thinking was that because so many had mothers who worked, many were also getting "too little affection, too little mother-child cuddling, too little conversation and play" (25, p. 39). Concern about this resulted in an emphasis on "the importance of doing what the child enjoys most or wants to do," and also on the idea that teachers of young children should assume a mother-like role (25).

Although many of the wartime schools closed in 1946—this was the year the federal government withdrew its financial support—the concepts of programs for young children which they promoted remained. In fact, throughout the 1940s and into the 1950s, nursery schools of all types continued to be characterized by goals like emotional and social maturity, by programs that were play oriented, and by teachers who were viewed more as mothers than instructors.

With the late 1950s came developments which had some effect on conceptions of the nursery school contribution. However, they also had an impact on kindergartens and so will be discussed in connection with them. First, though, it might be helpful to look at the kindergarten in its very beginning years.

THE KINDERGARTEN

The kindergarten is older than the nursery school. In fact, in the preface of a 1907 textbook the author states that kindergarten was then "an accomplished fact in American life and education" (37, p. ix). Usually Elizabeth Peabody of Boston is credited with establishing the first kindergarten in 1860; however, some authors point out that an earlier one was started in 1855 in the home of a Mrs. Carl Schurz of Watertown, Wisconsin (14, 37). Although the exact date of the first kindergarten might be debatable, all descriptions of the kindergarten movement in the United States agree that German immigrants and the philosophy and teachings of Friedrich Froebel were uniquely influential.

Froebel's earlier influence was in Europe. Consequently when well-educated Germans came to America because of the European Revolution of 1848, many brought with them Froebelian notions about education. As they settled in this country—and it was primarily in the larger cities—they not only established their own private German-speaking schools but also included the kindergarten in many of them. Mrs. Schurz, referred to above as the one who opened a kindergarten in her home in 1855, was among the newly-arrived Germans who had studied with Froebel. Although an American, Miss Peabody also had been influenced by Froebelian ideas when she opened her kindergarten in Boston. Earlier, she had learned about Froebel from accounts written by another American educator who had visited in Europe.

Whether first appearing in 1855, or 1860, the kindergarten spread relatively quickly in the United States. Even though in 1870 there were still less than a dozen and all but one had been founded by Germans and, in fact, were conducted in the German language, by 1880 there were about 400 kindergartens located in thirty different states (37).

Various factors account for the rapid growth. Although educators connected with private schools were the first to take an interest in the kindergarten, it was able to win fairly quick support in some public school systems, too. Primarily through the efforts of Susan Blow, the first publicly-supported kindergarten opened in St. Louis as early as 1873. By 1900, public schools were enrolling 131,000 kindergarteners (36).

Educators who were responsible for preparing teachers also showed prompt interest. As a result, a kindergarten training school opened in Boston as early as 1868. Providing considerable impetus, too, was the customary concern for young children of the poor:

> The mere fact that the children of the slums were kept off the streets, and that they were made clean and happy by kind and motherly young women—all this appealed to the heart of America, and America gave freely to make these kindergartens possible. Churches established kindergartens, individuals endowed kindergartens, and associations were organized for the spread and support of kindergartens in nearly every large city (37, pp. 19–20).

The same observer notes that "a new conception of education was necessary before the significance of the kindergarten could be comprehended . . ." (37, p. 9). What this new conception was is to be found in the teachings of Froebel.

Froebelian Teachings

To cite only the teachings of Froebel is to present an incomplete picture of the forces that affected nineteenth-century kindergartens in America. However, since this description is to be brief, giving special attention to Froebel seems justified because his influence was so great in that particular period of time.

To understand why Froebelian teachings were singularly influential, it is necessary to know how most kindergarten educators felt about Froebel himself. This is communicated very effectively in the introduction to one of the chapters in the 1907 Yearbook of the National Society for the Study of Education:

> A man who yields his entire being to his ideals, sacrificing every selfish interest to his spiritual tendencies of loving service for his altruistic ideals, the inspired enthusiast whose every thought and word and deed bears the imprint of his devotion to his mission, is a being whom no one susceptible of great and noble sentiments can approach without admiration and awe. Such a man was Friedrich Froebel (23, p. 32).

The same author also acknowledges that "the difficulty of understanding Froebel's writings in the original is so great that there are few persons who would attempt to interpret his meaning" (23, p. 32).

Among the more obvious meanings is Froebel's reason for calling his program a "kindergarten" (literally, children's garden). Symbolically he wanted to indicate that children are like plants in a garden, and in need of similar care (23). The care prescribed by Froebel grows out of a philosophy that is highly mystical and obscure and also out of a comprehensive theory about education for young children. In practice, part of the care took the form of what Froebel called "gifts" and "occupations." How these relate to his philosophy requires an explanation that would be far longer than the whole of this chapter; therefore let me just describe the referents for these two terms.

Froebel's gifts were what we would call instructional materials. There were thirteen kinds including six worsted balls, each a different color; spheres, cubes, cylinders, and cones; thin wooden tablets that were both square and triangular; sticks; wired rings of three sizes; and thread. Admittedly, naming a few of the gifts does not do justice to the way they fit into Froebel's theories about educating young children. However, even to describe how they were to be used and, secondly, why such use was considered mandatory, again would require a long explanation of a very complicated philosophy.

What was referred to as "occupations" were, in fact, eleven different activities that included "perforating" (pricking cards) and "sewing out" (following forms on a card with thread). Some others were mat weaving, drawing, coloring and painting, and paper folding and cutting. Such familiar terms as these latter ones might lead you to envision a classroom in which quite ordinary and informal activities were going on; consequently what must be added to these descriptions is the reminder that, like the gifts, Froebel's occupations were to be used in highly prescribed ways with little freedom in what was used, how it was used, or when it was used.

It is easy to imagine that in the hands of educators who idolized Froebel these methodically outlined ways of working with children would turn into rigid programs. Actually, it was just such rigidity that led to complaints which were sounded even earlier than the start of the twentieth century, and which led to two wings in the kindergarten movement. As Patty Smith Hill, a leader in the second and newer wing, put it: "History repeats itself in all ages and movements, and heresy has entered the paradise of the kindergarten world, destroying the peaceful satisfaction and pedagogical egotism of happier days in our early history" (20, p. 61).

In the less happy days of the early twentieth century, some of the disagreements about the kindergarten grew out of differences in the interpretation of Froebelian teachings. The more important ones, however, stemmed from fundamentally different ideas not only about the best way to educate the young child but also about how one arrived at this "best way."

Froebel had arrived at his way through what might be called introspection. "He believed that by studying his own mind he could determine the stages of development of the human race and of the individual child" (22, p. 21). He did observe children but, according to one author at least, he only saw in their behavior verification of his own preconceived notions about children (22). The result was a concept of childhood that viewed it as adulthood reduced in size. One further result was Froebel's belief that the meaning he himself assigned to the gifts and occupations mirrored the meaning they would have for a child. That this might not be the case was a factor that seems to have received little attention from Froebel's followers.

Contrary to the introspective way of proceeding, the new wing in the kindergarten movement supported what it believed to be a more objective and scientific way for arriving at programs for young children. This would involve deliberate variation in programs and the use of children's reactions as measures of their worth. And so began at least the possibility of a more experimental pedagogy for the kindergarten encouraged by individuals like Patty Smith Hill.

Development of the Progressive Kindergarten

To know what influenced Miss Hill is to know about some of the factors that led to the development of the so-called "progressive" kindergarten. For her, one of the first sources of influence was attendance at a training school for kindergarten teachers founded by Anna Bryan in Louisville, Kentucky. A member of the first class in 1887, Miss Hill apparently accepted the school's philosophy which, while not completely opposed to Froebelian teachings, hardly supported what had become almost a cult among kindergarten educators.

In 1893 Miss Bryan left Louisville to work at the University of Chicago where, a short time later, she was able to share her ideas about educating young children with John Dewey. Meanwhile, Patty Smith Hill assumed responsibility for the Louisville School. Later, courses taken with Professor G. Stanley Hall in the summer of 1895 turned out to be another important source of influence. At that time Hall was one of the foremost leaders of what was called the Child Study Movement. Essentially this was an attempt among psychologists to make their work less philosophical and more scientific and practical. It was an effort to move from the traditional introspective methods of study to more objective ways of collecting data.

Not to be overlooked in this discussion of what influenced Patty Smith Hill, and therefore influenced the development of the progressive kindergarten, was her move to Teachers College, Columbia University where, in 1910, she became head of its Kindergarten Training Department. Under her leadership, Teachers College became the center of the progressive kindergarten movement, a movement that won the support of such influential educators and psychologists as G. Stanley Hall and John Dewey.

In the meantime two other developments were affecting the public at large and also the viewpoints of educators about what constituted an appropriate school program for young children. One was Freudian psychology which was giving special attention to the emotional side of development and to the critical importance of a child's early years. Its contention that many adult problems are the result of earlier repression also was to have an effect on notions about appropriate classroom discipline for young children.

During some of the years when Freudian theories were receiving wide acceptance, World War I was being fought. On the surface such a calamity seems far removed from early childhood education; however the identification of many emotional problems among the servicemen—then interpreted as stemming form childhood problems—further highlighted the importance both of the early years and of considerations like social and emotional maturity.

Among other things, these developments encouraged public support of the kindergarten, making it part of the public schools in many areas. Combined with recommendations of the Child Study and Progressive Education Movements, these developments also fostered the emergence of a kindergarten program that kept something of the older Froebelian ideas but added new emphases as well. In keeping with traditional ideas, for example, the program continued to include music and art. Too, the kindergarten teacher continued to be viewed as a mother substitute. Within the newer progressive framework, however, the program she directed in the 1920s was to be much more free and flexible, always having as its goal the social and emotional development of the children it was to serve.

Evidently what was originally conceived of as being necessarily "free and flexible" jelled into a routine. I say this because for almost half a century the kindergarten program continued to be the same combination of free and organized play, music, art, stories, craft work, and snacks and rest. Why the continued sameness? For instance, why would a textbook for kindergarten teachers with 1951 and 1956 copyright dates still be proposing a schedule that divides into time for: opening exercises, work-play period, outdoor play and toileting, midmorning lunch, reclining rest, group experiences, and storytime (40, p. 96)? Even one more "why" seems called for when this listing of the 1950s is put side by side with another said to describe "Activities of A Typical Day" as of 1929: arrival, work period, stories, midmorning lunch, rest, music and rhythm, and outdoor play (39, pp. 253–257).

Factors Accounting for Unchanging Program

Even had I been an adult and a member of the educational profession during all the years of the 1920s to the 1950s, I still might not be able to explain just why the goals and program of the kindergarten remained relatively unchanged for so long.* Having to rely for many of those years on what others have written about the kindergarten, all I can do is to suggest what might have been some of the possible reasons for the continued sameness.

It seems safe to propose, first of all, that human nature was one of the factors impeding change. In the case of the kindergarten it might have been the general tendency among people to resist what is new and different, but it might also have been the tendency to hang on to what was dif-

* Why the 1950s are used as the terminal date in this discussion will be made clear later in the chapter.

ficult to achieve. Here I refer to the great effort required in earlier years to break out of the Froebelian rut. Once the new ideas won approval and the new program was accepted, it is easy to believe that those who worked hard for the approval and acceptance would not be eager to abandon what they had achieved in favor of something else. Further, once the newer ideas took the form of a program, then it is also very likely that the old evil of inertia took over. How much simpler to do what was done last year than to try something different!

In addition to our own human nature, what might be other reasons why the kindergarten remained relatively unchanged once the so-called progressive kindergarten took hold in the 1920s? From the literature about kindergarten it would seem that energies in the 1930s, besides being depleted by the hardships of the Depression, were also consumed by efforts to keep kindergartens open. Unlike nursery schools which actually expanded during the Depression years, kindergartens had to fight for their very life because, for the most part, they were publicly supported. Reflecting the struggle to exist are enrollment figures for the Depression decade (36, p. 46):

PUBLICLY SUPPORTED KINDERGARTENS

Enrollment

1930	1934	1940
723,443	601,775	594,647

When a publicly supported institution is struggling for its existence, proponents usually try either to remake it into something more attractive or to convince the public of its worth as it is. It would seem that kindergarten educators chose the latter course and wrote often about the "educational significance" both of behavioral goals like social and emotional maturity and of the program they had designed to achieve them.

When World War II broke out in the 1940s, justifying the importance of such goals was probably easier. Wartime as well as post-war instabilities included much disruption in family life. Father was away at war, and mother was busy with her work in the factory or office. And so once again educators saw in the kindergarten an opportunity to make up for deficiencies in home life. In the 1940s, some psychologists were even saying that:

> School also becomes a place in which there is an opportunity to correct some of the distortions which may have developed from excessively rigid feeding and toilet-training, excessively cold or excessively sentimental handling by mothers, and excessive competition with a sibling (25, p. 34).

Sometimes research findings have an effect on school programs; consequently it is relevant to ask what was happening in research during the decades of unchanging goals and programs. In this instance it is interesting to see that the social and emotional development that was being constantly emphasized and talked about by kindergarten educators also provided—along with physical development—the most popular foci for research done with pre-first grade children. In discussing this trend, a well-known early childhood educator once noted that an obvious dichotomy existed in school programs between what she called the play of the pre-first grade program and the formal learning of the elementary school years; and that such a division could be partially accounted for by research (15). She went on to explain, in the 1947 article, that research done with pre-first grade children was concerned with child development, while studies involving children of elementary school age dealt chiefly with "learning in the skills."

Actually, what is more interesting than this author's observations are her recommendations. Dealing only with the older children research, the recommendations point to the narrowness of these studies and voice the hope that the type done with the younger children would be extended to include the older ones. No mention is made of the possibility or desirability of extending the "learning in the skills" research to include the younger children.

Such an omission reflects what might be still another reason for the continued sameness of kindergarten programs and goals. In suggesting this one I am on shaky grounds for it is based only on the impression that for many decades educators of the young child were *satisfied* with what they were doing. I say this because in all the published material I have gone through in preparing to write this chapter, I found little—in fact, very little—self-criticism. When questions about what was being done did appear, they tended to focus on what seems like trivia. For instance, consider the following in a 1947 publication:

> Granted the security of the familiar, it is not in any sense proven that exposure to standard materials (such as blocks, five days a week, with an opportunity to make innumerable variations on the general theme of station, tracks, and skyscrapers) is the most constructive experience for the child of kindergarten age. An extension of materials the child handles to include some variety in textures, colors, and degrees of mobility would do no harm and might be a very important advantage, especially to children of superior potentialities (25, p. 35).

If a high degree of self-satisfaction did pervade kindergarten education for a long period of time, then it is one more reason why so little change occurred. It would also help to explain why the changes that have taken place in more recent years have been the result of forces and people outside the kindergarten group.

Before describing these outside sources of influence, let me first pull together some of the characteristics of both kindergartens and nursery schools that prevailed for so long and, secondly, the reasons for them. Such a synthesis will serve as a brief summary of the discussion thus far and will also provide a contrast for what has been developing in more recent years.

SUMMARY DESCRIPTION OF TRADITIONAL GOALS AND PROGRAMS

At various times during their histories, the nursery school and the kindergarten have been considered by some to be a means of providing custodial care for children of the poor. Even more frequently, the programs and emphases of both have been seen as a way of compensating for the emotional problems and deficiencies in a child's life at home. These two points of view, combined with one that sees the first six years of life as the "personality- and behavioral-building years," resulted in certain developments that have been noticeably influential for a long period of time.

Certainly one of these developments was the idea that a teacher of young children is to be viewed more as a mother than an instructor. Another was the idea that school programs should be of a type that promote physical and emotional growth and provide for helpful social experiences. Within the framework of these ideas, program goals were defined in such terms as "emotional stability," "self-acceptance," "ability to share," "acceptance of others," and so on. Within the same framework, programs comprised of group experiences, music and art, free play, and rest and refreshments came into existence.

Having established goals for pre-first grade programs that were different from those of the elementary school and, secondly, having established a different role for those teaching at pre-first grade levels, educational leaders also established different teacher training institutions which, at least in the beginning, were separate from those that prepared elementary school teachers. Even in later years, when physical separation no longer was common, a demarcation continued to exist between what was considered appropriate training for the pre-first grade teacher and what seemed essential for elementary school personnel. And so, instead of focussing on academic subjects and teaching methods, the education of the pre-first grade teacher has traditionally dealt with psychological concepts, child development, and such program goals as "good mental health."

These different viewpoints about the function of pre-first grade programs and the function of the elementary school years, along with related differences about the role a teacher was to play and the type of preparation that was necessary for carrying out that role, all combined to create school programs for pre-first grade children that were kept separate from those designed to educate the first-grader. Such a cleavage has often been discussed and lamented by both kindergarten and elementary school educators; yet it has continued to exist for many years. Whether it will diminish or even completely drop from sight as a result of some newer conceptions of young children is a question for the future to answer. Meanwhile, let me introduce into this discussion some of the more recent developments which have had an impact on school programs for pre-first grade children.

NEWER DEVELOPMENTS IN EARLY CHILDHOOD EDUCATION

To state the exact time a new development first appeared is difficult if not impossible. The new developments regarding young children are no exception. With these, however, one very exact statement about a related event can be made: The launching of the satellite Sputnik I by the Russians on October 4, 1957 resulted in an American inferiority complex creating an atmosphere that clamored for new developments in education. Among those to gain quick and widespread attention were some related to young children.

Publications Concerned with Young Children

One of the first things to have an effect on conceptions of early childhood education was the publication of *The Process of Education* by Jerome Bruner (3). Although appearing in 1960, his book describes a 1959 conference sponsored by the National Academy of Sciences to consider how science education in elementary and secondary schools could be improved. Among the dominant themes was the contention that a change in teaching method would allow for earlier contact with science. The proposed change highlighted the importance of the "structure of a discipline." According to Bruner it was this "fundamental character" of each discipline that made it possible "to narrow the gap between 'advanced' knowledge and 'elementary' knowledge" (3, p. 26).

Following this claim came a chapter on "Readiness for Learning." Introducing it was a statement that was to be quoted with great frequency: "We begin with the hypothesis that any subject can be taught effectively in some intellectually honest form to any child at any stage of development" (3, p. 33). For those who took the time to read all of

Bruner's report, this statement had a meaning that was hardly startling. It was, in fact, simply urging educators to take another look at how they organized and presented instruction in fields like science and mathematics. Quoted out of context, however, it encouraged what might accurately be called wishful thinking about the learning potential of young children.

Young children were to get still more attention as a result of another book by another psychologist. This one, *Intelligence and Experience*, was written by J. McV. Hunt and appeared in 1961 (21). Had publication been at another time, this particular book might have become nothing more than an item on a graduate student's reading list, for it is a highly technical description of the author's reinterpretation of findings from a collection of earlier studies. As it was, its appearance at a time when the intellectual possibilities of young children were just coming into the limelight turned it into something of a best-seller. In fact, quoting from *Intelligence and Experience* became almost fashionable. Although it is unlikely that all who quoted Hunt's book had read it in its entirety, the quotes were still listened to with rapt attention and wide acceptance. What they highlighted was the importance of a child's pre-first grade years; in particular, the crucial importance of early learning opportunities to his eventual intellectual development. Commonly overlooked, while Hunt was being quoted, was that his work offered no new research on children; that, instead, it was a reinterpretation of earlier research data, sometimes from animal studies. Overlooked more generally was that these reinterpretations were rich with hypotheses to be tested, not facts to be implemented.

Coming somewhat in the shadow of Hunt's book was another by Benjamin Bloom. Called *Stability and Change in Human Characteristics*, it was published in 1964 (2). Like Hunt's work, Bloom's was a detailed reexamination of earlier research—in this case, of longitudinal studies concerned with the development of certain measurable characteristics which included intelligence and achievement. The conclusions once again underscored the importance of learning opportunities in the child's early years. This time claims about their unique influence were rooted in the assumption that the most rapid period for the development of many characteristics, including intelligence, is in the first five years of life.

New Social Concerns

While the publications of individuals like Bruner, Hunt, and Bloom were helping to create an era of unprecedented excitement about the young child's learning potential and the special importance of the pre-first grade years to his intellectual development, another interest was coming to the surface. In this case it was a revived interest in age-old problems connected with poverty. During the 1960s the awakened interest had more dimensions than was usual for now it was closely associated with the civil rights movement.

Concern about children of the poor, who were described in the 1960s as "deprived" and "disadvantaged," took many forms. The one with relevance for this discussion is the special interest shown for young disadvantaged children. As has always been the case, part of this concern focussed on such basic needs as better nutrition. However, part of it also took the form of an interest in their intellectual needs. Certainly this was something new—but not unexpected given the temper of the times.

That this interest in children of the poor was, in fact, quickly joined with the new interest in the intellectual development of young children is reflected in the themes of a variety of conferences held during the 1960s. One of the earliest examples was the Arden House Conference on Pre-School Enrichment of Socially Disadvantaged Children held in December, 1962. The stated purpose of the three-day meeting was "to explore. . . the possibilities of accelerating the cognitive development of young children, beyond what might be expected from a standard nursery school situation" (7). That J. McV. Hunt was a participant in this conference should come as no surprise.

The next summer another conference was held at Teachers College, Columbia University, dealing with the more general theme, "Education in Depressed Areas." Among the conference papers was one by Martin Deutsch, a psychologist who became closely associated with efforts to provide earlier schooling for young disadvantaged children. In his paper Deutsch described research done under his direction at the Institute for Developmental Studies, part of the New York Medical College. The hypothesis being examined was that "early intervention by well-structured programs will significantly reduce the attenuating influence of the socially marginal environment" (8).

By the mid-1960s national interest in young disadvantaged children was very much apparent; yet there still was no accumulation of research findings that would provide definite guidelines for developing early school programs. The lack of data, however, had little effect on the move toward pre-kindergarten classes. As part of President Johnson's "War on Poverty," an aid-to-education bill was passed by Congress in 1965 which provided funds for what came to be called "Head Start" programs (33). Little time passed before they appeared in all parts of the country. Probably because of this swiftness, many were very much like traditional nursery school programs. A more than usual amount of attention, however, went to oral language development. When cognitive skills were considered a goal, most efforts seemed to go in the direction of trying to raise the children's IQ scores on intelligence tests (11). Unfortunately, carefully worked out programs, as well as efforts to coordinate them and systematically accumulate findings, were too rare.

Parent Involvement

For a variety of reasons, most of the attention given pre-first grade education during the middle and late 1960s centered on Project Head Start. During this time public schools altered existing kindergarten classes only in minimal ways; probably the most obvious and common change was the inclusion of reading instruction in some of them. Others also began to use the new K-12 math and science materials that bore some relationship to the proposals Bruner had made earlier in *The Process of Education* (3). Private schools, on the other hand, showed greater change in emphases, mostly because parents have more to say about what happens there. And, during the 1960s, it would not have been natural for educated parents to remain silent about traditional play-oriented programs when from all sides they were being bombarded by books and articles bearing titles like, "How to Raise a Brighter Child," "Why Waste Our Five-Year-Olds?" and "You Can Teach Your Baby to Read" (1, 9, 34).

The most obvious and widespread example of parent involvement in pre-first grade education was what might be called the American Montessori movement. Actually, this was a revival of interest in Montessori. Much earlier, during the initial decades of the century, other attempts had been made to implement Montessori theory in pre-first grade programs. At that time, though, it seemed too structured and academic to appeal to educators who were very much under the influence of the Progressive Education Movement. Life in the 1960s, however, was different.

Actually, it was in the late 1950s that attention began to focus again on Maria Montessori and her ideas about educating young children. At that time the Whitby School in Connecticut was putting Montessori theory into practice and also receiving attention in a nationally distributed magazine (4). It happens that I had the opportunity to visit Whitby and was very impressed with its inter-age groupings, team teaching, and very involved children. Popular descriptions of it, however, emphasized what was to be the title of still another magazine account, "Can Our Children Learn Faster?" (29).

By 1962 there was an American Montessori Society. In the same year its first president wrote *Learning How to Learn* whose theme was the adaptation of Montessori ideas to American education (32). Included was a lengthy bibliography of materials about Montessori and her work. Later, new editions of older, out-of-print books by and about Montessori became available (13, 28).

Lacking a systematic study of the many Montessori schools that sprang up throughout the United States during the 1960s, we now have only impressionistic accounts of what they achieved. My own personal impression is that like so many of the other new interests in young children that characterized the 1960s, this one developed too hastily. It became too popular too quickly. Among the unfortunate results was insufficient time to think through the details of a program and, most importantly, to provide for the careful training of teachers. For the Montessori movement this has meant that many classes are "Montessori" only in their use of the now readily available Montessori materials.

Early Childhood Educators

Noticeably absent as the years of the 1960s moved on was visible leadership from professional educators and organizations that had traditionally come to be associated with the education of young children. At the start of the decade their voices were heard, but inevitably the message they carried was what had been said so often before: School programs for young children should be concerned with their social and emotional development.

As other and quite different proposals began to come from individuals outside the field, the traditional message took on another dimension; namely, a "defense" of the young child. For instance, and as early as 1960, two early childhood education professors were warning:

> Recently pressure has been exerted to redesign the kindergarten program to attain fixed academic standards. The anxieties and tensions of our times create a sense of urgency that is likely to be transferred to the kindergarten child if we do not exercise caution (26, p. 59).

At the same time a similar message was appearing in *Childhood Education*, a publication of the Association for Childhood Education International:

> The restlessness and anxiety of our times have been expressed in trying to force down in the curriculum learnings for which the child is neither physiologically or psychologically ready and for which he sees no need (18, p. 316).

The titles of an article published in 1963 and of a book that came out in 1967 serve to illustrate how the early childhood education group continued to promote the same theme throughout the 1960s: "Is Play Obsolete?" and "The Conspiracy Against Childhood" (24, 38).

Why, it might be asked now, was there so little change in the thinking and writings of professional educators associated with the education of young children, even as the rest of the world was proposing and discussing almost revolutionary ideas? One reason, it must be assumed, was their honest conviction that the ideas they had been expounding for more than three decades were just as valid for the 1960s as they believed them to be for those earlier times. Another reason is reflected in materials they wrote in the 1960s, some of which were just quoted. They thought there was a special need, in the 1960s, to save the young child from individuals and groups who were making what they saw to be damaging proposals for his education. Aware, too, that many parents were reading and believing the promises held out in books like *Give Your Child a Superior Mind* and *How to Raise a Brighter Child,* they probably also felt some need to protect young children from their own parents (1, 12).

Still another reason for the lack of even minimal change has been suggested by one within the early childhood education group. In a 1967 article Bettye Caldwell asked her colleagues, "Why do we resist innovations in educational programs and teaching techniques?" Her own answer:

> Just below the surface in many teachers there appears to lurk a basic conservatism that is activated whenever anyone advocates a change in educational programs. In many ways teachers of the young seem to represent the far right in education and to be champions of the status quo. Whereas for more than a decade the field of education has been in a ferment of new ideas that has actively sought new approaches to old problems and ways of implementing change when new ideas come forth, within the field of preschool education there appears to have been active resistance . . . (5, p. 352).

WHERE ARE WE NOW?

Having looked at the major forces and ideas that were at work during the 1960s, it is time to ask, "Where are we now in the field of early childhood education?"

What the passing of time makes clear, first of all, is that the decade of the 1960s was more productive of excitement and hope than of well-documented facts or carefully worked out programs. It began with messages from psychologists—and these were quickly repeated in nationally distributed newspaper and magazines articles—offering a new conception of the young child's capacity for learning along with persistent reminders about the critical importance of an intellectually stimulating early environment. Within such an atmosphere, interest in providing earlier schooling as well as a different kind of program for four and five year olds was natural.

As it happened, in the 1960s the interest commonly went in the direction of a particular group of young children—the disadvantaged. This occurred for several reasons. National awareness of poverty and of the problems connected with it had never been so keen before. Pre-first grade schooling offered hope for children of the poor and, in fact, was seen as making a major contribution to President Johnson's "War on Poverty." Added to the concern for the poor were the educational demands connected with the civil rights movement. And, adding considerably to both, were federal funds.

Once the hope was engendered, the demands made, and the money became available, there seemed to be no end to early school programs for the disadvantaged. However, clearly apparent in spite of the growing pile of reports—or, perhaps, because of them—was that the hope and the demands and the money came on the scene before there had been sufficient opportunity to think through what needed to be done. Time shows the results: short-term programs, hastily developed programs, minimal coordination with existing programs.

To suggest that too much haste in developing programs was the only reason for some of the disappointments of the sixties would be untrue. The studies that were done also must accept blame, for like other research in education and psychology they were characterized by some serious flaws. In the 1960s, for instance, not enough time was taken to clarify what was and was not known about young children. The hypotheses and the facts were never sorted out. One became confused with the other. As a result, the relevant questions were not always asked, and so the relevant research was not usually done. Often, in fact, it was the easy-to-answer questions that guided studies, and so reports about them sometimes engendered the feeling, "So what?"

In addition—and this is so characteristic of research in education—there was practically no coordination among the individual researches and researchers. It was as if the right hand didn't know what the left was doing. The result of this was much needless repetition of studies, but also gaps and holes. Another result, therefore, is that we now know much less about what early childhood education ought to be than would have been the case had there been better questions, better programs, and better studies to evaluate them.

But, all is not gloomy. In spite of the shortcomings and excesses, what happened in the field of early childhood education during the 1960s can still make a positive contribution to subsequent decades. I personally think one of the lasting contributions will be a more realistic attitude toward the young child. By this I mean that we should now be in a better position to see him for what he is: a person living in a world that allows him to learn more, faster, and at an earlier age. At the same time, however, we should also be in a better position to see that attention to the young child's intellectual possibilities should never be so overwhelming that we forget what the traditionalists have been so fond of referring to as his "social and emotional needs." What we should have been reminded of also from the work done with the disadvantaged is that for some young children there are other overriding needs like good nutrition, sufficient rest, and adequate clothing.

In a sense, the lesson to be learned is one that was constantly preached in the heyday of the Progressive Education Movement: As educators we must be concerned with the *whole* child. If, in these current times, we can keep an eye on that whole child and therefore on all his potentialities and needs, then there is the possibility of developing programs that neglect none and nourish all.

Whether the possibility turns into a reality will depend upon other factors, too. One, certainly, is the development of research that allows us to learn more about the young child who is living now—not ten or twenty years ago. Another factor will be the willingness of school people to develop programs that reflect the life of the child now—not as it was lived in decades gone by. And, finally, the emergence of truly effective programs will also depend upon the willingness of researchers to take the time required to develop carefully worked out evaluations which continue for a length of time that allows for meaningful answers to meaningful questions.

REFERENCES

1. Beck, Joan. *How to Raise a Brighter Child.* New York: Trident Press, 1967.
2. Bloom, Benjamin S. *Stability and Change in Human Characteristics.* New York: John Wiley and Sons, 1964.
3. Bruner, Jerome S. *The Process of Education.* Cambridge, Mass.: Harvard University Press, 1960.
4. Burke, O. "Whitby School," *Jubilee,* VI (February, 1959), 21–27.
5. Caldwell, Bettye M. "On Reformulating the Concept of Early Childhood Education—Some Whys Needing Wherefores," *Young Children,* XXII (September, 1967), 348–356.
6. Davis, Mary Dabney. *Nursery Schools.* Washington, D.C.: U.S. Government Printing Office, 1933.
7. Deutsch, Martin. "Papers from the Arden House Conference on Pre-School Enrichment," *Merrill-Palmer Quarterly,* X (July, 1964), 207–208.
8. ———. "The Disadvantaged Child and the Learning Process," in *Education in Depressed Areas,* ed. A. H. Passow. New York: Teachers College Press, Columbia University, 1963.

9. Doman, G.; Stevens, G. L.; and Orem, R. C. "You Can Teach Your Baby to Read," *Ladies' Home Journal,* LXXX (May, 1963), 62ff.

10. Durkin, Dolores. *Children Who Read Early.* New York: Teachers College Press, Columbia University, 1966.

11. ———. "A Language Arts Program for Pre-First Grade Children: Two-Year Achievement Report," *Reading Research Quarterly,* V (Summer, 1970), 534–565.

12. Englemann, Siegfried, and Englemann, Therese. *Give Your Child a Superior Mind.* New York: Simon and Shuster, 1966.

13. Fisher, Dorothy C. *The Montessori Manual.* Cambridge, Mass.: Robert Bentley, Inc., 1964.

14. Forest, Ilse. *Preschool Education.* New York: The Macmillan Co., 1927.

15. Gans, Roma. "Young Children at the Turn of This Era," *Early Childhood Education,* Chapter II. Forty-Sixth Yearbook of the National Society for the Study of Education, Part II. Chicago: Distributed by the University of Chicago Press, 1947.

16. Gesell, Arnold L. "The Nursery School Movement," *School and Society,* XX (November, 1924), 642–652.

17. Goodykoontz, Bess. "Recent History and Present Status of Education for Young Children," *Early Childhood Education,* Chapter IV. Forty-Sixth Yearbook of the National Society for the Study of Education, Part II. Chicago: Distributed by the University of Chicago Press, 1947.

18. Heffernan, Helen. "Significance of Kindergarten Education," *Childhood Education,* XXXVI (March, 1960), 313–319.

19. Henry, Nelson B., ed. *Early Childhood Education.* Forty-Sixth Yearbook of the National Society for the Study of Education, Part II. Chicago: Distributed by the University of Chicago Press, 1947.

20. Hill, Patty Smith. "Some Conservative and Progressive Phases of Kindergarten Education," *The Kindergarten and Its Relation to Elementary Education,* Chapter IV. Sixth Yearbook of the National Society for the Study of Education, Part II. Chicago: University of Chicago Press, 1907.

21. Hunt, J. McVicker. *Intelligence and Experience.* New York: The Ronald Press Co., 1961.

22. Kirkpatrick, E. A. "The Psychologic Basis of the Kindergarten," *The Kindergarten and Its Relation to Elemetary Education,* Chapter II. Sixth Yearbook of the National Society for the Study of Education, Part II. Chicago: University of Chicago Press, 1907.

23. Kraus-Boelte, Maria. "An Interpretation of Some of the Froebelian Kindergarten Principles," *The Kindergarten and Its Relation to Elementary Education,* Chapter III. Sixth Yearbook of the National Society for the Study of Education, Part II. Chicago: University of Chicago Press, 1907.

24. LeShan, Eda J. *The Conspiracy Against Childhood.* New York: Atheneum Publishers, 1967.

25. Levinger, Leah, and Murphy, Lois B. "Implications of the Social Scene for the Education of Young Children," *Early Childhood Education,* Chapter III. Forty-Sixth Yearbook of the National Society for the Study of Education, Part II. Chicago: Distributed by the University of Chicago Press, 1947.

26. LINDBERG, L., and MOFFITT, M. W. "The Program and the Child," *National Elementary Principal,* XL (September, 1960), 50–125.
27. MCMILLAN, MARGARET. *The Nursery School.* New York: E. P. Dutton and Co., 1919.
28. MONTESSORI, MARIA. *The Montessori Method.* Cambridge, Mass.: Robert Bentley, Inc., 1964.
29. MORRIS, J. A. "Can Our Children Learn Faster?" *Saturday Evening Post,* CCXXXIV (September 23, 1961), 17–25.
30. PARKER, S. C. *A Textbook in the History of Modern Elementary Education.* Boston: Ginn and Co., 1912.
31. PINES, MAYA. *Revolution in Learning.* New York: Harper and Row, Publishers, 1966.
32. RAMBUSCH, NANCY McC. *Learning How to Learn.* Baltimore: Helicon Press, 1962.
33. SHAW, FREDERICK. "The Changing Curriculum," *Review of Educational Research,* XXXVI (June, 1966), 343–352.
34. SIMMONS, VIRGINIA C. "Why Waste Our Five-Year-Olds?" *Harper's Magazine,* CCXX (April, 1960), 71–73.
35. SYNGE, M. B. *A Short History of Social Life in England.* New York: Barnes, 1906.
36. UNITED STATES OFFICE OF EDUCATION. *Statistical Summary of Education, 1939–40.* Washington, D.C.: U.S. Government Printing Office, 1942.
37. VANDEWALKER, B. L. *The Kindergarten in American Education.* New York: The Macmillan Co., 1908.
38. WEISMAN, DOROTHY. "Is Play Obsolete?" *Saturday Review,* XLVI (November 16, 1963), 77ff.
39. WHIPPLE, GUY M., ed. *Preschool and Parental Education.* Twenty-Eighth Yearbook of the National Society for the Study of Education, Part I. Bloomington, Ill.: Public School Publishing Co., 1929.
40. WILLS, CLARICE D., and STEGEMAN, W. H. *Living in the Kindergarten.* Chicago: Follett Publishing Co., 1956.

3

Readiness for Reading

Continuing with the historical account of developments related to the education of young children, this chapter deals with some that are concerned with reading but more specifically with the question of when children are ready to learn to read.

How you yourself would respond were you asked that question is impossible for me to know. But let me make some predictions. If the bulk of your professional education took place in decades gone by, it is likely or at least very possible that you equate readiness with a mental age of 6.5 years. If your professional preparation was not that long ago but has been entirely in the field of early childhood education, it is likely that you entertain the same thought because it is communicated even in fairly recent books and articles written for early childhood teachers (31, 39, 49, 60).

On the other hand, if all your course work has been done within the past few years, then it is more difficult to read your mind because agreement about readiness—what it is, when it occurs, why it occurs—has hardly characterized these more recent times. Why widespread agreement did prevail in earlier decades and, secondly, why much less of it is evident today, ought to become clear as this chapter discusses the reading readiness concept from a historical point of view.

ORIGINAL INTERPRETATION

The term "reading readiness" first appeared in the professional literature in the 1920s. To explain how it was initially defined and, secondly, why it was assigned this definition, developments that occurred earlier need to be mentioned. At first they will seem far removed from the consideration of when children are ready for reading. Soon, though, you will come to see how all the pieces fit together and, further, how they account for the original interpretation of readiness.

Influence of G. Stanley Hall

It is entirely appropriate to begin this discussion by referring to a person mentioned in Chapter 2: G. Stanley Hall. In fact, it would be both difficult and inaccurate to leave him out of any consideration of education as it existed prior to the 1920s. In Chapter 2, Hall was discussed in connection with the Child Study Movement. Now it is more relevant to examine two of his ideas regarding the basic nature of man.

One of the points made in *Intelligence and Experience*, which was also discussed in Chapter 2, is that the eighteenth century ushered in two quite different explanations of the evolution of man and, further, that acceptance of one over the other had great and obvious effects on American psychology, especially during the first three decades of the twentieth century (34). One of the explanations, the earlier one, was proposed by Lamarck who maintained that evolution was the result of changes brought about by use and disuse. The other explanation, the one more generally accepted, was Darwin's. He contended that evolutionary change resulted from "variations in the progeny of every species or strain which are then selected by the conditions under which they live" (35, p. 210).

For this discussion the most relevant point in Darwin's proposal is his assumption that the characteristics of an individual are predetermined by genetic factors. Primarily because G. Stanley Hall accepted it, the assumption became part of the mainstream of psychological thought in America during the early decades of this century. One result was that the same decades gave attention to hereditary rather than to environmental factors, and to maturation rather than to learning and practice. Within the framework of the classical nature-nurture debate, it was nature that was honored in the early years of this century.

Still another of Hall's beliefs about man and his development is pertinent to this discussion. Here I refer to his acceptance of the doctrine of recapitulation. Perhaps you are familiar with this idea from courses in psychology. If not, let me explain it by quoting from Hall himself. In a 1904 text he wrote:

> The most general formulation of all the facts of development that we yet possess is contained in the law of recapitulation. This law declares that the individual, in his development, passes through stages similar to those through which the race has passed, and in the same order (27, p. 8).

This brief quote underscores the two basic tenets of the doctrine: (a) each individual, as he grows and develops, passes through certain stages, and (b) these stages follow each other in an inevitable, predetermined order. Because in the early years of this century factors like learning and practice were assigned only secondary importance, progress through these "inevitable stages" was generally explained with a reference to the maturation process.

Influence of Hall's Students

Why G. Stanley Hall's beliefs about man and his development enjoyed both widespread and long-lived acceptance can be at least partially explained by the fact that some of his students became prominent themselves and promoted his ideas in their own work and publications. Patty Smith Hill, as Chapter 2 mentioned, was one of them. And so were Frederick Kuhlmann and Lewis Terman who played well-known roles in the development of intelligence tests.

Of greater importance to a consideration of readiness is that Arnold Gesell also studied with Hall. It is likely that some of you—perhaps more as parents than teachers—are already familiar with Gesell's notions about children, for his views and interpretations of growth and development ruled supreme from about the time of World War I up until the 1950s (4, 34). Like Hall's earlier influence, Gesell's came about not only because of his own work and his prolific publications about it but also because of the work and writings of his many students. What everything added up to was continuous support for the earlier teachings of Hall that had derived from recapitulation theory: development occurs through stages whose sequence is predetermined and inevitable.

In describing these stages, but also in explaining progress from one to another, the publications of Gesell and his students commonly gave credit to such processes as "intrinsic growth," "neural ripening," and "unfolding behavior" (21, 22, 23, 24, 25). Whatever the language, the contention was the same: Growth and development are dependent upon inner processes which, in turn, are dependent upon spontaneous maturation or, put more simply, upon the passing of time. While neither Gesell nor his followers turned completely away from the influence of learning, none, either, showed any great excitement about its importance to a child's development.

Influence of Measurement and Testing Movement

One other characteristic of earlier decades needs to be mentioned before we turn to the reading readiness concept. This is the great interest in "scientific" measurement that was permeating both education and psychology by 1920 (55). As you will see, this enthusiastic attempt to get away from introspective and impressionistic research methods is relevant in two different ways.

The first reason for its relevance is that the interest in precise and objective measurement led to national surveys designed to uncover exactly what and how much children were learning in school. Common among the findings was that the rate of nonpromotion for first graders was considerably higher than for children at subsequent grade levels. That inadequate achievement in reading generally was the reason for the first grade retentions also became clear (13, 17, 33, 50).

While both findings probably described equally well the decades which preceded the 1920s, it was in the 1920s that they became widely known and, quickly afterwards, widely deplored. Concern was expressed for the children being retained, and also for the likelihood of behavior problems with the older first graders and of financial problems because of the extra years they would be spending in school. Many asked: *Why are these children not succeeding with reading?*

At another time, answers might have referred to the difficulties of teaching reading with large classes or uninteresting materials or, perhaps inadequate teacher preparation. However, it was the 1920s and that made a difference. The difference is that the first grade reading problems were singularly explained in terms of readiness: The children were having difficulty because they were not ready when reading instruction began at the start of the school year. The reasoning for this one-factor explanation is clearly related to Gesell's popular theories about growth and development, and seems to have been as follows:

(a) Development takes place in stages that follow one another in an inevitable order.
(b) Growth from one stage to another is the result of a maturation (internal neural ripening) that occurs with the passing of time.
(c) The ability to learn to read occurs at one of these stages.

(d) Reading problems disclosed by the surveys suggest most beginning first graders have not yet reached that particular stage of development and, therefore, are unready for reading.
(e) The solution is to postpone reading instruction beyond the start of the first grade year.

Because the passing of time, according to the above reasoning, would solve the reading problem, the same reasoning led to what came to be called a reading readiness program. Of varied duration in various schools, it was to replace efforts to teach reading at the start of first grade. Its goal was to make sure the children would be ready when reading was introduced later on in the year.

Mental Age Concept of Readiness

Given the circumstances of the 1920s, it would have been unusual to find complete contentment with a concept of readiness that related it to some rather vague stage in a child's development. After all, this hardly reflected the interest in exact measurement which characterized the times. With this in mind, it is not surprising that efforts were made to define with some precision that stage thought to insure a child's readiness for reading.

The form these efforts eventually took was influenced by the earlier development of numerous group intelligence tests because with their appearance came many reports about the relationship between a child's intelligence and his school achievement. Often the concern was for his achievement in reading. Frequently, too, the focus was on reading achievement in first grade. In fact, and as early as the year 1920, one author of a report was saying that the children who were having difficulty with reading and thus failing first grade were those with mental ages of less than six years (12). Subsequently other authors in the 1920s moved toward proposals that would establish a certain mental age level as a requirement for starting school instruction in reading (2, 13, 33, 61). Arthur, for example, writing in 1925, maintained that a mental age of 6.0 to 6.5 years was "necessary for standard first-grade achievement" (2).

The kind of thinking about readiness that is reflected in these reports of the 1920s seems to have been crystalized in an article which was published in 1931 and which became widely known and uncommonly influential for a long period of time (45). Written by Mabel Morphett and Carleton Washburne, the article described the reading achievement of first grade children when one particular method was used in one particular school system (Winnetka, Ill.). Based on the children's achievement as it related to mental age, the authors concluded:

> It seems safe to state that, by postponing the teaching of reading until children reach a mental age level of six and a half years, teachers can greatly decrease the chances of failure and discouragement and can correspondingly increase their efficiency (45, p. 503).

Why Morphett and Washburne specified a mental age requirement can be explained with another quote from their 1931 report:

> Mental age alone showed a larger degree of correlation with reading progress than did the intelligence quotient or the average of mental and chronological ages (45, pp. 502–503).

How seriously Washburne took his own proposal is reflected in an article he wrote in 1936 called—quite in keeping with the prevailing psychological views—"Ripeness." He observed: "Nowadays each first grade teacher in Winnetka has a chart showing when each of her children will be mentally six-and-a-half, and is careful to avoid any effort to get a child to read before he has reached this stage of mental growth" (57, p. 127).

Evidence of how seriously other educators took the Morphett-Washburne proposal can be found in reading methodology textbooks that came on the scene not too long after their report appeared and even in those published as many as ten and twenty years later (8, 11, 14, 29, 32, 41, 44). In fact, some textbooks with copyright dates of the 1960s were still taking it seriously (28, 46, 52). As was mentioned earlier in the chapter, this was especially true of early childhood education texts and articles in which this one-factor concept of readiness was often used to try to keep reading out of kindergartens (31, 39, 49, 56, 60).

REASONS FOR ACCEPTANCE OF MENTAL AGE CONCEPT

Knowing how influential and long-lasting the mental age concept of readiness has been, you might now be wondering why findings from a study of one teaching method in one school system were so readily accepted as being applicable to all children. Too, you might wonder why the acceptance continued for so long. A subsequent section in the chapter ought to help with the latter question. Here let me deal with the one that asks why the Morphett-Washburne proposal was so readily accepted.

A combination of factors suggests the answer. For one thing, their proposal fit in perfectly with the temper of the times in which it was made. It gave support to the "doctrine of postponement" because most children entering first grade have not yet reached the mental age of 6.5 years. It also supported the notion that development proceeds in stages, and it honored the measurement and testing movement by being precise and objective.

Probably another reason for the unusual influence of the mental age proposal is that it was based on correlation data. Because the whole notion of correlation was relatively new at the time Morphett and Washburne published their article, its importance and meaning were probably overrated. There was the tendency, no doubt, to see cause-effect relationships in the data rather than mere association.

Finally, any attempt to explain the unique influence of the mental age concept of readiness must take into account the prominence of Carleton Washburne. He was not only superintendent of the Winnetka schools —widely admired and copied in the 1930s—but also one of the most prestigious leaders of the Progressive Education Movement. As a result, what Washburne said was listened to—and not only in the field of reading. Even earlier than 1931, for instance, he had made very specific proposals about what was to be taught in arithmetic and at which mental age level (58). With all these facts in mind, neither his mental age description of reading readiness nor the influence it wielded should come as any great surprise.

EARLY OBJECTIONS TO MENTAL AGE CONCEPT

While there can be no doubt about the mental age concept of readiness being widely accepted, objections to it were still raised. The most important of the dissenters was Arthur Gates. Conclusions reached in two of his studies merit detailed attention not only because they raised questions about this concept but also because they were in reports that appeared not too many years after the Morphett-Washburne article.

In May of 1936, in a research report entitled, "Reading Readiness: A Study of Factors Determining Success and Failure in Beginning Reading," Gates described the reading achievement found in four first grade classes (19). Of particular relevance is that in March of the first grade year he identified the ten lowest achievers and assigned them tutors. By June all ten children were enjoying success. Referring to their success Gates wrote:

> The study emphasizes the importance of recognizing and adjusting to individual limitations and needs . . . rather than merely changing the time of beginning. It appears that readiness for reading is something to develop rather than merely to wait for (19, p. 684).

In another part of the same report he also pointed out:

> Correlations of mental age with reading achievement at the end of the year were about 0.25. When one studies the range of mental ages from the lowest to the highest in relation to reading achievement, there appears no suggestion of a crucial or critical point

above which very few fail and below which a relatively large proportion fail (19, p. 680).

In concluding his report Gates stated:

> The optimum time of beginning reading is not entirely dependent upon the nature of the child himself, but it is in a large measure determined by the nature of the reading program (19, p. 684).

Reaching the same conclusion was another study that Gates reported in March, 1937. This one had examined different methods of teaching reading and the achievement that resulted. Commenting on the findings Gates wrote:

> Reading is begun by very different materials, methods, and general procedures, some of which a pupil can master at the mental age of five with reasonable ease, others of which would give him difficulty at the mental age of seven (18, p. 508).

As you can see from these two research reports, a concept of reading readiness had emerged that was very much at odds with the Morphett-Washburne description. Within the Gates frame of reference the burden of responsibility was moved to the instruction and away from the child. In addition, questions were raised about the wisdom of postponement and of equating readiness with a particular mental age.

Essentially, Gates' message was a simple one: Improve your instruction and watch the children read! Apparently, though, the simplicity of the Morphett-Washburne proposal was more appealing. I say this because just as the publications of the 1930s and subsequent decades provide more than ample evidence of the wide acceptance of the mental age concept of readiness, so too do they reveal how little attention went to Gates' findings. His simply did not move with the stream of popular thought. What did, though, were further descriptions of the child thought to be ready for reading. Here I refer to what became the common practice of listing all kinds of attributes that were added to the mental age requirement. For instance, in the Thirty-Eighth Yearbook of the National Society for the Study of Education, which was published in 1939, the following were cited as being some of the "requisites of readiness for reading" (26, p. 195):

Keen interest in reading
Reasonably wide experience
Facility in the use of ideas
Ability to solve abstract problems

Ability to do abstract thinking of a very elementary type
Ability to remember ideas, word forms, and the sounds of words
A reasonable range of vocabulary
Command of simple English sentences
Good health, vision, and hearing
Ability to see likenesses and differences in word forms and to discriminate sounds of words
Normal speech organs
Emotional stability
Some degree of social adjustment

In glancing through such a listing, it is easy to forget that the concern was only for beginning reading. Probably the saving feature of such demands was that they generally were described in vague terms. With the vagueness they could be interpreted according to each person's particular prejudices.

READING READINESS TESTS

Still one more effort to describe the child who was ready to read came in the form of readiness tests. Actually, references to them appear in the literature as early as 1927 and 1928 (7, 53). The initial hope held out for these tests is portrayed well in an editorial in a 1927 issue of *Childhood Education:*

> In the field of reading it is essential that a joyous attitude of success shall be cultivated from the first. This necessitates a stage of development in which the learner is capable of getting meaning from the crooked marks which symbolize ideas. When does this period come? . . . In which direction shall we look to discover the truth regarding this confused situation? Fortunately the scientific method points the way toward the solution of this as of other baffling problems. The first steps have been taken. First, the problem has been recognized. Second, a name has been coined for the characteristic which is sought, Reading Readiness, a term not only alliterative but meaningful. Third, tests are in process of developing which shall be applicable to any young child. . . . So we may look forward to the day when the measure of readiness will rest in objective tests and parent and teacher will both be governed thereby (36, p. 209).

What did the tests, which were "in the process of developing," turn out to be? They were group pencil and paper tests made up of various combinations of subtests. All such combinations typically included items dealing with vocabulary development and visual and auditory discrimination.

If a subtest did focus on vocabulary, the children were usually asked to circle or underline a picture that went with a word named by the one administering the test, generally a teacher. Or, the administrator might be directed by the test manual to read aloud a particular sentence and again the children would be directed to select from a row of pictures the one pertaining to its content.

Subtests concerned with ability in visual discrimination also used pictures. In this case the assumption seemed to be: If a child notices similarities and differences in simple pictures, he has the ability required to see similarities and differences in letters and words. That the same assumption held for geometrical figures also seems to have been accepted because many of the early subtests included rows showing circles, squares, triangles, and so on. With these a child might be asked to look at the first figure in a row and then to underline or circle all the others that were the same (or different). When pictures were used in a visual discrimination subtest, the task was similar. Children would find in a row of simply drawn pictures the one that was like (or different from) the picture shown at the beginning of the row.

Evidently those who constructed the readiness tests figured that sooner or later the children would be taught phonics. This is suggested by the frequent inclusion of subtests that dealt with some type of auditory discrimination. The type most commonly tested focussed on rhyming words. Again, pictures would be used. In this case the administrator might be directed to name each picture in a given row and to have the children underline or circle all the pictures whose names rhymed with the name of the first one. Sometimes, but less often, an auditory discrimination subtest dealt with the initial sounds of words. When this occurred the one administering the test might say: "Put your finger under the picture of the table. (This would be the first picture in a row.) I am going to name the other pictures in this row. Listen, because I want you to draw a line around the one whose name begins the way *table* begins."

Test manuals, in addition to explaining how tests were to be administered, also offered suggestions about the way the results might be used. Almost without exception one suggestion was to use them diagnostically. That is, school administrators and teachers were urged to study subtest scores (profile scores) to identify each child's particular strengths and weaknesses. Lower scores would point out what needed to be taught;

high scores would indicate the way in which the child was ready for reading. What happened in practice, though, was something quite different. In practice, schools tended to use total scores (composite scores) to make global judgments. The end result was groups of first graders generally labeled "ready" or "unready."

What then? What came next depended on when the readiness test was administered. And dealing with that requires attention to reading readiness programs.

READING READINESS PROGRAMS

Once it was agreed in the 1930s that most children entering first grade were unready to read and, secondly, that postponing instruction would insure their being ready at a later time, a decision had to be made about what was to be done while the children were "growing into readiness." The term used to describe the product of that decision was "reading readiness program."

Content of Readiness Programs

Although called by the same name, what actually went on at the beginning of the first grade year showed considerable variation from school to school, especially when readiness programs were in the process of developing. Some of the variation, no doubt, reflected variation among teachers. But some also reflected differences in viewpoints about the very nature of readiness. Thus, educators who held staunchly to the notion that the passing of time would result in readiness also held to the idea that the content of a readiness program did not have to show an obvious and direct relationship to the reading process. On the other hand, those who believed that learning and practice made their own contribution to readiness would have quite different conceptions of what the readiness program was all about. Under their direction its content was more likely to focus on goals like those commonly assessed in the readiness tests.

What also promoted attention to what was being assessed—and this turned out to be uniquely influential over several decades—was the appearance of the reading readiness workbook. Often, the publisher of a readiness test was also the publisher of one or more of the workbooks. Whether or not this was so, however, the content of the tests and the content of the workbooks were very similar. In time, the content of the workbooks and the content of the readiness programs were remarkably similar, too.

Duration of Readiness Programs

In theory, a readiness program was to be for unready children and was to last until they became ready. In practice, things were not like that. In practice the typical procedure was to administer a readiness test—sometimes a group intelligence test was given, too—close to the start of the first grade year. Evidently the purpose was not to learn whether the children might be ready for reading but, rather, to see how much time they were to spend in a readiness program. The assumption seemed to be that it was good for everybody—ready or not.

If a school had decided that the shortest amount of time to be spent on readiness was, let's say, two months, then the first graders with the highest readiness and IQ scores would be in a readiness program for two months. The remaining children would participate for a longer amount of time, often determined somewhat arbitrarily and without consideration of particular children.

Other schools were more flexible in making decisions about the duration of readiness activities. For instance, they might administer readiness tests more than once in order to make more frequent decisions about whether the readiness program needed to be continued for individual children. In such schools, however, it was still the composite (total) scores that were of concern. Probably very few schools ever used profile (subtest) scores diagnostically, matching carefully what was taught with what individual children seemed to need.

Reasons for Questionable Practices

In retrospect, it is easy to be critical of practices like those just described. However one must keep in mind some of the reasons accounting for them. Such reasons do not endow the flaws with quality, but they at least make them comprehensible.

Certainly one reason for many of the questionable practices was the large number of children typically found in a first grade classroom at the time the readiness concept was receiving attention. Ideally, readiness programs should have been highly individualized and should have included only children who seemed unready. Being responsible for large numbers of children—forty or fifty or more—teachers were able to achieve the ideal only infrequently.

Further, the whole idea of readiness and of readiness programs was new. In addition, the programs were viewed not humbly but as a means of solving all the reading problems. No wonder, then, that they were greeted with what now seems like naive enthusiasm which, among other things, appears to have resulted in the notion that readiness programs were good for everybody, ready or not.

Why the content of the programs was often sterile and routine also has a very human explanation. When first grade teachers were suddenly called upon to do something other than teach reading at the start of the school year, many if not most must have felt insecure to say the least. After all, a good program—whether for readiness or something else—does not evolve overnight. It is no wonder, then, that readiness workbooks were greeted with enthusiasm and just about took over when decisions were being made about what to do with the time allotted to the readiness program.

Reasons for Maintenance of Questionable Practices

While it is fairly easy to see how questionable routines developed when the idea of readiness and readiness programs was new, it is difficult to understand why such practices continued for so long. I raise this question because what was going on in the majority of first grades not too many years ago was similar to what has just been described as characterizing the earlier decades. Why should this be?

Once again, no single reason offers a full explanation for the maintenance of some highly questionable practices. Among the many reasons, though, is the tendency of schools and teachers to be conservative (59). They often want to hang onto what they are doing and sometimes even actively resist change. Some of the resistance is part of what might be called "the human way," but some also is connected with instructional materials. At least this was so in the case of readiness programs. As was mentioned before, not long after the programs came into existence, readiness workbooks appeared. And they came—sometimes two and three to a set—as part of the various basal reader series.* Because basals have been used by the vast majority of elementary school teachers over many decades, readiness workbooks were used, too, and not always because their content taught what children needed to learn (3, 10). As one first grade teacher explained to me—and this was not too many years ago—"Our principal buys the workbooks and so we use them."

One more reason why certain practices connected with readiness continued for so long relates to another tendency among school people: to place too much faith in test scores. This has been true of readiness scores, by the way, even though researchers examining their predictive value have been raising questions almost from the time the tests came into ex-

* Basal reader materials are discussed in detail in Chapter 9.

istence (16, 20).* While the critics had some effect on their content, they had little effect on their use. Readiness tests continued to be published over the years—and still are—apparently because they continued to be used in a large number of schools.

Still one more factor needs to be mentioned in this attempt to explain why certain practices connected with readiness assessment and readiness programs were continued for so long. This moves the focus away from the schools and toward psychology because psychologists also were a reason for too little change over too many years. Here I refer to the fact that psychological conceptions of human growth and development changed very little from the early 1920s up until the late 1950s. Supported by Gesell and his students and his disciples, the popular view during the 1940s and 1950s was like the popular view of the 1920s and 1930s: Readiness for various tasks—including reading—results from maturation; therefore, the passing of time is the solution for problems connected with a lack of it.

In the 1940s and 1950s support for these contentions came from psychologists other than Gesell. Willard Olson, for instance, was especially popular among educators of young children and his ideas about child development, expressed in terms of "organismic age," did anything but go contrary to Gesell's (47, 48). Robert Havighurst, also well known to educators, offered no reason to question traditional practices as he wrote about "developmental tasks" and even referred to the notion of a "teachable moment" (30).

And so, having little reason to do otherwise, schools continued with what became the routine practice of administering readiness tests in first grade and of having all the children—ready or not—participate in readiness programs. But then came Sputnik and what might accurately be called a revolution in education.

THE POST–SPUTNIK ERA

Had Russia not launched a satellite in 1957, it is likely that major changes in education still would have occurred. The times were ripe for change if only because America was over the post-World War II adjustment period and, too, because school practices had remained the same for so long.

* While just about every educator will say he has little confidence in scores, daily practices say something else. Just recently, for instance, I was talking to a first grade teacher who expressed great surprise because one of the best readers in her room had received one of the lowest scores when a readiness test was administered at the beginning of the year. And then just last week I received a letter from an administrator who said he was considering the possibility of having reading taught in kindergarten and wanted an opinion about which readiness test to use when children were being selected for the instruction.

What the Sputnik event did was to increase the sound and quicken the tempo of educational debates already begun.

An important result both of the debates and of a collection of developments and publications, already described in Chapter 2, was an era in which unprecedented attention went to the young child—the pre-first grade child. Instead of repeating the earlier discussion of what produced the attention (pp. 25–27), let me now simply restate emphases of the post-Sputnik era that had special significance for early childhood education:

1. Environmental rather than hereditary factors were highlighted.
2. Growth and development were explained more often in terms of learning and practice than with a reference to maturation.
3. The young child's intellectual development was of major concern; discussions about social and emotional development were infrequent.
4. The child's early (pre-first grade) years were thought to be of unique importance to his later intellectual functioning.

As the above listing indicates, a quick way to describe the post-Sputnik era is to say that its emphases were completely opposite to those of prior decades. In contrast to times marked by Freudian influence, it was the young child's intellectual development that was of concern in the post-Sputnik years. (Like the Freudian times, however, the concern was again rooted in the assumption that what happens during the early years has a pronounced and inevitable effect on later ones.)

Also in contrast was the amount of excited attention given environmental factors. In fact, this was so great and exclusive at times that genetic endowment almost seemed unimportant. And related to this particular emphasis, of course, was the trust placed in the productivity of learning and practice as opposed to the maturation process.

Changes in Timing of Reading Instruction

Given this collection of emphases, it was only natural that post-Sputnik years heard many questions and complaints about the traditional interpretation of reading readiness. After all, an era which assigned critical importance to learning opportunities during the pre-first grade period was not likely to be patient with school practices that postponed reading instruction beyond the start of the first grade year and assumed the passing of time would insure a readiness for it.

As the years have shown, the typical response to the impatience was neither complicated nor imaginative. For the most part schools simply altered the timing of traditional practices. Readiness tests were administered earlier, often in kindergarten where readiness workbooks could be found, too. In first grade, reading instruction usually was started sooner than was typical for prior decades—although readiness programs still could be found in some first grade classrooms, especially in school districts that had no kindergartens. In a few places the change in timing was more radical: They introduced reading in kindergarten. In other areas, however, opposition to this was as great and as vocal as it had been in decades gone by.

Results of Changes

What was learned from these changes? Not much. The greatest change, reading in the kindergarten, was not usually accompanied by changes in materials or methodology. Instead, the latter tended to be like what would be found in a typical first grade (1, 5, 38, 40, 51, 54). As a consequence, limitations were placed on what could be learned about earlier reading and about the basic nature of readiness.* The end result is that the 1960s, with all their excitement about young children and earlier learning, contributed little to what could have been an enlightened discussion about the optimal time for beginning reading. Because of this, the concept of readiness to be proposed now cannot claim to have its roots in research-based facts. In spite of such a limitation, however, it still will get detailed attention because it is, in a sense, my reason for writing this textbook.

PROPOSED DEFINITION OF READINESS

The concept of readiness I offer is not an original one. It was articulated by Gates in the 1930s and at least inferred by others since then. In 1959 it was stated very effectively by Ausubel in an article appearing in the *Teachers College Record* (4). The concern of Ausubel's article was not reading; nonetheless his description of readiness for any learning is both valid and useful for the present discussion.

Readiness, Ausubel proposed, is "the adequacy of existing capacity in relation to the demands of a given learning task" (4, p. 246). Let us examine the details of this definition to see what they say about this chapter's theme: the timing of beginning reading instruction.

Existing Capacity. Nothing that we know about humans suggests that heredity alone accounts for an individual's capacity to learn nor, on the other hand, does anything or anyone suggest that only environmental

* A more detailed discussion of kindergarten reading research in the 1960s can be found elsewhere (15).

factors determine it. At various times, it is true, both nature and nurture have been placed on a special pedestal of honor by psychologists. Even amidst the adulation, however, the one not being raised on high was never cast aside completely. The assumption of this discussion, therefore, is that each child's capacity at any given time is the product of both nature and nurture. More specifically, it is the product of an interplay among genetic endowment, maturation, experiences, and learnings. Just how this interplay takes place awaits a definitive explanation. For now, though, it seems correct to say that a child's attained capacity at any given time is something he has inherited, grown into, and learned.

Demands of the Learning Task. What learning to read demands of children is not one thing—not a single collection of abilities, for instance. Many factors account for the variation and they include, certainly, the selected teaching method. A methodology that depends upon a child to memorize every word he is to read—to cite one illustration—has ability requirements that are not identical to what is demanded by another which might stress phonics. But even with the same methodology, demands are only rarely identical. Here the teacher enters the picture as a critical factor making it necessary to consider not only methodological differences but also differences in what a teacher does with a method. Just what she does and how well she does it always have an effect on what learning to read demands of children.

Adequacy of Capacity in Relation to Demands. One of the most helpful and important features of Ausubel's definition is the explicit attention it gives to the relational aspect of readiness. It reminds us, simply but effectively, that the question of a child's readiness for reading has a twofold focus: (a) the child's capacity in relation to (b) the particular instruction that will be available. Because differences in instruction make for differences in demands, what is adequate for dealing with them also differs. Therefore it is correct to think in terms of readiness*es* for reading and incorrect to assume that one and the same combination of abilities makes children ready for every conceivable kind of instruction. Conversely, it also is incorrect to assume that certain deficiencies make children *un*ready for every type of teaching.

Practical Implications of Definition

Before enumerating some of the practical implications of the Ausubel definition, let me lay it out before you again, this time in graphic form:

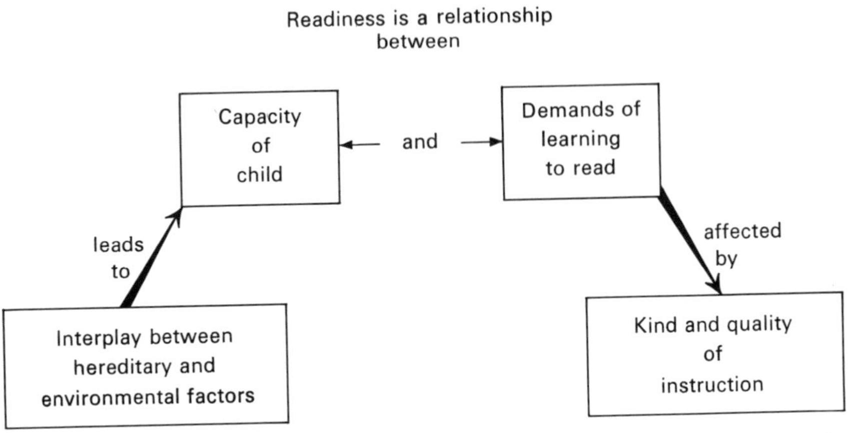

Ausubel: Readiness is "the adequacy of existing capacity in relation to the demands of a given learning task" (4, p. 246).

With its attention to the relational nature of readiness, one suggestion coming from the definition has to do with the way questions about readiness are worded. To ask—as is the common practice—"Is the child ready?" is to ask the wrong question because it is an unfinished one. Instead the concern ought to be, "Is the child ready for this particular kind and quality of instruction?" Even more ideally, of course, the educator's question would be: "Given this child's particular abilities, what type of instruction can we offer that will make use of them and thus allow the child to be successful with reading?" Commenting on this latter way of proceeding, another author once wrote—and maybe his thoughts are yours—"This concept is too beautiful and idealistic to materialize in practice, except in a tutoring situation" (9, p. 130). Perhaps his observation is correct. Even so, it takes nothing away from the correctness of the procedure.

Another implication found in the definition has to do with assessment; that is, with the way educators decide whether or not a child is ready for reading. If, as Ausubel suggests, readiness is the adequacy of existing capacity in relation to the demands of the learning task, then it follows that one very correct way to test for adequacy is to give children opportunities to learn to read in order to see what their capacity actually is. Ideally, these opportunities ought to vary in the methodology they represent because it is always possible for a child to be successful with some methods and unsuccessful with others. By observing what a child does or does not learn from each, much can be learned about his readiness and also about the instruction that makes best use of what he is able to do.

You might now be wondering what this recommendation looks like in a classroom—say, in a kindergarten classroom. Let me help with illustrations that use activities which seem to be a part of every kindergarten program.

Certainly some time in every kindergarten is given to the job of taking attendance. Mundane though it is, even attendance-taking can be turned into an opportunity for five year olds to learn to read, and for a teacher to learn something about existing capacities. For instance, the simple routine of beginning with the showing of first names by a teacher and concluding later in the school year with the children indicating their presence by selecting their name card and putting it on an attendance board, could teach the children to read their names and probably others' names as well. But, too, such an activity helps a teacher learn which children remember (read) names easily, which have more difficulty, and which remember few if any names.

Because opportunities for learning to read should be varied, art activities can serve as an example of another approach. In this case—and without diminishing their value as forms of free expression—finished products in art can be a reason for kindergarteners to learn to print their names but also to write captions and to read those composed by others. To be highlighted here is that the same activity gives an observant teacher the chance to identify children for whom writing and spelling might be an easy way into beginning reading, to identify those who remember whole words with a minimum of exposure to them, and also to become aware of children for whom the motor skill of writing is a formidable task or for whom it is difficult to compose even the briefest of captions.

Still another activity found in kindergartens is that of reading to the children. This should always be for enjoyment, but once in a while certain stories can become a vehicle for learning still more about the children's readiness for reading. Let us say, for example, that a couple of stories have been about Ping, a duck. Let us also say that two of the children in the class are named Paul and Penny. In such a case a kindergarten teacher might one day decide to print *Ping* on the chalkboard and then ask the children, "Does anybody (pointing to the *P*) have a name that starts the way *Ping* starts? If you do, I'll write your name up here with Ping's." And soon the board shows:

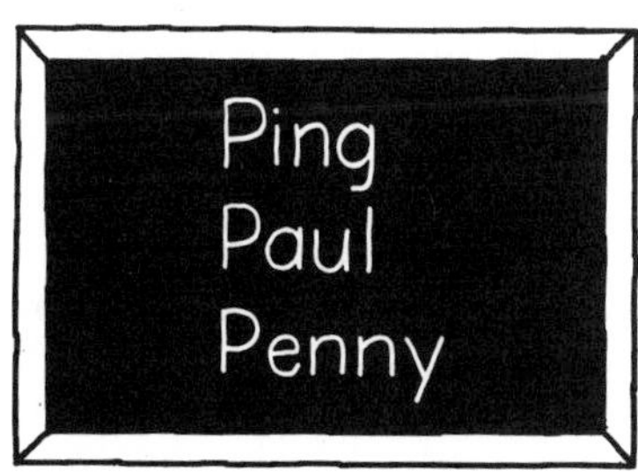

Other questions—their number and kind should depend upon the ability and interest of the children—would follow: "Does anybody know the name of the letter (pointing to *P*) at the beginning of these three names? . . . Have you ever seen any other word that begins with this letter *P*? . . . Now we have five words that begin with *P*. I'm going to read them all. As I do, listen to see if you can hear how they all start with the same sound. . . . Can someone tell us the sound that all these names make at the beginning? . . . I'm going to say these words again. Watch how I put my lips together when I start to say each of them. Listen to the way each word starts. . . . Can someone tell us the sound that's at the beginning of all these words? . . . Can someone think of other words that start the way *Ping* and *Paul* and *Penny* and *Punch* and *Pat* begin? If you can, I'll write them up here too." *

On another day another word and letter might be singled out for attention. Or, on the other hand, the teacher might decide to repeat the attention given *P* using a different collection of words to illustrate its sound. Whatever the decision, the opportunity is available for children to respond and thus for a teacher to identify who among them might know letter names and even have skill in auditory discrimination. At the same time, though, the teacher also is becoming aware of other kindergarteners who seem to have no knowledge of letter names or, more likely, no understanding of what is meant by the description "begin with the same sound."

Perhaps these few illustrations of very ordinary activities are enough to give specific meaning to what is being proposed as a way to assess a child's readiness for reading: Give him varied opportunities to begin and note what he is able to learn. Implied even in the few illustrations, however, are other ideas that are important for teachers of young children.

Assessment, Readiness Instruction, and Reading Instruction

Probably the best way to deal with these ideas is to describe two children in the kindergarten class just referred to who were present on the day the teacher wrote *Ping, Paul* and *Penny* and asked questions about them. We will call the children Paul and Mary Anne. Let us talk about Paul first.

Paul. Paul has all the signs of being mentally slow. Even his physical movements are slow and awkward. When the teacher wrote *Ping* on the board and asked whether anyone had a name that began with the same letter, he remained silent. Something like a concentrated look from the teacher plus a nudge from the child sitting next to him (Mary Anne) led to Paul's volunteering his name. It is uncertain whether he ever would

* A detailed discussion of phonics instruction comprises Chapter 10.

have mentioned it had there not been these "hints" from others. Once his name was on the board he seemed very interested in the discussion, although he remained silent during it all. The question now is: What meaning did the discussion and questioning have for both Paul and the teacher?

For his teacher the situation was one of assessment and gave further evidence of Paul's slowness. Even though the letter being highlighted was in his name, and even though he had seen it written many times before, he didn't appear—the teacher could not be certain though—to be aware that his name and Ping's both begin the same way. In addition, it was more than likely that Paul had no understanding—at least his behavior showed none—of the concept "sound alike" when applied to parts of words.

For Paul himself the situation was a very interesting one because everybody was talking about his name. He didn't remember anyone telling him before—they had actually—that the first letter in his name is *P*. And he didn't know until now that other words start with the same letter. For instance, he knows Penny but never knew until now that her name starts the way his does. For Paul, then, the situation was one from which he learned the name of a letter and the fact that more words than just his name start with it. He had received what would be considered readiness instruction because in some small way he was getting ready to learn to read. He was beginning to understand that letters have names and make words and that some of these words begin with the same letter.

Now, what about Mary Anne? What did the discussion and questioning mean for her?

Mary Anne. Mary Anne is a very alert child who does not believe in hiding her candle under a bushelbasket. What she knows she tells you. In the discussion of words beginning with *P* she was quick to inform the teacher that she already knew its name because it was in her big sister's name (Pat). She said she could write her sister's name, and her mother's and daddy's names, too. As the classroom discussion proceeded, she enjoyed making the sound of *P*—this seemed to be something new for her—and quickly recalled words beginning with it. *Punch*, *princess*, and *Pat* were her contributions when the teacher asked, "Can anyone think of some words that begin the way *Ping* begins?" (Mary Anne was eager to explain that *Punch* was the name of the detergent her mother used when she washed clothes.)

Obviously, what the discussion and questioning meant for Mary Anne was something quite different from what they had meant for Paul. With both children, though, the teacher had an opportunity to assess readiness. In the case of Mary Anne, much was learned—including the fact that she has already begun to read. She knew the name of *P*, enjoyed making its sound, and was able to name words beginning with it. That she did some writing at home and was attentive to words in her environment —*Pat* and *Punch,* for instance—also became clear.

While the teacher was looking for behavioral signs of readiness, what was Mary Anne herself getting out of the discussion and questions? Primarily they helped her recall what she already knew, and they also encouraged her to use what she knew. The two new learnings seemed to be the idea that words have a beginning sound and, secondly, that the sound of the letter *P* is /p/.* With Mary Anne, then, the teacher's assessment effort turned into an opportunity for her to have reading instruction; specifically, instruction in phonics.

What the discussion and questioning turned out to be for both of these children is summarized below:

	Assessment	Readiness Instruction	Reading Instruction
Paul	X	X	
Mary Anne	X		X

The summary above and the brief descriptions of the two kindergarteners offer some important reminders:

1. A productive way to assess readiness is to provide children with varied opportunities to begin to read. What is or is not learned offers information not only about readiness but also about ways to teach reading that seem to be easiest and of greatest interest.
2. Assessment carried out in this way provides more than just diagnostic information; it can, in fact, result in readiness instruction and even reading instruction itself.
3. What one and the same learning opportunity actually accomplishes depends upon the abilities and interests of the children. With some, an opportunity turns out to be preparation for reading. With other children it is reading instruction.

There is still one more important point to remember about readiness. Let me introduce it by telling about still another child in the kindergarten class that was just discussed.

Joey. Joey is a very willing participant in all kindergarten activities. At the start of the year he generally went to the blocks at free-choice time, but it was not long before quiet table games and puzzles became attrac-

* This isolation of sounds is discussed in detail in Chapter 10.

tive. He also is an inevitable "joiner" when the teacher makes available still other choices: "Today I'm going to be reading a story over in that part of the room" or "Today I'm going to be playing a game" (e.g., bingo played with numerals, letters, or words). When words are part of a game, Joey is very involved and always successful because of his wonderful ability to remember words with only minimal help. For instance, he learned to read all the days of the week as a result of quick, early morning discussions related to "What day is today?" Because of the attention given to *September, October,* and *November* in connection with the calendar displayed in the room, he can read those words, too.

In using words in games, Joey's teacher has heard him make interesting comments. When *Sunday* came up he observed, "Sandy's name looks like a short Sunday." On another day, when the teacher wrote *silk* on the board in connection with a discussion of fabrics and textures, Joey quickly observed, "That almost looks like salt." When asked, "Where did you see *salt?*" he explained, "It's on our salt shaker at home."

Interestingly, Joey's excellent visual memory is not matched by equal excellence in auditory discrimination. Thus, he only rarely responds correctly when the teacher makes requests like: "I'm going to say two words. Can you tell me whether they start with the same sound or a different sound: *ball, fence.*" . . . "I'm going to say some words. Would you tell me which of these words begin with the same sound: *mouse, table, mother.*" . . . "Can anyone think of another word that starts with the sound you hear at the beginning of *Ping* and *Paul* and *Penny?*"

What these and other observations indicate to Joey's teacher is that in some ways he is very ready for reading—in fact, he has already begun. In other ways, however, he is still learning to be ready. What the same observations mean more generally is that efforts to assess readiness should not have an either-or focus. That is, a teacher's thoughts ought not to be "Is he or is he not ready?" but rather "In what ways is he ready and in what ways is he not?"

This more correct concern has implications for the way we think about instruction. It reminds us—or should—that readiness instruction and reading instruction can go on simultaneously. With Joey, for instance, reading ability is developing as a result of help with whole word identification. At the same time, however, the attention being given to sounds is readiness instruction for him. Graphically, this point can be shown as follows:

September ——————————————→ June

r e a d i n e s s   i n s t r u c t i o n

r e a d i n g   i n s t r u c t i o n

How different the conception on the previous page is from the traditional all-or-none practice of separating the readiness program from the reading program:

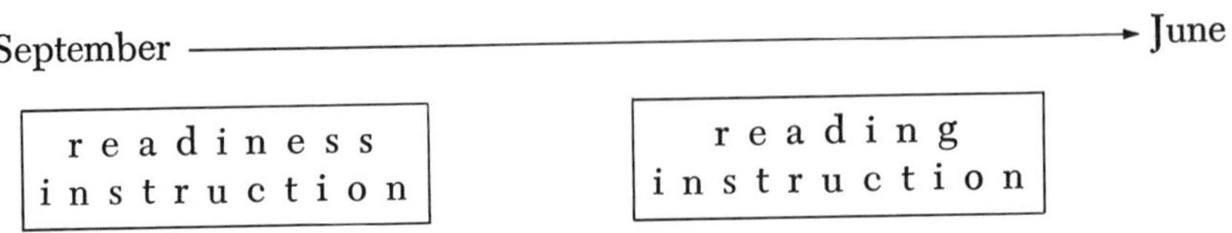

Still one more important reminder is to be found in the observations made about Joey and all other children, too. This also relates to readiness assessment; specifically to the idea that it is a daily occurrence, not a special event carried out once each year. All the reasons why this is so have been summed up perfectly by MacGinitie: ". . . when a child is taught a little, he is then ready for a little more" (42, p. 399).

A BRIEF SUMMARY

The timing of beginning reading instruction has been the concern of this chapter. Such a concern merits detailed attention because a child's initial experience with any activity always is of unique importance.

In considering the best time to start teaching reading, psychologists and educators whose views dominated the scene from the 1920s to the 1950s correctly gave attention to the concept of readiness. They asked, "When are children ready to be successful with reading?" Some answered, "When they have a mental age of about 6.5 years." Others, though, turned to special testing as a way of finding an answer and so was born the reading readiness test. Commonly, the interest of those who administered it was not in the possibility that some beginning first graders might be ready for reading but, rather, in the question of how long each should spend in a readiness program, conceived of as being separate and distinct from the reading program.

The chapter went on to identify some serious flaws in the early interpretations and use of the readiness concept. One was simply an exaggeration; specifically, an exaggerated appreciation of the contributions made by heredity and maturation. In contrast, everything said in this textbook assumes that whatever it is that constitutes readiness for reading is the product not only of genetic endowment and maturation but also of prior experiences and learnings. Within this context, much about readiness is teachable.

Another point emphasized in the chapter is the need to look at instruction as well as the child's abilities when readiness is being considered. With the twofold focus, the question the earlier psychologists and educators asked—Is the child ready?—also can be seen as having flaws. It seemed to assume that success with every type of reading instruction demands the same abilities and that readiness, therefore, could be assigned a single meaning. Or, maybe its assumption was that there is one way to teach reading and so the question to ask is, "When are children ready to be successful with it?"

Whatever the explanation, this chapter has tried to show that the correct question is more specific as it asks: Is the child ready to succeed with this particular kind and quality of instruction? Such questioning recognizes the equal significance of the child's abilities and of the instruction that will be available. Or, to put it somewhat differently, it reflects the relational aspect of readiness—an aspect effectively underscored in Ausubel's conception of readiness as being "the adequacy of existing capacity in relation to the demands of a given learning task" (4, p. 246).

This concept has implications for how readiness can be assessed: Give children varied opportunities to learn to read, and what they do or do not learn tells something about their readiness as well as the way of teaching reading that takes advantage of their particular abilities and interests.

This type of assessment, this chapter has shown, has the advantage of being two other things as well. It will be readiness instruction for some children and reading instruction for others. Further, as this way of assessing readiness makes use of different methodologies, teachers will also be able to learn that most children are neither totally ready nor totally unready for reading. Such an awareness ought to encourage schools to give up the idea that "getting ready to read" and "beginning to read" occur at separate points on a time line as well as the related practice of having a readiness program followed by a reading program. One of the happy results could be a lessening of the unfortunate gap that has always existed between kindergarten and the first grade.

REFERENCES

1. Appleton, Edith. "Beginning with Enthusiasm," *Education,* LXXXVI (February, 1966), 347–349.
2. Arthur, Grace. "A Quantitative Study of the Results of Grouping First Grade Children According to Mental Age," *Journal of Educational Research,* XII (October, 1925), 173–185.
3. Austin, Mary C., and Morrison, Coleman. *The First R: The Harvard*

Report on Reading in the Elementary Schools. New York: The Macmillan Co., 1963.

4. Ausubel, David P. "Viewpoints from Related Disciplines: Human Growth and Development," *Teachers College Record*, LX (February, 1959), 245–254.
5. Bacci, W. "Children Can Read in Kindergarten," *School Management*, V (May, 1961), 120–122.
6. Barton, A. H., and Wilder, D. E. "Research and Practice in the Teaching of Reading: A Progress Report," in *Innovations in Education*, ed. M. B. Miles. New York: Bureau of Publications, Teachers College, Columbia University, 1964.
7. Berry, Frances M. "The Baltimore Reading Readiness Test," *Childhood Education*, III (January, 1927), 222–223.
8. Betts, Emmett A. *The Prevention and Correction of Reading Difficulties*. Evanston, Ill.: Row Peterson and Co., 1936.
9. Brenner, Anton. "Nature and Meaning of Readiness for School," *Merrill-Palmer Quarterly*, III (Spring, 1957), 114–135.
10. Chall, Jeanne S. *Learning to Read: The Great Debate*. New York: McGraw-Hill Book Co., 1967.
11. Cole, Luella. *The Improvement of Reading: With Special Reference to Remedial Instruction*. New York: Farrar and Rinehart, Inc., 1938.
12. Dickson, Virgil E. "What First Grade Children Can Do in School as Related to What Is Shown by Mental Tests," *Journal of Educational Research*, II (June, 1920), 475–480.
13. ———. *Mental Tests and the Classroom Teacher*. New York: World Book Co., 1923.
14. Dolch, Edward W. *Teaching Primary Reading*. Champaign, Ill.: The Garrard Press, 1950.
15. Durkin, Dolores. "A Language Arts Program for Pre-First Grade Children: Two-Year Achievement Report," *Reading Research Quarterly*, V (Summer, 1970), 534–565.
16. Dykstra, Robert. "The Use of Reading Readiness Tests for Prediction and Diagnosis: A Critique," in *The Evaluation of Children's Reading Achievement*, ed. T. C. Barrett. Newark, Delaware: International Reading Association, 1967.
17. "Educational News and Editorial Comment," *Elementary School Journal*, XXXIII (May, 1933), 641–655.
18. Gates, Arthur I. "The Necessary Mental Age for Beginning Reading," *Elementary School Journal*, XXXVII (March, 1937), 497–508.
19. Gates, Arthur I., and Bond, Guy L. "Reading Readiness," *Teachers College Record*, XXXVII (May, 1936), 679–685.
20. Gates, A. I.; Bond, G. L.; and Russell, D. H. *Methods of Determining Reading Readiness*. New York: Bureau of Publications, Teachers College, Columbia University, 1939.
21. Gesell, Arnold L. *The Mental Growth of the Preschool Child*. New York: The Macmillan Co., 1925.
22. ———. *Infancy and Human Growth*. New York: The Macmillan Co., 1928.

23. ———. *The First Five Years of Life.* New York: Harper and Bros., 1940.

24. Gesell, A., and Ilg, F. *The Child From Five to Ten.* New York: Harper and Bros., 1946.

25. Gesell, A., and Thompson, H. "Learning and Growth in Identical Twin Infants," *Genetic Psychology Monographs,* VI (July, 1929), 1–124.

26. Gray, William S. "Reading," *Child Development and The Curriculum,* Chapter IX. Thirty-Eighth Yearbook of the National Society for the Study of Education, Part I. Bloomington, Ill.: Public School Publishing Co., 1939.

27. Hall, G. Stanley. *The Psychology of Adolescence.* New York: D. Appleton and Co., 1904.

28. Harris, Albert J. *Effective Teaching of Reading.* New York: David McKay Co., Inc., 1962.

29. Harrison, M. Lucille. *Reading Readiness.* Boston: Houghton Mifflin Co., 1936.

30. Havighurst, Robert. *Human Development and Education.* New York: Longmans, Green, and Co., 1953.

31. Heffernan, Helen. "Significance of Kindergarten Education," *Childhood Education,* XXXVI (March, 1960), 313–319.

32. Hester, K. B. *Teaching Every Child to Read.* New York: Harper, 1955.

33. Holmes, Margaret C. "Investigation of Reading Readiness of First Grade Entrants," *Childhood Education,* III (January, 1927), 215–221.

34. Hunt, J. McVicker. *Intelligence and Experience.* New York: The Ronald Press Co., 1961.

35. ———. "The Psychological Basis for Using Preschool Enrichment As an Antidote for Cultural Deprivation," *Merrill-Palmer Quarterly,* X (July, 1964), 209–248.

36. Jenkins, Frances. "Editorial," *Childhood Education,* III (January, 1927), 209.

37. Jensen, Arthur R. *Understanding Readiness: An Occasional Paper.* Urbana, Ill.: Distributed by the University of Illinois Press, 1969.

38. Keislar, E. R., and McNeil, J. D. "Oral and Non-Oral Methods of Teaching Reading," *Educational Leadership,* XXV (May, 1968), 761–764.

39. Keliher, Alice V. "Do We Push Children?" *Childhood Education,* XXVII (November, 1960), 108–112.

40. Kelley, Marjorie L., and Chen, M. K. "An Experimental Study of Formal Reading Instruction at the Kindergarten Level," *Journal of Educational Research,* LX (January, 1967), 224–229.

41. Lamoreaux, Lillian A., and Lee, Dorris M. *Learning to Read Through Experience.* New York: Appleton-Century-Crofts, Inc., 1943.

42. MacGinitie, Walter H. "Evaluating Readiness for Learning to Read: A Critical Review and Evaluation of Research," *Reading Research Quarterly,* IV (Spring, 1969), 396–410.

43. McKee, P.; Brzeinski, J. E.; and Harrison, M. Lucille. *The Effectiveness of Teaching Reading in the Kindergarten.* Denver: Denver Public Schools, Denver, Colorado, 1966.

44. Monroe, Marion. *Children Who Cannot Read.* Chicago: University of Chicago Press, 1932.

45. Morphett, M. V., and Washburne, C. "When Should Children Begin to Read?" *Elementary School Journal,* XXXI (March, 1931), 496–503.
46. Newton, J. Roy. *Reading in Your School.* New York: McGraw-Hill Book Co., Inc., 1960.
47. Olson, Willard. *Child Development.* Boston: D. C. Heath and Co., 1949.
48. Olson, W., and Hughes, B. "Concepts of Growth," *Childhood Education,* XXI (October, 1944), 53–63.
49. Rasmussen, Margaret, ed. *Reading in the Kindergarten?* Washington, D.C.: Association for Childhood Education International, 1962.
50. Reed, Mary M. *An Investigation of Practices in First Grade Admission and Promotion.* New York: Bureau of Publications, Teachers College, Columbia University, 1927.
51. Shapiro, B. J., and Willfred, R. E., "i.t.a.–Kindergarten or First Grade?" *Reading Teacher,* XXII (January, 1969), 307–311.
52. Smith, Henry P., and Dechant, Emerald V. *Psychology in Teaching Reading.* Englewood Cliffs, N.J.: Prentice-Hall, Inc., 1961.
53. Smith, Nila B. "Matching Ability as a Factor in First Grade Reading," *Journal of Educational Psychology,* XIX (November, 1928), 560–571.
54. Sutton, Marjorie H. "Readiness for Reading at the Kindergarten Level," *Reading Teacher,* XVII (January, 1964), 234–240.
55. Thorndike, Robert L., and Hagen, Elizabeth. *Measurement and Evaluation in Psychology and Education.* New York: John Wiley and Sons, 1969.
56. Trow, William C. "When Are Children Ready to Learn?" *NEA Journal,* XLIV (February, 1955), 78–79.
57. Washburne, Carleton. "Ripeness," *Progressive Education,* XIII (February, 1936), 125–130.
58. ——. "The Work of the Committee of Seven on Grade-Placement in Arithmetic," *Child Development and the Curriculum,* Chapter XVI. Thirty-Eighth Yearbook of the National Society for the Study of Education, Part I. Bloomington, Ill.: Public School Publishing Co., 1939.
59. Wayson, W. W. "A New Kind of Principal," *National Elementary Principal,* L (February, 1971), 8–19.
60. Wills, C. D., and Stegeman, W. H. *Living in the Kindergarten.* Chicago: Follett Publishing Co., 1956.
61. Zornow, T. A., and Pachstein, L. A. "An Experiment in the Classification of First-Grade Children Through Use of Mental Tests," *Elementary School Journal,* XXIII (October, 1922), 136–146.

4

Language Arts Approach for Beginning Reading

One major theme of the previous chapter was that readiness can be assessed most accurately by giving children a variety of opportunities to learn to read. This recommendation reflects the fact that what makes one child ready is not necessarily the same as what makes another ready. It also recognizes that what it takes to be successful with one methodology and one teacher is not always the same as would be required in the classroom of another teacher using either the same or a different method of teaching. What the recommendation indicates negatively, then, is that reading readiness is not one thing—certainly not something that can be neatly defined in terms of a particular mental or chronological age.

The last detail is interesting to note because it is chronological age which schools routinely use when making decisions about the time to start teaching reading. Though deserving of criticism, the continued use of this single-factor criterion is easy to understand if only because it wears the cloak of tradition—always difficult to discard. It can still be asked, though, why did the tradition develop?

One very apparent reason is that the schools have been using chronological age as the criterion for admission into first grade for a very long time, probably because it is the easiest and most obvious way to organize students. Even now it is not uncommon to have children turned away from first grade because the calendar indicates they are as few as one or two days "too young."

When this traditional admission policy is put side by side with the other long-lived one of introducing reading instruction during the first grade year, the end result is the idea that being six somehow means a time for learning to read. Such an association is especially interesting if only because nothing that is now known either about children or reading even suggests that the age of six is, in fact, the best time for all children to begin to read.

Relevant here are the observations of Kohlberg, who could be called a somewhat conservative or at least middle-of-the-road psychologist in his attitude regarding the learning potential of young children (4). In a paper characterized by careful caution about the benefits to be derived from pre-first grade programs, he still writes:

> A good deal of learning to read and to write in the elementary school is a tedious task for the six to eight year old, requiring drill, repetition, self-correction and considerable insecurity in comparing the child's own performance with that of other children in the classroom. Because reading and writing (especially reading) are relatively low level sensori-motor skills, there is nothing in the cognitive structure of the reading task which involves any high challenge to the older child. In contrast, the identification of letters and words can be challenging fun for younger children (4, p. 1038).

Probably Kohlberg's observations generate more thoughts about the advantages of a home start with reading than about an earlier school beginning. Yet they are useful in reminding us that there is nothing sacred and untouchable about the traditional practice of initiating school instruction in reading when a child is six. As a result, we should at least feel more comfortable in entertaining the possibility and even likelihood that some children, and for a variety of reasons, are ready to be successful with reading earlier.

NURSERY SCHOOL AND KINDERGARTEN STARTS

Because nothing in the fields of psychology or education suggests that the first grade year—and thus the age of six—is the best time for all children to begin reading and, secondly, because I personally have had the chance to observe groups of nursery school and kindergarten children *enjoy* learning to read, the recommendation of this textbook is to make available to pre-first graders opportunities to learn to read which represent varied methodologies and which are interesting and appropriate for this age level (2). Why such opportunities ought to represent different methodologies was discussed in Chapter 3 and will be re-discussed later in this chapter. For now, let me just deal with the qualifications "interesting" and "appropriate."

IMPORTANCE OF INTERESTING, APPROPRIATE START

Having raised many questions about the way educators once claimed unequivocally that beginning first graders were having problems with reading because they were unready when instruction got underway, I want to be sure that a possibility inherent in the recommendation I have been making is not overlooked. What I call to your attention is this. If nursery school and kindergarten teachers offer nothing but unimaginative, whole-class instruction in reading, it is very possible that most children will learn little or nothing—except, perhaps, to dislike school. An inevitable result would be widespread criticism. However, such criticism might not distinguish between a timing that could have been just right and a methodology that was all wrong. One further result, therefore, could be a return to the earlier and unfortunate belief that children didn't learn because they were not ready—they were "too young."

To discourage such a possibility of events from happening, let me restate some of the points I have already made, although I will add to them, too:

1. It is very likely that some children are more than ready to read before the first grade and would even enjoy learning.
2. Schools should offer interesting and appropriate opportunities for kindergarteners and even nursery school children to start to read.
3. If such opportunities turn out to be neither interesting nor appropriate, it is likely that few of the children will be successful.
4. If this occurred, the tendency might be to put the blame on the children; that is, on their lack of readiness.
5. Such an interpretation would take us back in time to the earlier notions about readiness and, perhaps, to some of the unfortunate school practices connected with them.

With all of these points in mind, I now want to make this very strong recommendation: *If pre-first grade teachers are either unwilling or unable to offer opportunities to learn to read that are interesting and appro-*

priate for young children, they should forget about reading and simply continue with their traditional programs.

On the assumption that some teachers are convinced of the readiness of their children and, further, want to learn how to introduce them to reading in a way that will be both productive and enjoyable, the rest of this chapter will discuss one such possibility: a language arts approach.

LANGUAGE ARTS APPROACH

The term "language arts" is school talk and refers to the combination of listening, speaking, reading, and writing. It thus encompasses all aspects of verbal communication. For this textbook it is a most important term because it is at the core of two of its assumptions: (a) the major academic responsibility of those who teach in the primary grades, but also in the school years preceding first grade, lies with the language arts; and (b) one productive way to promote skill in reading among younger children is through attention to all the dimensions of verbal communication.

Since reading instruction is the primary concern of this book, some of you might now be wondering why the broader language arts approach is recommended. Won't it be inefficient? Doesn't it take too much time away from the reading? Why not just teach children to read by concentrating on reading? Actually, my recommendation has to do with some facts.

Reasons for Language Arts Approach

The first fact is that the different aspects of language are not only interrelated; they also are interdependent. Those who rush to teach a child to read, even though he is barely able to speak or comprehend American English, learn about the dependent relationships quickly. But so, too, do teachers who work with more fluent children. With them, for instance, it is an everyday occurrence to see how readily they learn to read familiar words in comparison with those whose meanings are vague or simply unknown. Awareness of the dependent relationships also flourishes when reading comprehension is of concern. With this, teachers promptly learn that what cannot be understood when spoken cannot be understood when written. In fact, it seems accurate to say that the reading comprehension problems of many children are really symptoms of more basic deficiencies in language comprehension.

Another reason for my recommending the language arts approach—one directly related to the fact of interdependency—is that it encourages teachers to give time to whatever aspect of language needs attention. Thus, the teacher who carries in her head the broader language arts perspective is not likely to plunge children into reading, even though ability in reading might be one of her instructional goals, when it is obvious that their ability to deal with oral language suffers from serious limitations. I stress this point, by the way, because I have recently visited classrooms in which teachers seemed blinded by a very narrow view of what it means to teach reading or to prepare children for it. I recall one kindergarten class in which the teacher was fortunate enough to have the sweet combination of a teaching assistant and only eighteen children. Surrounded as this school was by extreme poverty and deprivation, my immediate thought as I entered the room was, "What a wonderful opportunity to help these children grow in their ability to use oral language." My second thought, however, was a combination of surprise and disappointment because in this classroom the assistant had assumed what I would call the role of a policeman. Both she and the teacher walked about the room, constantly reminding children not to talk—not even to ask questions—as they all completed the same two pages in a reading readiness workbook. Later, when I asked the teacher the reason for what had been observed, she explained without hesitation, "If these children are going to learn to read, they have to learn to be quiet." In this particular school an explanation like, "If these children are going to learn to read, they have to learn to talk" would have been easier to defend.

Because in the discussion thus far the dependence of reading upon oral language has been especially stressed, another idea—an erroneous one—might have been communicated unintentionally. That is, you might be thinking now that it is only after ability in oral language is an accomplished fact that a teacher turns her attention to reading. Not so! I say "not so" because oral language is never an accomplished fact with children if by this is meant that it is something which can be completed, boxed, and put away. Instead, think of it as an area of development that is constantly growing—or ought to be—but also in constant need of nourishment. And during the growth process a teacher can be giving some of her attention to matters like reading and writing.

Actually, all four of the language arts have this "unfinished" nature, and so all four continue to require attention throughout a school year:

September ————————→ June

l i s t e n i n g

s p e a k i n g

r e a d i n g

w r i t i n g

While the sketch on the previous page offers a reminder about the continuing, cumulative nature of the language arts, it also suggests an artificial separation. Therefore, a better portrayal of how a teacher moves back and forth among them might be shown this way:

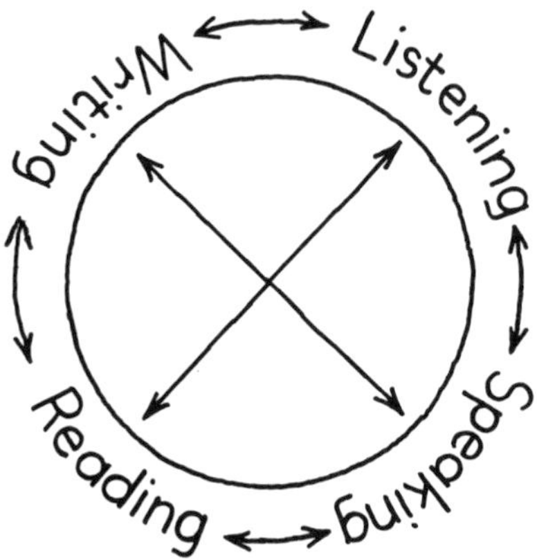

Just how a teacher moves back and forth among the language arts will be made clear as illustrations of teaching procedures are presented later on. For now the point to remember is that the various dimensions of language are interrelated and interdependent. To encourage teachers to take cognizance of the relationships is one reason for recommending the language arts approach to reading.

Still another reason for stressing the broader focus is that it allows for the likelihood that the easiest way into reading is different for different children. For example, you will recall from Chapter 3 the descriptions of some kindergarteners. From those descriptions you might also remember how Joey, with his wonderful memory, easily recalled the identity of written words; yet he had considerable difficulty with auditory discrimination. A language arts approach could accommodate him. It could give him multiple opportunities to learn to read words and also to prepare for phonics.

Another kindergartener—he was not mentioned in Chapter 3—could also be accommodated in the language arts curriculum. His name is Frank. Unlike Joey he shows little interest when there is the chance to learn to identify words, and he hardly gets excited when asked to think about others that begin with certain sounds. Frank, however, is very interested in learning to write and, in fact, has been doing some printing at home since about the age of four. Like other young "pencil and paper kids," his interest in writing is accompanied by a curiosity about spelling. Often his question in school (and at home) is, "How do you spell ———?" Although showing little interest as yet in reading per se, he is still doing some—thanks to the attention given printing and, when asked for, spelling. Eventually Frank's teacher hopes to use his interest in printing letters to teach him about the sounds some of them record. Meanwhile, his frequent decision at free-choice time is to write on one of the four small chalkboards in the classroom.

Paul must not be overlooked in this discussion of kindergarteners. He is the child, you will recall, who is slow in just about everything—even in physical movements. Yet he too can be accommodated in a program that puts reading into the context of the language arts. For instance, such a context takes pressure off his teacher in the sense that she feels no need to run to reading immediately and directly. It also helps her put Paul's particular needs into a correct perspective. He has a very long way to go with oral language, for example, and so needs a great deal of help and encouragement with that. Even while this is going on, attention is being given to such personally captivating words as his name. Paul recognizes its written form, knows the name of *P*, and gets excited whenever he sees it in other words displayed in the classroom. When instructional time goes to writing, his progress does not match his interest; however he is able to make *P* and *l*, and the *a* and *u* are gradually showing improvement. Thus, the more encompassing language arts approach is able to accommodate a child like Paul, too.

Still another important kind of accommodation is facilitated when all the language arts affect instructional goals and plans. This one has to do with the very obvious fact that young children love nobody quite as much as they love themselves. Whether this reflects what Piaget calls the "egocentric stage" is less important for this discussion than whether the teacher takes advantage of the fact that young children love to listen to, and talk, read, and write about themselves. Actually, the teacher who does not take advantage of these love affairs is foolish indeed.

The language arts perspective offers the wise teacher unending opportunities to use the factor of self-interest. Just consider the first names of children, for instance. I have watched one kindergarten teacher use a year-long interest in name cards (about 5 by 12 inches) not only for attendance-taking but also to give attention to such important instructional goals as:

letter names
capitalization
spacing between words
printing
letter sounds
alphabetical order

In this classroom one positive by-product of the children's involvement with names and attendance-taking was a heightened awareness of who was absent. As a result, an absentee's return to school was greeted with unusual enthusiasm which surely must have contributed to that child's positive feelings about school.

A more detailed description of what another teacher did with first names during the beginning months of a school year appears on pages 72–73. In this case the children were attending a nursery school for four year olds.

Still another nursery school teacher took advantage of her children's enthusiastic interest in themselves when she taught color identification. Some of the things she did are described on pages 74–75. In this case the children's clothes, art work, and birthdays were used.

The language arts approach, in addition to allowing for self-interest to be productive, also has the potential to make still another contribution. Why I name this one, by the way, could be rooted in nothing more than wishful thinking. I refer to the possibility of the broader approach becoming a means of steering away from the label "early reading program." This could be of monumental importance because such a label too often results in the expectation that every child participating in the program *will* read. Whenever this happens pressure is put not only on the children but on their teachers as well. The result, all too often, is exactly what nobody should want for young children: routine and uniform instruction.

To be sure, none of the foregoing comments implies that the other label, "language arts program," automatically eliminates expectations regarding reading; nor is there any pretense about a certain label being enough to guarantee good teaching. However, when the multiple goals of a language arts curriculum are accepted in deed as well as in word by teacher, parent, and administrator alike, they do offer every opportunity to teach each child what he needs and is ready to learn.

Because what is expected of the language arts program *can* have an effect on its quality, let me discuss that now.

Expectations for Language Arts Approach

All one has to do is visit nursery schools, kindergartens, and first grades located in a variety of communities to learn that no one set of goals can ever be established for any of these age groups. I personally have observed in nursery schools in which some of the children were more linguistically sophisticated than others I had seen in first grades. And similar discrepancies are found in behavior. Not very long ago, to cite one illustration, I used a day to observe in the kindergartens and first grades in a single school. In the kindergarten classrooms I saw children whose behavior suggested far greater maturity and independence than would ordinarily be expected of five year olds. Yet, as I visited the six-year-old groups I found others whose behavior patterns were those associated with considerably younger children and would thus be a deterrent to their learning. Therefore, and for all the reasons that account for human variability, the contention of this textbook is that the academic expectations established for any language arts program must vary from community to community, from school to school, and even from one group to another in the same school. In practice, such variation should result in programs in which no child is frustrated but, equally important, no child is bored. In fact, to have a program that either frustrates or bores is to have an indefensible program.

Applied to this textbook, the variability in expectations means that all it can do is suggest possible goals as well as some procedures for accomplishing them. In turn, readers must select from them whatever seems appropriate for the children they teach or will be teaching.

In choosing academic goals and making selections, it must be noted, factors other than a child's intellectual readiness have to be considered. In fact, anyone who works with children just starting school automatically learns that the very nature of the group situation requires attention to what early childhood education specialists have traditionally called "social and emotional development." Call it what you will. The point is that when a group of young children first arrives in school, some will need help in learning how to get along with others; to listen, when that is a requirement for whatever is going on; to take turns, whether with toys or during a conversation; to avoid bothering other children who are busy with an activity; and so on. What must be underscored about these kinds of needs, however, is that they do not force a teacher to make a choice. That is, she does not have to decide *between* behavioral goals and academic ones. It is not an either-or matter. Rather—except in extreme cases—children can learn appropriate behavior *while* they are learning a few of the academics. In fact, it frequently happens that a child's accomplishments in academic areas make a very positive contribution to more mature behavior. In spite of this, however, the point must still be made that what can be expected of the language arts approach will be affected not only by the children's intellectual and linguistic readiness, but also by what might be called the maturity of their behavior in the classroom.

Of course, what can be expected of a language arts program also depends upon the quality of the instruction. In fact, I would put that at the head of any list of requirements for success. But there are other prerequisites too, so let me deal with some of the more basic ones now, beginning with the teacher herself.

SUBJECT	GOALS	PROCEDURES
<u>Written Names of Children</u>	1. To introduce school with a personal emphasis	1. Used name tags ("Hello" tags) for each child during first week. Used sheriff's badges for boys, bracelets for girls, during second week. 2. Took Polaroid picture of each child. Displayed on bulletin board with first names under pictures. (Later, taken home in envelopes marked with children's names.) 3. Used placecards on tables at milk time during early weeks.
	2. To teach recognition of first name	1. Printed first names on all papers. Encouraged children to print all or part of their names themselves. 2. Displayed name cards on two bulletin board displays: a. on balloons b. on large red house 3. Gave smaller name cards to children to compare with cards on bulletin board.

		4. Let children take own attendance by removing name cards from card holder. 5. Each day had children read names of those who were absent (or present).
	3. To encourage attention to individual letters	1. Using large name cards, discussed names beginning with same letters. Named those letters. 2. Helped children look for words with letters that were in their names. Named them. 3. Gave each child white squares on which a letter in his name was written. Distributed name cards. Had children arrange letter-squares in a sequence to make their names. Had them paste letter-squares on paper. Later they drew a picture of themselves above their names. 4. Printed child's name at top of a paper. As each tried to copy it, identified letters.

SUBJECT	GOALS	PROCEDURES
<u>Colors</u>	1. To teach color identification	1. Named and discussed colors found in: a. name tags b. bulletin board displays* c. children's and teacher's clothing d. traffic signs e. calendar pictures f. crayons, paints, clay, chalk g. construction paper h. children's drawings i. cut-out train cars** j. autumn leaves k. soap bubbles made outdoors 2. Discussed colors during outdoor walks, giving attention to:

* For first week of school, bulletin board showed large cut-out figures of a boy and a girl. Every day their clothing was changed (paper doll method), and color of new clothing was discussed.

** Teacher made cut-out train of differently colored cars. Was first used to identify colors. Throughout the school year, each car became a month and children having a birthday during a particular month had their names placed on their car. The cut-out train was also used to show children names of the months.

a. houses
b. flowers
c. signs
d. train cars
e. rocks

3. Read books concerned with colors and discussed pictures; for instance:

   Color Kittens
   Color Wheel
   Book of Colors
   Come and See the Rainbow

Requirements of Language Arts Approach

Competent Teacher. "It's the teacher who makes the difference" has become something of a cliché in education. And no wonder. Whether one is doing research or observing in classrooms, what always becomes apparent is the unique importance of the teacher. Consequently when I maintain that what can be expected of the language arts approach is determined in no small way by the teacher who uses it, I am not suggesting anything new or startling.

Because of the key importance of the teacher, Chapters 5 to 10 in this book will deal with topics directly related to her instruction. Chapter 5 looks at the young child in a classroom, pointing out some of the characteristics that make working with him both difficult and uniquely rewarding. Chapter 6 then singles out the teacher of young children and describes with many classroom illustrations some of the behaviors that seem to make for success. Because empty-headedness has never been known to be a contributor, Chapters 7 to 10 deal both with the content of instruction in the language arts and with some of the ways for teaching it. Just how helpful those four chapters turn out to be, however, still depends upon the teacher; for she is the one who must make selections from the specifics in accordance with what particular children are ready to learn.

Small Group Instruction. In making selections—and this becomes even more obvious as a school year moves on—an inevitable result will be the need to teach different things to different children. One consequence of this, in turn, is the need to teach small groups rather than the entire class. This does not mean that a teacher must always be working with less than her whole class; but it does mean that if a program is to succeed in matching instruction with what children are ready to learn—and this, after all, is the very reason for having the language arts focus—then some of the teaching must be carried on in small groups.

Admittedly, a variety of factors often impedes a teacher from working with less than her entire class, even when she knows that nothing else is educationally defensible. One very obvious deterrent, for instance, is large classes. Generally, the more children there are the more difficult it is to work with some while others do other things. For the kindergarten teacher it is doubly difficult because she has both morning and afternoon groups. With so many children it is a problem not only to find ways to work with smaller groups but also to learn just what each child is ready to be taught. In visiting schools, however, I have been very impressed with the way many kindergarten teachers do manage both to know their children and to offer what they are ready to learn. But, it must be noted, with two groups of children this requires heroic efforts.

Because teachers of young children should not be required to make such efforts, more and more schools are going to have to move in the direction of supplying teaching assistants. Here I do not have in mind college graduates or even, necessarily, high school graduates. Rather, I refer to women who are looking for worthwhile ways to spend free time; who would like to add, even modestly, to their family's income; and, most of all, who enjoy young children. Such women are available in every community. And in every community in which schools expect teachers to be more than baby sitters and supervisors of play, they also must expect to supply them with help in the form of another adult.

How this extra adult could facilitate small group instruction can be shown with illustrations. For example, listed below is a schedule one nursery school teacher used. She had nineteen children and the help of a teaching assistant.

8:30– 8:45 A.M.	Conversation groups
8:45– 9:00	Attendance-taking; attention to date, weather, and current interests
9:00– 9:20	Academic period for one group Free-choice for other group
9:20– 9:40	Groups reversed for above activities
9:40–10:00	Music
10:00–10:30	Playtime, bathroom, milk
10:30–11:00	Art
11:00–11:15	Storytime
11:15–11:20	Preparation for home

With this schedule, the nursery school children divided into two groups of about equal size at conversation time, although on some days the boys would make up one group while the girls comprised the second. The teacher sat around a table with one of the two groups, while the teaching assistant conversed informally with the other.

The next fifteen-minute period began with attendance-taking and ended with current interests. All the children were together for this, sitting on the floor in front of the teacher. Meanwhile the assistant was able to prepare materials for use later on in the morning.

At approximately nine o'clock, the academic goals of the program received explicit attention. (A less structured type occurred at other times.) Each week the five "academic periods" focussed alternately on: color identification, printing, reading (word identification), letter identification and phonics, and numeral identification. During the early months of the school year the two academic groups were based simply on numbers and so were comprised of nine and ten children. As the year passed, however, and differences in ability and achievement were apparent, they became the basis for the composition of a group and, too, for what and how much would be taught.

While the teacher carried on instruction with one academic group, the assistant was responsible for the remaining children. Her work with them centered on choices made by the children from among prescribed possibilities. At the beginning of the school year these generally included toys—for instance, blocks, trucks, dolls, dishes, telephones, and so on. As time passed, possible choices were altered to include more quiet activities such as writing on small chalkboards or slates, working puzzles, or playing with sequence picture cards, concept cards, or bingo cards which at different times displayed colors, numerals, letters, and words. When games were selected, the assistant played, too. In fact, in observing the children they seemed to be choosing the chance to have the attention of the assistant as much as they were choosing a game itself.

Following the academic and free-choice periods came music which was followed by playtime. For this the children went outdoors whenever weather permitted. Bathroom and refreshment needs were taken care of afterwards.

For art, which lasted approximately thirty minutes, both the teacher and assistant worked with the children. Usually the teacher gave directions and then both she and the assistant distributed materials and, later, helped or talked with individuals. During art the atmosphere was relaxed but never rowdy. Conversations among the children and between teacher and child were taken for granted.

Next came a story, and then it was time to prepare for home.

In case some of you are now wondering about the omission from this schedule of the traditional rest period, I would like to make two comments. The first is that I was a frequent visitor in the nursery school class using the schedule, and I cannot recall ever seeing evidence of a need for daily rest periods. Perhaps the schedule had sufficient variety and, in addition, perhaps each period was sufficiently short that fatigue was no problem.

The message of the other comment was stated well in an article by William Martin, an educator whose name has been closely associated with nursery school education for a long time. After quoting from another article in which its author portrayed four year olds as somewhat fragile creatures in need of tender care, Martin responded with:

> I confess I find it difficult to accept this description. The typical nursery school child is a rugged, vigorous, almost inexhaustible creature as I see him. Of course, he gets tired. Of course, he can be overstimulated. But, at the end of a nursery school session, it is not the child who arouses my sympathy. He is jumping, shouting, racing, pulling, and pushing. It is his teacher and his mother who is trying to get him home who look as if they need rest, care, and indulgence (5, p. 94).

Regardless of how one chooses to portray four year olds—or fives or sixes for that matter—an inevitable characteristic is that there will be differences in what they are ready and able to learn. And it is just these differences that require some small group instruction. With a teaching assistant whose time is used well, the more individualized approach is very possible. In fact, I have seen it function beautifully in many classrooms. Without the teaching assistant there is no question but that it is difficult to achieve. And so to readers of this book who have large classes but no assistant, all I can do is to urge you to do whatever you can under the circumstances. Even while you are being forced to compromise and even while you are aware that your program is not perfectly matched to individuals, there is always the hope that as the learning potential of young children becomes more widely appreciated, teaching assistants will become more common.*

Flexible Scheduling. Whether or not a teacher does have an assistant, she must keep in mind a few important ideas about schedules. For instance, when young children are having their first experience with going to school, they must be given ample time to learn its routines as well as some of the do's and don't's of behavior. Later, as these learnings are accomplished to some degree by most of the children, then more attention can go to academic goals. When this first occurs, it must be remembered, it usually takes a long time for the children to do just a few things. Then, as time passes, more will be done more quickly. The usual result of such natural change and growth is the need for a change in scheduling. In fact, not to make the change can lead to idle, mischievous children and then to a frustrated teacher.

Even when teachers do examine their schedules regularly and make changes whenever they seem necessary, there still will be occasions when what was planned for a group takes either less or more time than was originally predicted. This requires another type of flexibility—a willingness to disregard the clock and to alter somewhat the day's routine.

Still another important kind of flexibility is not nearly as common as it ought to be. Here I am thinking of the many teachers who persist in

* Teaching assistants are discussed in greater detail in Chapter 6.

carrying out a certain instructional plan even when it is obvious that it is not going well. The children are not the least bit interested or perhaps they are frustrated or, maybe, just bored. And yet the teacher persists.

Once, when I was working with a group of new teachers, one among them had this characteristic to the point that it was causing discipline problems. When we talked about her tendency to persist—come what may—she was very honest, said she was aware of the problem but didn't know what to do about it. She explained that she panicked every time she had the feeling of losing the children but, not knowing what else to do, just continued with the original plan. Since I was not about to suggest that she have one plan plus three emergency plans for each instructional period, I offered a much simpler alternative.

This particular teacher had a kindergarten class and was following a schedule something like that shown a few pages earlier. Consequently she gave planned attention one day each week to goals like numeral and letter identification. For these and the other academic goals I suggested she keep a book close by, which could serve as a "security blanket." Thus, on the day set aside for letter identification it would be appropriate to have an alphabet book available. Should it happen that what was planned for helping with letter identification did not work out or, perhaps, did not take as long as was anticipated, she could gracefully shift to the book to look at illustrations, name letters, talk about them, and so on.

Later, it was interesting to see how the available book added tremendously to this new teacher's security; in fact, in a very short time the "blanket" was unnecessary. As she gained self-confidence and began to know the children better, her plans were almost always successful probably because she was learning to use them with just the right amount of flexibility.

Pervasive Language Arts Concern. In discussing the need for flexibility, an inflexible idea might have been communicated unintentionally. Here I refer to the possibility that as a result of the foregoing discussion of instructional periods, you might have picked up the erroneous notion that language arts goals only get attention at stipulated times each day. Again, not so. In fact, the language arts focus that is the concern of this chapter is one that pervades the whole of a program. It is a focus that permeates the thoughts of a teacher reminding her to be constantly searching for interesting and natural opportunities to give attention to any and all aspects of language. Because of the special importance of this point, let me make it more graphic with illustrations which show that listening, speaking, reading, and writing need not be confined to specified periods.

No matter what changes occur in future curricula for young children, it is highly unlikely that art will be eliminated. For that reason let me describe a few of the ways I have seen teachers use art projects to give attention to some aspect of the language arts.

One kindergarten teacher, on the day she discussed the sound of *v* with about half the class, had all the children make paper vases when art was scheduled. On each, she herself carefully printed the word *vase* and called the children's attention to the fact that it started with *v*. One child enthusiastically called everyone's attention to the fact that he knew its sound, which he promptly identified. Since the vases seemed empty without flowers, the teacher suggested that on the following day paper flowers could be made to fill them.

As the art period began the next day, the vases were brought out. All the children were asked to look at *vase*, to spell it and, if they could, to make the sound of *v*. Then the teacher commented about how appropriate it would be to fill the vases with a flower whose name also started with *v*. Thanks to a grandmother who had a collection of some thirty violet plants, her grandson immediately suggested "violets." Not by accident, pictures of violets were in a drawer. They were soon taken out by the teacher and thumbtacked on a bulletin board. Beside the pictures went the word *violets*, and then the children began to make some for their vases.

With another kindergarten group—the date was early April—the teacher was especially pleased with the number of words most children had learned to read during the year, but also uncomfortable about the possibility of their forgetting everything they knew over the spring vacation. To encourage the children to "play with words" at home, she decided to have them make Easter baskets which, during the course of the week before vacation, were gradually filled with small, egg-shaped pieces of construction paper of various colors. On the day set aside for color identification, the children—in small groups—reviewed colors and then, as each successfully named one, an egg of that color went into his basket. The same review and reward were used on subsequent days in connection with numeral identification, letter identification, and, for two days, word identification. Thus, the week ended with a review of material pertaining to four instructional goals—and, in addition, with well-filled Easter baskets.*

Presumably music is another subject that will continue to be in school programs for young children. While enjoyment always is its main concern, music still can be used occasionally to give attention to the language arts. Again, let me use some illustrations taken from actual class-

* I learned about this particular art project not from the teacher but from a parent of a girl in her class. Without any urging on my part, the mother told how the Easter basket and eggs became one of her daughter's most treasured possessions and of how it was frequently used when she and her older sister played school together. Because "playing school" is a common occurrence with young children and older siblings, teachers should keep it in mind as they make plans for materials that will be taken home.

rooms to show how instruction need not be confined to a prescribed period of time.

In one nursery class of four year olds, the children began the year completely unfamiliar with the Alphabet Song. Consequently it was taught early and, by the way, learned quickly. Sometimes the children sang it while they were having a midmorning snack. When this happened, the teacher used it as an occasion to discuss and hang up one more alphabet card. In fact, this was the way all the cards eventually got on the wall. Later, either the teacher or a child would point to the letters as the song was sung or listened to on a record.

One morning, as a special surprise, each child received his own alphabet book. It was a three-page dittoed copy of the Alphabet Song arranged in the way shown on the next page. At first the teacher and children talked about the page numbers 1 to 3 because they were known by almost everyone. Then the children were asked to point to the letters as the teacher sang part of the song very slowly. When they got to page 3, a few of the children quickly identified *I* and *me,* which were part of several earlier bulletin-board displays, so the teacher wrote those words on the board for all to see. Following this, she slowly sang the words shown on page 3, again encouraging the children to point to each as she sang it. Then the books were collected, but given out again on subsequent days. Eventually, most children learned to point to each letter and word as they sang the song. Before the books were finally taken home, a cover was added. These were made by the children during an art period and often incorporated letters of the alphabet.

Later, when this group of children arrived in kindergarten, most were able to name all the letters. Recognizing the omnipresent need for review, their kindergarten teacher soon found a rich opportunity to name many letters in connection with a popular song of the times—which, again, the children learned readily. You probably will remember the song if I just note the word that was written by the teacher and then spelled by quite excited children:

s u p e r c a l i f r a g i l i s t i c e x p i a l i d o c i o u s

Music, of course, can be used to give attention to words as well as letter names. In fact, because so many songs for young children have numerous verses, the combined use of words and pictures fits in naturally. Take "Old MacDonald," for example. With all of its verses, how natural to show a picture of an animal as a cue for the next verse to be sung. For the teacher who also has the language arts in mind, the same pictures might later be labeled with the animals' names. And as a final step, why not show the labels alone to indicate the next verse to be sung? All this,

Name________________________________

a b c d e f g

h i j k

l m n o p

-1-

q r s

t u v

w x y z

-2-

Now I know my a b c's.

Tell me what you think of me.

-3-

of course, would take place over several weeks, and would be interspersed with opportunities for the children to examine and discuss the pictures and to look carefully at the written names of the animals. Later, perhaps when the teacher decides to extend listening-speaking vocabularies by calling attention to pairs of words like *cow-calf* and *pig-piglet,* the pictures would again be useful to promote discussion and questions and, perhaps, to add to a bulletin board display entitled "Animal Words."

Probably these few illustrations are sufficient to make the point that the academic goals of a language arts program are given attention at more than just the periods of time especially set aside for them. Hopefully the illustrations have suggested also how young children can be given many opportunities to learn language arts skills in ways that are interesting and free of pressure.

Instructional Materials for Language Arts Approach *

Thus far, three of the most important requirements for a successful language arts program have been mentioned; a competent, knowledgeable teacher; opportunities to work with small groups of children; and flexible scheduling allowing for attention to the language arts at times other than specified periods. Not to be omitted when essential prerequisites are being discussed are instructional materials. Are there any "musts" for them?

Actually, in discussing materials for any kind of instruction or type of program the first point to consider is goals, not materials. Such a sequence is required by the fact that materials are one of the means a teacher uses to achieve instructional goals. Thus, her *initial* task is to select a goal or goals for a particular group or individual (e.g., meanings of *calf, piglet, colt;* ability to print *o* and *c;* an interest in learning to read). It is only after a selection is made that the teacher is ready to consider: What materials might I use to help achieve this goal with these children?

I immediately call your attention to the priority of goal selection because of an experience I once had with undergraduates enrolled in my reading methods course. Because I was convinced at the time—and still am—that one of the best ways to learn how to teach is to teach, I had the students tutor children while they were taking the course. I thought I had stressed the importance of relating materials to goals, but subsequent discussions about the tutoring showed I had been anything but successful. Repeatedly I heard the students explain their selection of materials—they had a rich source to choose from in a Materials Center—with words like, "Oh, it looked interesting," or "I had heard about them and thought I'd see how they worked," or "I remembered you had talked about that in

* Much more attention to materials is given in connection with the topics covered in Chapters 7 to 10.

class." Only rarely did I hear an explanation like, "I knew Richard had trouble remembering the different short vowel sounds and thought this practice material might help him." Together, all the explanations demonstrated that a wealth of materials does not automatically result in good education. For me, they also were a personal reminder of my failure to get across an important point about teaching: Instructional goals ought to be selected before thoughts turn to materials.

Assuming the means-end connection between materials and goals has now been stressed sufficiently, let me move on to a discussion of materials for a language arts approach to reading.

"Homemade" Materials. What the illustrations of teaching procedures scattered throughout this chapter ought to have underscored is the usefulness of "homemade" materials. The violets in a vase, the Easter basket with eggs, the bingo cards showing words, the name cards, the typed alphabet song book, the birthday train—these and the other examples serve well in pointing out how helpful, and interesting, homemade materials can be as a teacher works with young children. To further highlight this point, let me list a few other descriptions of materials, each to begin with a statement of the goal for which they were selected. Once again the illustrations represent something of what I have been fortunate enough to see during classroom visits.

Goal: To review the sounds of *m* and *t* in an initial position in a word.

Materials: Two old plastic clothes baskets, one showing a card with *m* and the other displaying a card on which *t* has been printed; two large balls.

Procedure: When inclement weather requires indoor play, a game called "phonics basketball" can sometimes be used. Two teams are selected and a member of each is given a ball. Members take turns listening to the teacher say a word that begins with either *m* or *t*. If a child throws his ball into the correct basket he moves to the end of his line, eventually getting another turn. Otherwise he has to sit down. At some stipulated time, the team with the most members is declared the winner. Then other children become two more teams and the game continues.

Goal: To provide practice in identifying numerals from 1 to 5, and counting from 1 to 5.

Materials: Using heavy paper, cut out five cards shaped like a house. On one side print a numeral from 1 to 5; on the other, paste the corresponding number of square windows on the house.

Procedure: Have children begin either by counting windows or naming a numeral. Looking at the opposite side can verify the correctness of the counting or the identification of the numeral.

Goal: Same as above.

Materials: Collections of paper squares, pebbles, buttons, straws, toothpicks, popsickle sticks, etc.

Procedure: Distribute one of the above collections among a group of children. Show a numeral and have them count out that number of items.*

Goal: To help children learn to read *family* and to provide practice with printing.

Materials: Store catalogues.

Procedure: Following a discussion of families, have children cut out people figures to match the makeup of their own family. After figures are pasted on a sheet of paper, each child can lablel his collection "family." **

Goal: To add baby animal words to children's speaking vocabulary (e.g., *lamb, piglet, calf, colt*).

Materials: Clay; small rectangular pieces of paper for labels.

Procedure: Following attention to animal vocabulary through pictures and stories, have each child make one pair of clay animals, for instance a horse and a colt. Later, display all the pairs on a

* Once I saw a kindergarten teacher follow such a procedure—only she used pennies. One child's reaction is worth quoting. She said, "Mrs. ———, you're the richest lady I know!" What made the child's comment especially interesting was that her family had the reputation of being the wealthiest in the community.

** Again I must comment about the reaction of a child. In this case it was tears. As it happened, the crying child was an only child, and she was unhappy because sitting next to her was a girl who had four brothers and two sisters. Evidently she felt slighted.

large table, each with a printed label showing its name.

Goal: To reinforce the concept "circle" and to provide practice in printing children's first names.

Materials: For each child: three white circles of different sizes, and enough smaller circles to match number of letters in his first name.

Procedure: On a wintry day, after listening to a recording of "Frosty the Snowman," have children make their own version of Frosty by pasting on a sheet of construction paper the three white circles of different sizes. Each child should then be encouraged to add eyes, nose, mouth, hat, etc. Later, on each small circle, the children print a letter found in their first name. These can then be arranged in correct sequence and pasted at the bottom of the Frosty pictures.

Goal: To provide practice in identifying letters from *a* to *g*.

Materials: Piano, and a cardboard keyboard made the same size as an actual one with each white key labeled *a* to *g*. Also, dittoed copies of the following sequence of letters: *c c g g a a g f f e e d d c*.

Procedure: Have children read aloud the names of the letters on the dittoed sheet. Then place the cardboard keyboard, standing up, behind the corresponding keys of the piano. Ask the children to reread the letters so that you will know which keys to play. Play as they read. The result will be part of two familiar songs ("Twinkle, Twinkle, Little Star" and "Alphabet Song") and a group of delighted children. Over several days, give each child a chance to play the tune on the piano as the others read the names of the letters.

Goal: To reinforce the sound recorded by *f*.

Materials: Paper, from which hand fans can be made by the children; small dittoed pictures of objects whose names begin with *f*. (Depending on the teacher's artistic ability, illustrations might include: *face, fence, flower, foot, football, frog, fountain, feather, flag, fire, fan.*)

Procedure: Have children make fans with fairly wide folds. Dittoed pictures can then be distributed, named by all, colored, cut out, and pasted in the folds of the fan as a decoration. (In doing something like this, be sure the connection between the fan, the names of the pictures, and the sound of *f* is made explicit. Otherwise the instructional potential of the activity may go no further than the teacher's mind.)

Goal: To review colors, and the concepts "circle," "square," "rectangle," and "triangle."

Materials: Small, multicolored pieces of paper cut in the four geometrical shapes; black construction paper.

Procedure: Have children identify shapes and colors. Distribute varied collections of shapes to each child, who can then make a pasted design on the black paper.

Goal: To provide practice identifying words.

Materials: Box painted blue to represent pond; fish-shaped pieces of paper on which words are printed and to which a paper clip is attached; long, thin stick (like what a florist uses in arranging flowers) with a string tied to one end; a magnet, which is tied to the end of the string.

Procedure: Individuals from a group of about five or six children can take turns fishing for a word. If it is correctly identified, the child gets to keep the fish; if not, it goes back into the pond. (To maximize practice, have the group look at and identify every caught fish, after the fisherman has his chance to identify it.) This same procedure can be used for practice in letter identification and/or phonics. With the latter the fish would show letters, and the fisherman's job would be to name the letter and say a word whose name begins (or ends) with it.

Goal: To provide practice in printing numerals from 0 to 9.

Materials: Telephone (old one can be obtained from telephone company); dittoed pictures of telephone; individual cards on which the children's phone numbers are printed.

Procedure: Using the telephone, show children the numerals on the dial and then demonstrate how some of them could be called at home. Distribute pictures of telephone and, to each child, a card showing his telephone number. The pictures can be colored and, underneath, each child would copy his phone number. Later, they could be assembled in alphabetical order and used as a telephone directory.

In addition to homemade materials like those just described, bulletin-board displays can also put ordinary things to good use. In fact, in a language arts program I once directed for four and five year olds, such displays turned out to be sources of great interest and even excitement for the children. In addition, though, they became productive vehicles for instruction. Some examples of bulletin-board displays, along with descriptions of how they were prepared and used in a variety of classrooms, can be found on the following pages. Other possibilities will be mentioned in connection with the topics of Chapters 7 to 10.

When bulletin-board displays are prepared for young children, it is a good practice to place them fairly low. In this way all their details can easily be seen and touched; for, like a book, the best display is one that is used. In fact, if a teacher feels compelled to couple her bulletin boards with warnings of "Do not touch," it is possible that she is one who should not have them—at least not if she teaches young children.

(*This text is continued on page 106.*)

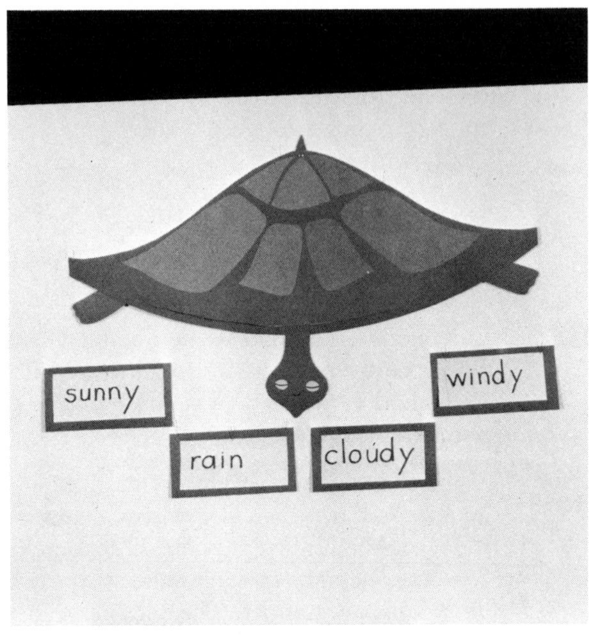
sunny
windy
rain
cloudy

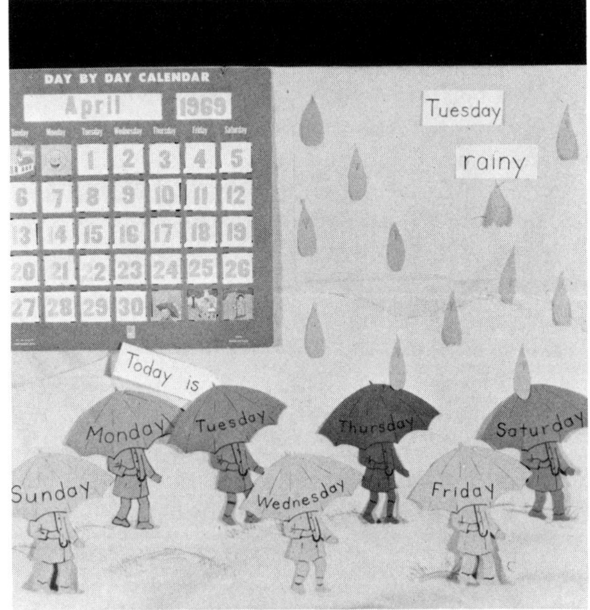
DAY BY DAY CALENDAR
April
1969
Tuesday
rainy
Today is
Monday
Tuesday
Thursday
Saturday
Sunday
Wednesday
Friday

Practice with Word Identification

A school day usually began with attention to the weather. Words like *windy* and *rainy* were used to describe it and also to teach the children to read *wind, windy; rain, rainy;* and so on. Once a description of a day was selected, the children took turns moving the turtle's head so that it pointed to the appropriate word.

Attention also went to the names of months and days. For every month a bulletin-board display was prepared to provide practice in reading these names. Figures of children carrying umbrellas were used for April. At other times of the year such things as leaves, turkeys, Christmas trees, snowmen, houses, and birds were displayed.

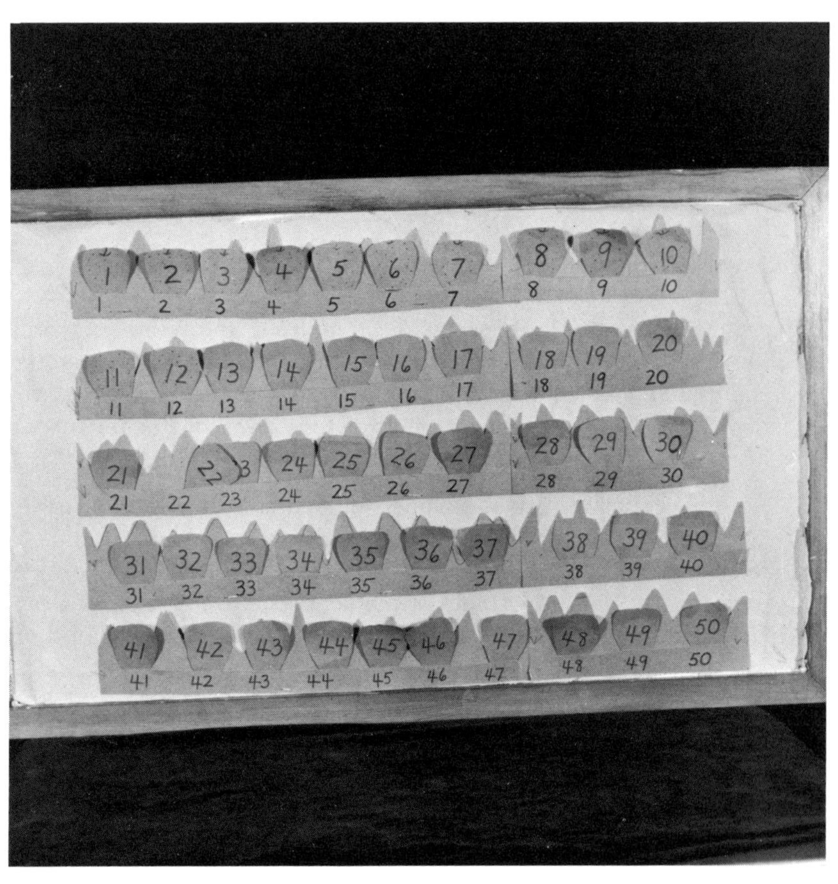
1 2 3 4 5 6 7 8 9 10
11 12 13 14 15 16 17 18 19 20
21 22 23 24 25 26 27 28 29 30
31 32 33 34 35 36 37 38 39 40
41 42 43 44 45 46 47 48 49 50

Numeral Identification

Strawberries placed in rows on a portable bulletin board were used in a variety of ways to help with numerals. At the start, children were each given numbered strawberries; the task was to put them in the correct place on the board by matching numerals.

Later, as the children learned the names of numerals, the strawberries were again used for practice. This time the teacher called out a number and a child would volunteer to pick that particular strawberry.

As the children learned to write numerals, the same bulletin-board display became useful again. In this instance individual children were directed to pick certain strawberries and to practice making the numerals printed on them.

Still later, the display was useful in helping the children understand the concept "ten."

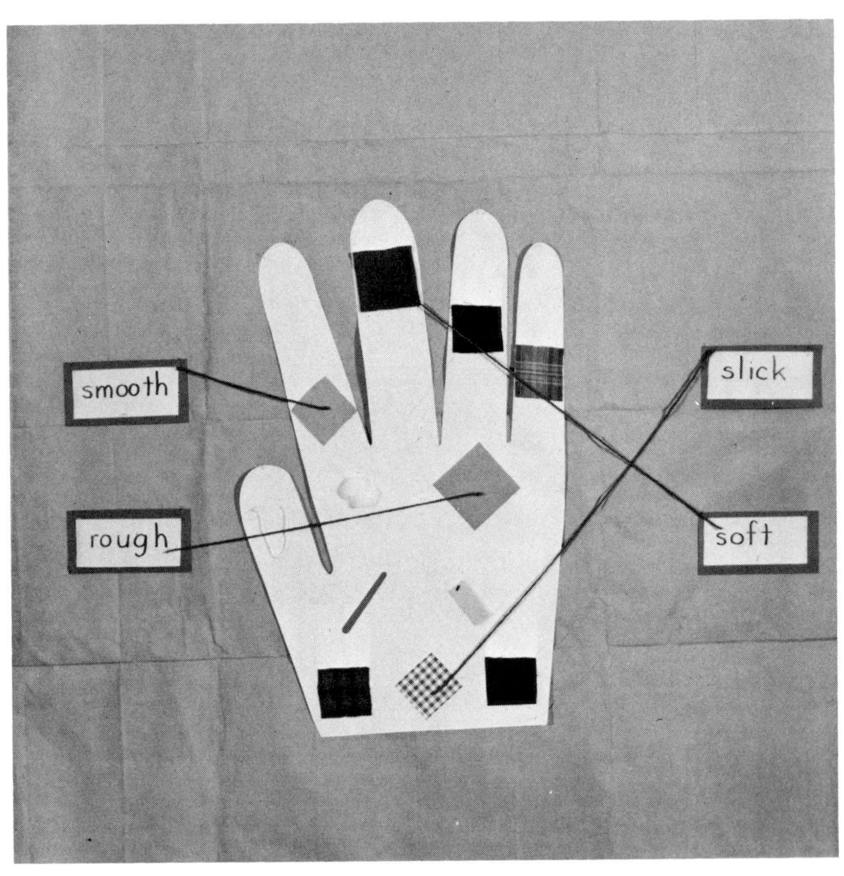
smooth
rough
slick
soft

Word Meanings

How things feel was used to teach the meanings of words like *rough* and *smooth*. To introduce some of these descriptions and to create interest in them, a bulletin board showed a hand. Pasted to it were pieces of fabric as well as things like a nail file and piece of string. As individual children took turns touching the fabrics and objects, they told the others how they felt. Their descriptions—for instance "rough"—would then be connected to the objects or fabrics with yarn.

Although this was not a preestablished goal, some children had no difficulty learning to read the descriptive words. Eventually they were allowed to play with the display. On their own they would connect appropriate descriptions to objects, again with yarn.

down
chicken
said
this
yellow
jump
eat
something
barn
man
This is up.
fast
pig

Practice with Word Identification

After the children had become acquainted with Humpty Dumpty, a bulletin-board display was prepared to provide practice with word identification. Some of the bricks in the wall had flaps which could be opened to show printed words or brief sentences. Pretending to be Humpty, a child would hold one of the paper figures in his hand and try to climb the wall by reading the words and sentences. An incorrect response meant that, like Humpty, he took "a great fall." Another child would then be given the chance to climb. If he was successful, a miniature figure of Humpty Dumpty on which his name was printed would be placed at the top of the wall.

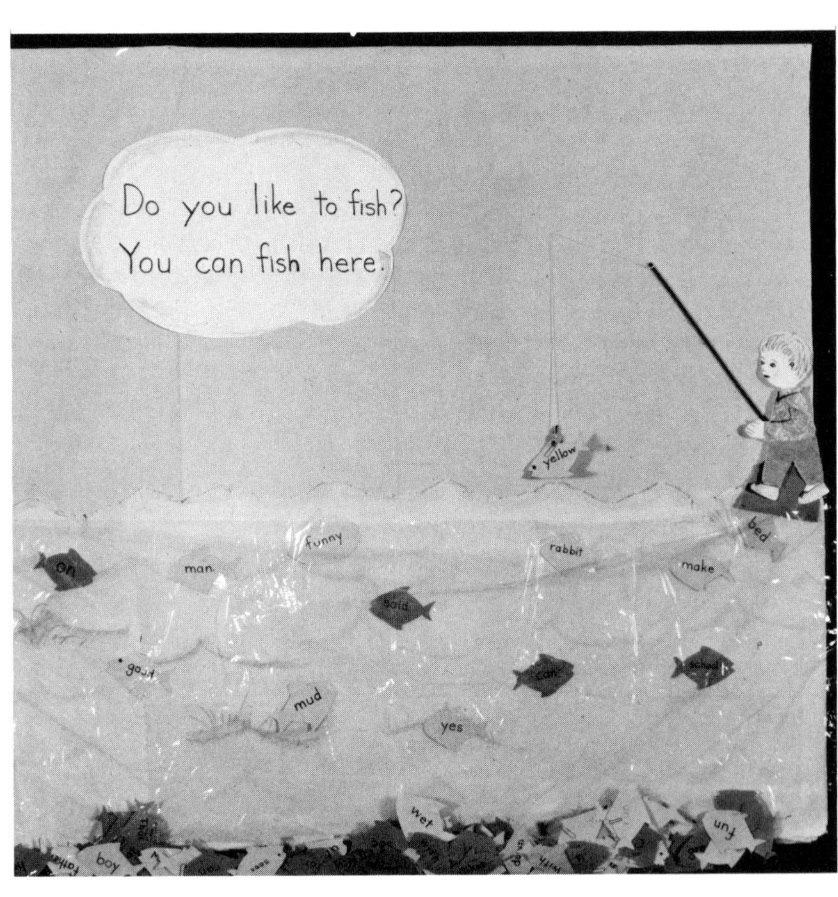
Do you like to fish?
You can fish here.
yellow
funny
rabbit
bed
on
man
make
said
can
school
mud
yes
wet
boy
fun

Practice with Word Identification

A fishing pond was prepared by covering the lower part of a bulletin board with cellophane paper that was attached on three sides. (The top was left free to allow for "fishing.") A fishing pole, which could be removed from the hands of the boy shown holding it, was a stick obtained from a florist. A string was tied to it, and at the end of the string a magnet was attached. Words from the children's reading vocabulary were printed on construction paper cut in the shape of a fish. To each, a paper clip was fastened.

The fishing pond was used in a variety of ways. Sometimes the teacher would be the fisherman, and as she caught a fish the children named it. The fish were then thumbtacked to another bulletin board and later, to provide for review, all the caught fish would be named again by the children. On other occasions the children were the fishermen, and a similar procedure was followed. At other times, two children would be allowed to play with the display. In this case they would take turns fishing for and naming words. (When this latter procedure was used, the teacher saw to it that one of the children was an able reader, thus making sure that words were being identified correctly.)

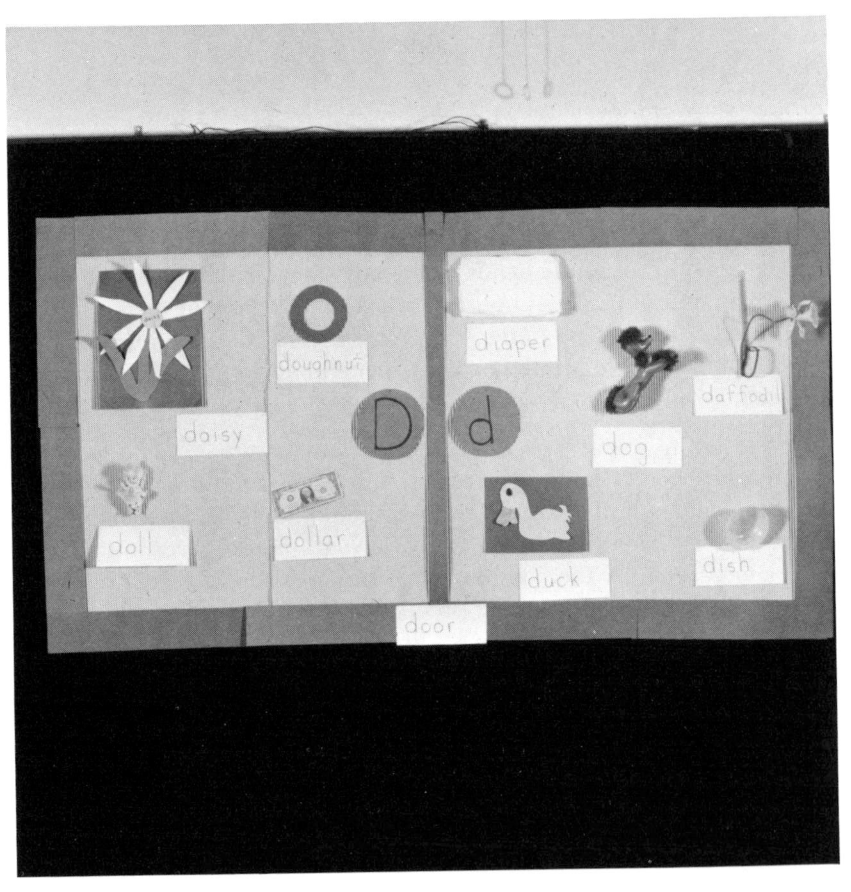
doughnut
diaper
daffodil
D
d
daisy
dog
doll
dollar
duck
dish
door

Teaching the Sound Recorded by D

To start a discussion of the sound which *d* records at the beginning of words, the teacher prepared a background for a bulletin board: the outline of two doors, each with its own doorknob. Once the children identified the doors and talked about the meaning of "doorknob," the teacher wrote *door* and *doorknob* on a chalkboard, pointed out that they began with the letter *d*, and then asked the children—as she said the words aloud—to listen for the sound at the beginning of each. Following this, the children named other words that began with the same sound. As correct examples were given, they were listed on the chalkboard by the teacher. To summarize the lesson, she read the total list.

When the children arrived at school the next day, the same bulletin board was covered with labeled objects whose names began with *d*. And so that particular school day began with phonics and with very excited children. Individual reactions were interesting:

Object	Child's Response
dollar	"Wow!"
diaper	"Ick!"
dog	"That's not really a dog. It's a poodle."

Moon
Mars

Practice in Associating Letters and Sounds

This bulletin-board display took advantage of the children's enthusiastic interest in space exploration. Letters whose sounds had been taught were printed on paths leading to the moon and Mars. Children took turns traveling the paths by pointing to each successive letter with a small rocket and by naming a word that began (or ended) with its sound. Correct examples allowed a child to reach the moon or Mars. An incorrect response meant a rocket had lost its way and fallen off into space.

(Earlier in the year the same display was used to provide practice in naming letters. At another time words were printed on the paths, allowing for reading vocabulary practice.)

get
hit
pad

Practice with Initial Consonant Substitutions

To encourage use of the letter-sound associations that were being taught, the teacher would write a list like the following on the chalkboard:

Consonant sounds would be reviewed first and then *get* would be identified. (A list like the above always began with a word the children knew.) Next, individual children would be given the chance to figure out the other words by using both their knowledge of *get* and the sounds recorded by *m, b, l,* and *j*. The meanings of the words would then be discussed.

To add interest to sound substitutions, a display of flowers was assembled on a bulletin board. Parts of common one-syllable words were printed on the stamens. The petals, which were cut out in one piece and were moveable, displayed consonants whose sounds had been taught. By rotating the petals, further practice with consonant substitutions was possible.

Materials from Children's Environment. Closely related to what I have been calling homemade materials are those found in a child's everyday surroundings. Here I am thinking of materials like labels on cartons, packages, and cans of food which always display a rich variety of words and numerals. That young children learn to read some of them on their own becomes obvious to anyone who takes the time to listen.

To cite one example, just recently I was visiting in a first grade classroom and found the teacher working with a group of seven children. She wrote *water* on the chalkboard and quickly commented, "This is a new word that's in our story for today." Equally quickly a boy responded with, "I know that. It says 'water.' " Curious about the way it had been learned, I asked him how he knew it. His explanation, like so many offered by young children, was breathless and long. Briefly translated, it told how the box for a cereal called "Frosty Flakes" explains the way a toy car can be obtained with some box tops. This car was special, for it could go either on land or in water.

In another classroom—this was occupied by a nursery school group—the teacher was planning to help the children learn to print the letter *O*. To create interest, she decided to show them many different packages and cans of food whose descriptive labels included *O*. She thought a package of Jello would be a good beginning because the way its name is printed (JELL–O) highlights *O*. Especially interesting was the response of a boy. As soon as the package of Jello was shown he called out, and with such excitement that he jumped out of his chair, "It's in my name! It's in my name!" What had caught his attention was not *O* but *E*, for his name was Eddy and he was just learning to print it. Taking her cue from his response, the teacher later used the same packages and cans for letter-naming and for encouraging individual children to point to and identify letters that were in their names.

In thinking about useful materials in the child's everyday environment, it would be impossible to name a total list. Instead, let me just suggest that one way to bridge the gap between a child's school life and his out-of-school life is to make use of materials like food labels, menus, newspaper advertisements, weather reports, labels on phonograph records, and so on. When taking a walk, other materials become available—labels on cars and trucks, for instance, or street signs or words displayed in store windows. When numerals are the concern, still other materials offer help; for example, birthday cards, calendars, measuring tapes, television dials, clocks, store catalogues, telephones, and telephone directories.

Commercial Materials. Because teachers tend to move too quickly—even automatically—to textbooks and workbooks when they make plans for instruction, the discussion of these commercially available materials has been kept until the end. Postponement seemed wise in order to show first, and with many illustrations, how other materials can make rich contributions to a language arts program for young children.

In any discussion of materials, whether they are commercially prepared or are of the homemade variety, the first point requiring emphasis is one that was made earlier: Materials are a means for achieving instructional goals. As such, decisions about them ought to be made *after* certain goals have been selected as appropriate and important for the children being taught. If the materials selected turn out to be helpful, then they can be considered "good." On the other hand, if they make little or no contribution to the achievement of goals, then they should be laid aside so that other more helpful materials can be found and tried out.

This emphasis on the means-end relationship between materials and instructional goals is, I believe, especially important when commercially prepared materials are the concern. I say this because of the frequency with which I have seen teachers assume the role of assistant to them. By this I mean they have allowed materials like textbooks and workbooks to dictate not only what they will teach but how and when they will teach it. Without commenting on what this does to children, I would like to suggest that such a role is unbecoming for a professional person.

Because commercial materials like textbooks and workbooks *can* be assigned their proper role—assisting the teacher—they should not be bypassed when materials for a language arts program are being considered. For example, because the language arts program discussed in this book has reading ability as its primary goal, it is both natural and right to wonder about the place of basal readers in it. What this place might be will be discussed in detail in Chapter 9. For now let me just say that because the very purpose of these texts is to teach reading skills, they often are useful as one means of achieving certain instructional goals. Problems like routine and rigidity develop, however, when they are viewed as *the* means; for it is within this context that they often dictate both the what and how of instruction.

As valuable or, perhaps, more valuable to a language arts program for young children are commercial materials related to what is generally called a "language experience approach" to reading. As the name suggests, this is a way of teaching reading that makes extensive use of what is happening to children. Typically, they are first encouraged to tell about some experience which the teacher then writes about, using very simple language. The two lines of text on the next page demonstrate this simplicity, and also the simplicity of possible content.

Vincent lost his shoes.
They are in his boots.

The hope and expectation is that children will soon do their own composing and writing. The material that results, presumably of special interest to them, would then be used to teach reading and related skills.

Good teachers—especially when working with young children—have always made some use of experience materials. However, during the past two decades widespread attention to a more extensive use has been fostered by publications and films connected with work done in the San Diego County Schools. From there, language experience programs have spread to other schools in other areas.

Researching the relative value for reading achievement of these programs has always been difficult. One obvious problem is that by their very nature they differ from school to school and from class to class. Noticeable wherever they are used, though, is the interest of the children. And this is reason enough to suggest ways for learning more about experience material to teach the language arts.

Some fairly recent publications are particularly helpful because, while avoiding prescriptions, they still include many specific ideas that would be useful to teachers. A few are described below in no special order.

Herrick, Virgil E., and Nerbovig, Marcella. *Using Experience Charts with Children.* Columbus, Ohio: Charles E. Merrill Books, Inc., 1964, 116 pp.

The quickest way to define "experience chart" as it is used in this booklet is to say it is all written material except what is commercially produced. And so the examples are of many kinds, beginning with what the authors call "one of the first charts": a list of children's names. From such a humble beginning this paperback moves on to show the variety in experience charts as well as the variety in how they can be used in classrooms occupied by either young or older children. Frequently the authors' descriptions are coupled with photographs. Often, too, the charts they show include drawings and paintings done by children. As a result, a teacher can get many ideas for reading and writing, and also for art projects.

Stauffer, Russell G. *The Language-Experience Approach to the Teaching of Reading.* New York: Harper & Row, 1970, 260 pp.

The assumption of this book exemplifies the contention of those who advocate a language experience approach: The majority of children entering school have sufficient ability in language and a sufficient amount of experiences that materials for teaching them to read can be and even ought to be based on their experiences told with their language. It then goes on to show how such an assumption works to produce a reading program at and beyond the first grade. The way a teacher might get started is treated in a chapter called "Dictated Experience Stories." Subsequent chapters—there are ten in all—deal with such topics as "Building a Word Bank" and "Creative Writing."

Because the author has been working with the language experience approach since 1952, his account includes numerous examples of children's materials and, in addition, many specific reminders and guidelines for teachers who want to try using it.

Darrow, Helen F., and Allen, R. Van. *Independent Activities for Creative Learning*. New York: Teachers College Press, Columbia University, 1961, 110 pp.

The popularity of a San Diego County Board of Education publication called "A Handbook of Independent Activities Which Promote Creativity in Children" led to the above paperback. Like the original, the newer publication is written for all classroom teachers in the sense that all need to be constantly searching for ways to keep children profitably occupied so that they themselves can give uninterrupted attention to individual and small group instruction.

Available in this paperback edition are many interesting ideas—some illustrated—for assignments in the language arts and other curriculum areas, too. How to make bulletin-board displays which will help with instruction also is considered, often with the assistance of pen and ink drawings. Especially valuable for busy teachers are the detailed reminders about "the teacher's part" in each activity, which are then followed by a listing of what the children are to do.

Many, but by no means all, of the suggestions are for children beyond first grade. In most instances, though, they can be adapted for the younger ones.

Lee, Dorris M., and Allen, R. V. *Learning to Read Through Experience*. New York: Meredith Publishing Co., 1963, 127 pp.

This paperback is concerned more with reading than with a total curriculum; however its emphasis is on reading closely tied to other communication skills including art. Within the broad communication focus, many suggestions are offered about ways to use children's experiences to teach reading in a more personal way. Highlighted is informational and narrative material, either dictated or written by the children, which is used to create interest in reading and also to teach skills dealing with punctuation, spelling, reading vocabulary, phonics, and so on. Creative writing by the children, sometimes accompanied by related paintings and drawings, gets attention, too. More ideas for bulletin boards, charts, and scrapbook collections also are to be found.

Again, many of the suggestions would have to be adapted for use with younger children. However, because it is so much easier—and more productive—to begin with something than with nothing at all, teachers who work with the younger ones should find this book helpful as they make an effort to turn the education process into something more personal than it usually is.

Hall, Mary Anne. *Teaching Reading as a Language Experience.* Columbus, Ohio: Charles E. Merrill Publishing Co., 1970, 109 pp.

Compared to the other short paperbacks, this one gives more attention to background material and explanations, and less to suggestions for activities and assignments.

A topic not included in the others is the name of one of its chapters: "Literature as a Language Experience." Themes of other chapters (e.g., "Experience Stories," "Writing Creatively") are like the topics typically found in a publication dealing with the language experience approach.

Allen, Roach Van, and Allen, Claryce. *Language Experiences in Reading.* Chicago: Encyclopaedia Britannica Press, 1966, Level I, 280 pp.; Level II, 339 pp.

This publication is divided into two loose-leaf notebooks, each comprised of six units of work that have themes like "Growing Up," "About Me and My Friends," and "Sounds Around Us." The authors call them a "Teacher's Resource Book," which turns out to be a very accurate description for the notebooks are filled with helpful ideas. In fact, of all the materials dealing with the language experience approach, these turn out to be the richest in terms of the number of ideas offered. Among them are suggestions not only for using children's experiences but also for extending them.

BEYOND KINDERGARTEN

Because so much of what has now been said in this chapter refers to nursery schools and kindergartens, first grade teachers might feel like forgotten people. Hopefully, this is not so.* The attention given the pre-first

* Chapter 11 deals with language arts programs beyond the kindergarten level.

grade school years was deliberate for those who teach at that level sometimes need special encouragement to offer children the chance to learn to read. However, it was never meant to suggest that what was being said did not have relevance for first grade. Indeed it does. For instance, what was said about the advantages of a language arts emphasis during the pre-first grade years applies equally well to first grade:

Advantages
Reflects dependent relationships among the language arts
Encourages different methodologies for teaching reading
Can put to good use the children's interest in themselves

Just as the advantages of the language arts emphasis have meaning for first grade, so too do its requirements:

Requirements
Competent, knowledgeable teacher
Some small-group instruction
Flexibility in day's schedule
Pervasive language arts concern

While nursery school, kindergarten, and first grade programs have much in common when each utilizes the language arts approach, there will still be differences, of course. In first grade, for example, the children are older and, in general, more mature. They also have a school day that is about twice as long. Together, these important differences allow a first grade teacher to do more and to do it more quickly. Even still more can be done—or ought to be—in first grade classrooms occupied by children who had an earlier opportunity to advance in all the language arts in kindergarten and maybe even in nursery school.

This last point merits special attention, for it offers a reminder that is very necessary for these current years: *First grade teachers, unlike earlier times, should no longer assume that children come to them with no ability in such things as number and letter naming, printing, and reading.* Another way of making this same important point is to say that as nursery school and kindergarten change, so too must first grade. In fact, to change the earlier school years without making corresponding changes in the first grade curriculum is to carry on an educational program that makes no sense at all.

What always makes sense, regardless of what one's point of view about early childhood education might be, is to know some of the behavioral characteristics of young children which have special relevance for teaching them. With this in mind, the next chapter discusses children as they have been observed in numerous visits to nursery school, kindergarten, and first grade classrooms.

REFERENCES

1. Batinich, Mary Ellen. "Language-Experience Activities," *Reading Teacher,* XXIII (March, 1970), 539–546.
2. Durkin, Dolores. "A Language Arts Program for Pre-First Grade Children: Two-Year Achievement Report," *Reading Research Quarterly,* V (Summer, 1970), 534–565.
3. Hirst, Wilma E. "Entrance Age—A Predictor Variable for Academic Success?" *Reading Teacher,* XXIII (March, 1970), 547–555.
4. Kohlberg, Lawrence. "Early Education: A Cognitive-Developmental View," *Child Development,* XXXIX (December, 1968), 1013–1062.
5. Martin, William E. "An Armchair Assessment of Nursery Education," *Journal of Nursery Education,* XVI (April, 1961), 90–96.

II

Classroom Observations

5

Behavioral Characteristics of Young Children in Classrooms

What a child is affects what it takes to be successful in teaching him. To be more specific, what a child is away from home—that is, how he behaves with other children and an adult who is not a parent—affects what it takes to be successful in teaching him in school.

That this textbook considers the behavior of the child in one chapter and the behavior of his teacher in another is not a denial of the dependent relationships just described. Rather, the separate treatment is required by the inability of language to deal simultaneously with two things, even when the two are closely connected and at times interdependent.

Because the topics considered in this and the next chapter *are* so closely tied together, it was sometimes difficult to decide what material to put in this one and what to keep for the other. In writing the second of the chapters, it was also impossible to avoid referring back to some of the material in the present one. But, this is to be expected and should reinforce the fact that teaching—whether successful or unsuccessful—constitutes a relationship among many variables which include both the behavior of children and the behavior of their teachers.

SOURCE OF INFORMATION ABOUT YOUNG CHILDREN

Ideally, the material comprising this chapter would come from a collection of carefully executed studies of the behavior of young children attending school. The children studied would have varied in chronological age, intelligence, sex, race, and home background. Further, they would have attended schools with varying philosophies regarding the education of young children and, therefore, with varying goals and curricula. In addition, these children would have been in the classrooms of teachers who also differed in such relevant factors as professional preparation, number of years of teaching, age, sex, personality, and expectations regarding behavior and learnings. Unfortunately, such studies are still to be done. Lacking the data which could come from them and which would be so very useful to teachers, I have based the material in this chapter on observations made in countless numbers of nursery school, kindergarten, and first grade classrooms.

When first observing I had no idea that what was being seen would end up as material for a teacher's textbook. However, the more I visited classrooms—and I have been in schools in a variety of geographical and socioeconomic areas—the more I began to realize that children of these age levels share certain characteristics that ought to be taken into account by those who work with them. In some cases, the characteristics make that work uniquely rewarding; in others, uniquely difficult. But in either case a teacher should know about these characteristics and keep them in mind as she plans schedules and instruction, and as she makes decisions about important matters like goals and materials.

As the behavioral characteristics of young children are discussed in this chapter, no attempt is made to label some as being especially true of fours, others of fives, and still others of sixes. I have no reason to make such distinctions because I learned from classroom visits that the behavior of some fours is like that of some sixes, that the behavior of some sixes is not yet up to that of some fours, and so on. This is not meant to deny that a group of six year olds, as a whole, will be more mature and able than a group of fours. However the job of a teacher, whether in nursery school or first grade, is to deal with individuals. And, individually, children of the same age can differ tremendously. Because of this, the characteristics discussed in the chapter are viewed as being common among young children; but there is no pretense about their adding up to a description of each and every young child.

Because my own research has given me the chance to learn about young children as they behave with parents as well as with teachers, there can also be no assumption about behavior being the same at home as it is in school. That parents treat their children differently is one reason for the variation. In fact, I was reminded of this difference somewhat dramatically just the other day. I had been visiting in a nursery school of four year olds and was especially impressed with one girl's mature behavior and advanced learnings. Physically she was the smallest in the group but certainly the "biggest" in the way she behaved and in how easily she learned everything. This was why I was surprised—even shocked—by what happened when her mother came to get her at dismissal time. The mother met her at the door, picked her up as if she were about a year old, and carried her to a nearby car. My immediate thought: "I wonder how that child behaves at home."

In another case I came to know a four-year-old boy quite well. At school his behavior could only be described as docile, always displaying an obvious eagerness to please. I once even commented to his teacher, "I think if you told that child to jump out the window, he would." Yet, as his mother later described him in a home interview, he was willful, had frequent temper tantrums when he didn't get his own way, and spent most nights sleeping on the livingroom sofa because of his refusal to stop watching television.

The comment of still another mother is worth quoting. She was speaking to me about her son, who was then in first grade, and noted, "Why, when his teacher talks about him, it's as if she's describing a child I don't even know."

What follows are descriptions of young children as they have been known in classrooms only.

TRADITIONAL TEACHINGS VERSUS OBSERVED BEHAVIOR

That we often see what we expect to see cannot be forgotten in a chapter concerned with descriptions of behavior based on classroom observations. Although the earliest of the observations were not made in order to examine behavior, it still is likely that I had certain expectations for it based on what I had read or heard or had been taught in early childhood education courses. Let me call them traditional teachings about young children in school, some of which are stated below:

1. Young children have difficulty relating to more than one adult.
2. Young children require a daily rest period.
3. Young children have short attention spans.
4. Young children have great need for help with social and emotional development; in fact, that is the primary reason to have school programs for them.

A discussion of each of these traditional teachings in relation to observed behavior follows.

Do Young Children Have Difficulty Relating to More Than One Adult?

In the majority of classes visited there was only one adult, the teacher. With these groups, therefore, it might be relevant to comment about the reactions of the children to me, an adult visitor who in most instances was also a stranger.

How the children reacted probably was affected by the role I played —or tried to play. My intention was to be a quiet, unobtrusive visitor who was not to get in the way of the teacher or the children. For that reason I made no effort to communicate with either or to become part of what they were doing. However the children went out of their way to make me a part of it.

Typically, when I first entered a room the children would look at me but, if any caught my eye, they would quickly turn away as if shy and self-conscious. Within a short time, however, I became an object for study. Later, when the children were used to my being in the room, some individual would come over to show me something: a toy or paper or, perhaps, new shoes. Even when I made only a minimal response, others would soon do the same. If, as I tended to do when just a neophyte observer, I made some positive comment about what was shown, then many children inevitably brought me something. There were times, in fact, when I quietly had to tell them I could not talk.

As the sequence of responses described above occurred over and over again becoming something of a pattern, it became clear that for the children the second adult was a potential source of extra attention and praise and, therefore, a welcome addition to the classroom. When there was a teaching assistant, she seemed to have the same value. Children were eager to be with her, to have her attention, and to win her approval.

To sum up: Based on my observations it would seem that the more adults there are, the better the children like it. In fact, I saw *no* evidence of young children having difficulty relating to more than one. There were, to be sure, individual children who were extremely shy and who found it hard to approach anyone. However, when it happened that I had the chance to visit frequently in classrooms that had these children, they too—but still shyly—eventually came to show or tell me something. Once the initial contact was made, future "visits" usually were common.

Do Young Children Require a Daily Rest Period?

As was expected, daily rest periods were scheduled in the nursery schools and kindergartens which I visited, but not in the first grades. This practice, and it is a very traditional one, seemed to assume great differences between five and six year olds in the sense that the fives attended school for half a day and were given a rest period while the sixes went to school for a full day and were not. Did my many observations lead to support for, or rejection of, such an assumption?

Actually, what the observations led to was an awareness that the so-called rest period was anything but restful. Usually children were asked to lie on the floor on some type of mat or rug. Often but not always, quiet music was played and the window shades drawn. Almost inevitably, though, the children wiggled or talked or bothered a neighbor. Frequently, a teacher had to discipline individuals. And if, by chance, she made the mistake of naming some unacceptable behavior ("Kim, keep your hands to yourself") it inevitably spread among the children, and further scoldings and admonitions followed. Conclusion: As typically carried out, rest periods provide little rest for the children and still less for their teachers.

Eventually, because of what had been observed in so many classrooms, certain teachers were urged to omit rest periods and, instead, to provide relaxation with schedules that allowed for fairly frequent changes of pace. These changes were in the form of quiet periods followed by more active ones and by concentrated activities followed by more relaxed types. Because of a young child's tremendous—sometimes unbelievable—energy, teachers were also reminded of the need to provide outlets for that. Influenced by the current interest in physical fitness, one kindergarten teacher introduced a brief period of calisthenics each day. Only one child objected, a chubby girl, and she objected because, "These exercises bend me too much."

To deny the need for regularly scheduled rest periods is not also to say there were never any children who were tired. Indeed there were. In fact, during one of my first visits to kindergarten classrooms, a boy fell asleep fairly early in the morning while the teacher was reading a story. She said later that he was always tired but this was the first time he actually slept. The teacher also mentioned his mother allowed him to watch television every night until he fell asleep on the livingroom sofa. Verification of this came in a subsequent conversation with the boy's mother.

Also verified, as I listened to numerous classroom conversations between children, and between children and teachers, was the frequency with which far too many young children watch television late into the evening. This became evident as they commonly referred to programs that ended at ten o'clock and even later.

Insufficient rest, then, is not rare and can be a problem; but the rest periods still scheduled by most nursery school and kindergarten teachers probably are not helping. Certainly they are not helping in communities where it is very common for large numbers of young children to come to school not only tired but even hungry. What must be recognized in these areas is that basic physical needs must be taken care of before other goals are considered; and, secondly, that the traditional rest period combined with the equally traditional juice and cracker are hardly sufficient to take care of the needs.

Do Young Children Have Short Attention Spans?

That the length of time children attend to anything is affected by a great many factors is what was learned from classroom observations. As a result, general statements describing the attention span of a group or even of an individual do not seem to reflect the realities of life in classrooms.

For instance, when the attention spans of individuals of the same age and in the same class were compared, they always varied—sometimes considerably. Complicating the comparisons, however, was that for each child a single description or judgment often was inaccurate. Here I cannot help but recall a boy in a kindergarten that was visited regularly. In general, I had classified him as a "hop-skip-and-jumper" for, when allowed to do so, he flitted from one thing to another. Yet, put paper in front of him and some crayons in his hands, and he was a different child—or so it seemed. Always the last to finish an art project, this boy produced meticulously executed pictures.

Curious about the ever-present details in his art work, I once talked with him about a picture he had drawn of his parents. From the conversation I learned that he had taken the time to curl his mother's hair, to make her dress a floral print, to put gloves on her hands and bows on her shoes. Naturally she was carrying a nicely detailed purse. And with the father he had been just as careful: best hat with band and a tiny feather, handkerchief in suitcoat pocket, wide stripes in tie, laces in shoes.

Had a visitor come into this classroom at any time other than the art period, he surely would have assigned descriptions like "giddy" and "restless" to this child's behavior. Yet, had the same person observed only during art there is no doubt that he would have been impressed with the steady, patient attention this boy gave to his work. While the work and play of other children in that same classroom were not characterized by such extremes, it was still difficult—but also inaccurate—to label the attention span of each with a single description. More correct and realistic is the contention that each had a collection of attention spans.

Classroom observations led to the conclusion that each child has a collection of attention spans for some of the same reasons that every adult has a collection. Factors like fatigue, illness, and mood, for instance, play important roles. In fact, in classrooms that were visited regularly over a period of a year or more, the relevance of the moods of the children became especially pronounced. Some children, of course, were far less moody than others, but all had their good days and bad days. I often thought that wet weather brought out everyone's bad mood; for whenever there was a series of rainy days, there usually was a great deal of restlessness, too.

Other factors had a positive effect on the amount of time a child was willing to give to something. If it related to himself or at least had a connection with what was familiar, it was likely to get and keep his attention. Too, if previous involvement with something had led to achievement or praise for the child, it was likely to succeed in involving him again. Successful, too, was whatever the child himself selected. In classrooms in which teachers were wise and able enough to keep such factors as these in mind when they planned a day's activities, an observer could be nothing but impressed with the way children became involved and stayed involved. It was in these classrooms in particular that traditional teachings about the short attention span of a young child seemed highly questionable.

While there were, as I have noted, innumerable times when I was pleasantly surprised at the sustained attention of four-, five-, and six-year-old children, there were other times when I was equally surprised at how easily they could be distracted; and this was true even of the older-acting ones.

The greatest distraction, I learned, is another child. If left alone, an individual might stay with something for what seemed like an endless amount of time. But then along would come another child, and the picture changed. The more I observed the more I also noticed that in just about every classroom there is at least one boy or girl who spends a considerable amount of time interrupting children who are busy and occupied.

Other common distractions in classrooms are new acquisitions. In fact, I watched a boy with new cowboy boots and a girl with a new watch turn into intermittent sources of distraction for the whole of a school day. At other times in other classrooms irresistible attractions were bracelets—especially those that dangle—bandages, combs, rings, and jewelry pins.

Once I even learned that a piece of string could get in the way of a successful morning in school.

To sum up, then, classroom observations uncovered variety rather than uniformity in attention spans. Such variety was characteristic not only when children were compared but even for one and the same child. What seems like an accurate conclusion, therefore, is that children have a collection of attention spans, each determined by many factors which work together to affect its depth as well as its length.

Should Social and Emotional Development Be the Major Goal of School Programs for Young Children?

Traditionally, as Chapter 2 pointed out, a child's social and emotional development has been of major concern to educators responsible for planning pre-first grade programs. Consequently goals like emotional stability, self-acceptance, independence, and ability to get along with others have been emphasized for nursery schools and kindergartens. The question to consider now is: Did visits to pre-first grade classrooms verify the need for such emphases?

To be stressed immediately is that classroom observations are not a prerequisite for appreciating both the importance and the necessity for helping four and five year olds with the various aspects of what might globally be called "good mental health." One simply has to be alive to know there is always room for growth in this area whether a person is a child or an adult. Therefore, the need to justify concern about a young child's social and emotional development is nonexistent.

What still remains questionable, nonetheless, is what seems to be the traditionalist's tendency to artificially separate social and emotional goals from what might be called academic or intellectual ones. A question about this is raised because the unfortunate result of such a tendency has been either-or thinking and, therefore, either-or decisions. Should we emphasize getting along with others, or should we be teaching readiness for reading? Should we help a child grow in independence, or should we introduce simple mathematical concepts? These are the kinds of either-or questions that have been asked, and traditional answers moved in the direction of the social and emotional goals.

What classroom observations suggest is that goals like these should not be isolated, as has been traditionally done, because they are not achieved in isolation. That is, they are not attained in a vacuum but, rather, as children participate in activities connected with other goals.

Why traditionalists have given such special though, unfortunately, isolated attention to social and emotional goals is made clear during classroom visits, especially when they occur close to the start of the children's first year in school. It is at that point in time that matters like "learning to be a good group member" seem to be of crucial importance. But even and, perhaps, especially at that point it must be recognized that such learnings are never *achieved* if by this is meant that they are fully and permanently realized in children. In fact, as adults we ought to be very much aware that the many behavioral goals that have been named in the past by early childhood educators are only rarely achieved to the fullest even in the most mature of adults. Consequently, to hold them up as goals for nursery school and kindergarten children in a way that isolates them from academic goals cannot be justified.

OTHER COMMONLY OBSERVED CHARACTERISTICS

Characteristics other than those already mentioned were observed often enough to be named. An outstanding one, for instance, was the open self-interest of the children, a trait discussed in Chapter 4. Still another was their great excitability.

Excitability

The tendency of young children to get excited about anything and everything became very apparent as classrooms were visited. The source of excitement could be icy sidewalks, a child's loose tooth, or a birthday party scheduled for after school. It did not have to be of monumental importance; young children are interested in just about everything and with the interest comes their excitement.

Teachers accustomed to working with the older and more blasé child would consider it a treat to get the response that is common for those who teach the young ones. What a joy, for instance, when children get excited because a teacher decides to use last names for attendance-taking rather than the customary first names. How rewarding, too, when children get excited because they suddenly see in books words they can read: *go, the, some*. Equally refreshing is the enjoyment they find in acting out the meanings of words; *jump* and *hop,* for instance.

While this easily aroused excitement has obvious rewards for teachers, it must be noted that it has its problems, too. A teacher once pinpointed the major one when she commented, "You sometimes get more than you bargained for." Earlier in the morning, in preparation for a story about frogs, this teacher had introduced a group of children to a large stuffed frog who was to sit on a chair and listen to them read. The children were delighted. New words in the story were *hop* and *jump*. After they had been written, identified, and discussed, the teacher asked certain children to act out their meanings, which they promptly did with great gusto. Later, after the story had been read, the children were allowed to jump and hop back to their desks, which they again did with obvious enjoyment. The problem? The whole class jumped and hopped for the rest of the morning.

On another day in another classroom, children had reached the point where they could print their names quite well. They could also read a number of words including *me*. To promote further interest in reading and printing, the teacher typed and dittoed a simple letter which began, "Dear Me." Each child received a copy, plus a stamped envelope addressed to himself. What excitement!

It happened that a postoffice was close to school. The weather was good, so off went the children and teacher to mail the letters. It was a small office, and arrangements had been made for the children to get a quick tour and explanation of the facilities.

Upon their return to the classroom, excitement was everywhere. As the teacher observed, "They're really high now." And they were for the rest of that morning.

Many other examples of the excitability of young children in classrooms could be given. Together, though, they would lead to the same conclusions that might be drawn from the two mentioned:

1. Excitement is easily aroused in young children. It also is very contagious.
2. The amount of excitement is not always in proportion to its source. Often, what seems small and unexciting to an adult can lead to great excitement among young children.
3. The excitement of young children commonly continues after the reason for it no longer exists. With them, excitement is not something that is easily turned off.
4. The great excitability of young children, combined with its tendency to persist, can result in overly stimulated children. It is then that some become undisciplined and rowdy.

To sum up, classroom observations make it clear that young children are very responsive and easily excited. Such tendencies can be an advantage for those who teach them and a source of great reward. However the same observations highlight the relationship between too much excitement and discipline problems. Thus, "a little goes a long way" seems to be a good motto for teachers of the young to keep in mind.

Imagination

The excitability of young children is the result of many factors, one of which must surely be their rich imagination. Classroom observations have shown that imagination also brings reality and fantasy very close together, thus allowing young children to be an interesting combination of sophistication and naiveté.

Such a combination first became noticeable in a kindergarten classroom occupied by what I always thought were unusually sophisticated five year olds. They were highly verbal, learned easily, and showed a surprising awareness of what was happening in the world. Then one day, after they had sung and enjoyed a song about a jack-in-the-box, their teacher suggested they become one. Without hesitation all of these "sophisticates" did just that, hiding their heads in nonexistent boxes. The teacher then commented about seeing nothing but boxes in her classroom and asked, "But where are the children?" Of course the "lost" children were delighted and tried all the harder to curl up in their boxes. And the harder they tried the more I thought, "Such an interesting combination of sophistication and simplicity."

The same thought became increasingly common as more and more classrooms were visited. With a first grade group, for instance, a teacher was using a bulletin-board display to review words the children were learning to read. At the bottom, the board showed an airport. Over it were clouds and attached to them were small word cards. With this display children took turns "flying." It was done by holding a small paper airplane that took off into the air, touching cards and naming words as it flew up and down in a variety of directions.

To create interest in what was to be done, the teacher had first talked to the children about the trip they were going to take to the airport and of how they would have the chance to be pilots. And then the flying—and vocabulary review—began.

From the comments children were making to one another, it appeared that some thought a real trip to a real airport was in their future. That this was true of at least two of them was verified later. In the evening the teacher received phone calls from two mothers who wondered when the trip to the airport was to be, and how much it would cost. Before the teacher could explain, one even volunteered to go along.

At another time, in a semi-rural nursery school, I had the chance to observe a teacher create great interest in numeral identification with the help of a cloth, stuffed hen and a group of imaginative four year olds. The hen had been placed on a pile of straw; under her were egg-shaped pieces of paper on which numerals from 1 to 10 had been printed. As the teacher took out the eggs one by one, the children named the numerals. After each was correctly identified, that egg was thumbtacked to a board. At the end, all the eggs were counted. Following this, the numerals were named again by the children as the teacher took down all but three. The three eggs remaining on the board displayed 3, 5, and 8.

Next came a writing lesson. Three numerals (3, 5, 8) had been selected for additional practice because most of the children had difficulty forming them correctly. As they began to do the printing there was a considerable amount of noise because, of course, they still had much to say about the hen. Quickly but kindly the teacher reminded them that the hen was tired from laying so many eggs and needed to rest. No further disturbances occurred as the children proceeded with their work in what was an amazingly quiet room—considering it was filled with four year olds who had a sleeping hen in their midst.

Other examples of young children who had imagination and enjoyed using it were many. Once, for instance, a group was fairly restless when the teacher wanted them to listen to some directions. Their hands seemed especially busy. Instead of making the more usual request to fold their hands, the teacher suggested they be trains and that they hook their hands together the way they had seen train cars being attached. The willingness of the children to do this was immediate and lasted long enough for the teacher to finish the directions.

At another time in another classroom, trains had also been discussed. Later, as the teacher collected pictures of trains drawn by the children, she told them she was a conductor and was collecting tickets. The children loved the idea. Still later, a little girl who always seemed to have trouble sitting for more than two minutes stood up. Instead of chastising her the teacher suggested, "Oh, you had better not stand up. The train might start and then you'd fall and hurt yourself." Very agreeably the child sat down.

In cases like these one might ask whether it is the teacher or the children who have the greater imagination. In others, however, it is the children who do the imagining quite on their own. Here I am recalling the number of times parents have told how their young children—especially girls—play school when they get home. Their imagination freely allows them to use dolls as students. Once the teaching begins, however, imitation rather than imagination takes over. According to the parents at least, both the words and the gestures of the teacher at school are imitated by the children with perfection.

Imitation

The tendency of young children to imitate is well known, so it was hardly surprising to find them in classrooms copying the behavior of others. With some, the tendency seemed almost like a compulsive need. I can recall a variety of individuals—usually the less mature in a group—who, at least on certain days, copied everything they saw and heard. If the child next to them looked at a picture displayed on a board, they looked at it, too. If he accidentally fell off his chair, they fell off theirs. With the majority of children, however, imitative behavior was less frequent and seemed normal. For example, to see one child blowing bubbles while drinking milk with a straw and then to see all the others do the same thing seemed very natural indeed.

Fortunately, young children copy the good as well as the bad. I can recall one incident in which a kindergarten girl suddenly discovered that the color of each of her crayons was printed on its label. With considerable enthusiasm she began to copy each word with the appropriate color, a somewhat awkward task since the crayon being used was the one from which the copying had to be done. But she persisted printing *red* in red, *blue* in blue, and so on. Meanwhile a classmate came along and asked what she was doing. It wasn't long before the second child was busy with the same task. However, she wasn't nearly so successful. Her first carefully printed word in purple was *crayola*.

At another time in another classroom I saw imitative behavior spread throughout the entire group. These kindergarteners were busy drawing a picture of a dog like the one in a story that had just been read by their teacher. Before they started, each paper had been labeled with the word *dog* at the bottom. When one of the boys finished his picture, he added what looked like a circle close to the dog's foot. Soon he was asking the teacher, "Will you write *food* here?" Soon, food was being added to everyone's picture, as well as the second label.

Suggestibility

Similar to imitative behavior is what might be called the suggestibility of young children. I mention this trait because over and over again while visiting schools I have been reminded of how easily they are influenced by suggestion.

Often, I learned, the suggestion comes from a teacher—and causes problems. At storytime, for instance, with all the children sitting on the floor in front of her, a teacher might simply comment, "Can you all see?" Suddenly, once contented children say they cannot see and must move about. Or, as I heard recently in a kindergarten class, the teacher says, "John, I don't think you can see the pictures from where you're sitting." Predictably, *everybody* decides he cannot see them and so, once again, everybody must move. Or, to cite another example, because the teacher allows one child to examine a picture in detail, demands can soon be heard from all the children to look at the same picture.

At other times I have observed still other teachers create needless problems with a suggestion. With a four-year-old group, for instance, I watched one distribute numeral cards to each child and, as this was being done, she warned, "Now I don't want any of you to put these cards in your mouth." Very quickly, cards were in mouths. On another day—this was in a first grade room—I watched as the children were just about finished with a writing paper. One child in fact had already completed his, so the teacher suggested, "Jeffrey, as long as you're finished you can stand by the door." (It was almost time for outdoor recess.) Suddenly, children who at first seemed intent on being careful and correct changed into children who hastily scribbled the last few words on their papers and then eagerly asked, "Can I get in line, too?"

No reason for surprise is the fact that some of the problems connected with suggestibility are initiated by children. One child says she's cold and needs to get her sweater. Quickly, others who have a sweater need to get it to keep warm. Or, one child gets a paper tissue to blow his nose and, predictably, several children suddenly have colds and also need to go to the tissue box. Or, on another day, one child declares he doesn't like white milk and then many say they don't like white milk.

Again, fortunately, this great power of suggestion also works for the good. A teacher participates in a word game with a group of children and says for all to hear, "I'm going to listen carefully so that I'll be ready when it's my turn." As a result, at least some in the group listen a little more attentively than might otherwise have been the case. Or, a teacher says to a child, "I certainly like the way you put that *e* on the line," and then many *e*'s are very carefully placed on lines.

What also led to *e*'s on lines, of course, was the praise they received. Like all humans, young children respond positively but also very openly to praise, sometimes adding a little of their own. Here I especially have in mind a little girl who, after being complimented by her teacher for offering a good suggestion, was heard to say, "That was good head thinking, wasn't it?"

Impatience

Unlike praise, what is *not* relished by young children is the need to wait. Yet, in classrooms occupied by large numbers of them and only one adult, waiting is the rule rather than the exception. Waiting to have a turn, for instance, is a common occurrence in school. And in this case practice does not make perfect. Repeatedly I have watched children become inattentive and get into trouble because they are unwilling, or perhaps unable, to be patient and wait their turn.

Not long ago, to cite one example of problems connected with waiting, I observed a first grade class as the teacher was working with a group of about ten children. Each had been given a number of word cards, and the teacher was building sentences by naming the words. Thus she might say "the" and the child holding *the* would bring it to a card holder hanging in front of the group, where he would tuck it into a slot. All went well, as long as a child was having a turn. When he was not, and especially when all his cards were gone, restlessness and inattentiveness resulted. (In this case, had the teacher been the one who placed the cards as they were brought to her, the routine would have moved along more quickly and the children would have had more and faster turns. In addition, more words and sentences could have been read.)

In still another first grade classroom the teacher was also working with a group of about ten. In this case she was combining writing and phonics. She would name a word and one child would be chosen to write its initial letter on the chalkboard. For the child doing the writing, life was great. For all the others, however, it was a little dull. Why? For one thing, the selected child often took a long time to write a letter; and, for another, his "audience" was unable to watch as he made it because he was standing in the way. Eventually, as might be expected, more and more children lost interest and the procedure became an obvious failure. (What might have been used in its place was one that would allow all the children to write at the board at the same time. Again the result would be less waiting, a greater amount of practice and, more than likely, a greater amount of attention from the group.)

Although taking turns often requires an amount of patience that most young children do not have, it is also true that once the process is begun, none is willing to have his turn skipped. I can recall one kindergarten teacher who took advantage of this concern about getting a turn to introduce and use alphabetical order. The practice in her classroom was to have a child hold the flag each morning while the others said the pledge of allegiance; turns for this were assigned in alphabetical order. To help, a large alphabetical list of the children's first names was discussed and then displayed low enough for all to see. Never did a child not know when it was his turn to be the flag holder.

Later on, when the children's eagerness to be first in line began to cause problems, the teacher used another alphabetical list, this one comprised of the children's last names. Predictably the teacher never once had to ask, "Whose turn is it to be first in line today?"

Sporadically, when difficulties arose because several children wanted to do or use the same thing at the same time, it was common to have one of them say something like, "Let's take alphabet turns." However, it was equally common to hear objections from children whose names might be Tommy or Vicky or, perhaps, Wilson or Zimmerman. Clearly the concept of alphabetical order had been learned well.

Misuse of Words

What is not always learned well is the meanings of words. At a time when television-educated children are occupying our nursery school, kindergarten, and first grade classrooms, it is important for teachers to be reminded of this. Otherwise they will assume these children know more than they really do.

I stress such a point because often during classroom visits I learned that children who at first seemed highly sophisticated verbally turned out to have many misconceptions. These became apparent most quickly when free and unstructured conversations took place. In one such conversation, a group of children was talking about the occupations of their fathers. A teaching assistant guided but did not force the discussion. At one point a child mentioned that his father was a carpenter, so the assistant asked, "Do all of you know what a carpenter is?" Eagerly one girl volunteered, "I know. He brings your carpet." During the same conversation the discussion turned to occupations the children themselves would like to have when they grew up. The usual ones were mentioned: policeman, cowboy, nurse, mother, and so on. One boy's choice, though, was unexpected. He told how he was going to be an angel because he liked the wings.

During another conversation that took place on a Monday morning, children were telling what they had done on Sunday. One girl mentioned that her mother and father had taken her little brother to church to be advertised. Nobody objected. Apparently to that group of five year olds an advertised baby was just as acceptable as one who had been baptized. (For adults the message might seem to be: "Speak a little more clearly, please.")

In another conversation in another kindergarten, a group was very involved in a discussion of events which they must have learned about from watching television because they were referring to such things as campus riots and the highjacking of airplanes. One also mentioned the killer of Bobby Kennedy which, in turn, led to a discussion of the electric chair. Among their many interesting observations: "That's just like the dentist's chair."

Misconceptions related to numbers and age also turned out to be common occurrences in classrooms occupied by young children. In one, a teacher was discussing the approaching presidential election and explained how a person had to be twenty-one years old to vote. "Twenty-one!" exclaimed a boy. "If you were twenty-one you'd be a grandpa." * In another kindergarten which I visited regularly, misconceptions about age came closer to home when a girl said to me, "You're just a kid, aren't you?" Delighted—but curious—I asked why she thought I was a kid. Her explanation? "You don't wear buttons on your ears."

* Obviously, this conversation took place before the age requirement was changed to eighteen years. For the child in question, however, it is likely that an eighteen year old would be ancient, too.

Self-awareness

While there were these very interesting misconceptions, young children in classrooms also displayed a surprising amount of astuteness regarding themselves and their abilities. For example, I can recall a four year old who had been taught to print his name and who, for the first time, was looking at a typed version of it. His reaction? "That looks gooder than the way I make it." While cutting out the outline of a house another four year old observed, "I'm having trouble steering." At another time, during a visit to a kindergarten class, one little girl looked at the S she had just printed and then complained, "I can't make S. Up here it's bigger and down there it's littler." As he watched a group of children print numerals on the chalkboard, a kindergarten boy in another school was heard to say, "I make good 5s now. I used to make messy ones."

Similar awareness of one's ability in reading was noted in still other classrooms. For instance, quite on her own a girl lamented, "I'm having trouble with *house* and *horse*. Is that *house* or *horse*?" Another was observed reading to several other children from a book that included pages with pictures and very few words, and pages with nothing but words. With her still quite limited ability, she did fine with the first type but seemed to know she had met her Waterloo each time she came to the second. But she found a solution. Whenever she came to the more densely worded page she simply explained, "Oh, I don't like this. I don't think I'll read it."

Other kinds of awareness also became apparent during visits to classrooms, some of which—I must admit—surprised me. In one nursery school class a teacher had dittoed pictures of a telephone which were to be used in connection with practice in printing phone numbers. Approximately one second after a boy received his copy he was objecting, "That's wrong. The zero should have the word 'operator' next to it." Somewhat embarrassed, the teacher explained that there hadn't been enough room to print it. At another time in another nursery school, a four year old had been coughing. As soon as she could catch her breath she was also saying—and with considerable disappointment in her voice—"I don't even smoke and I still have a bad cough."

How television has entered the lives and thoughts of young children became apparent many other times but never so strikingly as in a conversation between a kindergartener and his teacher. Like the others in his class this boy had been practicing making a *d*, but he was forming it incorrectly. When the teacher stopped at his desk and noticed this, she commented about it and then showed him the correct form. A child who always had to get in the last word, he said back to her, "I like to do it my own way." Patiently the teacher explained that in school he was supposed to learn how to do things the right way, which might not always be his way. Not about to go down in defeat, this five year old proceeded to tell about the campus fights he had seen on television and to point out that people sometimes learn to do the wrong things in school.

Fortunately, other instances of young children being so aware of everything seemed more childlike. Complaints about books like, "The story says the top is red but the picture makes it look orange," or "Kittens don't say mew mew. They say mow mow," were easy to accept. So, too, was the comment of a girl who, when her teacher spoke softly, was quick to say, "Mrs. T———, you sound so weak!" And in this connection the comment of a boy cannot be bypassed. When he arrived at school one morning he looked at the teacher and immediately observed, "I bet you put curlers in your hair last night. That's how come you've got curls on the top of your head."

Independence

Although dependence is part of the very essence of childhood, it is still true to say that the more young children learn to do, the more they want to do on their own. I say this because in so many ways this move toward independence was seen in classroom behavior. Even among five year olds who were just learning to print their names, it was not uncommon to find some who refused to use models (small name cards) made by the teacher because, they explained, "I know how to do it." Or, after many classroom visits I was hardly surprised to hear a first grader complain because the teacher was labeling objects in her picture. "Why can't we do that our own selves?" was the way she phrased her disappointment. And even four year olds are not about to accept help when it is not needed. One time, for example, a nursery school teacher was calling the children's attention to certain numerals and their names. She did this by writing and then naming them, all the while asking the children to watch. In response one boy said with pride rather than boldness, "I don't have to look because I know what it looks like."

Art projects also brought out the growing independence of young children. Once, I recall, a nursery school class was drawing pictures of a dog who had been described earlier in a story. He was brown and white and, presumably, the children would make their pictures the same colors. However, one boy told the teacher that he was going to make his "a rainbow dog." In response, she explained that the dog was to be the one in the story and so had to be colored brown and white. The boy seemed resigned. Later, when he brought his picture to the teacher, the dog *was* brown and white—but he was wearing a rainbow-colored sweater.

On another occasion, this time in a kindergarten, the children were making pictures of Indians. One mentioned that Indians never wore clothes, so he wasn't going to put any on his. The idea spread and was quickly accepted by the others. Probably concerned about what parents might think when their children brought home pictures of naked Indians, the teacher insisted rather firmly that Indians *did* wear clothes. The children, however, were not about to change their minds. Sensing this, the teacher left the visitor "in charge" and went out of the room. A few minutes later she returned with a library book about Indians which, with many colorfully illustrated pictures, portrayed Indians wearing clothes. She showed the children the pictures, and she also reminded them of how chilly it was outside and of how they must not let their Indians catch cold. The last point seemed to be taken quite seriously by the children; at least they proceeded to dress their Indians.

Enjoyment of Challenges

In addition to independence, another characteristic of young children as they are learning more and more is their enjoyment of a challenge. For instance, all a teacher has to say is, "I bet I can fool you," and suddenly all eyes and ears are working. When, on the other hand, it is the teacher's error that is caught, even more delighted children are the result. With this in mind, a first grade teacher was able to add interest to a review of the written names of colors simply by saying, "I'm not sure I can remember all these words. I'll try to read them, but tell me if I make a mistake." Predictably, everybody watched with great attention and then was obviously pleased to catch and correct the teacher's "errors."

Of course, teachers' errors are not always deliberate. I recall a kindergarten discussion of a very attractive display of Halloween pictures, each coupled with a simple label. At the time of the visit the teacher was using the display for practice in counting, so things like pumpkins, ghosts, and bats were being counted by the children. Reaching a picture that was labeled *3 bats,* the teacher asked, "How many bats are on the board?" Almost in unison the children eagerly informed her that the label was wrong because there were four bats. And there were. One appeared in another picture and was almost made invisible by its small size. A child in the group probably expressed the feelings of all when she said to the teacher, "I like it when we caught you."

Nonpredictability

It is possible that an erroneous conclusion might be drawn from this discussion of the characteristics of young children; namely, that their behavior is predictable. Actually, as any parent or experienced teacher will verify, it is not. For example, what we know about children would suggest that if a group of four year olds is taken to a hatchery, they will be willing and even eager to discuss what they saw the next morning. Yet I was in a nursery school classroom the morning following just such a trip and heard one boy object as the group began to discuss it. "How come we're still talking about chickens?" was his complaint.

Probably the greatest number of unexpected behaviors occurs when a school program for young children has academic goals. I suggest this because their accomplishments do make the children seem older than their age. As a result, when they display behavior that reflects actual age, it is a cause for surprise. In this connection I can recall one kindergarten girl who burst into tears when, unintentionally, the teacher passed her by as she was distributing little rhythm band instruments during music. Such a response seemed so out of character because the weeping child was one who learned everything that was ever taught—or merely mentioned. Consequently she did seem "too big" to cry about some triviality, but cry she did.

I saw another able girl in another kindergarten also take everyone by surprise with her tears. At the time, the children were printing each letter in their last names on a small square piece of paper. Eventually the squares were to be pasted in correct sequence on a large sheet of paper. This particular girl, as would be expected, had no trouble with the printing nor with the job of arranging the letters in order. However, when she went to paste her unusually long name on the paper, it wouldn't fit. And then came the tears.

Other behavior not expected by teachers often shows up as young children respond to "lessons." I remember one teacher—always a careful planner—who used an interesting collection of colored pictures to introduce a discussion of clouds. Later, the children were to be taken outdoors to look at some but, at the start, they examined and discussed pictures of them. Once curiosity was aroused, the teacher read from a book that told some interesting facts about cloud formations. As I watched, the children listened attentively and seemed interested. Then, just before they were to go outside, the teacher held up still another picture which, in addition to having clouds, also showed stars. One child's immediate and excited response? "Oh, it's the Fourth of July." And soon everyone was talking at once about fireworks and sparklers. Gone was the carefully nourished interest in clouds.

Even with games, children can react in unexpected ways. I first learned this while watching a group of children play Musical Chairs. Inclement weather had made indoor recess necessary, so the teacher lined up chairs and the game began. But then problems developed when everyone wanted to be a loser. Why a loser? Because in some unplanned way the loser got to carry away a chair, and that was very special for a reason not at all obvious to the adults who watched.

Probably all these accounts of the nonpredictable behavior of young children, as well as of that which is highly predictable, can be summed up with a simple prediction directed to their teachers: *Never* will there be a dull moment in a classroom filled with four-, five-, and six-year-old children.

6

Classroom Behavior of Teachers of Young Children

Attempts to learn about factors that affect a child's achievement in school inevitably lead to the conclusion that the teacher is the most influential one. And, it might be added, such a conclusion is common whether these attempts are in the form of somewhat casual classroom visits or carefully designed studies (2, 3). One consequence of this widespread awareness of her special importance is that "It's the teacher who makes the difference" can now be listed among educators' pet clichés.

Unfortunately, those who ponder such a proclamation and then ask, "Just what is it about a teacher that makes the difference?" or "What are the specific behaviors of a good teacher?" must go unanswered for the educational profession still lacks the information which would allow for a factual response. A promising note in this otherwise disappointing state of affairs is that the profession is very much aware of its ignorance. Thus, there is the hope that one day it will be replaced by reliable cause-effect data. Meanwhile, observations like the following will continue to be common:

> While it is clear that the teacher and the methods he or she uses are important to the learning process, we cannot yet say just what it is that the effective teacher is or does (1, p. 40).

Recognition of the difficulty of learning about effective instruction will also continue to be found in the literature in forms like:

> Instruction is a complex process. . . . we cannot detect the ingredient that is present in optimum proportion; we cannot tell what is active and what is inert and what is catalytic; we cannot tell what is *causing* what (7, p. 41).

Although both of the above quotations put the spotlight on the teacher and her instruction, it still is safe to predict that neither author would deny the student's importance. As was emphasized in the previous chapter, teaching always involves a relationship between the instructor and those to be instructed; consequently, whether any instance of instruction turns out to be successful is dependent not only upon factors pertaining to the teacher but also upon some having to do with the student. This is why the underlying theses of Chapter 5 were (a) young children display certain behavioral characteristics in classrooms; and (b) successful teachers take them into account when instructional decisions and plans are being made.

Before discussing this and still other characteristics of successful teachers of the young, it is first necessary to explain what is meant by "successful." Now that the little that is known about the specifics of successful instruction has been admitted, it also seems necessary to explain why such a discussion is included in this textbook.

SUCCESSFUL TEACHERS OF YOUNG CHILDREN

As a result of my many visits to nursery school, kindergarten, and first grade classrooms, a picture of the successful teacher has gradually evolved. It is possible, of course, that many of the pieces comprising it were selected for subjective reasons. However, even if they do suffer from all the limitations of subjectivity, they can still make a contribution if they succeed in getting you to think more carefully about your own teaching or, perhaps, your current conception of what the "good" teacher is and does. The possibility of this occurring is, I believe, reason enough to discuss what might only be personal, subjective judgments.

My own conception of the successful teacher of young children began to develop as I watched not the teachers but, rather, the children. For instance, when I saw children who appeared to be pleased and happy about attending school, I assumed their teachers must be doing something right. When I had the chance to observe children who were not only content but also busy and involved with school activities, then it seemed even more likely that they had "good" teachers. Finally, when I saw children who liked school and wanted to come, who were interested and involved with what was going on and, in addition, who were learning what had been planned for them to learn—and even more—I was convinced that their teachers merited such laudatory descriptions as "successful" and "effective."

What were these particular teachers like? What behavioral characteristics were common among them? Before answering, let me first be explicit about a problem that can develop whenever the specifics of instruction are made visible—whether in a demonstration or on television or, for instance, through the silent language of the written page.

"Problem?" you might be thinking. "How can specific descriptions of successful teachers create problems?"

Having thoughts and questions like the above is natural and to be expected, especially when they are put side by side with the fact that the traditional complaint about methods courses in any subject matter area has been their *lack* of specificity. "Too general!" "Too theoretical!" is the way the disappointment has been phrased over the years. Why then, you might be wondering, has the warning about a problem been issued? In this case, to name and discuss the problem is to offer an explanation.

The problem I refer to is the tendency—and this is particularly prevalent among those who are preparing for teaching—to want to imitate specifically described behavior. But again you might be thinking, "Why is this a problem?"

It is a problem because effective instruction is never the result of copying what a successful teacher is doing and for a variety of reasons. One reason, for instance, is that what turns out to be successful teaching with one group of children will not always be equally successful with another. To know this is to take one step toward being a "good" teacher.

Another reason is that while it is at least somewhat possible to copy what another teacher does and says, it is never possible to copy what she is. This distinction is an especially important one, by the way, for it recognizes that every teacher is a person as well as an instructor and that both play important roles in what will constitute successful teaching *for her*.

For me, the key role played by what might be called the personality of a teacher has become very clear whenever I combined teacher education—or what I thought was education—with classroom observations. For example, I can recall working very closely with two teachers whose personalities could not have been more diverse. What remains particularly vivid about that experience is how differently the two put the same suggestions into practice. In the case of one, I could feel nothing but pride as I observed her using an idea or procedure that had been recommended in a conference. Yet, when I visited the other teacher—and she had attended the same conference—I felt some chagrin that I might have contributed to what she was doing.

At another time I was trying to help just one teacher. In this case tremendous amounts of help were required because for many years her first grade program had been characterized by dull routines, too few materials, and many rules about talking, raising hands, keeping a straight line, and so on. Probably my most vivid and lasting recollection of that particular experience is the way the teacher used my suggestion to turn at least some word identification practice into games for the children. The suggestion had been developed with many specific ideas that had already been used successfully by other first grade teachers; thus I had hope for some success in this classroom, too.

When I next visited, I found the teacher using one of the suggestions. She began by announcing to the group of children with whom she was working—and in her typically stern voice—"I want absolute silence because you've got to learn to play a game today." Following this wholly unexpected introduction, she proceeded to lay down the various rules and regulations, again with the customary sternness. Finally the game began and proceeded surprisingly well, thanks more to the children than the teacher. At the end, each child was holding word cards he had identified correctly and so, as would be expected of any young children who can count, all started to count their cards aloud in order to see who had the most. Immediately the teacher responded with, "This is not a game for counting. I want that talking stopped."

I had two reactions: (a) This is a game? (b) Am I the cause of this? More lasting reactions have been in the form of a clearer recognition of the important role played by personality and, secondly, of the uselessness of imitating the behavior of a successful teacher as a way of becoming one.

With these observations in the background, it should now be clear that the descriptions of successful teachers to be presented in this chapter are not meant to turn readers into "copycats." Rather, they are included as a way of making the act of teaching more visible and specific with the hope that this will be of special help to those who have not yet taught. For those of you who are now teaching, the descriptions might offer suggestions that could be incorporated into your work *in your own way*. The descriptions might also portray a few standards against which you might want to evaluate some of your current procedures and practices.

CHARACTERISTICS OF SUCCESSFUL TEACHERS

What becomes apparent most quickly whenever successful teachers are observed is that they work hard. To be sure, experience does reduce the amount of work required. Still, in every classroom in which I had the privilege of observing a good teacher, it was very clear that what she did and was able to accomplish resulted from much work and careful planning. This underscores the fact that successful instruction is not an accident. Or, to make the same point positively, good teachers work for their success.

What else describes good teachers of the young?

Take into Account the Characteristics of Young Children

Actually, the importance of taking young children's characteristics into account has been highlighted as much by poor as by successful teachers.* For example, one of their characteristics is the tendency to turn everything into a toy and, therefore, to see everything as something to play with. Consequently it is not surprising that when materials like pencil and paper are distributed *before* directions for using them are given, the children will play with them—perhaps even scribble—*while* the teacher gives the directions. Inevitably the result is misused materials, directions that are not heard, an impatient and perhaps angry teacher, and chastised children. Over and over again I have watched this same sequence of events occur, simply because teachers did not take into account very normal characteristics of the children they were teaching.

Another observable characteristic of young children is the ease with which they can be distracted. Call it their lack of self-discipline, their inability to resist temptation, their immaturity. The label is not too important. The simple fact is that young children can easily be distracted; therefore teachers should take this into account as they work with them. But, do they?

I recall being in one first grade classroom at a time when the teacher

* This and subsequent references to less than excellent teachers are not intended to be criticisms. Rather, they reflect the fact that it often is easier to learn about the requirements of success by watching the obviously unsuccessful person. Effective teachers, I learned, typically go about their work with such ease that they would encourage an observer who had never taught to erroneously conclude that it is easy to be a good teacher.

was working with a group of about six children on word identification practice. She was printing words on a chalkboard; the children were sitting in front of the board and were expected to be looking at and identifying them. However, there was a problem. Next to the board was a small, low table. On it were clay figures of animals which the children had made the day before. *Naturally* they were an attraction, even though they had been discussed the day before. *Naturally* two children in the group of six were more interested in looking at the animals than at the words on the board. Instead of taking into account and dealing with a very normal response—this could have been done simply by moving the table to another part of the room—the teacher instead chose to scold the children for not paying attention. The final result was much wasted instructional time, an annoying repetition of reminders from the teacher and, as might be expected, two children who continued to give more attention to clay animals than to words on a chalkboard.

How another first grade teacher—a more successful one in everything she did—handled a similar situation also merits a description. In this case the teacher had given two written assignments to a group of children with whom she had just finished working. One made use of Indian headbands that had been made earlier in the week. This assignment required the children to select from a page of small pictures those whose names began with the short sound of *i*, to cut them out, and to paste them on the headbands as a decoration. Children being children, as soon as the headbands were distributed the group became Indians, apparently forgetting the work that was to be done. Aware of her mistake in passing out the headbands too soon, this teacher wisely bypassed chastisement and said instead, "I don't think you'll have enough room on your desks for the headbands. Maybe it would be a good idea to put them back on the table until you finish the two workbook pages. When I check them and find that all your answers are correct, you can put the workbooks away and then there will be plenty of room to do a good job with the headbands." No child objected, and the work period proceeded without further disruptions.

Actually, how a teacher deals with behavior that is disruptive or, perhaps, simply in need of change, has a great deal to do with whether or not she will be successful. For instance, those who are successful have learned to deal with it in ways that are effective but also acceptable to the children. Thus, the teacher who instead of ordering a child to put an annoying trinket away simply suggests, "It might be a good idea to put that in your pocket; otherwise you'll lose it," tends to be more successful both in her relationship with the child and in changing his behavior. Or, in connection with writing practice, the successful teacher of young children would avoid negative and discouraging comments and in their place say things like, "Oh, that *t* got in too much hot water and shrank. You'll have to make it bigger." When numerals are the content for practice, she might say to a child who is having problems, "That five is a shorty. He needs to grow taller so that he'll be as big as the other numerals. You don't want him to be sad, do you?"

A somewhat dramatic example of how another successful teacher dealt with undesirable behavior occurred in a kindergarten classroom. In this case one of the boys displayed a boldness to her that startled everyone—including, I thought, the boy himself. For a brief moment his behavior brought total silence to the room. Then, with poise and calmness, the teacher looked at him and started to sing—with just the right amount of sternness—a song called, "Watch What that Little Tongue Says." Within a very short time, everything and everybody were back to normal.

On another occasion I saw this same teacher quiet a group of children who were all talking at once with another song, this one called, "Only One Can Talk at a Time." She also turned out to be a teacher who, rather than ordering a group to listen and pay attention, was more likely to say something like, "I'm looking for closed doors (mouths) and open windows (eyes)."

What was always apparent and even striking about the way this particular teacher dealt with disruptive or undesirable behavior was that her methods were both effective *and* acceptable to the children. It would seem she not only knew and took into account the characteristics of the young but also enjoyed or, perhaps, had learned to enjoy all or at least most of them.

This is not the case with every teacher. Visits to classrooms suggest that some who are now working with young children might do better and be happier in classrooms occupied by older students. Here, for instance, I am thinking of one who commonly scolded children for doing things like stamping their feet when a child in the story being read stamped his; or because they asked, "Where's the cowboys?" after she read, "They played Indians." In another classroom I observed a teacher who became quite perturbed with a child because, just briefly, he pretended his paste bottle was binoculars and proceeded to examine objects scattered about the room. In addition to magnifying the trivial, this same teacher also tended to argue with children. One brief conversation typifies what could be heard in her classroom:

Teacher: These are new books.
Child: I've seen them before.
Teacher: No, you have not.
Child: My brother had them.
Teacher: I said these are new books.

At another time I watched another teacher as she was working with a group and explaining with considerable detail the meaning of "train," used as a verb. My immediate thought was, "How patient these children are," because the explanation did seem unnecessarily long. Eventually she added, "It's also something you can ride on." Apparently this second meaning was more interesting; at least a few of the children immediately responded by making train noises. But that was promptly stopped with, "That's enough of that." As an observer, I could not help but contrast the great patience displayed by the children and what appeared to be a lack of it in the teacher.

Personally, I have always thought that one of the most appealing characteristics of young children is their unexpected answers; consequently the behavior of another teacher was a constant source of surprise because she seemed so unaccepting of anything unusual. Once, for example, she was discussing the color red and asked the children to name things that were red. At first, ordinary responses like "fire truck" and "traffic light" were given, and they were accepted with a smile. They were also printed on the board so that soon the following list appeared:

After the response of "strawberry," an interesting but disappointing thing happened. One child eagerly contributed "sore tonsils," which was not greeted with a smile and was never added to the list.

On another day another child received a similar response to his unexpected answer. In this case he and some of the other children were reading a story about bakers, pictured as being clothed entirely in white. The teacher asked them, "Why do you suppose bakers wear white clothing?" As the children proceeded to offer explanations it became clear that the teacher wanted them to refer to the need to be clean when working with food. However, one boy seemed to ignore the "hints" for he explained, "If the baker drops flour on his clothes, nobody will know they're dirty." I was not surprised when his answer failed to receive a positive response. I had come to expect that, after a series of observations.

Happily, most visits to classrooms occupied by young children provide opportunities to watch teachers who seem not only to understand their particular characteristics, but also to enjoy them. This is why I have been able to see teachers who:

> Prepared a trayful of small objects and trinkets whose names began with *t* as a way of helping children enjoy phonics instruction.
>
> Used a puppet to make counting a little more interesting.
>
> Promised the children a rectangle surprise when they were talking about rectangles; and later carried in four small, rectangular chalkboards to the delight of the children.
>
> Prepared for use in Monday morning's phonics instruction a bulletin-board display portraying a Saturday night television program called "The Mouse on the Mayflower."

While there are many teachers who take the time to do things like this, the presence of others who probably would not bother with such "extras" is enough to warrant the suggestion that those of you who are now considering teaching the young should ask yourselves whether you have thought sufficiently about their characteristics and, equally important, whether you enjoy them. That enjoyment, classroom observations repeatedly point out, inevitably enters into the behavior of successful teachers.

Are Sensitive to Individual Needs and Problems

Successful teachers, as has been emphasized, are knowledgeable about young children and also enjoy them—at least most of the time. Another related characteristic is what might be called their sensitivity regarding the needs and problems of individual children.

I became consciously aware of this particular trait early in my observations. Its importance was initially made clear in a kindergarten in which there was an exceedingly bright girl—in fact, I would say she was one of the brightest young children I have known. Yet, for reasons I would not pretend to understand, she became tense and anxious whenever she was asked to do something alone. It could be as simple as reading a word or pointing to a particular card or picture. The nature of the task did not matter, nor did her outstanding ability and accomplishments. She simply could not cope with situations that called attention to herself. Luckily she was in the classroom of a teacher who quickly sensed the problem and went out of her way to avoid placing the child in any situation that called for a solo performance. Eventually but very slowly this girl was able to overcome the problem, although at the end of the year she still was not one who would go out of her way to "perform."

What on the surface also looked like excessive shyness appeared in a boy in another kindergarten. With him, having to do anything physical seemed like an unbearable burden. At music time, for instance, when the other children would be merrily skipping or, perhaps, dramatizing the words of a song, he acted as if his greatest desire at the moment was to find a hole and hide. Sensitive to the problem, his teacher never commented about it and said nothing when he chose to remain apart from an activity. Occasionally she would offer encouragement, but nothing more. Again, little by little, this child was able to join the others—although with great hesitation at first.

Other combinations of sensitive teachers and children with problems were found in many other classrooms. In a first grade group, for instance, one girl seemed unusually intimidated by children who knew more than she did. The teacher took cognizance of this when she organized instructional groups, always placing her in one in which she was likely to know either as much as or more than the other children. Such careful placement seemed to bolster the child's self-confidence; at least by the end of the year she was not so readily squelched by children who knew more than she did.

Whole groups of children were also found benefiting from sensitive teachers. With the young ones this became especially noticeable on days when restlessness pervaded an entire class. On such days these teachers allotted a longer amount of time for recess and, for example, planned a music period in which the children sang but also marched, skipped, jumped, and hopped. As one of the teachers noted, "On a day like this I always make sure there's plenty of wiggle music."

Another kind of sensitivity is required when children first come to school. Here I refer to the fact that for some, leaving home and starting school is a frightening experience; and, as a result, teachers must be ready to provide a situation that is nonthreatening and even pleasureable. All of us have lived long enough to know that the nature of our initial contact with anything—including school—has a lasting effect on all subsequent ones. Consequently there is no need here to elaborate upon the special importance of a teacher's sensitivity during the early part of a child's first year in school.

Use Common Sense

In addition to being sensitive to the needs and problems of individual children, I would like to suggest that successful teachers also make abundant use of common sense. Admittedly, "use common sense" is neither an informative nor a scholarly description of teacher behavior. However, I hardly know how else to categorize certain requirements for success. In this instance they were identified indirectly by watching poor rather than good teachers. Therefore let me describe certain behaviors of the former and, at the end, you can assign your own descriptive heading for this section of the chapter.

The heading "Use Common Sense" was chosen because in the course of visiting schools I sometimes found myself wondering, "What happens to common sense in the classroom?" You might be amazed to learn that one of the most frequent reasons for asking such a question is that much too often I watched teachers who failed to make sure that children were able to see what was going on. Surprising?

To describe some of the ways this lack of attention to a very important detail was noticed, let me reproduce below a few of the notes I made immediately following observations. In all instances, the teachers' names have been changed.

> In her work with small groups today, Mrs. White used words that had been printed on a large chart. The chart was hung so low that most of the children were unable to see the words at the bottom.

> Today Miss Hutchins played a game with small groups of children as a way of providing word identification practice. A group divided into two teams whose members lined up on opposite sides of the room. The game proceeded by having team members take turns identifying words shown on cards held by Miss Hutchins. Unfortunately, she held up each card in such a way that only the members of one team could see it. This reduced by half the amount of practice that could have been possible.

> Each reading group in Miss Marlan's class is made up of about eight children who sit in one row of chairs at the front of the room when it is time for instruction. This morning, instruction for each group began with a review that had individual children identify words printed on cards held by Miss Marlan. Because of the length of the row of chairs, children sitting at one

> end were never able to see words being identified by children at the other end.
>
> As she works with a group, Mrs. Banlon inevitably shows pictures, cards, charts, etc., in such a way that only those sitting directly in front of her can see them. The other children either strain to see, or simply do not bother to look.
>
> Today it just so happened that some of the tiniest children in Mrs. Ray's room ended up sitting in the second of the two rows of chairs used when small-group instruction takes place. This created obvious problems whenever Mrs. Ray wrote words on the chalkboard. However no effort was made to have the shorter children sit in the front row.
>
> Today Mrs. Wonder had children identify words as they framed them.* (The words were printed on the chalkboard.) To do this, they had to stand in front of the word, thus preventing others from seeing it as it was being identified. In addition, a table was in front of the chalkboard which meant that the children had to lean across it. The end result was much stumbling and giggling, but little practice.

Other notes about observations pointed out still other procedures that raised questions about the use of common sense in classrooms:

> Today, as Mrs. Green placed word cards in the slots in the card holder, the bottom of the cards in one row was commonly covered by the cards placed in the next row. This created problems whenever the covered words included letters like *g* and *y*. In fact, when partially covered the *g* looked like a manuscript *a*, while the *y*'s looked like *v*'s.
>
> As she holds up word cards Miss Ninsley's fingers frequently cover the bottom of letters like *g*, *j*, *p*, and *y*. Sometimes this is enough to give a word a distorted appearance.
>
> Today Mrs. Winters had a number of word cards which she held up and then showed to the children, one at a time. All the cards were the same size except for a longer one on which she had printed *something*. This created two problems. First, the

* "Framing" requires a child to place a hand at the beginning and end of a word. It has been a traditional recommendation in basal reader manuals even when the reason for it (presumably to emphasize that one word = one symbol) no longer exists.

> unusual length of the one card could be used as a cue in identifying *something*. Secondly, because all the cards were being held together, the *ing* in *something* extended out from the rest. This meant that as each word was shown to the children they saw that word but they also saw *ing* at the end of it.

Other notes raised questions about other teacher-made materials. For instance, one practice sheet composed by a teacher showed a list of ten typed sentences. The job for the children was to read each and underline the one word that contained a short *o* sound. The surprising feature of this assignment was that all the words to be underlined appeared at the ends of the sentences. It was also surprising to find other dittoed assignment sheets in which letters were not printed clearly or, perhaps, parts of them were simply not visible. Such imperfections always caused problems for the children; yet they appeared repeatedly, often in the same classrooms.

In other schools, teachers were giving a great deal of time to preparing very interesting materials. Nonetheless, flaws appeared which again were surprising because they were so obvious. For instance, one teacher had taken the time to print words on paper apples. (The apples would be placed on a bulletin board tree, if the words were correctly identified.) Unfortunately the red chosen for the apples was quite dark; as a result, it was almost impossible to read the words because they had been printed with a black crayon.

The great difficulty of seeing what a teacher had so carefully printed also became apparent in another classroom in which the cars of a train, each a different color, were hanging on a wall. The intent was to display different colors and the word for each. Thus, *red* had been printed on the red car, *yellow* on the yellow car, and so on. In this instance the obvious problem was that the words were so small they could not be read from where the children sat.

A similar yet different kind of problem connected with being able to see was observed in still another classroom. In this case the teacher had drawn the face of a clock on a paper plate. It was to be used for practice with numeral identification, so the numerals from 1 to 12 had been carefully printed around the edge. There also was a hand, made from paper and attached to the center of the plate so that it was movable. But there was one problem. The hand was so long it covered the numerals as it pointed to them. With this, the flaw could have been eliminated with the snip of a scissors, but instead—again surprisingly—the teacher used the plate without making the small but important adjustment.

Other surprises underscored the importance of "Be prepared!" In fact, a few new teachers habitually demonstrated its importance because, as they habitually had to look for this and that, they were also losing the attention of the children with whom they were working. It would seem that these teachers had failed to think through the requirements of a particular assignment or type of instruction; the result was the need to get or find something right in the middle of a lesson or explanation. Predictably the children lost interest in the job at hand and, commonly, it was not regained when the necessary materials were finally collected.

Failure to think about necessary materials was displayed in other ways, too. For example, one assignment in a first grade classroom required the children to read color words in order to know what color to make certain objects in a dittoed picture. Not all the children knew every word but the teacher reminded them that all they had to do was look at a chart in the front of the room, should they have trouble. This chart showed rectangles of various colors, each labeled with the appropriate color word. An obvious shortcoming, however, was that the assignment used two words (*purple* and *brown*) which were not included in the chart. As a result, the "independent" assignment turned into an occasion for many question, all of which would have been unnecessary had the teacher considered its requirements.

In another classroom the importance of being prepared became clear again as a teacher worked with a group. In this case she commented about having just a small amount of time for review, and then proceeded to write a sentence on the chalkboard. The children read it, then waited while another sentence was written. With this procedure, and with the time that was available, a total of only four sentences was read. Thus, an observer could not help but wonder why the teacher had not prepared differently for the review, either by writing sentences on cards or, perhaps, a chart. With such materials available, many more than just the four sentences could have been read in the same amount of time.

Another group of teaching procedures which always raised questions were those that demonstrated something—backwards. Here I am recalling teachers who, as they faced a group, demonstrated a left-to-right movement in a way that turned it into a right-to-left direction from the children's point of view. It would seem that common sense would suggest to a teacher that if she wants to act out the meaning of left to right for children who are facing her, she must display a right-to-left movement. Or, for instance, if children are to see the correct movements for making a certain letter or numeral by watching a teacher form it in the air, then she must go through movements that are opposite to what she wants the children to see.

Still other observations that provoked the question, "What happens to common sense in the classroom?" could be cited. However, probably enough have been related to support the contention that it is not always apparent in classroom procedures and, secondly, that the lack of it impedes learning. Another and more positive way of making the same point is to suggest that effective instruction is made up of many component parts and that one of them is giving attention to small but important details.

Have Diagnostic Ability

Like members of the medical profession, those who teach and want to be successful must learn to be astute diagnosticians. In fact, a brief yet accurate description of the skillful teacher is to say she is a skillful observer. It is this ability that enables her to carry on a maximum of individualized instruction. What is individualized instruction?

Individualized instruction is any instruction that is a match for what is needed. That is, what is being taught is what children need to learn. Sometimes individualized instruction is carried on with just one child; however it is not that feature which merits the description "individualized." Rather, it is the correspondence between what is being taught and what needs to be learned—or, perhaps, relearned or reviewed—that makes it individualized. And this, after all, is what good teaching is all about: selecting instruction that is a match for what children need and are ready to learn.

Because of its basic importance to individualized instruction, diagnosis will be discussed in all the chapters in this textbook that deal with the specifics of teaching. Here it will be dealt with only briefly in order to emphasize its close connection with the central theme of this present chapter: behavioral characteristics of successful teachers.

One basic ingredient of diagnostic ability is a willingness to listen to children as they respond, explain, ask questions, and so on. To be emphasized immediately is that such willingness is rooted not in any desire to criticize or blame but, rather, in the spirit of wanting to help.

What is especially helpful to teachers, by the way, are *in*correct responses (4, 8). In fact, it very often is the mistakes of children that provide the best insights not only into their learnings and mislearnings, but also into the flaws and shortcomings of a teacher's instruction. Remember: To hear a child's response is to have an opportunity to learn something about yourself *qua* teacher.

Having underscored, though just briefly, the importance of listening to children and of having the desire to help rather than criticize, it now seems timely to ask: What actually happens in classrooms? What do teachers do with erroneous or confused answers? How do they react?

Sometimes, *not* in ways that are ideal. Let me cite an example. Not long ago I was visiting in a first grade. The teacher was working with part of the class and, in fact, had just distributed readers to the children as I entered the room. She asked them to read a story silently and then added, "If you come across a word you don't know, I'll help you." Shortly after the reading began a boy raised his hand to indicate the need for assistance. How did the teacher respond after he pointed to the troublesome word? She said, "You should know that. We talked about that yesterday. Don't you know it? You should." Perhaps it is unnecessary to mention that no other hands were raised, for even six year olds are quick to discern the contradiction between a promise that offers help and a response that seems critical. Such happenings as these are regrettable not only because they assign to teachers the role of a person who blames and criticizes, but also because they are unused opportunities for learning about a child's achievements—or problems—and a teacher's successes—or failures.

Fortunately, as I visit classrooms occupied by young children, I see many more teachers who display a desire to help rather than to censure. Still, it must also be said that not enough use children's responses diagnostically; that is, as a means for learning more about the children and their own instruction. All the attention seems to go to judgments about wrongness and rightness rather than to a consideration of the clues a response might offer for improving the teaching-learning process. Much too frequently, as a matter of fact, a child simply learns—directly or indirectly—that his answer is "wrong." Not often enough is he told why it is wrong, and even more rarely does a teacher use the incorrect or confused response to identify what still needs to be taught. This is too bad because, for example, the child who reads *eat* as if it were *cat* is telling the teacher something about his particular learning problems, but he is also telling about some necessary content for future instruction. Or, to cite other illustrations, the child who responds "nine" when a *g* is shown, or who says "red fire trucks" when asked to identify *red* is revealing something about his particular shortcomings but, equally important, he is identifying material that still needs to be taught. Reflecting another flaw in instruction is the child who, after *find* is written and identified by the teacher and a request is made to use it in a sentence, offers, "It is a fine day."

Probably the quickest way to describe what is here being called "diagnostic ability" is to say it is a combination of attitudes and knowledge which allows and even prompts a teacher to see in every child's response an opportunity to learn more about that child and also about her own instruction. In this case both sides of the coin are equally important if instruction is to be improved.

Have Ability in Selecting Appropriate Instructional Goals

Closely related to ability in diagnosis is another which also marks the behavior of successful teachers: ability to select appropriate goals. Because the importance of such an ability is self-evident, classroom procedures should show evidence of being guided by carefully chosen goals; yet this is not always the case. In fact, a few observations tempt the visitor to ask a teacher, "*Why* are you doing what you're doing?" Often the answer could only be, "This is what the manual said to do." While the manuals that come with textbooks *can* be useful, they cannot guarantee that the goals they enumerate are the most appropriate for particular children. And even when they are, what a teacher does with them makes for important differences.

I have often been reminded of this during the course of visiting classrooms. For example, in first grades it is common to see a type of reading instruction that follows very closely the suggestions found in a basal reader manual. Among those commonly included is review vocabulary. Generally such a goal is quite appropriate and even necessary; what a teacher does with it, however, makes for obvious differences in what is actually accomplished. For instance, I have watched teachers who had a group of children go over certain words but then did nothing about common errors except to mention what the responses should have been. It was as if teaching is merely a matter of telling rather than of helping children understand errors in order to minimize them. To be more specific, to say to a child that *eat* is "eat," not "cat," is telling—*not* teaching. On the other hand, to point out both the similarity and the difference between *eat* and *cat* and, further, to explain why *eat* could not be *cat* is to teach and, therefore, ought to be a part of the goal designated as "review vocabulary."

In other classrooms I have found teachers who seemed to know the meaning of a goal like "review vocabulary," but failed to learn from the children's responses that it was inappropriate—for them. In a kindergarten, to cite one example of this, a teacher was reviewing words that had been introduced earlier in connection with outdoor signs, and so they included *stop, go, slow,* and so on. She first worked with the lowest achievers. The words were written and identified and discussed; then a game was played in which the children had to act out the meanings of the words, now appearing on homemade signs. With this group, the goal *was* appropriate and the means taken to achieve it were effective. At least the children seemed to be both learning from and enjoying the game.

When the same procedures were next used with the brighter children, it immediately became clear that they knew the words as well as the teacher; consequently "review" hardly seemed necessary. Nonetheless, the teacher went right on and repeated everything that had been done with the others. Now, however, the results were quite different. In a matter of a few minutes the children lost interest in the game, probably because unlike the other group it offered them no challenge. But still the teacher persisted. Here, of course, is an example of a teacher who did select a goal and did select effective procedures to achieve it. It just so happened, though, that the goal was inappropriate because, in this instance, its purpose had already been achieved.

Other classrooms reveal other types of inappropriateness. I readily recall one in which the teacher was found giving time to a child who, unlike the rest of the class, had great difficulty learning the names of letters. Unfortunately—this was a new teacher, by the way—instead of selecting just a few letters, she apparently had chosen to work on all of them. Needless to say, the child was just as confused at the end of the tutoring as he was at the beginning.

Even when goals *are* appropriate, failure to keep them in mind can get in the way of reaching them in the most efficient way. Exemplifying this shortcoming is a common occurrence in classrooms in which young children are learning about the sounds letters record. To reinforce a certain letter-sound association (goal), teachers often have the children underline pictures whose names begin with the selected sound and then, typically, they are directed to color these pictures. Such an activity might take about twenty minutes, five of which are spent on sounds while the remaining time is consumed with the coloring. Teachers who keep their goal in mind spend the fifteen minutes helping individual children with the sound. Those who do not are more apt to spend it supervising the coloring.

Because children *will* be children, the point must also be made that even when both goals and the procedures for accomplishing them are appropriate—and also kept in mind—things still do not always go as planned. A boy in a kindergarten reminded me of this just recently. He and some of the other children were playing "bingo" with the teacher. This had been selected as a way of reviewing words which were printed on the cards. As in any bingo game, the children received markers; in this case, paper squares. As it happened in this particular game, the boy referred to above became much more interested in counting and comparing squares than in covering words. And the interest spread to the entire group. Since it became clear from their responses that practice in counting and comparing also were appropriate goals, the teacher was wise enough to switch the focus temporarily. After a while, interest in the words returned and the bingo game proceeded in the way the teacher had originally planned to play it.

Are Flexible

This incident identifies another characteristic that prevails when successful teachers are observed. They have definite plans; yet they are flexible and are able to see in a situation a potential not originally thought about or planned for. Call it "flexible structure" or "structured flexibility." The point is that teachers who are successful in their work with young children are well organized, yet always open to unforeseen possibilities.

In a somewhat striking way the significance of such a trait was once highlighted for me while observing a group of four year olds during outdoor play. It happened that the play area was close to a railroad track; it also just happened that at the time of the observation the longest and most colorful freight train I had ever seen came along. Just as it was passing by, the teacher was explaining the details of a game to the children. Although all wanted to watch the train she scolded those who did, reminding them that she was explaining something. Evidently she had a plan and was determined to follow it, come what may—including a train that provided a rich opportunity for color identification and the extension of speaking vocabularies. Here, quite obviously, was a teacher with a goal —but not much flexibility.

It is likely, of course, that seeing the potential in situations requires more than what I am calling "flexibility." For instance, what was lacking when:

> A teacher taught the song "B–I–N–G–O," but never once wrote any of those letters on the board even though letter identification was one of that year's goals.
>
> A group of children was talking about a recent PTA Carnival during a conversation period; yet the teacher never pointed out that "PTA" was an example of what had recently been discussed: abbreviations.
>
> A child observed, "So many begin with J!" while attendance was being taken with the help of first-name cards tucked into the slots of a word card holder; yet, in spite of the fact that the children were learning about letter-sound associations, the teacher never mentioned or demonstrated that these names also began with the same sound.
>
> After a teacher asked a boy, whose name happened to be Paul, to put a library book called *Ping* on the table, one child immediately commented, "Oh, that's a good idea. Paul and Ping both begin with the same letter." Yet, once again, nothing was done with the fact that they—but also *Peter* and *Patsy*—began with the same sound.

In concluding this discussion of the importance of being able to see the instructional potential in accidental happenings, I must not forget to mention an experience I once had while working with a teacher, for in this lies a reminder about another of the requirements for successful instruction.

This particular teacher taught kindergarten. My purpose in working with her was to show how everyday happenings often give a teacher opportunities to expose young children to written words and that, as a result, some learn to read them. As a start, I suggested that whenever words of special interest came up, some might be printed on the board so that the children could see as well as hear them. Apparently I was totally unsuccessful in communicating my idea because when I next visited this teacher's classroom she was writing practically every word she spoke. The result was a group of children who were being deluged by many words rather than exposed to just a few special ones. For me, the result was a new awareness of the importance of, "A little goes a long way."

Know the Meaning of "Enough"

Once more I am at a loss to know exactly how to label the characteristic or ability that allows a teacher to appreciate that a little goes a long way; to have a sense of the right proportion; to know when it is time to quit. I have called it "knowing the meaning of 'enough.'" A description of a few teachers who did too much or went too far should help clarify both the meaning of what I am trying to name as well as its importance for teaching.

The first teacher who comes to mind is one who was unusually successful in assembling interesting bulletin-board displays that had much instructional potential. The children's enthusiastic response to each one probably was a reason for an unfortunate development. As the school year progressed, one attractive bulletin board was replaced by two. Gradually the two were replaced by three until, at one point, everything in the room was covered including the one chalkboard.

Two consequences of this failure to appreciate the importance of "enough" are worth mentioning. One was that the lack of a chalkboard interfered with instruction, at times making it impossible to show what the children needed to see. Another consequence was a room in which the displays were an unsettling distraction rather than an interesting aid. Obviously being demonstrated was that four good bulletin-board displays are not four times as helpful as one. Also shown was the ease with which means can become ends in themselves.

In another classroom I had suggested that an attempt be made to help the children become more consciously aware of the written words in their everyday surroundings, including those appearing on television and in newspapers. In response the teacher developed what she called the

"News Bulletin Board." For this, the children were encouraged to find and bring in words in newspapers which they could read. For about a week the group's response to "news time" was one of considerable interest and involvement, and they eagerly named letters, read words, and even talked about current news. But then it became obvious that with the passing of each day this interest waned. And yet the teacher continued to have news time every morning. By the end of about three weeks, however, it had turned into a time of discipline problems and was finally discontinued. Once again, the meaning of "too much of a good thing" became crystal clear.

It was also made clear in a classroom in which there was both a teacher and a teaching assistant. This was a kindergarten and, among other things, the children were learning to name letters and to read some words. Toward the end of the year, as a way of helping with both goals, the teacher used an alphabet record in which the narrator spent considerable time on each letter. This enabled the teacher to write a letter on one chalkboard as she discussed it while, on another, the assistant printed a word—a familiar one whenever possible—which began with it. To an observer it seemed that the children enjoyed both the record and the extra touches added by the teacher and her assistant. In addition, from an instructional point of view the procedure offered interesting review as well as an opportunity to expose the children to some new words. But then something else was done.

Probably encouraged by the children's positive response, this teacher later decided to use the same procedure with another record, this one dealing with the months of the year. But there was an important difference, which apparently was overlooked. With the second record each month was considered much more briefly, requiring the teacher to print the letters and the assistant the names of the months so quickly that the procedure turned into something quite ludicrous. Once more the message that came through was the importance of appropriateness, of knowing when to quit, of sensing what is too much.

Actually, what is for me one of the most difficult things to communicate to teachers is this sense of knowing what is the right amount. Even when I work closely with individual teachers, communication seems to break down when it comes to this. As a result, things like the following have occurred. I mentioned to one teacher—and we discussed in some detail specific ways for carrying out this suggestion—that children's names could be very useful in teaching and reviewing the names of letters. A subsequent visit to her classroom showed a procedure in which she was having *every* child, one after the other, spell his name. Probably I do not have to point out that the procedure outlasted the children's patience with it.

At another time I mentioned to another teacher that children are interested in their homes and that such an interest could be useful in teaching word meanings and some reading vocabulary. The next time I visited her room I found that *everything* was dealing with homes. In fact, toward the end of the morning's visit I had serious questions about ever making that suggestion again. By the end, I was determined never to make it for when it came time to close the morning with a story, the teacher began reading from—you guessed it—a book about houses and homes.

Are Knowledgeable

The last characteristic of successful teachers to which attention will be given is the requirement of being knowledgeable. Had this chapter been written earlier such a requirement probably would not have been discussed, not because it is unimportant but because its importance is so obvious. However, not long ago I overheard a conversation in which the most persistent thought expressed was: "You don't have to know very much to teach young children." Because others may hold the same opinion, this part of the chapter will conclude with a few comments about the need for teachers of the young to be very knowledgeable.

Traditionally, as has been pointed out before, individuals and professional groups connected with early childhood education have stressed the need for teachers to be knowledgeable about what might be called the psychology of young children. Because they considered social and emotional development to be the major goal of school programs, such an emphasis was natural, as was the fact that teacher education programs were heavily weighted with courses in child development.

Now that the child's early years are considered to be uniquely important for intellectual development, other emphases have come to the foreground. Nonetheless—and this has been underscored throughout this chapter as well as the previous one—the need to understand and even enjoy the behavior and the psychological characteristics of young children continues to be an essential requirement for their teachers. Added to this one, however, is the need to be knowledgeable about subject matter and how it might be taught to the young.

Because there is no agreement about the best subject matter for early childhood programs, there also is no agreement about what teachers must know. The contention of this textbook is that the language arts comprise the most important foci for instruction; consequently the subject matter chapters deal with content designed to help teachers to know what is necessary for teaching skills concerned with listening, speaking, reading, and writing.

What is necessary, incidentally, is much more than what will actually be taught. In fact, a basic requirement for successful teaching is an amount of knowledge that allows for selections; more specifically, for selections of content which is appropriate for the particular children being taught. And this brings the discussion right back to individualized instruction.

Individualized instruction, you will recall, is instruction that corresponds to what children need and are ready to learn. Thus, its basic concern is to match content with children, *not* with the grade level sign that happens to hang on the classroom door. Because a maximum of individualized instruction is the aim of this textbook, chapters dealing with subject matter do not prescribe what must be taught to all children attending nursery school or, to cite another example, they do not lay down what are to be the goals of all kindergarten programs. Clearly, any such prescriptions go contrary to the very essence of individualized instruction. Instead, the chapters consider language arts content in a way that should allow nursery school, kindergarten, and first grade teachers to select from it whatever seems appropriate for the particular children who happen to be in their particular classrooms. Because one selection must be followed by another, these chapters also consider the matter of sequence by pointing out what tends to be easier or more simple than something else. As with these present chapters, those dealing with subject matter also try to make the act of teaching as specific as possible. Once again, what has been learned from both good and not so good teachers should help with this.

TEACHING ASSISTANTS

Of obvious help to those who teach young children is another adult who provides the extra hands, the extra ears, the extra eyes, and all the other extras that are needed when every effort is being made to carry on a program marked by individualized instruction. Often, in fact, it is the absence of just such extras that makes individualized instruction very difficult to achieve. Here I am thinking of the teacher who is keenly aware of what individual children do and do not know and who is sufficiently knowledgeable to select appropriate content for them but who, because of the differences among the children, simply cannot do what she knows ought to be done—without help. It is then that the second adult can make a substantial contribution as, among other things, she spends time with children who are not working with the teacher. Well prepared, an assistant can even be the difference between a very ordinary program and a truly excellent one.

What is meant by "well prepared"? As I see it, an assistant's clear understanding of the role she is to play is one important part of being well prepared. I stress this immediately because I have learned that having an assistant who does not know what she is supposed to be doing is very much like having one more child to worry about.

Right now, what she should be doing has not been prescribed or agreed upon; consequently teachers who are lucky enough to have an assistant can themselves establish her role. In practice, the full role generally evolves as time passes. However, even at the start of a school year, some decisions should have been made about what the assistant will and will not do.

Some Possible Contributions

Assuming the assistant is not certified to teach and, in fact, is simply an adult who has some free time and likes young children, let me enumerate a few of the way in which she might help.

Supervise Children not Working with the Teacher. Because it is a fact that children in the same classroom are inevitably different in what they can and cannot do, it also is a fact that individualized instruction can only rarely be achieved by working with the entire class. With young children the need to work with less than the whole class often presents problems because they commonly need some type of supervision, especially when being in school or working alone is a new experience. And this is where an assistant can help because as the teacher works with some children, she can be with the others.

Exactly what she does with the others often is a part of the assistant's role that evolves over time. For instance, at the start of a school year her contribution might simply be her presence, although it is likely that she would also make sure the children have understood directions, are completing assigned work, and so on. In time she probably would enter more directly into their work by offering reminders, answering questions, or, maybe, raising some that the children ought to be considering.

Direct Practice or Review Periods. Often, an assistant can help when practice or review is needed. For instance, when certain children require practice—its details would be determined by the teacher—the assistant might supervise it, direct it, or, in the case of games, play them with the children. If it should happen that an entire class has need for the same practice—printing certain letters, for instance—both she and the teacher might move about the room, examining work, making suggestions, offering encouragement. Depending on the assistant, she might also be able to take on the role of tutor, offering aid to individual children who need more explanations and practice than most. Or, for example, I have seen assistants who were especially helpful when children returned to school after being away for one or more days. Inevitably absentees need varying amounts of help in catching up.

The most important point about all these possible roles for the assistant is that she assume only those for which she has the necessary ability and knowledge and that, with each, she knows exactly what she is and is not to do. This means that the teacher must take the time to learn about her abilities, perhaps add to them, and then assign only those roles in which she can function successfully. Once this has been done, the most important next step often is one of helping the assistant grow in self-confidence.

Assist with Materials. Among a teacher's many responsibilities is that of making certain the right materials and supplies are available and at the right time. An assistant can also help with this by making sure materials are returned to the proper place, by keeping track of supplies that are left and then ordering what is needed, by duplicating ditto sheets selected by the teacher, and so on. Often, too, homemade materials are necessary for instruction. While it is the teacher who must decide on their details, an assistant usually is able to help make them. Once, in fact, I visited in a first grade in which the teacher was full of good ideas for materials but lacked the ability to execute many of them. Her assistant, on the other hand, had a great deal of artistic ability; so, together, this team was able to produce some of the most attractive—and productive—materials I have ever seen. Unfortunately, not all assistants have the talent of this one.

Guide Conversations and Read Stories. Once children know something, they want to talk about it. Yet, in classrooms in which there are many children but only one adult, opportunities for conversation are too few. An assistant can help with this too, either by guiding a planned group conversation or simply by being available when a child just has to tell something to somebody.

At least some of the time, an assistant might also be the one who reads to the children. Or, for example, as a way of accommodating boy-girl interests, a teacher might choose to read a story especially selected for the boys while, in another part of the room, the assistant reads a story to the girls that was especially chosen for them.

Help with Clerical Duties. To visit regularly in classrooms is to be reminded of the many things a teacher has to do that hardly come under the heading of "instruction." In case you have forgotten, teachers still have to count money for milk, money for lunches, money for bus service, money for school pictures, and money for outings. They also must turn in attendance data, record test scores, and make out report cards. In one kindergarten, a teacher even had to keep track of which children were brushing their teeth with a fluoride preparation.

When a teacher has one group of children, such extras as these are very time consuming. However when she has two, as is common at the nursery school and kindergarten levels, they become a nuisance. They also take considerable amounts of time away from mornings and afternoons that are already too short to accomplish all that needs to be done. Clearly an assistant could help with many of the clerical duties now performed by people who are supposed to be teachers. In fact, without this assistance an observer can only conclude that teachers spend far too much time with matters that have little to do with teaching.

Other Contributions

As I have observed in classrooms in which there was both a teacher and an assistant, still other contributions have been noticeable. For instance, an important one is the extra source of praise, sympathy, and rewards made available with the second adult. For young children these extras are very important because they provide more of what is always needed: personal attention.

I have also watched as assistants were able to reduce the amount of time children spend waiting for things ranging from milk to a turn to talk. In addition, I have observed assistants who, because their personalities were quite different from that of the teacher, reduced the number of problems related to teacher-child personality clashes. And, finally, I have been reminded of the time it takes, and therefore of the time saved by the assistant, to do things like help with shoes that have come untied, zippers that are stuck, boots that are too small, and mittens that are lost.

As assistants in classrooms become more and more common, it seems safe to predict that we will become increasingly aware of still other contributions they can make to the development of a school program that is worthy of the many talents and abilities of four-, five-, and six-year-old children.

REFERENCES

1. Boocock, Sarane S. "Toward a Sociology of Learning." *Sociology of Education,* XXXIX (Winter, 1966), 1–45.
2. Chall, Jeanne. *Learning to Read: The Great Debate.* McGraw-Hill Book Co., 1967.

3. Dykstra, Robert. "Summary of the Second-Grade Phase of the Cooperative Research Program in Primary Reading Instruction," *Reading Research Quarterly,* IV (Fall, 1968), 49–70.
4. Goodman, Yetta M. "Using Children's Reading Miscues for New Teaching Strategies," *Reading Teacher,* XXIII (February, 1970), 455–459.
5. "Manpower in the Classroom," *Reading Newsreport,* IV (February, 1970), 60–61.
6. Robb, Mel H. *Teacher Assistants.* Columbus, Ohio: Charles E. Merrill Publishing Co., 1969.
7. Wardrop, James L. "Generalizability of Program Evaluation," *Educational Product Report,* II (February, 1969), 41–42.
8. Weber, Rose-Marie. "A Linguistic Analysis of First-Grade Reading Errors," *Reading Research Quarterly,* V (Spring, 1970), 427–451.

Instruction

7

Extending Listening-Speaking Vocabularies

Not much teaching experience is required to appreciate the close connection between language skills and learning ability. In fact, the mere recollection of personal experiences probably is sufficient to identify their interdependent relationship. Because of the interdependence, it seems unnecessary to defend the position that curriculum goals pertaining to language always merit special and persistent attention.

Of course, language ability makes contributions of a more personal nature, too. As a start, it helps a child establish contact with his world and then, for the rest of his life, allows him to communicate something of himself to that world. Thus, it is for both intellectual and personal reasons that teachers ought to do whatever is possible to help children grow in their ability to use language with precision and richness.

LANGUAGE AND THE DISADVANTAGED CHILD

While the importance of language ability to school success has always been recognized, only in relatively recent years has it become a much discussed topic. Accounting for this new attention is the unprecedented concern now being shown for age-old problems that go along with poverty. More specifically, as the link between impoverished homes, impoverished language, and failure in school has become more widely understood, the basic importance of language has been getting an amount of attention that is justified and also long overdue.

As researchers and authors representing various disciplines tell about the language of children from impoverished homes, they are in unison in pointing out that it is at odds with classroom language and expectations (6, 7, 14, 15, 16). For example, they describe how it is different both in individual words and in the way these words are put together. The frequency of poor articulation problems is mentioned also. In addition, we are reminded that children from economically and socially marginal areas are restricted in what they see, hear, touch, and taste; consequently their ability to name or label objects and experiences also is restricted. Overall, then, they use a smaller number of less varied words than do other children of comparable ages.

Some authors rightfully remind us that "the measures of verbal ability and the incentives provided by the school for talking and otherwise using language may not tap the verbal ability of the culturally disadvantaged or culturally different child" (15, p. 388). Still, it seems indisputably correct to conclude that children from low socioeconomic backgrounds come to school with deficiencies in language which, if nothing special is done to help, preclude academic success.

LANGUAGE AND THE YOUNG CHILD

Surrounded as teachers now are by the very vocal attention being given to language deficiencies of the poor, it is easy for them to forget that all children—certainly all young children—are in need of continuous help with language. It is true that many of today's young children appear to be more sophisticated and advanced in the way they speak. Often, however, their seemingly adult-like words and expressions are only a façade, behind which lies a great variety of shallow understandings and even totally erroneous concepts. Examples of the latter are easy to find; for instance, some comprised an interesting *New York Times* article written by the parents of a young son. Among other things the authors mentioned that:

> A 3-year-old who knows more about rockets and jets than his grandfather was absolutely disbelieving when told that milk comes from cows. "Oh, no," he said indignantly. "Comes from the frigerator." And a little girl, who on her first visit to a farm was taken to see how the flowers and vegetables grew, was most interested in another crop. "I want to see where the lamb chops grow" (13, p. 39).

A different kind of deficiency also is found among the modern generation, whether they be urban, suburban, or rural children—and whether they are rich or poor. I can recall hearing somebody allude to this particular one with the comment, "For today's kids, a spinning wheel is what keeps you from getting the car back on the road." If only because the concern of academic areas like social studies and literature is for the past as well as the present, this kind of deficiency also merits the attention of teachers. In fact, *not* to give attention to concept and language deficiencies is to deny children the right to develop to their full potential.

Because with every young child there is so much that can be done in the area of language, it is the wise teacher who makes specific selections from among the long list of possibilities. Otherwise, everything might be attempted but not much will be accomplished. The selection made for this chapter has to do with the extension of listening and speaking vocabularies; therefore a good beginning is a definition of these terms.

Listening vocabulary refers to all the words a child understands when they are used by another. His *speaking vocabulary* would be smaller for it is comprised only of those words that he understands well enough to use himself. Thus, this present chapter deals with the important goal of helping children learn the meanings of a maximum number of words, hopefully with a sureness that will make them part of their speaking vocabularies. The assumption is that such a goal is of primary importance and should receive systematic and persistent attention in every school program planned for young children.

CONTRIBUTIONS OF LISTENING–SPEAKING VOCABULARIES

Highlighting the acquisition of vocabulary is not to deny the significance of other aspects of language growth. Assumed, for example, is that teachers will always assist young children with the correct pronunciation of words and, too, that they will help them put words together in acceptable ways. Another assumption of special importance is that when teachers do give attention to word meanings, they will see this not as a time for developing showcase vocabularies but as an opportunity to improve the children's ability to think; that is, to observe, note differences and similarities, infer, classify, and conclude.

For teachers who keep an eye on the future school lives of children, attention to the lexical aspect of language will also be seen as one effective means to insure that reading success continues throughout all the grades. I emphasize this point because limitations in a child's collection of meaningful words often explain a common phenomenon: He starts out successfully with reading, only to develop problems once he moves from simply told stories to subject matter textbooks. All one has to do is skim through middle- and upper-grade texts to become aware of one of the reasons why this happens. Even the quick survey would reveal how comprehension of their content depends upon the ability to cope with an abundance of terms likely to be unfamiliar, but which are introduced at rapid rates. For example, consider the following sentences in a third-grade social studies textbook:

> After the chlorine is thoroughly mixed with water in mixing tanks, the water goes to settling basins. The water is very still here so that any solids in the water settle to the bottom of the basins. From the settling basins the water goes through the sand filters (11, p. 291).

That words and ideas which hardly are a part of the modern child's prepackaged and mechanized world still need to be understood is brought out in this paragraph from another social studies textbook:

> Soon each plantation was a busy little village. It had a large house where the planter lived with his family. Some distance away were the small, plain cabins occupied by the workers. Then there were barns and stables, and the blacksmith shop where iron tools were made. Near the large house were storerooms, spinning and weaving rooms, the laundry, the blacksmith shop, and sometimes several kitchens (4, p. 30).

It would be unfair not to mention that authors of subject matter texts give help with word meanings through definitions that often are repeated. In a fourth grade science book, for example, the following appears:

> Water is a substance. This means that water is made of those tiny bits of matter called molecules. You remember that there are molecules in the air and that they move back and forth when an object vibrates. A solid, too, is made of molecules that are packed tightly together. Sunlight also makes molecules move back and forth, and objects become hot. Any substance—solid, liquid, or gas—is made of molecules. Water, a liquid, is made of molecules, and they can be made to move (2, p, 62).

At the sixth grade level, terms are still being defined but along with the defined words come others that might interfere with comprehension:

> The principle of alloys was discovered by chance and has remained unchanged through the centuries. Some primitive alloys survive today. Today, however, man knows a great deal more about the chemistry of metals, their microscopic structure, and their properties. He produces hundreds of different types of alloys ranging from the bronzes and brasses to the alloys of steel (3, p. 80).

A safe prediction is that anyone who is willing to skim through elementary school textbooks for social studies, science, and health can only come to these conclusions. First, all are characterized by the introduction of *many* new terms. Second, authors of all offer help with their meanings through some combination of definitions, examples, photographs, charts, diagrams, and maps. Third, with the science texts, extra help comes from the numerous experiments which are suggested for clarifying certain concepts. And, finally, in spite of these helps the number of new terms a child is expected to learn and remember is overwhelming, especially if he has a limited listening-speaking vocabulary to begin with. The message of these conclusions seems clear: Only when teachers are willing to give planned instruction in word meanings that will begin as soon as children start school is there any hope that they will be able to cope with the reading demands made of them as they move through the middle and upper grades.

CLASSROOM ATMOSPHERE AND LANGUAGE DEVELOPMENT

Providing the right atmosphere hardly is sufficient to equip each child with a vocabulary that will serve him well, both academically and personally. Yet the classroom climate established by a teacher cannot go undiscussed for it either hastens language development or gets in the way. It is never neutral. A recent experience pinpoints the most important thing to be said about classroom climates. As its details are being related below, you might note a ring of familiarity about them.

During a social gathering of a group of adults, a teacher was the last to arrive. When one of the other guests learned what her occupation was, he quickly commented, "Oh, I had better watch what I say." Although spoken in jest, his remark evoked some thoughts worth noting. For instance, it accurately suggested the tendency of some teachers to be too quick to correct language. While the eagerness stems from their desire to improve it, constant correction is not likely to accomplish the end they have in mind because children soon learn to stop talking when whatever they say seems to be wrong. And, children who do not talk do not learn to talk well.

Because teachers *are* responsible for improving language, they can hardly adopt an "I don't care" policy. If neither this nor constant correction is the answer, what is?

From what I have observed, the best answer begins with a teacher whose own language provides children with a model worthy of both admiration and imitation. With young children this means she neither talks down to them, nor over their heads. Probably the natural tendency is toward the former; therefore let me give some attention to that, again through a personal experience.

In this case I was interviewing teachers for a kindergarten position and went to the home of one because illness in the family made it difficult for her to be away for the interview. What especially impressed me about this candidate was the way she talked to her two youngest children, both of whom were present during our conversation. Her choice of words seemed just right; they were neither unnecessarily difficult nor childishly simple. This impressed me enough to recommend that she be hired.

The next time I was to see this teacher was the following fall when I visited in her classroom. Naturally I was both surprised and disappointed to hear her converse with the kindergarteners in a way that could only be described as "talking down." I cannot explain why she changed from a most acceptable way of communicating with young children; however I can and do want to urge other teachers to avoid such talk because, first of all, it is unnecessary and, secondly, it deprives children of the chance to reach up to a language which, if imitated, will bring improvement to their own.

In addition to the language model provided by a teacher, another relevant factor is her general attitude toward words. Ideally, again because attitudes are so readily picked up by young children, it should be one that is marked almost by an excitement about them. I say this not because research data support such a statement—studies dealing with this have not been done—but because classroom observations continually point out that the children's response to words mirrors that of their teacher. Find an interested teacher, I learned, and you will also find interested children.

More difficult to verbalize is still another feature of the ideal atmosphere. Here I have in mind what a teacher communicates to children about her role and responsibilities in relation to *their* language. Ideally, what ought to be communicated is acceptance combined with a desire to help. Such a message has its beginnings in certain understandings about young children and language—for instance, that they must be encouraged to use it and that, essentially, they learn to use it well through trial and error efforts. While it is somewhat difficult to describe this message in the abstract, in practice it looks very different from the one of, "You are wrong. I am here to correct you." It also is different in what it can accomplish.

WHICH WORDS TO TEACH?

What can be accomplished when vocabulary development is the concern is affected by such variables as the ability of the children and the state of their existing vocabularies. As was mentioned earlier, the teacher's interest and her own facility with language are of considerable relevance, too.

While these and still other factors like insufficient time sometimes place limits on possible accomplishments, what can only be described as *limitless* are the words that can be selected for attention. In fact, with young children the options are so numerous that the problem is not what to teach but, rather, what to select from all that might be taught. This is why it always is surprising to hear teachers ask, "But what would I teach?" when they are being urged to give attention to word meanings. I can recall one in particular who was so ill at ease with the prospect of making plans for extending vocabularies that she said she could do nothing, until she found a book that would help. It just so happened that on the very day she expressed the anxiety she taught a song about a brook and read a story about a duckling.

What she but also others need to be reminded of is that everyday things and everday happenings offer an abundance of possible subject matter. Searching for words—in a teacher's manual, for instance—simply is unnecessary. Even something as common and near as shoes offers possibilities like: *pair, size, sole, heel, tongue, arch, lace, buckle, strap, leather, canvas, rubber, oxford, sandal, moccasin, tight, loose, comfortable, uncomfortable*. Admittedly, not every teacher might want to start with shoes; nonetheless they do exemplify the ease with which subject matter can be found in the most commonplace objects.

Because of the abundance of possibilities, certain criteria should serve as guidelines in making word selections. Usefulness, for instance, suggests that the meanings of esoteric or seasonal words—*cornucopia*, for instance—should not be among the first to get attention. Difficulty is still another factor to consider—nouns, for example, are easier than qualifying terms which, generally, are simpler than relational words.

The children's background bears on selections too, and in many ways overlaps with another criterion; namely, their interests. With young ones, the great interest is themselves. Other concerns are what is already somewhat familiar. This means that what is close at hand and occurring in the present is what captures their attention.

While, in theory, it is easy to list these distinct criteria for selecting words, in practice they are not clearly separate and different. For that reason it is difficult to make statements about the relative importance of each. Were such a judgment requested, I would list the criteria just mentioned in the following order:

1. Children's interests
2. Children's backgrounds
3. Difficulty of word
4. Usefulness of word

INSTRUCTIONAL PROCEDURES

Sometimes the very selection of words automatically results in ideas for teaching them. To cite one illustration, let us say a teacher decides to use the five senses as a way of organizing some of her instruction. Let us say she also chooses to begin with the sense of touch and thus plans to give meaning to words like *soft, hard, smooth,* and *rough*. Having chosen this sense and these particular words (presumably the meanings of all or some are unfamiliar to the children) she automatically knows that verbal explanations or pictures are not appropriate or at least not sufficient. Instead, instructional procedures must include opportunities for the children to feel different textures. This points to the usefulness of pieces of cotton, sandpaper, fur, velvet, wool, and so on. In addition, contrasts like the one existing between a powder puff and a fifty-cent piece would be helpful.

The next decision—how to provide the kinesthetic experiences—could be made from a variety of possibilities. One teacher, for instance, might choose to use a story about a rabbit and a word like *cottontail* as vehicles for initiating attention to *soft*. This could be followed by the distribution of a small piece of cotton to each child and then by individual comments from the children about how it feels. In turn, each might be given a pebble so that it could be felt and contrasted with the cotton. And so the "lessons" would go.

Because the selection of many other words would not be nearly so helpful in defining instruction and suggesting materials, I want to name and discuss some teaching procedures that are generally useful. Exactly how useful they turn out to be, of course, depends upon a variety of factors including both the words being taught and the skill of the teacher.

Before cataloguing individual possibilities, it might be helpful to present first a broader picture of what can be done. To provide this, descriptions of instruction found in classrooms are given on the following pages.

GOALS	PROCEDURES
To teach the meaning of <u>fall</u> and <u>autumn</u>. To introduce sequence of seasons.*	1. Used first day of fall season to introduce <u>fall</u>. Wrote it on board and pronounced it carefully. Mentioned names of other seasons too. Also talked about different meanings of <u>fall</u>. 2. On the following day, introduced <u>autumn</u> as a word which can be used in place of <u>fall</u>. Read a story about the fall season as a time of changing colors in leaves. 3. The next day, took children to the park to collect leaves. Upon return to school, used them to re-mention <u>fall</u> and <u>autumn</u>, and to provide practice in counting and naming colors. (Learned children are confused both about colors and counting. Future instructional plans will thus give attention to both.) 4. A week later, read story about squirrels gathering nuts to prepare for winter. (Also showed children some nuts.) Used story to review <u>fall</u> and <u>autumn</u> and to introduce the fall season as one that is followed by winter. Also mentioned that summer comes before fall.

* The teacher chose the second goal because of an answer from one of her more sophisticated kindergarteners. When she asked her, "When does spring come?" the child responded, "In the fall."

GOALS	PROCEDURES
To call attention to words related to homes: <u>door</u>, <u>window</u>, <u>stairs</u>, <u>porch</u>, <u>roof</u>, <u>chimney</u>, <u>TV antenna</u>, <u>gutter</u>, <u>rain pipe</u>. To call attention to names of materials from which homes are often built: <u>wood</u>, <u>brick</u>, <u>stone</u>.	1. Used magazine pictures to name parts of house. Discussed reasons for chimney, gutter, and rain pipe. 2. Children drew pictures of their own homes or apartment buildings. 3. The next day, children were taken for a walk to look at different parts of houses. 4. The following day, story about a wooden house was read. Explained that other houses are brick or stone. 5. After the story, children were taken for a walk to find wood, brick, and stone buildings.
To give meaning to <u>measure</u>, <u>ruler</u>, and <u>inch</u>.	1. Introduced idea of measurement by asking, "If I wanted to know how tall you were, how could I find out?" This led to idea of measuring. Tape measure used to demonstrate how child might be measured. The word <u>inch</u> was introduced. It was printed on the board; under it, a one-inch line was drawn. Then, using a 12-inch ruler, measured length of comb, pencil, and sheet of paper. 2. Later, reviewed <u>measure</u>, <u>ruler</u>, and <u>inch</u> by demonstrating measurement of toy car. Distributed sheets to children on which were drawn simple dittoed outlines of a comb, pencil, straw, and crayon. Children were to

GOALS	PROCEDURES
	measure each and write the number of inches it measured beside the picture. (Comb was measured with much guidance and help to make sure children understood the task. Major problem: tendency to put ruler to edge of paper rather than to edge of picture being measured.) When measuring was completed, answers were checked. 3. For several weeks afterwards, rulers were kept in a box on a table. Whenever there was free time, children could choose to measure various objects in the room.
To teach the meaning of: orchestra, orchestra leader, baton, violin, trumpet, flute, trombone, clarinet, saxophone.	1. Once children were accustomed to their own band instruments, used collection of pictures of orchestral instruments to introduce them to names of others. During three-week period gave attention to each with the help of pictures and a musical recording that highlighted it. Summarized with bulletin-board display of labeled pictures. 2. High school orchestra leader visited classroom, bringing with him students who played the instruments that had been discussed. Each played a brief selection. The leader also explained and demonstrated use of the baton. 3. Children visited high school when orchestra was practic-

GOALS	PROCEDURES
	ing. One selection was played especially for them. Upon returning to the classroom, children played their own selections with the help of triangles, sticks, bells, and tambourines.
To teach names of baby animals: <u>calf</u>, <u>colt</u>, <u>chick</u>, <u>piglet</u>, <u>duckling</u>.	1. Showed children picture of a woman holding a baby. Talked about it, mentioning that animals have babies too and that each has a special name. Talked about the familiar names <u>puppy</u> and <u>kitten</u>. Read a story which named and told about other baby animals. Discussed each picture and counted the number of animals shown. Repeated their names. 2. Prepared bulletin-board display of animals, each labeled. Talked about pictures to introduce art project, which was to make figures of a mother animal and her baby from clay. Later, each was labeled and put on a table for display. 3. Periodically, read a story about each animal that had been discussed. Later, to provide a review, reread story used to introduce the baby animal terms.
To teach the concept <u>circle</u>.	1. Began by asking, "Who knows what a circle is?" Later, showed circular objects: bracelet, clock face, penny, button, jar cover. Printed

GOALS	PROCEDURES
	circle on board, identified it, then showed children a small paper circle on which the word circle had been printed. Said each would receive a circle like this to take home, to serve as a reminder to look for circular objects or pictures of them. The next day these were discussed. 2. For the day circular objects and pictures were to be discussed, prepared bulletin-board display showing paper circles of different sizes and colors. Each was labeled circle. Used display for practice in counting and naming colors; and, with the help of questions and paper squares, to teach that the concept circle encompasses variation in size and color, but not shape. 3. For the next day's art project children were given paper circles of different sizes and colors, which were to be pasted on black paper to make a design. 4. Pictures of circular objects brought in earlier by the children were assembled in a scrapbook cut in the shape of a circle. Each page was shown to them. Later it was added to the collection of books that children can select at free-choice time.*

* These same procedures, with some variation, were used later to teach the concepts *rectangle, triangle,* and *square.*

Some observations about these illustrative procedures:

1. Like all instruction, teaching word meanings *begins* with the selection of specific goals. In this case goals are appropriate if, among other things, they deal with words whose meanings are unfamiliar to the children.
2. Sometimes other goals can be achieved with the same instructional procedures. For instance, when *fall* and *autumn* were the concern, attention was also given to practice in counting and identifying colors. Too, achieving goals related to meanings provided many opportunities to expose the children to written words and, in this way, to give them the chance to learn to read them.
3. Teaching meanings requires the careful pronunciation of words.
4. Selections of instructional procedures must consider their prerequisites. For instance, if children are not yet able to identify numerals, they are not yet ready to use rulers to measure.
5. Selections of instructional procedures should also reflect use of the familiar to get to the less familiar. This was illustrated when *puppy* and *kitten* were introduced prior to terms like *calf* and *duckling*.
6. Generally, combinations of teaching procedures are used to realize a goal. Combinations in the illustrations included use of explanations, discussions, objects, stories, pictures, walks, and bulletin-board displays.
7. Even with young children, word study can make use of homographs—for instance, *fall*.*
8. Teaching word meanings is not to be confined to a specified period. In the illustrations, for example, time set aside for art was used to reinforce the attention given earlier to names of baby animals.

PLANNED VERSUS UNPLANNED INSTRUCTION

While this textbook is a very open supporter and even promoter of careful planning, no assumption is being made that it *automatically* results in successful instruction with word meanings. Let me describe just one in a long list of classroom observations that helps explain why this is the case.

The visit was in a first grade, and I was there at the request of the teacher. She wanted me to see and react to one of her initial attempts to extend listening-speaking vocabularies. The attempt I witnessed focussed

* Homographs are words that are spelled and pronounced the same but have different meanings.

on *happy* and *joy*. (The selection of an adjective and a noun created problems that became apparent when the children later suggested sentences using these words.) The method chosen to teach the meaning of *joy* (*happy* was already familiar) might be described as a mini-lecture to which the children responded with little interest.

As it happened, I remained in the room for the rest of the afternoon and was glad I did because of what occurred during the art period. It was the fall of the year so leaves were to be traced. In preparation, the teacher distributed a real leaf to each child—enough to create noticeable excitement. The children were encouraged to feel it and, as they did, the teacher talked about its veins and theirs, and also about the stem. But all of this was done quickly in order to get to the tracing.

Because I knew this teacher was genuinely interested in teaching word meanings, I was naturally surprised that she seemed unaware of the potential in the art work and, therefore, failed to take advantage of it. As a result, it was likely that only a few of the children acquired new words for their vocabularies (*vein, stem, trace, outline*) when, in fact, there had been the opportunity to be successful in teaching them to all the children if only because all were so interested in their leaves.

As a result of this and still other observations, several reminders assume importance for instruction in word meanings. The first has to do with the need to have *regular* instruction. Even simple resolutions like "I'm going to teach a word every day" or "I'm going to highlight one new word each week" are helpful. In addition, when instruction *is* scheduled, careful planning should precede it and ought to reflect awareness of the fact that young children are most responsive and interested when instructional procedures involve them in some active way. The lecture method, for instance, cannot be expected to win and keep their attention.

Another reminder is that opportunities to teach word meanings often occur in connection with other goals. Sometimes they turn out to be of greater interest and, as a result, are even more desirable than when vocabulary development is the selected focus. Because of the basic importance of vocabularies, the potential of these opportunities should always be utilized.

Still another reminder is that sometimes things just happen which suddenly present a wonderful chance to teach word meanings. Again, teachers should be flexible enough to take advantage of these situations.

In summary, then, these means are available for extending listening-speaking vocabularies:

1. Through regularly scheduled instruction
2. In connection with the achievement of other goals
3. Through unexpected happenings

Having mentioned three general ways to teach meanings, let me now name and discuss some specific possibilities.

SOME TEACHING POSSIBILITIES

As was mentioned before, the words that can be selected for attention seem almost unlimited when young children are the concern. Ways to teach them, however, are fewer than what would be possible with older children. Nonetheless the possibilities are sufficient to supply every teacher with an abundance of ideas.*

Because of the importance of talking for vocabulary development, let me discuss that first of all, initially under the heading of conversation.

Teaching Words Through Conversations

In visiting classrooms, great contrasts are found when the amount of child talk is noted. In some, keeping silence almost seems to be the teacher's greatest concern while in others the amount of constant noise is more than I personally could tolerate. Somewhere in between, I would like to suggest, lies a teacher attitude about talking that is just right for young children in school. The hope is that by the end of this discussion its details and standards will have been communicated.

To begin, it must be recognized that children in school—whether young or older—cannot be allowed to talk all the time, nor is it possible to let them talk whenever they feel like talking. Still, within the limits imposed by such factors as large classes, there should be many opportunities for young children to express themselves orally. In fact there *must* be, because of the importance of talk for language development.

One such opportunity can be in the form of a conversation period. This should be part of the daily schedule, ideally coming at the beginning of each day since that is when children are most eager to talk both to the teacher and to other children. With a teaching assistant available, arranging for conversation groups is no problem.** The class can be divided into two groups—periodically into a group of girls and a group of boys—so that each includes an adult and not so many children as to make conversation impossible.

When an assistant's help is unavailable, arrangements are always less desirable but still feasible. For instance, a teacher might choose to

* More teaching procedures are described in another of the author's texts, *Teaching Them to Read,* which was prepared to help throughout all the elementary school grades (9).

** See page 77 for an illustration.

converse with one group of children while another is busy with something else. After about fifteen minutes, the groups would exchange activities. With this kind of arrangement—particularly when it is a nursery school or kindergarten class—conversation periods cannot be scheduled as soon as the school year begins because the children first have to learn that there are times when they must busy themselves with something while the teacher is occupied with something else. For this reason the suggestion must be: *Just as soon as possible* include a regularly scheduled time for conversation.

In carrying on a conversation with a group, certain guidelines are helpful. One, certainly, is to keep it as informal as possible. Sitting around a table and avoiding the requirement of raising hands often help with this. Another especially important guideline is that teacher talk should be *minimal*. In fact, the essential role of the teacher is to listen and, when necessary, to clarify or perhaps supplement.

Typically, when conversation groups first get underway the children seem shy and many are reluctant to talk. This is when it might be necessary for the teacher or assistant to ask a question, show a picture, or make some comment in order to get conversation started. As time passes, a different problem is likely to develop: everyone wants to talk at once. Ideally such a problem should be turned into opportunities to help the children understand that only one can talk at a time and that all will get a turn—should all want one. Obviously no child should ever be obligated to talk just as no child should be allowed to talk all the time.

While, in theory, it might also appear desirable to use conversation periods as a time to teach the importance of staying with a topic and of making only relevant comments, in practice such a goal seems less desirable because attempts to achieve it inhibit the very thing that is to be encouraged—talk. Actually, when I first began listening to children's conversations, I simply assumed that problems connected with the goal of relevance were related to their age. But then I began to listen somewhat analytically to adult conversations and quickly learned that they were more alike than different from those of young children. For instance, participants commonly said what was of interest to themselves, whether or not this related to what had just been said by another. In fact, it was as if each one was waiting to have his turn, often merely tolerating what others were saying. While this concentration on self does not make for ideal conversations, it ought to remind teachers that they should not try to get from children what is uncommon among adults. Thus they should expect to hear many topics mentioned even in a fifteen-minute conversation period.

Occasionally, interesting connections between topics will be apparent. For instance I recall one conversation in which a discussion about encyclopedias being big books led one child to tell the others about the big bruise on his leg. Most of the time, however, topics will be many and varied and will bear little relationship—or at least not any that is obvious and certain—to one another. Exemplifying their winding course are some that were covered during one morning's conversation in a kindergarten:

picture of harp shown by teacher
Batman
birthday party
spot on the table
men building a bridge
acquisition of real horse
chocolate milk
television cartoons
cows are not for riding
clean fingernails

When young children are the participants in a conversation, other characteristics also are identifiable. Almost always, for example, a child will introduce his contribution with either "Guess what?" or "You know what?" Common, too, are speech hesitations and repetition of words. And sometimes, especially when the contribution is a long one, the speaker will almost seem to be gasping for breath as he mentions one thing after another. For all of this, the only desirable response is patience, acceptance, and attentiveness.

Other responses from the adult should reflect her awareness that conversation time presents opportunities to teach word meanings. Thus, if on a rainy morning a child mentions that her coat is reversible, it would be appropriate to ask, "Does everyone know what 'reversible' means?" This gives the teacher or assistant a chance to repeat the word so that all hear its correct pronunciation. Answers or the lack of them might also tell her a correct explanation is required.

Although this procedure of explaining one word with others is not the best for young children, it does have to be used some of the time. Still, its shortcomings ought to be recognized:

> One difficulty with this procedure is the danger of relying on superficial verbalizations. Meanings that are clear to the teacher may be quite hazy to the child. Many of the classical boners are due to superficial and inadequate grasp of word meanings. It is not sufficient to tell a child that *frantic* means *wild*, or that *athletic* means *strong;* he may try to pick *frantic flowers* or pour *athletic vinegar* into a salad dressing (12, p. 409).

One way to minimize superficial verbalizations is to let the children have their say when words are being explained. What will be heard will be interesting is all that can be predicted when this is done. I recall being in one classroom, for example, when the teacher was explaining *freedom*. Among other things she said that children are "not free to do bad things, such as take somebody else's coat." Immediately one of the children objected with, "Sometimes it's OK to take a coat. When you have company you say to them, 'May I take your coat?' "

Often, of course, children's responses are helpful for diagnostic purposes because they are so revealing. Misconceptions about age and time, for example, are common; consequently it hardly comes as a surprise to hear a question like, "When you get to be a very old man, say about nineteen years old, does your body stop growing?" Nor is it surprising to get quite different definitions for a word like *manners* from two children whose backgrounds are anything but similar. When asked for its meaning one was heard to explain, "It's something you have to use very nicely when you use it" while the other believed, "It's if you don't push anybody down and give them a bloody nose."

Other responses from children reveal what they have been learning, consequently are highly rewarding for a teacher. Relevant here is a first grade class in which a unit on "Helpful Animals" had been used to extend vocabularies. Among the animals studied was the lamb; especially highlighted was its double contribution of food and clothing. About a month after this unit ended, some of the children were talking about Christmas during a conversation period. Evidently the holiday reminded one child of lambs which reminded another of woolen clothing. This soon led to a discussion about the frequency with which woolen mittens are given as Christmas presents. Such a conversation could have been nothing but satisfying for the teacher who was listening.

In one kindergarten, the children were learning to recite the pledge to the flag. Each day the teacher talked about the meaning of some word likely to be unfamiliar, beginning with *pledge*. About a week after it had been discussed, she happened to say to a conversation group, "I brought a special picture to school today. Promise you won't look while I go get it." Quite agreeably one child commented, "I pledge *I* won't look!" At another time—this also was in a kindergarten—the teacher had read a story about frogs and gave some attention to the word *speckled* because of its frequent appearance in the story. Some of the illustrations helped by displaying its meaning. On a subsequent day, again at conversation time, she happened to show the children a large photograph of some new puppies, one of whom was dotted with spots. This time the rewarding response heard was, "He's sure speckled, isn't he?"

Teaching Words Through Question-Answer Sessions

A more structured procedure for getting children to talk is what might be called "question-answer sessions." If done well, they can foster thought as well as talk. For example, once children are accustomed to the question-answer technique, queries like these might be posed to small groups:

> What would happen if . . .
> everyone forgot to write his name on his paper?
> everyone sang a different song?
> everyone fed the fish on the same day?
> What would you do if . . .
> the clock at home stopped running?
> the bus broke down on the way to school?
> two pages in your reader were stuck together?
> Tell me why . . .
> I wore a coat today.
> we go to school in the morning rather than at night.
> people buy fans.

Used with pictures the questions, "Which go together?" and "Why?" can be productive. In this case sets of pictures might show objects like:

bird, boy, house, nest
fence, clock, spoon, wall
bush, book, flower, ant

Deliberately, pictures would be combined in ways that would promote conflicting answers and, as a result, some group discussion.

Combinations of pictures and questions also are helpful in teaching the meanings of such pairs of words as *alike* and *different*. In this case the question would be, "Are these alike or different?" and it would be posed while the children were considering pairs of pictures that might show:

cup, glass
clock, watch
mittens, gloves
large plain ball, small striped ball

The meanings of other pairs of words could also be taught with pictures. Here I refer to combinations like:

fat, thin
wide, narrow
close, far
tall, short
happy, sad
full, empty
dark, light
heavy, light

A question, this time combined with demonstrations, can offer assistance with relational words. Using something as simple as a button along with the question, "Where is it now?" a teacher or child could demonstrate the meanings of such words as: *in, on, under, over, between.*

Depending on the children, it might also be possible to use questions like, "Could you hear this?" in connection with such statements as:

An ant walking on dirt
A fence running around a yard
A clock telling time

Whatever the focus, the important thing to keep in mind—should you elect to use question-answer sessions—are the reasons for having them. The first, of course, is to encourage children to talk and thus to use the words they already know, while the second is to teach them new ones. The third reason, mentioned earlier, is to get them to respond in more thoughtful, analytical ways. All in all, the possible accomplishments of question-answer sessions do make them something that should at least be tried.

Teaching Words through Experiences

I can think of no more effective way to communicate about the importance of experiences for word meanings than to quote some mind reading appearing in a textbook by Dolch:

> The average adult tries again and again to tell children with words what things are. . . . The child asks, "What is a snake?" The adult says, "An animal that crawls along the ground." The child imagines such an animal and asks, "But his legs will be in the way." The adult says, "Oh, he hasn't any legs." So the child takes off the legs and sees a legless body lying there. "But how does he crawl around without legs?" "He wiggles," says the adult. The child tries to make the legless body wiggle. "How does that get him to go forward?" The adult loses his temper. The peculiar way in which part of the snake pushes the other part cannot be described. It has to be seen. Let us go to the zoo (8, p. 309).

The effectiveness of this quote might have one drawback. It could lead you to conclude that "providing children with experiences" necessarily means taking them on some kind of trip or at least taking them out of the classroom. Actually, this is not so. For instance, should a selected goal be the one of giving meaning to *pair,* teaching procedures might begin with a brief verbal explanation, perhaps with a reference to the children's shoes, stockings, gloves, and so on. Following this, a procedure like the following could provide an experience to solidify its meaning:

> Fill two boxes with identical collections of small objects and trinkets (e.g., toys, pencils, crayons, erasers, pennies, pebbles, buttons, straws). Have children take turns selecting an object from one of the boxes, which is then named. Following this, the child finds the same object in the second box, then places both side by side on a table. The eventual result is a display of pairs of objects.

To reinforce this point about not having to take children out of classrooms to provide experiences for word meanings, let me describe what occurred in one kindergarten. In this case the teacher brought the experience into the classroom by inviting a policeman to talk with the children. In preparation for the visit, she had read a story about a policeman in which the words *crest* (for the badge on his hat) and *uniform* were especially highlighted. She mentioned this to the visitor prior to his coming so, as he talked, he used these words several times. And then an interesting thing happened in connection with his use of *crest.* It reminded one of the children of the name of his toothpaste which, of course, he mentioned. In turn, others named theirs. To the amusement of the adults—the children went right on naming brands—one girl said her toothpaste was "sex appeal."

This particular experience, in addition to reminding us that life with young children is rarely dull, offers other reminders too. One is that vocabularies are enlarged through experiences only to the extent that this is planned for. In fact, the richest ones may be fruitless insofar as meanings are concerned if the teacher does not see to it that certain words are selected and then given explicit attention—sometimes before, during, and following the experience.

This same point has been made very effectively by Frazier (10). He puts it this way:

> Experience may be said to have been fully experienced only when it has been worked through in terms of language. The meaning of experience has to be extracted, clarified, and codified, so to speak. Perhaps, then, one of our chief challenges in working more produc-

> tively . . . with all children is to attend more carefully to the development of vocabulary from whatever experiences they are having (10, p. 176).

Of special value in Frazier's article are the lists of words he has categorized in relation to the five senses. About these lists he says:

> Perhaps their chief use is to remind us as adults of what there is to be learned. Perhaps we need to spell out more clearly our ends in vocabulary development as we have in other aspects of language learning (10, p. 184).

Since one means for vocabulary development is a maximum of experiences, it is important for teachers to keep in mind—and this was exemplified in the policeman's visit—that elaborate ones are in no sense necessary. After all, a walk through the community might be the best of dictionaries for *shingle, dormer, cupola,* and *shutter*—or, *rain pipe, gutter,* and *chimney*. And something as ordinary as the nearby grocery store offers help with words like *yam, parsley,* and *cabbage*. This does not mean, of course, that special trips should never be taken. For instance, a trip to an airport is very effective in changing the meaning of *airplane* from a noisy spot in the sky to a structure of unexpected size, while that trip to the zoo can change *snake* from an unbelievable creature into something starkly simple. Probably the most generally useful reminder in this regard is that the productivity of an experience is not dependent upon its elaborateness or exotic quality, but it is very directly related to what a teacher does to insure that word meanings are clarified as a result of it.

Still another reminder is to be found in the description of the policeman's visit. This has to do with the importance of planning with those who are involved in an experience. With the policeman, this merely required asking him to talk about his uniform and, more specifically, the crest on his hat. With other resource people, preplanning may take different forms. Why *some* type is always necessary is explained well by a teacher:

> The first year I taught I knew it was important to provide children with experiences, and I guess I assumed they would automatically result in new words. I remember very well the first trip I planned. It was to a greenhouse and, other than to get permission from the owner to come, I made no special preparation. The result was a tedious tour that seemed more appropriate for botanists than my first graders. It was sufficiently disappointing that we didn't do much more with trips for the rest of the year.
>
> By my second year of teaching—thanks to some things I had read—I was more aware that the good that comes from excursions is not an accidental happening. What comes, I learned, must be

> planned for ahead of time. For that reason, at the start of the second year I spent some time with the florist before I took my new group to see his greenhouses. Because of the time we spent together, this second tour was most productive. It started by calling the children's attention to the word *greenhouse*. Many of them knew *green*, some recognized *house*, and all seemed to know why it was an appropriate name—once we arrived at our destination. On this particular tour the florist showed the children how all the plants were kept warm in winter and how each one was individually watered by a tiny hose connected to a larger one. At the end of that particular discussion, he turned on the entire sprinkling system. Need I mention how much this delighted the children?
>
> They were also delighted when, at the end of the tour, each received a bag of crocus bulbs. Earlier, the florist had demonstrated some planting and also showed pictures of what their bulbs would look like in the spring.
>
> The end result of all of this, combined with some discussion and showing of pictures when we got back to school, was new or more specific meanings for: greenhouse, florist, sprinkle, hose, bulb, temperature, mum, and crysanthemum. (The connection between the last two words was brought out during the tour. At first the florist used "crysanthemum," then switched to "mum." One of the boys picked this up immediately commenting, "That's not what you called it before." Very nicely the florist explained the connection. Fortunately, when we got back to the room I remembered to write both on the board so that the children could see how *crysanthemum* included *mum*.)

Encouraged by the successful trip to the greenhouse, this teacher followed it up with one to the postoffice. Out of class, preparations began by talking with the worker who was to be the guide; in class, by having the children compose a "thank you" letter to the florist. This was later typed by the teacher, shown, and reread to the children. She then addressed an envelope, stamped it, and off everyone went to the postoffice to mail the letter.

At the postoffice, the group was met by the guide. The tour itself began dropping the letter in the "city" slot; it proceeded by tracing what would be done with the letter in order to get it to its destination.

Preparation for the next trip, this one to a firehouse, began when the children were taught to read *red*. In talking about it, fire trucks naturally were mentioned. This was followed by some stories about fire trucks and firemen. Then it was timely to ask the children, "Would you like to go to the firehouse some day?" The next day they went and not only learned about a variety of equipment but also got to stand on the rear of the trucks. In this case the climax came when the fireman who was acting as guide ran the motors and let all the sirens ring.

As it happened, this trip offered many opportunities not only for vocabulary development (*fireman, firehouse, fire truck, axe, pick, siren, ladder, hose*) but also for practice in other academic areas. For instance, while discussing the trip the teacher wrote *red* and all identified it. She also wrote *fire* and then showed how it was part of *fireman* and *firehouse*. Because the children had already been introduced to the sound recorded by *f*, these same words were used to review that. Later, at art time, each child received a copy of a typed, two-sentence caption:

```
Look and see the boys and girls.
See the fire truck.
```

This was read, again providing review of vocabulary, and then the children drew pictures to go with it.

This particular trip, along with others (newspaper office, lumber yard, pharmacy, jewelry store, hatchery, grocery store), effectively demonstrate how different goals can be worked on simultaneously. This is an important point to remember because, in talking or writing about teaching, only one thing can be mentioned at a time; consequently there always is the possibility of giving the impression that a teacher does this *or* that—for instance, she either works on word meanings *or* reading *or* phonics. What the descriptions of the trips correctly point out is that most of the time a teacher meshes goals and works on more than one. With the trip to the firehouse, for example, the selected goal was vocabulary development. However, in both the preparation and follow-up periods, the children learned to read *red;* were exposed many times to *fire;* were introduced to compound words (*firehouse, fireman*); and reviewed what they had learned earlier about the sound recorded by *f*. Because teaching requires attention to numerous goals it should be a consolation to know that often more than one can be dealt with at the same time.

Teaching Words with Audio-visual Aids

If it happened that clarifying the meaning of a word such as *shell* was an instructional goal, everyone would agree about the desirability of having the children see crustaceans in their natural habitat. Since that is likely to be impossible except in rare cases, the next best experience would be a trip to an aquarium. If that too had to be ruled out, probably the next best thing would be an excursion on a beach to find empty shells; less desirable would be a collection of shells in the classroom. If even that was unavailable still another substitution would have to be used—in this case, pictures.

To take another and briefer illustration, if a teacher wanted children to learn the meaning of *siren,* what more effective procedure could be used than that trip to the firehouse where sirens could be both seen and heard? Were this impossible a recording might be played, but that still would only be a substitution for the real thing. That is, in fact, what all audio-visual aids are: substitutions. Saying this, by the way, is not meant to be critical but is done to put the present discussion into a correct and realistic perspective. And, realistically, audio-visual aids are never as effective as the real thing. Still, if chosen well they can be very helpful with the job of enlarging vocabularies.

Some aids, of course, will be more helpful than others. Photographs, slides, and films, for instance, typically are better than illustrations. And, colored photographs, slides, and films generally are more effective than those in black and white.

With visual aids, the word or concept selected for attention also has something to do with effectiveness. Thus *square* can be pictured more accurately than *cube*. In fact, three-dimensional objects always suffer, leading to the tale of the child who, when seeing a cow for the first time, was absolutely amazed to find it was not flat.

Sometimes other factors also reduce the effectiveness of visual aids. For instance, while it is fairly easy to illustrate or photograph an apple or banana, the same type of picture would communicate little about the unique textures of a peach or pineapple. The same comment would apply to a picture of a dog in contrast to pictures of a raccoon or fish.

On the positive side it must be noted that visual aids can be helpful with more than just concrete things. One effective illustration of how a picture displays the meanings of relational words is shown on page 191. I have also been in classrooms in which scrapbook collections of magazine pictures communicated very effectively the meanings of words like *devotion, serenity,* and *anticipation.* Although being used with middle-grade groups of children, the collections successfully demonstrated that pictures can pinpoint the meanings of abstract terms with an accuracy and even emotional overtone that could never be matched by verbal explanations.

Still one more point must be made about pictures used with young children; this can be done with a classroom illustration. It was a first grade and because there was an assistant the children had been divided into boy-girl groups for conversation. On the morning of the visit the teacher was with the girls and had chosen to get things started by displaying a picture of a small child holding a doll. The group showed interest, but almost immediately one girl called attention to the pin she was wearing on her own dress. From that point on everyone talked about pins, apparently forgetting the picture of the girl with her doll. This was no problem for the teacher, however. She simply used the unexpected interest to teach more about *pin*. She displayed the girl's pin. She also showed a straight

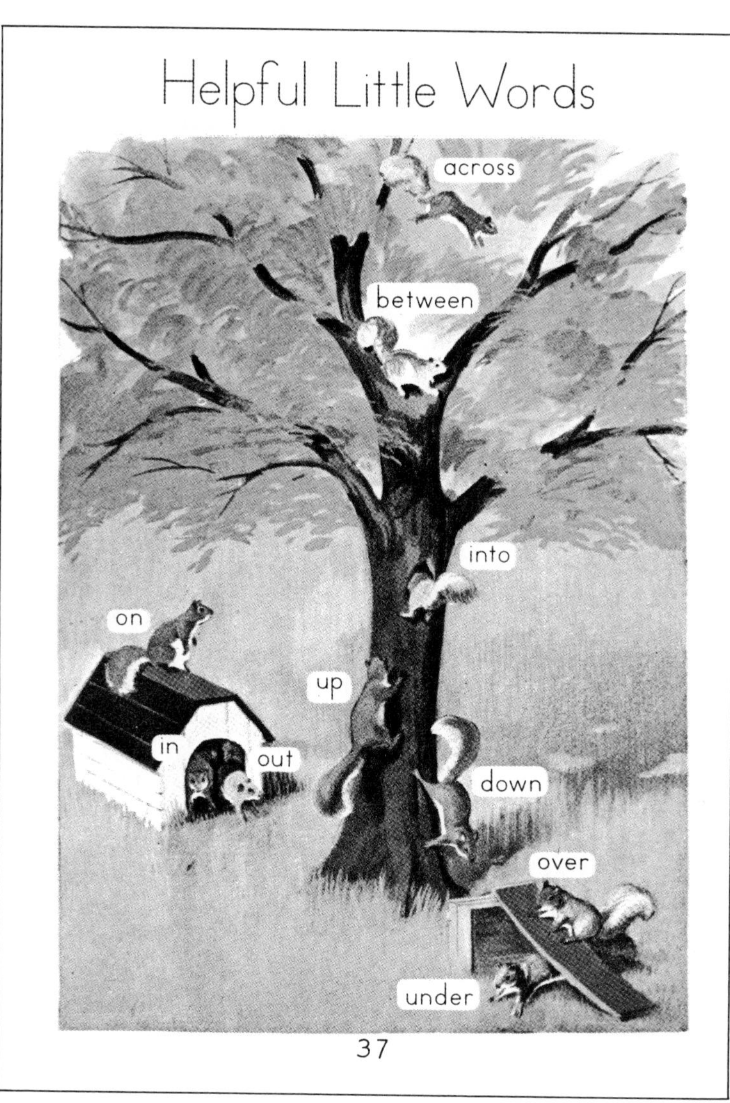

For page 37 from *My Picture Dictionary*, by Hale C. Reid and Helen W. Crane, of the GINN ELEMENTARY ENGLISH SERIES, © Copyright, 1965, 1963, by Ginn and Company.

pin and safety pin and the children discussed their uses. Knowing that they could read *in*, this teacher also printed that on the board and demonstrated how she could change it to say *pin* by adding an initial *p*. Being demonstrated again, of course, was the productivity of instruction that is grounded both in flexibility and an awareness of educationally significant goals.

Teaching Words by Reading to Children

It would seem that nobody ever gets too old to enjoy a story. Classroom visits to nursery school, kindergarten, and primary classes further suggest the younger the child, the greater that enjoyment is. In fact it never ceases to be surprising to see a group of children become one—no matter what their differences in ability and behavior—as they listen with ears *and* eyes to a story. Occasionally the interest will be less, but that only happens when the wrong book was chosen.*

Reading to young children serves a variety of purposes. It offers enjoyment first of all, thus promoting positive feelings about school. It can also encourage nonreaders to want to become readers. In addition, it provides models of book language which is an especially important contribution for disadvantaged children. In choosing books and planning time for reading—it should be a daily occurrence—it is only the first goal that must be kept in mind because accomplishing that automatically takes care of the other two.

Even with such important goals as these three, additional ones might be considered which could be accomplished at the same time. The one I have in mind, of course, is vocabulary development.

When vocabulary development *is* a goal, a variety of options is available for book selections. The most common procedure would be to select one without consideration of this extra goal and thus with total concentration on the factor of enjoyment. This was what was done when a teacher who was mentioned earlier chose to read a book about frogs. As it happened, *speckled* was used frequently and it was also explained well with pictures. Therefore, calling the children's attention to its meaning was natural and in no way interfered with enjoyment.

Sometimes, but less frequently, vocabulary development might play a more active role in book selections. This results in reading one which still is of interest to the children but which deals more directly and fully with certain concepts. An example would be *Let's Find Out What's Big and What's Small* (see pages 193 and 194). In this book, clarification of

* If inexperience leaves you feeling insecure about choosing books, you might want to read an *Elementary English* article in which the author lists and briefly describes books found especially suitable for young children (17). Another article in another issue of the same journal lists books and also notes the concepts each teaches (1).

Next to an elephant, a rabbit looks small.

From *Let's Find Out What's Big and What's Small* by Martha and Charles Shapp, copyright 1959 Franklin Watts, Inc., p. 11.

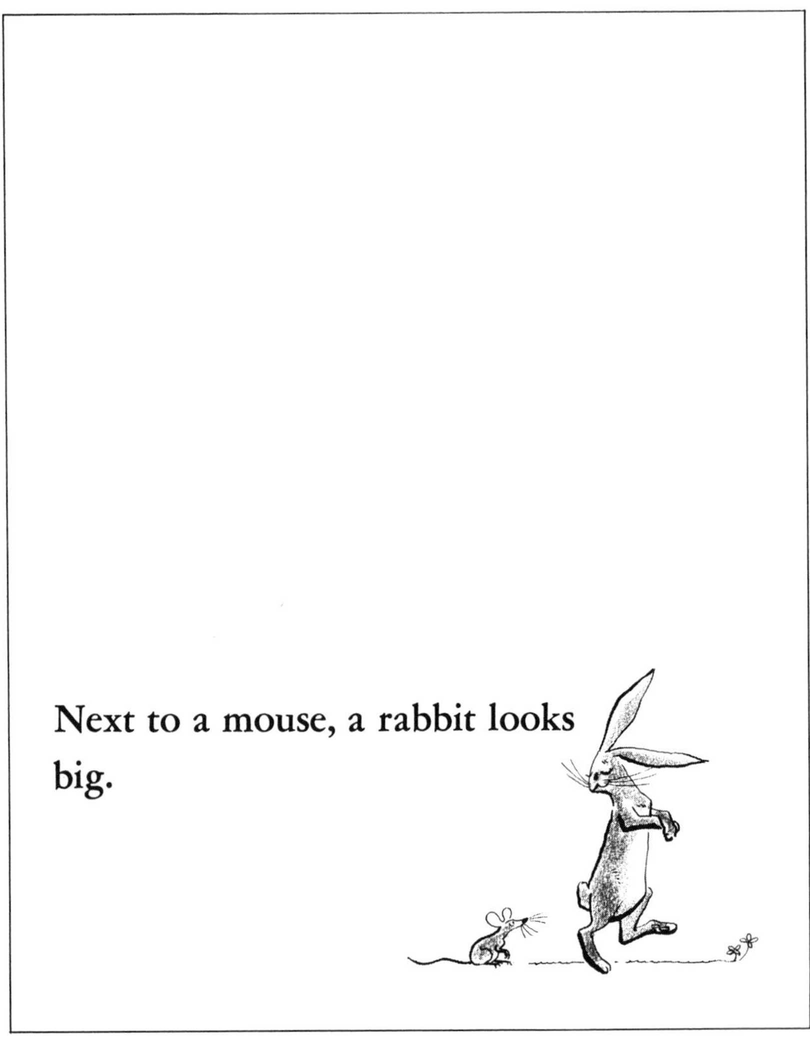
Next to a mouse, a rabbit looks big.

From *Let's Find Out What's Big and What's Small* by Martha and Charles Shapp, copyright 1959 Franklin Watts, Inc., p. 12.

Used by permission of Golden Book Educational Services, Inc. Art by John P. Miller from *Adventures with Color* by Seymour Reit, p. 8. Copyright 1970, 1963 by Western Publishing Company, Inc.

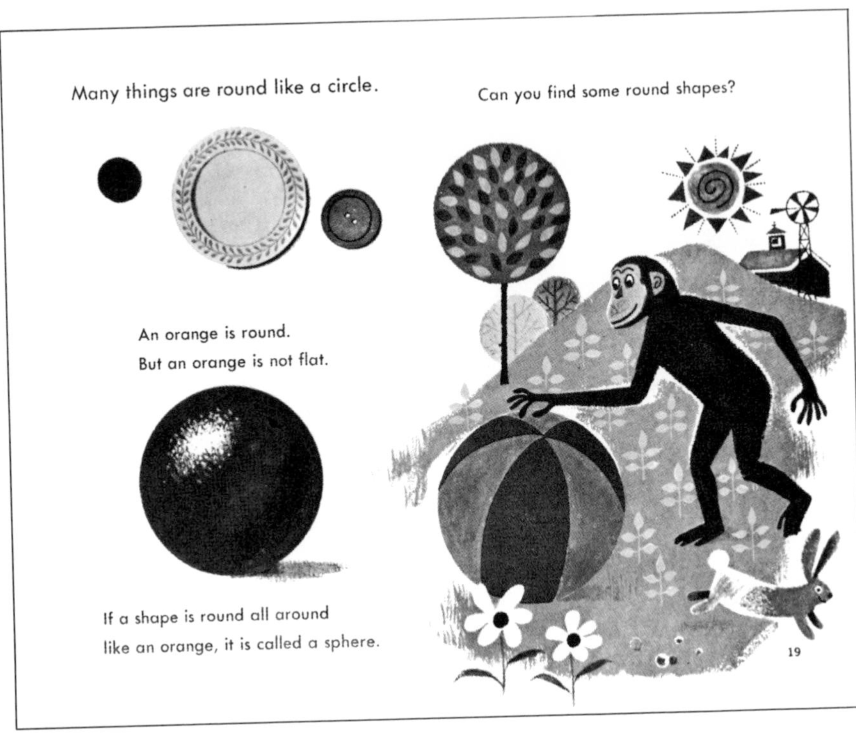
Many things are round like a circle.
Can you find some round shapes?
An orange is round.
But an orange is not flat.
If a shape is round all around
like an orange, it is called a sphere.
19

words is built into the content and illustrations; it is not "stuck on" as sometimes happens, nor is it preached. Having read it to many children, I also know they enjoy it.

Other selections might be made from series of books now available which were written explicitly to help with concept development. Illustrative of these is one published by the Golden Press called, *First Adventures in Learning Program* (see pages 195 and 196). Probably the best way to describe this series, and thus suggest themes commonly found in others, is to list a few of its individual titles:

Listening for Sounds
Adventures with Color
Understanding Numbers
Time and Measuring
Discovering Shapes
Learning about Sizes
Adventure with Words

No matter how good the concept books might be—and quality varies greatly—young children usually are not as interested and involved as when they are being treated to a story. This suggests two things. First, when a book is primarily concerned with concepts rather than characters and plot, it generally is a good practice to read only part of it at one sitting unless it happens to be very short. Or, to make this same point differently, do not expect the same attention span that is typical when a story is being read. And certainly never expect to get the response sometimes heard when an especially good tale has just ended—"Read it again, please."

The second suggestion has to do with the wisdom of reading concept books to small groups rather than an entire class. This is wise because the small numbers allow for discussion and also make it easier for children to look carefully at illustrations, which usually are an integral part of the concept books.

Teaching Words in Subject Matter Areas

In other chapters as well as this one, the point has been made that just about every activity and subject matter area allow for growth in one or more of the language arts. That this holds true for vocabulary development seems too self-evident to warrant any discussion. What does merit discussion, though, are illustrations.

Easy to find are illustrations connected with a subject like music, for just about every song offers opportunities to teach meanings. In addition, there also is the chance to give attention to words like *introduction, solo, duet, chorus, lullaby,* and so on.

Art projects also can be productive for vocabulary development. Names of colors, including those for the more subtle shades, offer possibilities as do art materials and techniques.* Basic terms such as *top* and *bottom,* and basic feelings like *happy* and *sad,* can also take on meaning with the help of art. However, in considering art for vocabulary development—and music, too—it is important to remember that nothing should ever be done with meanings that would take away from the enjoyment each offers young children. That always is of greater importance and should receive initial attention.

Other curriculum areas provide still more opportunities to extend vocabularies. In fact it would be accurate to say that subjects like social studies and science are directly related to concept development, as is clearly shown in textbooks. To exemplify this, passages from first grade teachers' manuals, one for social studies and the other for science, are reproduced on pages 199 and 200. As these samples illustrate, instruction in content fields is basically concerned with enlarging a child's understanding of himself and his world, and thus with enlarging his listening-speaking vocabulary.

Not all schools have subject matter textbooks for younger children, and not all teachers elect to use them even when they are available. Whether or not this is the case, the manuals that come with them can be helpful in pointing out ways to teach word meanings. And, even when what they recommend is not what you would want to use, the descriptions often have a way of suggesting other possibilities that seem better for the particular children with whom you work. For that reason it is a helpful practice to glance through manuals periodically, even though you might not be using them on a daily basis.

Teaching Words in Relation to Classifications

Earlier, when some teaching observed in classrooms was described, you were reminded that even with young children word classifications can provide a focus for vocabulary development efforts. In the example cited, *fall* was the word and the classification was "homograph." Other classifications also are suitable. They, plus "homograph," are listed on page 201 to suggest one of the ways in which you might want to organize your own thinking about words.

* Just recently I was in a classroom in which the teacher had collected literally hundreds of small plastic squares used by decorators to help customers select paint colors. Various sorting jobs were most effective in demonstrating that even a "simple" color like blue can get very complicated.

Using Page 49

TO THE STORE

Points to Be Stressed

Shopping in a department store
Being courteous to others

Terms to Know and Use

directory escalator advertise

Creating Interest

Discuss with the children the meaning of *department store.* Explain that each department in a store specializes in a particular product. "What departments have you visited in a large store? How does this help the customer?"

The children may wish to talk about the toy department, children's department, furniture department, etc. Help the children realize that the departments make it easier for the customer to find the special item he wishes to buy. If the children mention dishes and glassware, point out that children must not touch or handle these breakable items.

Guiding the Learning Activities

"Look at the picture at the top of the page and read the three sentences. What is Lee doing? Is he being polite? What did Mother say to Lee? What can you see in the store window? Why do stores have windows?"

Explain to the class that the stores display in the windows some of the items one may buy inside. It is one way to advertise what the stores have to sell. "In what other ways do stores advertise?" Help the children to think of newspapers and magazines as means of advertising.

"Look at the picture at the bottom of the page. Read the sentences. Who can answer the question? What is this type of a stairway called?" Tell the class that the moving stairway is called an *escalator*. "How is it different from an elevator? What safety rules are the children following?

"What do you think Mother will buy for the children? How will Mother know where to find that department?" Explain to the class that at the store entrance there is a *directory*. The children may be familiar with a telephone directory. Tell the class that a directory is a listing of names and places. It will tell customers how to find the department they wish to visit.

Related Enrichment Activities

Reading a Directory. Help the children to understand and use a *Directory*. Place on the chalkboard a simple directory using known words from the children's basic sight vocabulary. It may resemble the following:

	FLOOR
CHAIRS	5
DRESSES	2
HATS	2
LOST AND FOUND	1
PAINT	4
TOYS	5

"On what floor of the department store will you find dresses? toys?" Review the meaning of "lost and found."

Collecting Ads. Suggest that the class cut ads from newspapers and magazines. The collection may be classified into departments. The children may wish to have labels printed to identify the different departments.

The class may begin by collecting ads for children's clothing. Allow the collection to follow the particular interests of the group. It may be the desire of the class to collect ads for automobiles, farm equipment, foods, etc.

Designing an Advertisement. Allow each child to pretend that he is the proprietor of a store. Have him select the type of store he would like to own. Suggest that each child draw an ad which they will pretend to have printed in a newspaper. If the class wishes to include prices with their ads, help the children to write the dollars and cents correctly.

Some children may prefer to draw pictures of a window display for their imaginary store. When the drawings have been completed, allow each child to tell the class about his picture.

Poetry Book. "E is for Escalator," in *All Around the Town.*
Filmstrip. *Going Shopping.*

UNIT FIVE: CLOUDY OR SUNNY

Section 1: Clouds

CONCEPT
Evaporation and condensation are changes in the state of matter.

LESSON 1, page 40

SUBCONCEPT: Clouds and precipitation result from the cycle of evaporation and condensation.

Aim of the Lesson

To help children to understand that a cloud can be formed from water that has evaporated and gone into the air.

Introducing the Lesson

REQUIRED: a bulletin board display of pictures of clouds.

Invite children to look at, discuss, and ask questions about the cloud pictures. Take them outside (or let them stand at the windows) to look at the sky for evidence of clouds. Encourage them to tell what they know about clouds — differences in shape, color, and how they move across the sky. Lead the discussion to the question:

What are clouds made of?

Let us see if we can find an answer by considering water boiling in a teakettle.

Developing the Concept

(by emphasis on the subconcept)

1. Have children look at the picture on page 40 and describe what is happening. Refer to the water as a liquid, and ask what happens to a liquid when it is heated. Help the children to recall from Unit Four that heat can change a liquid to a gas: *heat changes water to water vapor*. When water in the kettle is boiling, it is changing from liquid to water vapor quite rapidly.

Children will wonder what it is they see coming out of the teakettle. Some, undoubtedly will say "steam." This is a popular notion, but more precisely, steam is water vapor and, therefore, is invisible.

2. At this point, call attention to the gap between the spout of the teakettle and the little ***cloud.*** Water vapor is coming out of the spout; like all water vapor, it is invisible. Have children point to the place where the water vapor is coming out of the teakettle.

3. Point out the little cloud just beyond the gap and explain as follows, how it is formed.

a. Heat changes the water in the teakettle from liquid to gas. The gas is water vapor.

b. The water vapor comes out of the teakettle spout and into the air. We cannot see it.

c. The water vapor is hot. The air around it is *not* hot. Water vapor loses heat when it touches the cool air. **What happens to water vapor when it is cooled?**

d. Since water vapor changes to water when it loses heat, the cloud must be made up of tiny droplets of water. We can see the cloud formed by the tiny droplets.

Check for understanding by asking children to respond to the following questions:

Why can we see the cloud in front of the teakettle when we cannot see water vapor?

Would there be any clouds in the sky if there were no water?

What happens to the water vapor from the teakettle to make it change to water?

Encourage answers that reveal an understanding that the cloud is formed when water vapor in the air changes to tiny droplets of water.

Extending the Concept

Through Actual Observation. Use a teakettle, water, and an electric grill to do the investigation on page 40.

CAUTION: Teach children the danger of touching the grill, the teakettle, the invisible gas coming out of the spout, and the hot cloud. Explain that a very painful and serious burn can result from touching hot things.

Do **not** let children assist in doing this demonstration.

Through Key Concept Words. Add *cloud* to the Science Vocabulary Chart.

Through Activity. Have children bring in pictures of clouds. Let them use their cutout pictures to make a chart or scrapbook of different kinds of clouds.

What makes the little cloud?

40

CONCEPTS IN SCIENCE: 1

From First Grade Manual for *Concepts in Science,* Teacher's Edition, by Paul F. Brandwein, Elizabeth K. Cooper, Paul E. Blackwood, Elizabeth B. Hone, p. 40. Copyright 1966 by Harcourt, Brace & World, Inc.

CLASSIFICATION	EXAMPLES
synonym	little, small bloom, blossom
antonym	dry, wet tiny, huge
homophone *	bear, bare flower, flour
homograph	fair cobbler

Generally the classification terms themselves—"synonym" for instance—need not be used with young children. I say "generally" because I never cease to be amazed at the way many young ones take to "big words," using them with both accuracy and pride. While showcase vocabularies is not the aim of instruction with word meanings, what children enjoy should never be passed over lightly because what *is* enjoyed is learned with ease.

That many words in our language are comprised of roots plus affixes (prefixes and suffixes) provides still another way for organizing thoughts about vocabulary instruction. Here I refer to examples like:

ROOT **	PREFIX	SUFFIX	EXAMPLE
obey	dis		disobey
teach		er	teacher
read	un	able	unreadable

To be aware of prefix-suffix possibilities is to be ready to take advantage of still more opportunities for teaching meanings. Because of this, page 202 shows a list of some of the easier and more common affixes. It is included as reference material; whatever in it turns out to be useful will depend upon the particular children with whom you work.

INSTRUCTIONAL MATERIALS

In the just completed discussion of instructional procedures for extending vocabularies, many references were made to materials. That is to be expected because of the close connection between the two. In those references, you will recall, attention frequently went to homemade materials,

* These are also referred to as "homonyms."
** The root is sometimes called the "stem" or "base."

Some Common Prefixes and Suffixes *

Prefix	*Meaning*	*Example*
un	not	unhappy
ir		irregular
il		illegal
im		impatient
in		inactive
a		atypical
non		nonhuman
dis	not	disobey
	remove	disarm
re	again	remake
	back	recall
mis	wrongly	miscount
pre	before	preschool
fore	before	forewarn
	in front	foreword
co	with	coauthor
counter	against	counteract
anti		antiwar
under	below	underage
semi	half	semicircle
	partly	semitropical
	coming twice	semiannual

Suffix	*Meaning*	*Example*
er	one who; doer of action	teacher
or		actor
less	without	spotless
able	capable of being	readable
ful	full; characterized by	careful
y		oily
ous		joyous
ful	amount that fills	cupful
ic (ical)	connected with	poetic, historical
ist		humorist
ness	state of	softness
hood		childhood
ship		friendship
ance		tolerance
ence		dependence
tion (ation)		action, starvation
ment		enjoyment
ward	in the direction of	homeward

* This is an illustrative rather than complete listing. Instructional materials will identify other affixes. Also available to provide help are dictionaries in which you would learn, for example, that the prefix *un* means "not" (*unhappy*) and also "to do the opposite" (*untie*).

often the best to use because they can be constructed to match the interests and learning needs of particular children. Because of their special value, let me start this discussion of materials with some comments about the homemade kind.

One type meriting immediate and special consideration is the bulletin-board display. Such consideration seems warranted because these displays (a) can be very helpful with vocabulary work; but (b) too often are used as a "Do Not Touch" decoration rather than a type of instructional material. It is within the latter context that they are being considered now, and in that context they function especially well in introducing and/or summarizing instruction.

Probably the best way to help you think about bulletin-board displays is to describe a few seen in classrooms:

> One teacher had been giving attention to homonyms (homophones). They were introduced with a bulletin board showing two paper trees appropriately labeled, "A Pair of Pear Trees." At the start, a picture of a pear was pasted to one while the other held a picture of two shoes. Nothing more was done with the board while homonyms were being taught, although the children did know that eventually they would fill up both trees with pictures.
>
> At the conclusion of the instruction the bulletin board was again used, this time to summarize. Now the trees also showed pictures depicting: *one, won; sea, see; break, brake; blue, blew; Mary, merry.**
>
> * * * * *
>
> In another classroom a teacher used a similar procedure to introduce and summarize other work with homonyms. In this case it was October so the bulletin board theme was, "Which Is Witch?" The board itself was divided into two sections. At the conclusion of the instruction one part displayed pictures for: *ate, aunt, red, meet, wee.* The other had pictures depicting: *eight, ant, read, meat, we.***

* In this dialect area, "merry" and "Mary" were pronounced the same and so would be homonyms. In some areas, however, their pronunciations would differ.

** It happened that both teachers chose to label the pictures displayed on their boards. This is one time, however, when I would *not* endorse labeling because for children who are either getting ready to read or are just beginning, the idea "sound alike but are spelled differently" might be an unnecessary source of confusion. It would be important that they realize the sounds of homonyms are the same even though their meanings are different; but they need not be told *yet* that their spelling is different. This additional characteristic could be mentioned later, when reading ability is somewhat established and more homonyms are being taught.

* * * * *

In a kindergarten where there was an assistant, the class divided into two groups to make cookies. Although each worked separately, preparations were the same: a simply-composed recipe was listed on a large sheet of chart paper. With each group the teacher (or assistant) read the ingredients, giving particular attention to *teaspoon* and *tablespoon.* To help clarify their meanings, both were shown and the children talked about their uses.

Later, while the children were enjoying the fruit of their labor, the teacher put one of the charts on a small bulletin board to which she also attached a teaspoon and tablespoon. Eventually a fork and knife were displayed too, after their uses had been discussed.

* * * * *

In a kindergarten a teacher had been working with the children on the names of animals and their homes. To summarize, she prepared a bulletin board showing pictures of: cage, nest, bowl, stream, barn, jungle, cave, and pen. At the bottom of each picture a pocket had been made by stapling to it three sides of a rectangular piece of construction paper. The teacher also had a collection of animal pictures.

The display was used by having individual children name an animal shown by the teacher. After it was identified, the child named his home and then placed the animal's picture in the correct pocket. (Later, playing with the display could be selected by any two children at free-choice time.)

* * * * *

In another classroom the teacher prepared bulletin boards for each month. They were used every morning to teach the children to read the names of the months, to practice naming numerals and colors, and to teach word meanings.

For April, to cite one example, the board showed a large tree in the background and flowers and bushes in the foreground. For use with this, the teacher had cut out thirty tiny birds.

Before the display was assembled, spring had been discussed in order to introduce *migrate,* a term used frequently during

April. As each of its days passed, one bird was added to the board, attached either to the tree or a bush. Daily the birds were counted and *migrate* was mentioned. (Unexpectedly the children became very interested in birds; consequently April also turned out to be a month for bird watching and naming.)

* * * * *

Calling attention to such homemade materials as the bulletin-board display is not intended to be an indirect criticism of commercial materials, and it certainly is not meant to suggest that only the homemade kind should be used. Actually, such a suggestion would never be made because, first, teachers do not have time to make everything they will need and, second, many of the commercially available materials are excellent. In fact, problems with the commercial type often relate more to the way they are used than to built-in flaws. For this reason, any discussion of commercial materials ought to begin with what might be called a philosophy about their use.

The philosophy underlying all that is said about them in this textbook begins with the recognition that it is the teacher who must make the important instructional decisions. Essentially these have to do with *what* will be taught to *whom, how* it will be taught, and *when.*

Part of the philosophy is that many of the commercially available materials can help with these important decisions. For instance, it is recognized that some materials describe important content which, as a matter of fact, might never have been considered by teachers had they not seen the materials. Many also offer assistance with the how of instruction by proposing ways in which content might be taught. In addition, some help with its timing by outlining a possible sequence for reaching certain goals. In spite of this potential, however, the important limitation even of the very best of material is that it cannot deal with *appropriateness* for that always depends upon the particular children being taught. Because it is the teacher who knows them, it also is the teacher who must make selections as well as the necessary adjustments.

Probably the best way to summarize the philosophy being recommended is to say that commercial materials can be of valuable assistance, sometimes in their existing form but more often as they are modified and supplemented. They become a liability, on the other hand, whenever teachers assume the role of "assistant to materials," carrying out their suggestions to the letter and without regard for the characteristics of the children in their classrooms. Having stated this philosophy, let me now mention a few commercial materials that could help with vocabulary development.

LANGUAGE DEVELOPMENT ACTIVITY

Specific Objective

Syntactical understanding: Discovering various meanings for the words park, bill, and can

Write on the chalkboard: Lad is at the park.

Ask someone to read the sentence aloud. Then have the word park underlined.

NOTE: This activity provides an opportunity to review the underlining of words from left to right, just below the base line on which the letters are written.

Have the children discuss the meaning of the word park in the above sentence. Then ask them if they can think of different ways this word could be used. If necessary, give assistance in developing oral sentences:

Where did Dad park the car?

He can't park here.

Ask the children to state specifically what is meant by the word park in the above context.

Continue, by discussing the multiple meanings of the words bill and can through the use of written and oral sentences. As you do this, ask the children to underline Bill and can in the written sentences.

Written sentence: Bill is at the park.

Oral sentences: The white duck has an orange bill.
Our telephone bill came today.
I wish I had a dollar bill.

Written sentence: Lad can get the ducks.

Oral sentences: Sometimes coffee comes in a tin can.
Mother is going to can some peaches.

SKILLS HANDBOOK

ADJUSTING TO INDIVIDUAL NEEDS

DECODING ACTIVITY 1

Specific Objective

Phonemic analysis: Discriminating between /k/ and /g/ in final position

Special Materials

A bulletin board divided into two sections, with a picture of a dog in one section and a picture of a duck in the other section. Example:

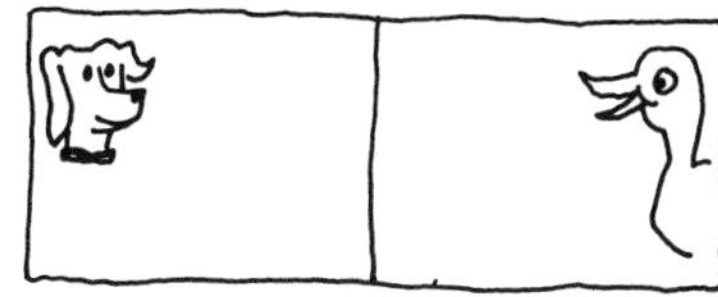

Drawing paper, one sheet per pupil

As the children examine the bulletin board, ask them to pretend that Dog lives on half of it and that Duck lives on the other half. Explain that Dog will allow in his territory only things that have names ending with the same sound as dog. Duck will allow in his territory only things that have names ending with the same sound as duck.

Tell the children they can make some pictures of objects or animals that have names ending with the same sound as dog, or duck. Provide ideas for the pictures by making a zig zag sketch ( ) on the chalkboard. Identify. Then ask the following questions:

Could you make a picture of a zig zag?

Where could you put a picture of a zig zag, with the dog or the duck? dog

Recall the story about the pink spook and ask:

Who would like to make a picture of a pink spook?

After you draw a pink spook, should you put your picture with the dog, or the duck? duck

Continue in the same way, suggesting other ideas, as:

black sock	big frog
big bug	rag rug
thick stick	cook book
zig zag	dark park

63

For page 183 of the Teachers' Edition of *My Sound and Word Book*, by Theodore Clymer and Thomas C. Barrett, and page 63 of the Teachers' Edition of the Skills Handbook for *A Duck Is a Duck* and *Helicopters and Gingerbread*, by Theodore Clymer and Billie Parr; both of the READING 360 Program and © Copyright, 1969, by Ginn and Company.

Unit 1 · **LESSON 14,** Urban Scene 7 (right)

Purposes

To give the child practice in hearing and using standard language patterns by talking about what can be seen from the top of a tall building in the city.

Necessary Materials

Big Book for *Getting a Head Start*, page 7 (right)

Talking About Scene 7 (right)

Vocabulary:	airport	river	skyscraper
	bridge	runway	highway (freeway)

This is a picture of a city. Where would you have to be to see the city this way? . . . *(On top of a tall building or in an airplane.)* . . . Come and point to the airport. . . . How do you know it is an airport? . . . (*runways, airplanes*) How could you get from the city to the airport? . . . What are the wide roads called? . . . (*highways or freeways*) Who will point to a building that probably has an elevator in it? . . . Why do you think there is an elevator in that building? . . . A very tall building has a special name. It is called a skyscraper.

Who can find the bridge? . . . **Have several children come and trace it with a finger.** Yes, the bridge and the highway go over some water. Do you know what this water is called? . . . **If nobody knows, tell the children that this is a river.** How many boats do you see on the river? . . . Come and point to them. . . . Where do you think these boats are going? . . . **Develop with the children the idea that boats bring things to the city. You may wish to expand the idea, depending on the abilities of your group, that many of the things you eat, and wear, and use are brought into the city by large trucks, or trains, or by boat.**

Continue to discuss with the children what can be seen from the top of a tall building in the city. Encourage the children to ask questions. This will give more oral practice in the sentence patterns which is the aim of this material.

Using Related Activities

Your class will enjoy looking at and talking about *The Boats on the River* by Marjorie Flack, published by Viking.

Study prints, *How People Travel in the City*, published by SVE include a picture of a jet airliner and a ferryboat that will interest the children.

74

From Teachers' Guide for *Getting a Head Start*, p. 74. Copyright 1969 by Houghton Mifflin Company.

Looking Down on the City

From Teachers' Guide for *Getting a Head Start*, p. 74. Copyright 1969 by Houghton Mifflin Company.

Unit 1 · LESSON 5, Rural Scene 15 (left)

Purposes

To give the child practice in hearing and using standard English by talking about pets; to help him increase his vocabulary by learning names of animals he may not know; to help him become aware that some animals make good pets and some do not.

Necessary Materials

Big Book for *Getting a Head Start*, page 15 (left)
Picture cards from the *Picture and Key Cards for Getting Ready to Read*: duck, goose, pigeon, turtle, dog, and kitten

Talking About Scene 15 (left)

Vocabulary:	goose	dog
	geese	kitten
	duck	animal
	ducklings	bird
	pigeons	pet
	fish	turtle

Language Pattern:	**Example:**
What kind of (vocabulary) is this?	What kind of bird is this?
It's a (vocabulary).	It's a goose.

Before opening the Big Book, discuss the pictures listed under "Necessary Materials."

Hold up the pictures of the duck, the goose, and the pigeon. Say: These are all birds. **Help children to name each picture by saying:** What are the names of these birds? . . . (*It's a duck, goose, pigeon.*) **If children cannot tell these birds apart, point out some differences among them: the goose has the longest neck, the pigeon has the roundest breast, and this duck is the most colorful. Talk about where these birds live. Use such phrases as "near the water," "on the farm," "in the city," "in the park."**

Introduce the pictures of the fish, turtle, dog, and kitten. Say: Here are some other animals. **Talk about where each animal lives. Use such phrases as "in the water," "near the water," "in the house."**

Place all the pictures along a ledge. Say: Some of these birds and animals make good pets. Do you have any of these animals for a pet? **Encourage each child who has one to talk about his pet. With children who have no pet say:** Which animal would you like for a pet? . . . Why? . . . Do you know anyone who has one of these birds or animals for a pet? . . . Where

92

does he keep his pet? . . .What does he feed his pet? . . .

Name some other animals that make good pets.

Open the Big Book to page 15 and use the scene on the left. Say: What is this boy doing? . . . What does he want to catch? . . . What will he do with a fish if he catches one? . . .

What do you think he is using to catch a fish? . . . Where do you think he got his fishing pole? . . . How do you know he didn't buy it in a store? . . . Why can't you see the fishhook the boy is using? . . . (**Urban children may need help with the concept of fishing pole and fishhook.**) Have you ever gone fishing? . . . Tell us about it. . . .

Point to the geese and say: What kind of birds are these? . . . Where do they live? . . . Do you think the geese belong to anyone? . . . (*Yes, they probably belong to the boy.*) **Point to the ducks and say:** What kind of birds are these? . . . What are they doing? . . . Where do you think they live? . . . Do the ducks belong to anyone? . . . (*probably not*) They could be wild ducks. If they are wild ducks, they won't belong to anyone. How can you tell that the big duck is a mother? . . . (*She has some babies swimming beside her.*) Baby ducks are called ducklings. Come and point to the ducklings.

Select pupils to play the roles of the boy and his mother. Develop a dialogue by getting the children to verbalize what "mother" might say when the boy tells her he is going fishing. (*Don't get wet. Be careful not to fall in. Don't get your clothes dirty, etc.*) **Another dialogue can be developed by verbalizing what the boy's family would say if he caught a fish and brought it home to show everyone.**

Using Related Activities

For pupils who lack experience with birds and animals, take time to look at picture books of farm animals, other common animals, and birds. Identify some of the animals and birds, but try to get the pupils to name as many as they can among those listed.

For pupils who have difficulty understanding the language pattern "What kind of (vocabulary) is this?" give extra practice in matching classifications — such as vegetables, tools, foods, animals, birds, and pets — with objects with which the pupils *are already familiar.* Use the pictures and objects you and your pupils have collected. For example, hold up a picture of some tomatoes and say: What kind of vegetables are these? . . . (*They are tomatoes.*)

A field trip to a park, or a zoo, would be a good idea at this point. The more pupils see, hear, and experience at first hand, the easier it becomes for them to talk freely.

The kind most obviously related is the picture dictionary. Page 191 showed a sample page from one of many now available for use with young children. Others (pages 193–196) showed pages from two additional types, the concept books and the subject matter texts.

Still more help with word meanings can be found in materials designed to teach reading. Illustrations of some of the help they offer can be found on pages 206–211. Pages 206–207 shows a passage from a manual offering suggestions for teaching the homographs *park, bill* and *can.* The section from another manual shown on pages 208–209 pertains to word meanings but also demonstrates how themes in the newer materials are dealing more with urban areas and much less with life on a farm or in suburbia. Pages 210–211, showing another section from the same manual, displays still another characteristic of current materials: much specific attention to oral language patterns. This reflects the current interest in disadvantaged children and their need for great amounts of help with language.

A SUMMARY

Having dealt in this chapter with many different aspects of vocabulary development, let me now summarize some of the more important points.

Any such summary ought to begin by highlighting what was an assumption of the entire chapter: Language should be an asset to a child, not a liability. Stated explicitly was that facility with language is important for both personal and academic reasons; as a result, every aspect should receive attention just as soon as he starts school.

The aspect selected for attention in this chapter was the extension of listening-speaking vocabularies for they are of *basic* importance to achievement in reading. In fact, problems with reading comprehension commonly are a reflection of vocabularies that are too limited. In discussing their development, sources for finding words were named; these ranged from everyday things and happenings to word classifications to sources like music, art, social studies, and science. Hopefully one result of this discussion is the awareness that a teacher's problem is not one of finding words to teach but, rather, of trying to decide what to select from all that might be taught. To help with selections, four criteria were discussed. They included the interest and background of the children as well as the usefulness and difficulty of the words themselves.

Procedures for teaching word meanings were described next. These included oral language activities centering on conversations and question-answer sessions. The discussion of instructional procedures also outlined contributions made by experiences, audio-visual aids, and books that would be read to the children. In all of this the point was made repeatedly that the best of procedures—providing children with experiences, for instance—will be fruitful for vocabulary development only to the extent that teachers *plan* for them to be fruitful.

Although materials were seen to be an integral part of instructional procedures, they were discussed separately in order to present more examples and to make additional comments about them. In the end they were generally divided into homemade and commercial types so that the advantages of each could be mentioned. The conclusion reached was the wisdom of using some combination of both.

Although careful diagnosis is at the heart of all successful instruction, little was done with it in this chapter except to point out with examples how much can be learned about children's vocabularies simply by listening to what they say and ask. This skimpy treatment seems justified because reliable procedures for learning exactly what any given child's vocabulary actually is have not yet been found; even learning what it might be in some approximate way would be an impossible task for a teacher who would have to collect the information for many children.

Recognizing these problems, the chapter assumed that young children have so much to learn when it comes to vocabularies that teachers need not worry about spending too much time on what is already known. Such an assumption does not sidestep the importance of finding out about misconceptions. Underscored, in fact, was that the speech of TV-educated children frequently suggests a level of understanding which overestimates what actually exists; and that, because of this, the responsibility of their teachers is to deal with misunderstandings as well as with new concepts and the new vocabulary that goes with them.

REFERENCES

1. Adams, Ruth R., and Litwin, Zelda. "Talking Typewriter—A Study in Concept and Attention Growth of Young Children," *Elementary English,* XLVII (February, 1970), 250–256.
2. Brandwein, Paul F., et al. *Concepts in Science,* Grade 4. New York: Harcourt, Brace and World, Inc., 1966.
3. ———. *Concepts in Science,* Grade 6. New York: Harcourt, Brace and World, Inc., 1966.
4. Brown, Gertrude S. *Your Country and Mine.* Boston: Ginn and Co., 1965.
5. Cohen, Dorothy H. "Word Meaning and the Literary Experience in Early Childhood," *Elementary English,* XLVI (November, 1969), 914–925.
6. Dale, Edgar. "Vocabulary Development of the Underprivileged Child," *Elementary English,* XXXXII (November, 1965), 778–786.

7. DEUTSCH, MARTIN. "Facilitating Development in the Pre-School Child: Social and Psychological Perspectives," *Merrill-Palmer Quarterly,* X (July, 1964), 249–263.

8. DOLCH, EDWARD W. *Psychology and Teaching of Reading.* Champaign, Ill.: The Garrard Press, 1951.

9. DURKIN, DOLORES. *Teaching Them to Read.* Boston: Allyn and Bacon, Inc., 1970.

10. FRAZIER, ALEXANDER. "Developing a Vocabulary of the Senses," *Elementary English,* XLVII (February, 1970), 176–184.

11. GOETZ, DELIA. *At Home in Our Land.* Boston: Ginn and Co., 1965.

12. HARRIS, ALBERT J. *How to Increase Reading Ability.* New York: Longmans, Green and Co., 1961.

13. HECHINGER, FRED M., and HECHINGER, GRACE. "Before the Age of Discretion," *New York Times,* January 31, 1965, p. 39.

14. JOHN, VERA P., and GOLDSTEIN, LEO S. "The Social Context of Language Acquisition," *Merrill-Palmer Quarterly,* X (July, 1964), 265–275.

15. PETTY, WALTER T., and STARKEY, ROBERTA J. "Oral Language and Personal and Social Development," *Elementary English,* XLIII (April, 1966), 386–394.

16. PONDER, EDDIE G. "Understanding the Language of the Culturally Disadvantaged Child," *Elementary English,* XXXXII (November, 1965), 769–774.

17. TAYLOR, MARIE E. "Instant Enrichment," *Elementary English,* XLV (February, 1968), 228–232.

8

Teaching Writing

A combination of reasons explains why this chapter about writing is in a reading textbook. One of them also explains why the writing chapter precedes the two which deal with the specifics of reading instruction.

Accounting for the sequence are data from this writer's series of longitudinal studies. (A longitudinal study follows the same children over an extended period of time.) The first two were concerned with preschoolers who learned to read at home and one of the findings common to both was the children's early interest in writing (4). For many, attempts to write began at the age of four; for more than half, they came prior to any reading ability.

Subsequent to these two studies another was done in which the focus was a two-year language arts program that started with four year olds (5). Classroom observations again uncovered interest in writing that often appeared before any was shown for learning to read.

What must be underscored immediately is that the findings from the three studies pertain only to trends among the groups studied; they are not a description of each child nor, certainly, are they now offered as inevitable characteristics of all children. Therefore the only claim of this chapter is the likelihood that *some* young children will be more interested in writing than in reading and that to accommodate this, school programs ought to provide opportunities to learn to write as well as to read.

Another claim of the chapter—this stems from the two-year experimental program mentioned earlier—is that instruction in writing can achieve more goals than just the one of writing ability. It is assumed to be helpful with the visual discrimination required by reading. As described here, writing instruction also is being viewed as a vehicle for teaching letter names; for demonstrating that words are comprised of letters; for introducing and then repeating the idea that letters represent sounds; for pointing out, again with numerous illustrations, that the writing (spelling) of a word is related to its sound; and for teaching the sounds of some letters. For multiple reasons, then, writing instruction is assumed to be directly related to reading and is, therefore, a relevant topic for this textbook.

MANUSCRIPT VERSUS CURSIVE WRITING

Throughout the chapter "writing" will refer to what is commonly called printing and to what is technically called *manuscript writing*. The latter contrasts with *cursive writing*, the type commonly used by adults.* That cursive writing *is* what adults customarily use prompts a question about why schools teach manuscript first.

In answer, it might be helpful to point out that a different question was being raised in earlier years. At the start of the century it was cursive writing that was taught to beginners and the question at that time was: Why teach *any* kind of writing to six year olds? What accounts for this query is very much like the reasons why reading for six year olds was also being questioned during that earlier period. Because they were described in detail in Chapter 3, only a brief reference will be made to them now.

During the early years of the century, you will recall from Chapter 3, recapitulation theory was widely accepted. As a result it commonly entered into educational discussions, including those about writing. Patrick, for example, reminded his readers in an article published in 1899 that writing should never be taught before the age of ten because ". . . it will demand a considerable maturity in the child before he is ready for that which has developed so late in the history of the race" (15, p. 390).

* Apparently either poor enunciation or careless listening is frequent in classrooms. I recall a parent of a seven year old who once asked, "What in the world is 'cursed' writing?"

Further evidence of the influence of recapitulation theory appears in an article by Dewey published in 1898. In this case he was criticizing both reading and writing instruction as he observed:

> There is an order in which sensory and motor centres develop—an order expressed, in a general way, by saying that the line of progress is from the larger, coarser adjustments having to do with the bodily system as a whole (those nearest the trunk of the body) to the finer and accurate adjustments having to do with the periphery and extremities of the organism. The oculist tells us that the vision of the child is essentially that of the savage; being adapted to seeing large and somewhat remote objects in the mass, not near-by objects in detail (3, pp. 319–320).

The early years of the century, as Chapter 3 pointed out, also were marked by singular attention to the maturation process and such related phenomena as neural ripening. Consequently it is not surprising that educators of the times were saying, "It is a well-known fact that a child's powers, whether physical or mental, ripen in a certain rather definite order" and that "the child's mind, before ten, has not ripened sufficiently for tasks like reading and writing" (15, pp. 386–387).

Still another reason for the earlier criticism of writing instruction is one Dewey commonly discussed. Characteristic of his viewpoint is what he wrote in an article in which he was attempting to encourage teachers of the young to move away from symbols—and thus from reading and writing—toward what he called nature study:

> Originally, when authority and tradition were the ultimate sources of knowledge, learning how to read and write soon was important. But now science has given importance to other sources of knowledge: observation, experimentation, testing (3, p. 316).

Even though—as these various quotes point out—all writing instruction was being criticized and even though the critics were well-known educators and psychologists, the change that eventually came about was one which replaced cursive with manuscript writing. Why?

During the years when American educators were advocating postponement of all writing, one in England was saying that manuscript is easier than cursive and so should be taught to young children (7). As the facts show, the influence of English educators upon early childhood education was considerable (see Chapter 2); thus it is not surprising that manuscript writing was imported to America in the early 1920s. Once here, it was used with gradually increasing frequency and now is the kind commonly taught to school beginners.*

* In the 1970s, the sudden popularity of the "open classroom" is another example of British influence upon American education.

In what sense is manuscript writing easier for beginners? It is easier primarily because it is made up of letters which, in addition to being separated from one another in words, are themselves comprised of separate strokes. Or, as another author has put it: With manuscript writing the child can "stop, rest, and get his bearings before making the next stroke or the next letter" (7). Interestingly, the very features that make manuscript writing easier for young children also make it a slower process than cursive. This, in turn, explains its infrequent use among adults who, for everyday purposes, are interested in quick communication.

In addition to being easier, another reason commonly cited to explain why manuscript writing is taught initially is its close correspondence with the print found in beginning readers (10). The thinking here is that manuscript writing and text print go hand in hand, while the cursive type would only introduce differences at a time when everything should be done to simplify learning. And so for a combination of reasons, manuscript writing is what is now taught to beginners and what is discussed in this chapter.

WRITING INSTRUCTION

The method of writing instruction to be described here is recommended because it links writing with beginning reading skills. Nothing in the recommendation, however, suggests it is the best or the only method. In fact, the more I visit classrooms the more firmly convinced I become that there is no such thing as one best way to teach anything. I say this because what is successful and of interest to some children can be either boring or frustrating for others. And, a method that works well with one teacher seems doomed to immediate failure when used by another. What is being described, therefore, is simply a way of teaching writing which you might want to consider for your own work with young children.

Initial Decisions

One of the first questions a teacher needs to answer has to do with which manuscript system to use. Many are available from a wide variety of publishers who market writing workbooks; two samples are reproduced on pages 220 and 221. Comparisons between these and still others show that differences are minimal and deal either with the shapes of a few letters or the direction in which some strokes are made.

Research has nothing to say about which of the available systems is best for young children. Consequently selections usually are made for reasons that have to do with such factors as familiarity and convenience.

They also are commonly made by people other than the teacher; thus you might find yourself using what has already been chosen.

Regardless of how such decisions are in fact made, the important thing for teachers is that they have some system and that they use it with facility. I emphasize this because I have observed a few who either confused children by being inconsistent in the way they made letters or simply lost their attention because their own printing was much too slow. The lesson seems clear: Have a system and learn to use it with skill.

Once a particular way of writing letters has been selected, the next decision has to do with the sequence for teaching them and with whether the capital and lowercase forms of each letter will be presented together or separately.* When writing workbooks are used, both questions already have answers—assuming the teacher chooses to use them exactly as they are assembled. When this is not the decision, or when workbooks are either unavailable or simply bypassed, a teacher does need to give some thought to sequence. To help, a number of criteria can be considered.

One is the factor of difficulty. This would immediately suggest beginning with the more easily made letters such as *i, l, t,* or *x*. Mentioning *x*, however, suggests still another criterion: usefulness. Because writing letters is simply a means to an end—the end in this case being ability to write words—attention to less frequently used letters like *x, q,* and *z* could be temporarily postponed.

Likelihood of confusion is still another important consideration. Here the notorious problem with *b* and *d* comes immediately to mind suggesting that attention to each be separated by time. The same would apply to pairs like *p* and *q*.**

The last criterion to be mentioned is, in my opinion, the most important. Here I refer to interest and the observable fact that some letters are more appealing than others. Those in a child's name, for example, always are special for him but others can be made special. In this context I recall a nursery school class in which *s*, often difficult to make, presented no problems when introduced on the day that brought winter's first snow. Thus, and on the basis of many classroom observations, I would suggest you put interests at the top of your list of criteria and remember that even the best of commercial materials for writing cannot take advantage of them to the degree that you can.

What kind of paper to use is still another of the practical concerns. At the start, when children's efforts result more in scribbling than writ-

* The terms "capital" and "lowercase" will be used throughout this textbook. Hopefully "big letter" and "small letter" will be avoided in your instruction.

** Children often have their own solutions for problems with closely similar letters. One girl, as she compared *b* and *d*, was heard to observe that *d* is the one with "its stomach in the back."

From *Handwriting with Write and See,* Book 1, Teacher's Edition, by B. F. Skinner and Sue-Ann Krakower, p. 5. Copyright 1968 by Lyons and Carnahan, Inc., Educational Division, Meredith Corporation.

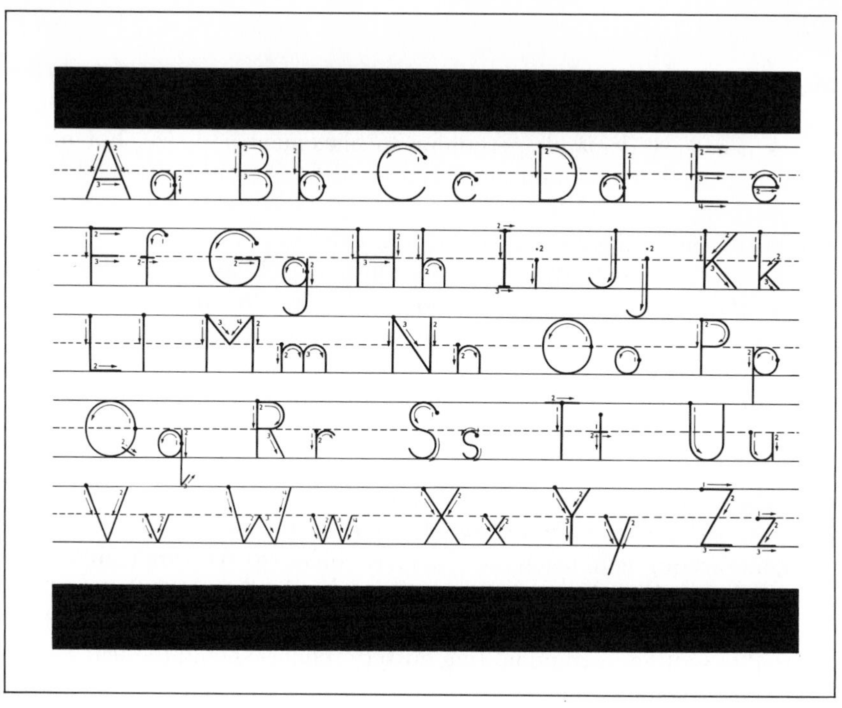

For page 52 from the Teachers' Edition of *Grade I, Part 2,* by Hale C. Reid and Helen W. Crane, from the GINN ELEMENTARY ENGLISH SERIES, © Copyright, 1970, 1965, 1963, by Ginn and Company.

ing, it often is helpful to use large unlined paper; but soon a shift should be made to manuscript paper which, with its uniformly spaced lines, makes necessary demands pertaining to placement and size. For manuscript writing, paper should be placed squarely in front of the child with its lower edge parallel to the edge of the desk or table. His nonwriting hand is placed at the top to keep it from moving.

At the start, help should be given in how to hold a pencil correctly: between the thumb and first finger, resting on the others. And, even though earlier decades had a great deal to say about the need to use oversize pencils with young children—this was one outgrowth of the exaggerated attention given maturation—observation indicates they are awkward to handle. Consequently, regular size pencils are what you should have available.*

One other question has to do with the pace of instruction. Here, too, correct answers can be found by observing the children. In general the guideline would be to teach the letters as quickly as they are comfortably able to learn them—but no faster. What turns out to be a comfortable pace will be affected by the children's age, but also by the amount of time allotted to writing instruction. In a nursery school—should the teacher decide to have some writing—this might be as limited as one or two weekly periods of about fifteen or twenty minutes' duration. At the first grade level, on the other hand, it would probably be daily periods of about the same length.

Another factor that affects the pace of instruction is a teacher's ability which, among other things, is affected by the number of children being instructed. In general, the smaller the group the better the teaching and the faster the pace because of increased opportunities to give individual assistance as well as generous amounts of praise and encouragement.

Getting Ready for Writing

Whether you teach (or plan to teach) nursery school, kindergarten, or first grade, remember that individual children might have done some printing before starting school. For the most part they will only know about capital letters and often will be using incorrect strokes. (Comments about home help with printing can be found in Chapter 12.) Nonetheless they *have* begun and usually do not require the basic preparation that is essential for others.

Beginners, for instance, frequently have to learn such basic things as how to hold a pencil and how to keep paper from moving. Sometimes

* A finding from the research with preschool readers is relevant here: the children routinely used regular pencils before they started school but then, in first grade, were given the extra large ones because official school policy said they were "unready" for the regular size (4). Isn't it unfortunate that we do not pay more attention to the children when we make decisions or issue proclamations about them?

they also need to learn referents for "top" and "bottom," and for "left side" and "right side." If their preschool experiences did not include the chance to use pencils, crayons, and paper, they should also be allowed to do some scribbling in order to get a feel for these materials and to experience "pencil power." Once it is experienced and some control is achieved, the scribbling can be channeled somewhat. For instance I recall one kindergarten teacher who, by having children color the spaces resulting from a limited amount of scribbling, turned their paper into interesting mosaics—or as one child aptly described them, "windows like my church has."

Following the somewhat aimless scribbling, beginners should next be encouraged to try to copy or make objects. Of special relevance for writing are round or oval shapes such as would be found in: wheels, doughnuts, pumpkins, snowmen, eyes, and eggs. Straight lines also have importance. How children might get initial practice with lines as well as circles is demonstrated in the reproduced material on page 224. Being demonstrated, too, is the way workbooks offer ideas for instruction, even when they are not being used by the children. In fact, as you think about preparing children for writing, you might want to further prepare yourself to teach it by at least glancing through some of the manuals that accompany the workbooks.

Thus far attention has gone to physical preparations but this is not meant to overshadow the psychological; for getting children interested in learning to write is of major importance, too. Some, of course, already are interested. They have watched parents or perhaps older siblings write at home; as a result they want to learn. When it happens that such an interest has not been acquired, probably the quickest way to foster it is to entice the children with the prospect of learning to write their names, always a perennial favorite not only with the young but, as Dale Carnegie tells it, with adults, too (1).

Finding occasions to call attention to names is no problem. Just the combination of a teacher's taking attendance (done with cards held by her) and signing first names to the children's papers and possessions (e.g., crayon boxes and coat hooks) is enough to highlight them. Before long, the children will want to write their names themselves; thus it is not long either before writing instruction can get underway.

Initial Writing Lessons

All instruction should aim toward the achievement of one or more goals. Therefore let me begin this discussion of writing lessons by mentioning what they can eventually accomplish:

1. Writing ability
2. Knowledge of letter names
3. Awareness that words are comprised of letters

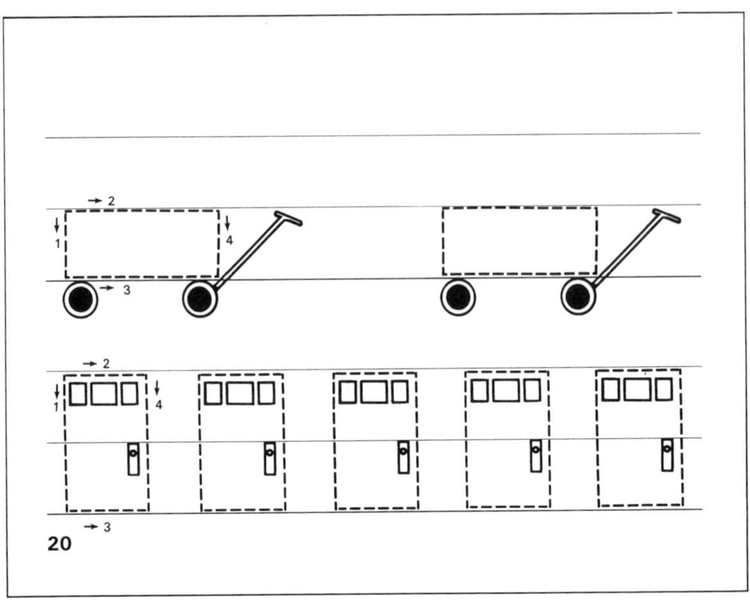
2
1
4
3
2
1
4
3
20

4. Awareness that letters represent sounds
5. Awareness that the writing (spelling) of a word is related to its pronunciation
6. Understanding of "beginning sound"
7. Knowledge of letter sounds

As with any collection of instructional goals, there is no assumption here that all the children will reach all of these. In fact, they have been listed simply to remind you of the potential of writing instruction and because they directly affect the type to be described now.

Selecting the letter to be practiced is the first step in any instruction. One of the many ways this might be done will be explained with a description of a kindergarten teacher.

In this case she did nothing with writing until early November. Prior to that the children had been getting accustomed to using pencils and paper and, among other things, had made straight and slanted lines (fences, houses, tepees) and also circles (faces, suns, clocks). Meanwhile the teacher had decided to get writing started by giving attention to *T* and *t*. When it was time, this is how it began.

On the first Tuesday in November, as had become the daily practice, the morning started with comments about the weather, what day it was, and so on. Although a card showing *Tuesday* ordinarily would have been on a bulletin board it was not today in order to give the teacher a reason to say, "I forgot to put up Tuesday," and to print it on the chalkboard as the children watched. This was followed by the question, "Does anyone know the name of the first letter I made to write Tuesday?" Nobody did so the teacher answered her own question. She also mentioned it was a capital *T* because *Tuesday* was the name of a day and, like their names, began with a capital letter.

She next printed and named a lowercase *t* and asked whether anyone could find a word in the room which started with that. (About a week earlier a small chart showing *1* and *2* with *one* and *two* written beneath had been displayed and discussed.) Several children immediately pointed to the number chart; then *two* was printed. Following this the teacher mentioned the possibility of everyone learning to make *T* and *t*. The children were enthusiastic, so it was time for the first writing lesson.

In this class it began with the teacher's suggestion to try some "skywriting." (This led to comments about airplanes that write messages in the sky.) For this the children stood and held up their writing hands. The teacher faced them and proceeded to demonstrate the correct way to make *T*. Then, as she made it again, the children followed along making their own *T*'s in the air. While they did this, the teacher watched to make sure the direction of their strokes was correct.

Following the air writing, the children sat down and each received a pencil and a piece of unlined paper. After reminders about how to hold the pencil and where to place the paper, they proceeded to make *T*'s wherever they chose but only on one side of the paper. As they did this the teacher circulated among them, correcting strokes that were being made either in the wrong sequence or the wrong direction. Subsequently the same general procedure was followed for lowercase *t*, made on the second side of the paper.

The next day, following some preparations, these kindergarteners were treated to a visit in a first grade room where, as had been planned, the children were having a writing lesson and using lined manuscript paper. This was enough for the kindergarten teacher to suggest, after they had returned to their own room, that she would get some of the special paper used by the first graders. On the following morning, of course, it was available and "big kid" writing lessons began, the first dealing only with capital *T*.

As before, words beginning with *T* were mentioned and written on the chalkboard:

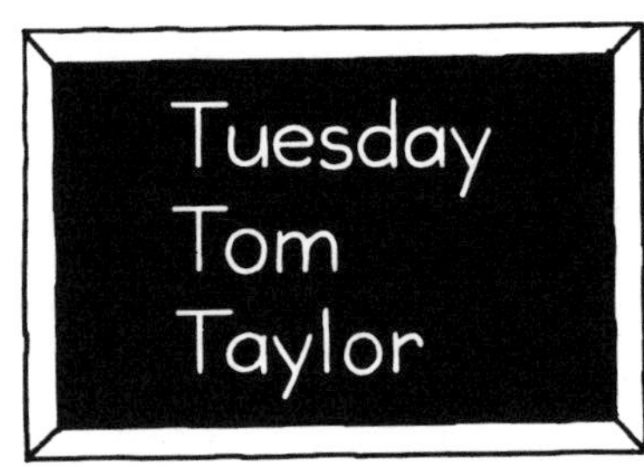

Also as before, instruction began with skywriting, after which pencils and half sheets of manuscript paper were distributed:

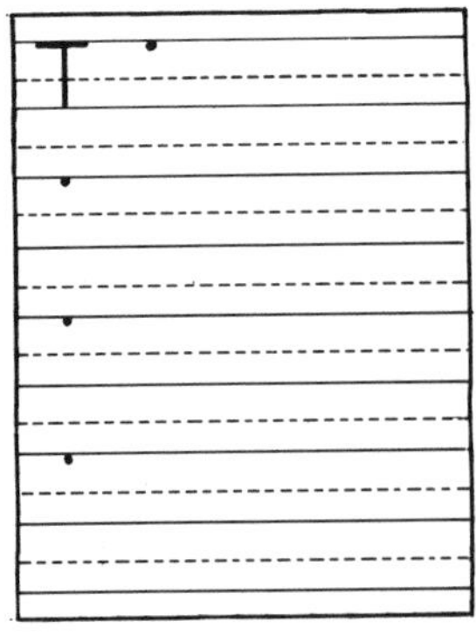

One *T* had been printed on each sheet so that the children would have a close-at-hand model as they made theirs. Dots were added to show where to make their first *T* and, further, where each new row of *T*'s was to begin. The half sheets of paper were used because earlier experiences with other kindergarteners had shown that a whole sheet was discouraging for some in that it took too many letters to fill it up. Finally, a model of a completed paper had been prepared which now was hung up for all to see:

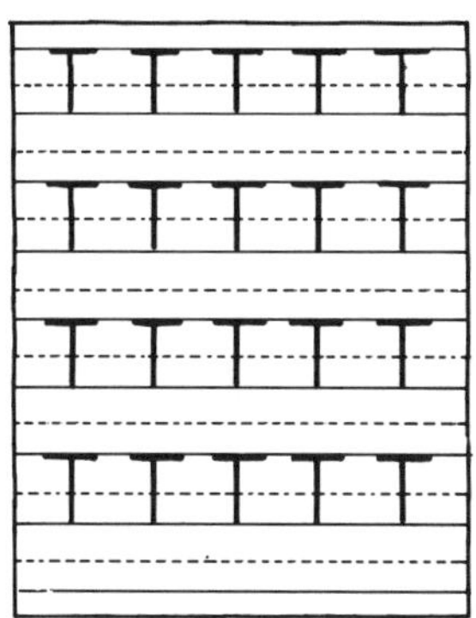

This had been done because, again from past experiences, the teacher learned that like a picture a completed model is better than a thousand words for explaining the nature of a task.

As soon as pencils and paper were ready, the children began their first attempt to use lined paper. With the help of the dot, the teacher made sure everyone started his first *T* at the right place. She also offered reminders for making each of the other *T*'s in the first row. When that was completed, the second row was undertaken; once more the dot showed the children where to begin. And so this lesson proceeded.

The next writing lesson came several days later, after the children had been talking about Thanksgiving and turkeys. In fact, *turkey* was used to initiate work on lowercase *t* and to remind the children that once they knew how to make several other letters they would be able to write their own words.

To show words that started with *T* and *t*, the teacher listed:

Prior to rereading the four words, she casually mentioned how they not only started with the same letter but also with the same sound. (Knowing she would be calling the children's attention to the beginning sound was the reason why familiar and interesting words like Thursday and Thanksgiving were not part of the *T* list.)

The lesson with lowercase *t* was similar to the one for capital *T*. It began with air writing. A finished paper also was displayed, while one *t* plus the helpful dots appeared on the children's sheets. And so another writing lesson was underway.

Features of Writing Lessons

Admittedly, not all teachers would choose to initiate writing instruction in the way this one did. Nonetheless the illustration exemplifies practices which are pertinent for any that aims toward the goals listed earlier on pages 223 and 225. For that reason, let me specify them now:

1. A special effort should be made to insure that early experiences with writing are both pleasurable and purposeful. In the illustration, visiting the first graders coupled with the "privilege" of using the paper they used were designed to turn writing into a special and enjoyable occasion. To help make the first efforts with it successful, the teacher chose *T* because it is easy to make. Although both its lowercase and capital forms were introduced together, writing on the manuscript paper dealt with one at a time, again to insure a maximum of success. To provide a purpose for writing, the teacher explained to the children that the ability to make letters would allow them to write their own words.

2. Young children require a certain amount of physical activity. Thus skywriting was used both to get them out of their chairs and to allow the teacher to look for and correct erroneous strokes. Because it was compared to the writing done by airplanes, the skywriting also added to the children's enjoyment of the lesson.

3. As was mentioned in an earlier chapter, young children commonly view materials as something to play with. This is why the teacher in the illustration waited to distribute pencils and paper until it was time to use them.

4. That the children *were* young did not prevent her from using correct terminology; in this case, "capital letter" and "lowercase letter." The teacher also made sure the name of the letter being taught was mentioned many times.

5. When writing is demonstrated to children, it should be done with special care. For this reason the completed page of *T*'s plus the sample that was printed on the children's papers were perfectly formed. In addition, when the teacher was skywriting and facing the children, she was careful to make her strokes in a way that would display them correctly.

6. Beginners experience difficulties that can be minimized by taking certain precautions. In the illustration, a fully completed page of letters was prepared in order to clarify the exact nature of the job at hand. It was hung up so that it would be a continuous reminder of that job. Half sheets of paper were used to prevent the discouragement that can develop when a task is viewed as being too extensive. Because where to get started, both with a letter and with a new row, is a common problem for beginners, dots were printed on the children's papers to provide guidelines.

7. When writing instruction is viewed as a means for helping with phonics, certain steps should be included. In the illustration, words that began with *t* were highlighted because the teacher wanted to mention the similarity in the beginning sound of each. (Generally the initial sound in a word is the easiest to hear as a distinct sound; therefore it makes sense to start with that.) Although the attention given sounds was very casual during these early lessons, it would become more concentrated as time passed.

What else happens as time passes and both writing instruction and writing ability progress?

Subsequent Lessons

Even with later lessons, it is a good practice to begin with some type of demonstration of how a letter is formed. Thus skywriting might continue to be used, at least some of the time. In one class in which it was used all the time, the teacher intermittently added little touches to maintain interest. On some days she would print a very large form of the letter on the board; then she and the children would pretend to trace it in the air. At other times she might have her assistant play "A Tisket, A Tasket" on the piano while she and the children made *T* and then *t*. (The same song was used with letters like *C*, *I*, *J*, and *L*). *A*, *B*, and *F* were sometimes written to the tune of "Three Blind Mice," while "Twinkle, Twinkle, Little Star" helped with *b*, *h*, and *d*. The children's reaction? They loved it. Meanwhile their teacher was having ample opportunities to make sure letters were being formed correctly in the air before the children started to cope with the more demanding lines of the manuscript paper.

As lessons progress and greater facility with letter making is achieved, more time can also be given to the phonics dimension of the instruction.* For example, after the children's attention has been called to the fact that all the *f* words in a given list start with the same sound—all would be read to emphasize this characteristic—the teacher might ask, "Can you think of some words that begin the way *fast, food, fish,* and *fun* start?" In some cases they might not yet be ready to respond; that is, they still do not have sufficient ability in auditory discrimination or, perhaps,

* Many more details about phonics comprise Chapter 10.

do not yet understand the meaning of "begin with the same sound." In other cases, however, teachers are in for a pleasant surprise. I recall one nursery school group, for instance, in which the teacher had been carrying on writing instruction much like that being described here. By early spring I encouraged her to see whether the children could give examples of words beginning with a certain sound but even then she was hesitant, doubting that they could. Nonetheless she gave it a try and soon found herself facing children who just about fell out of chairs in their eagerness to name words, in this case words beginning with the sound of *b*. The first contribution? *Bourbon*.

While observing other groups of young children, I have seen the same type of auditory ability displayed. Samples of their contributions follow, along with comments about some of the things that were done when the designated letter received attention during a writing lesson:

M

As was her practice, the teacher wrote and named *M* and *m*, then wrote and read some words starting with them. An added attraction was a tray of objects (mask, mitten, magnet, map, picture of a man, table mat) covered with a cloth. The teacher said she was a magician—*magician* was dramatically added to the list of words on the chalkboard—and that she was about to make some *m* things appear. With that, the objects were uncovered after which the children named them with much enthusiasm. As each was identified, still another word was added to the now extensive list. One especially interesting comment from a boy pertained to the table mat which showed a picture of Donald Duck. He objected saying, "For *M* it should be Mickey Mouse."

Following the board work and the effective use of a magic tray, these kindergarteners were able to contribute on their own: *medicine, milk, monster, magic.*

L

When *L* and *l* were introduced in another classroom, words contributed by the children were numerous and quick to come. They included: *laugh, lamp, look, lap, lawn, ladder, lemon, lantern, leaf, letter, lettuce, Lee.* The children—and I have seen this in other rooms, too—took special delight in the fact that the teacher was running out of space on the chalkboard because they could name so many words that began with the same sound as her original examples: *love, lie, lollipop, Larry, Lincoln.*

On the day *L* and *l* were being highlighted, art time provided a special surprise for the children because they had been "so smart" earlier. It was the chance to make paper lollipops. Small circles were first cut out of construction paper. Since these were to be the lollipops, the teacher explained, *L* was to be printed on one side and *l* on the other because that was the first letter in *lollipop.* (The latter point was made explicit to insure that the children understood the connection between the letter *L* and what they were so eagerly making. Without the direct explanation, some might never see it.) Afterwards, each child received a straw through which a piece of pipe cleaner had been pushed in order to make it firm. (Notice that the teacher did not distribute "sticks" until it was time to use them. Had they been handed out earlier, it is likely that some of the children would have played with them when they were supposed to be printing *L* and *l.*) Quickly the teacher stapled each child's stick to his lollipop. The result was a group of very happy children.

It should also be noted that one among them had strenuously objected to calling his a "lollipop." He insisted it was a "sucker." The teacher accepted this as a correct name, then proceeded to write *lollipop* and *sucker* on the board. She identified each and asked, "Does anyone know why we're using 'lollipop' today even though some of you do call what we made a 'sucker'?" Quickly one child rementioned the connection between *lollipop* and *l.* Then the teacher continued, "Can anyone think of a reason why I didn't ask you to write the whole word 'lollipop' on the circles?" Again responses came quickly from these kindergarteners. One said she didn't know how to make all the letters. Another said it was "too fat" to fit. And so an interesting writing-phonics-art lesson came to an end.

H

To provide some variation when *H* and *h* were being introduced, another teacher drew the outline of a large house on the board and asked the children what it was. They knew immediately so, next to the outline, *house* was carefully printed and the letter *h* identified. The teacher then asked, "What else could we call this house? The word I'm thinking of also begins with *h.*" Nobody responded so the teacher continued, "Let's play detective. I'll give you a clue. When you leave school you don't say, 'I'm going house.' You say, 'I'm going ——.'" And, of course, everyone responded with "home" so that was printed under *house* while the *h* was again named.

Following this, the teacher suggested it might be a good idea to write other *h* words inside rather than outside the house in order to keep them warm. (It was January.) Everyone agreed. Eventually the following were contributed by the children and printed within the outline: *hammer, hat, Halloween* (this word gave the teacher the chance to identify capital *H*), hot ("hot dog" was the suggestion, so the teacher explained why only *hot* could be printed), *hunt, harness, hand, head, heart.* To stress the similarity of their beginning sound, the teacher concluded the phonics part of the lesson by reading all the words named. Then the writing instruction itself began with some air writing.

P

On the day I was visiting in one kindergarten, *P* and *p* had been selected for a writing lesson. In order to write the *forty-one* words suggested by the children, the teacher—with much fanfare—covered three chalkboards. Rather than take the space to list all forty-one, let me just say that the examples included such modern words as "Peyton Place" (at the time of the visit it was a television program) and such long responses as, "Peter, Peter, pumpkin eater."

T

How one teacher dealt with *T* and *t* was described earlier in the chapter. Let me mention now what another chose to do. In this case much more was done with its sound because the lesson came at a more advanced stage of writing. This meant the children would learn to make *T* and *t* more rapidly and, by this time, they also were more adept at hearing initial sounds.

As was her custom, this particular teacher began by writing a capital *T*. She named it and soon heard from Tommy that it was the first letter in his name. Consequently under *T* went *Tommy.*

She then mentioned that she knew another name starting with *T*. She said it was not a child's name but, instead, the name of a tuba. This immediately led to questions about a tuba, all of which were answered with the help of a picture of one. Following this, the children tried to guess its proper name. They were unsuccessful, so the teacher told them as she wrote it. As a result the board now showed:

This lesson also had a special surprise. It was a recording of a song called "Tubby the Tuba." After it was played and obviously enjoyed, a request was made to name other words that started like *Tommy, Tubby,* and *tuba*. The following were offered by the children and written by the teacher: *television, telephone, table, turkey, tea, teeth, tongue, train, tiny,*

trick, tent, tonsils, towel, truck. To summarize the phonics part of the lesson the teacher read all the words, commenting again about the similarity of their beginning sound. Then the writing instruction began.

To illustrate still other words I have heard young children suggest during writing lessons, let me list some in the order in which they were mentioned. It happens that all were named by kindergarteners.

F

flower, flea, Flipper, floor, feather, fan, Friday, first, French, fur, fish, fork, flag, four, father, fence

W

wagon, wasp, wine, worm, waiting, water, watermelon, wife, wiggle

N

newspaper, nickel, napkin, nursery, numeral, nurse, needle, nail, nun, nest, Nixon, nothing, name, nap, no, neighbor

V

violet, vegetable, Venus, vacation, vase, Valentine, vacuum, valley, volcano

U

umbrella, umpire, under, ugly, uncle, usher, us, up

C

cute, coffee, coffee cake, coke, comb, carrot, cookie, candle, cap, coat

Mentioning *c* is a reminder of the fact that the same sound can be recorded by different letters. This leads to the need to comment about children's erroneous responses—for instance a response that names *king* as a word starting the way *cat* and *cough* begin.

If a lesson is dealing only with sounds and the teacher's question is, "Who can think of another word that starts like *cat* and *cough*?" then contributions such as *king*—or even *queen*—are correct. However, once the focus of instruction shifts to letter-sound associations and thus becomes visual as well as auditory, they no longer can be considered correct. Still, explanations are required so that the children who offered *king* and *queen* will understand that in one respect they are correct (initial sound) but in another they are not (initial letter). Meanwhile, all the children involved in the instruction are being given the chance to learn that letters other than *c* are sometimes used to stand for the same sound.

Additional Practice

Commonly heard is that "practice makes perfect." This is true, assuming it is the right kind. The purpose of this section, therefore, is to outline characteristics of practice that fosters perfect writing ability among young children. It goes without saying, of course, that what is perfect for them is different from what would merit the same description among older children or adults. It also seems unnecessary to say that not all will achieve perfection, even after a year or more.

The best kind of practice begins in the mind of the teacher who views it not as the mere repetition of the same thing done in the same way but, rather, as a repetition done in different ways—with different trimmings, if you will. This means that teachers must look for ways to vary the repetition that happens to be necessary for the development of a motor skill like writing. With young children, this is not overly difficult. Just changing temporarily from black pencils to red ones—or adding some music—is enough to give them the feeling of doing something different, even though the basic task is the same. I have also seen other successful variations in the form of making letters at the chalkboard or in sand in a paper plate.

Another feature of practice that is productive but also tolerable, is an amount of repetition that is neither tiresome nor more than what is actually needed. Here I cannot help but recall two kindergarteners, both boys but in different schools, who were willing to practice a letter only until they knew—and knew they knew—how to make it well. If the letter happened to be an easy one—*I* and *i*, for instance—they would write it just a few times and no more. On the other hand, if the selected letter was difficult, one could expect to find them trying to squeeze into every line of letters more samples than were required. While no generalization can be drawn from just two five year olds, the behavior of these boys succeeded in reminding me to remind teachers to avoid unnecessary practice.

And this suggests the next characteristic from the teacher's point of view: select only those letters that need to be improved. This means that when writing lessons get underway, they should be interspersed with practice sessions focussing on what turned out to be difficult-to-make letters. With certain ones, just about all the children will need the extra practice. With others, some or only just a few will require it. During practice periods, therefore, different children often will be working on different letters. It also is likely that some will be doing something else.

As writing lessons progress, words as well as single letters will need to be practiced. In one classroom the teacher initiated a change to words by taking advantage of the children's perpetual self-interest. Thus, she started with *me*. First she printed it on the board; some children knew what it said and spontaneously identified it. Then, at the direction of the teacher, the two letters were named. (Each had been identified and practiced in an earlier writing lesson.) Next the teacher suggested it would be a good idea to practice writing *me* because, at art time, self-portraits were to be made—one of the Christmas presents being prepared for parents—and *me* would be a good label.

After practicing *m* and *e* in the air, each child received paper:

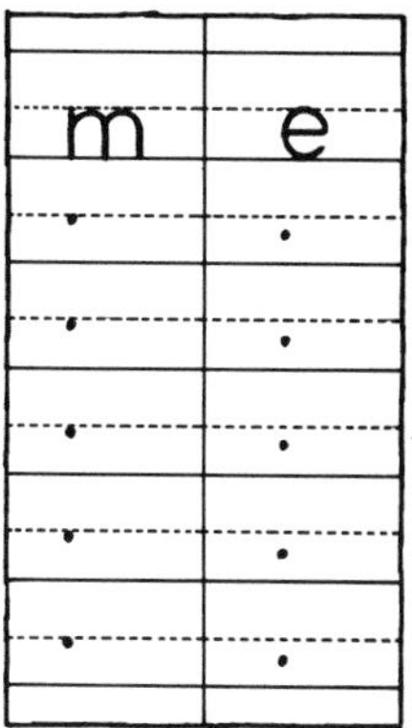

To specify the task and to serve as a reminder of it, a finished model was displayed in the front of the room:

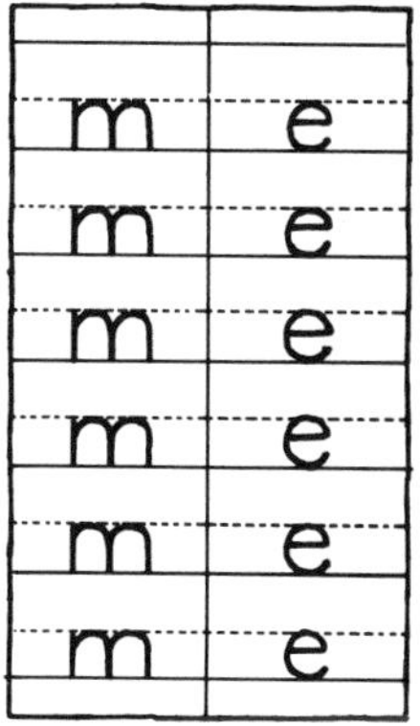

The directions were to print *me* six times on both sides of the paper. Then, at art time, each child would select his best *m* and *e*, cut them out, and paste these two rectangular pieces at the bottom of his self-made portrait. Motivation and enthusiasm were high; in addition, each letter had been introduced and practiced earlier. The result was a first attempt at writing words that brought both enjoyment and success.

Maintaining motivation and, therefore, continuing success, can be helped by keeping folders for the children's work. Especially valuable are samples of the earliest efforts with printing because, by contrast with later ones, they offer the children concrete evidence of their progress.

In addition to fostering motivation for practice, a teacher must also make certain that the practice itself is correct. This is one reason to have the children write in the air or on a chalkboard at least some of the time because both provide an opportunity to watch them in the act of making a letter. As a result, there also is the opportunity to change immediately what needs to be changed. This contrasts with another practice common in classrooms. I refer to times when children are directed to trace a letter which appears on manuscript paper or in a workbook, but then are not watched as they do the tracing. Almost inevitably some carry on a hit-or-miss type, which only helps them learn to do the wrong thing well. This suggests that the most effective and, in the long run, the most efficient practice is *supervised* practice.

In summary, then, the following points have been made about practice that will be productive:

1. It involves the repetition that is necessary if writing ability is to progress.
2. Although essentially concerned with this repetition, it still offers some variation. In addition, it is never excessive in amount.
3. It is carried on only when deficiencies are noted.
4. It is supervised in order to eliminate the perfection of errors.
5. It is made at least somewhat pleasant by being related both to the children's interests and their progress with writing.

WRITING NAMES

Because his name is a child's favorite word and, too, because the ability to write it is a useful one, time should be given to the development of that achievement. In fact, even teachers who choose to bypass writing instruction would still be wise to allot time for practice with names if for no other reason than the enjoyment young children experience when they learn to write them.

Generally, attention to names begins with efforts to get the children to recognize them in print. Generally, too, only first names are used at the start. Chapter 4 has already described a collection of ways for achieving name recognition with young children; a few are repeated below:

1. During the early weeks of the school year, use a variety of name tags; for example, "hello" tags, badges, and bracelets.

2. Take attendance by using name cards which are held up for all to see and then identified.
3. Use place cards at milk or juice time.
4. Print first names on the children's art work.

The fairly quick and typical result of these and similar procedures is that each child will recognize his own name plus the names of others.

The actual writing of first names can begin with attention to initial letters. One teacher in whose room I visited started with the first letter plus a period, explaining to the children that the period would take the place of the remaining letters until they learned to make them. What she was doing, of course, was paving the way to an understanding of the concept "abbreviation."

Practicing initial letters can be carried on much like the writing practice already described in this chapter; now, though, the teacher will be printing different letters on different papers, all of which continue to serve as close-at-hand models as the children attempt their own versions. To replace air writing, impossible now because of the variety of letters, the teacher will move from child to child, offering suggestions and, in some instances, changing erroneous formations.

Soon the children can practice the first two letters and, before long, all of them. During the time the various letters are being added, they can also get some practice in noting their sequence. For this, a small name card might be given to each, plus an envelope containing all the letters in his name. The job would be to arrange them in the order in which they appear on the card. Actually, name cards should be a permanent possession for each child because they serve as useful models and reminders when the children begin to sign their names to work papers and art projects.

Once children are writing their names many possibilities are available for practice, in addition to the daily routine of putting them on completed work. A few are described below:

> Paper can be ruled in squares, according to the number of letters in each child's first name. At the top, his name would be printed, one letter in each square. Under the models the children would practice their names. To make a design, remaining squares could be filled in with various colors.
>
> At the top of a sheet of construction paper each child's name would be printed. Now, without the help of the squares, he would copy it just beneath. The paper would then be folded from the bottom and stapled to form a pocket just below the name. On Friday, the week's papers could be tucked into the pockets to be taken home.

> Periodically, simple messages to parents can be composed by the children, then typed, duplicated, and reread. After each child receives a copy to take home, he signs his name at the bottom.

As time passes and the children routinely sign their names to many things, they usually get somewhat careless in forming letters. This is why it is a good practice to schedule time periodically for attention to more careful efforts. With these, it is helpful to have the name cards for models, even though they might not have been used for some time. Helpful, too, are samples of the children's earlier attempts at name writing which were done more carefully.

INSTRUCTIONAL MATERIALS

Pencils and paper are the most obvious kinds of materials for writing practice, but chalkboards should also be available because their use gives a teacher the chance to note and correct errors before the children have time to incorporate them into their writing habits. For young children, chalkboards should be placed sufficiently low on a wall. It is helpful, too, if they are lined. And, to avoid what might be called "chicken scratching," the children should also be taught how to hold chalk. (It is held between the first two fingers and the thumb. The other two fingers rest lightly on it. For young children, half pieces of chalk are the best.) Without instruction, the tendency is to grasp chalk as if it were a pencil; one result is the unbelievably tiny, pinched writing that is seen in far too many classrooms.

What often turns out to be a special attraction are the small chalkboards that can be found in many homes. Typically these have an alphabet printed at the top. If it happens that some of its letters are formed differently from the way they are being taught in school, the entire alphabet can be covered with a strip of paper that shows the letters as they are made in the adopted system. With these portable boards, it is a good practice to make them available only some of the time; this tends to make their appeal a continuing one.

For further variety sandpaper letters might be traced occasionally or, as was mentioned earlier, once in a while practice might be carried on by using sand in something like a paper plate. I have also been in classrooms in which the children formed letters with clay. While this does call attention to their shapes, it does not provide practice with correct stroking.

Workbooks also are available to help with practice. Pages 240 and 241 show the instruction one series gives for introducing *T*. The special feature of these particular workbooks is explained in the Introduction:

Tom	Rita
Karen	Bob
Lori Jo	Amy
S Scott	David

Eight samples of name writing at mid-year in kindergarten.

3. Forming Capital Letters

The child now begins to form letters. He works from a model and at first has only to fill in a small part of the letter next to it. As he proceeds, he must complete more and more of the letter, until he completes the whole letter with only a small clue to guide him. (Make sure the children understand that the letters appear in pairs—the first being the model, the second the one which they must complete.)

Letters of the alphabet are presented in order of increasing difficulty. The letters F and E are separated by H and Z so that the child will not confuse them. The section ends with V, which is difficult because of the diagonals.

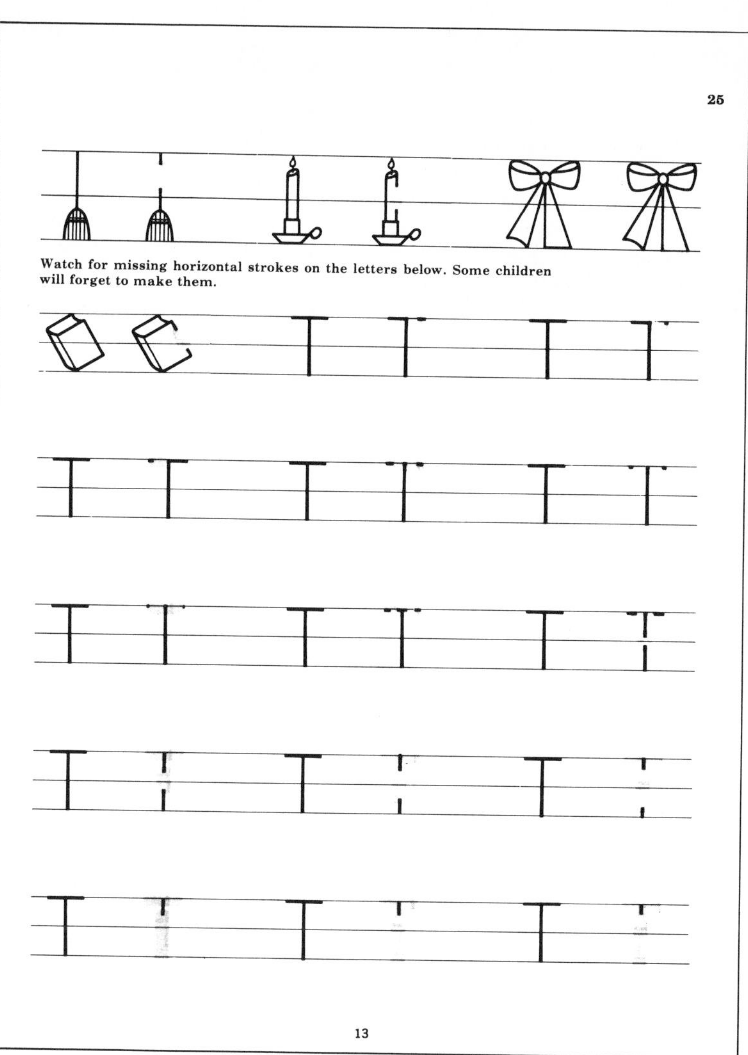

25

Watch for missing horizontal strokes on the letters below. Some children will forget to make them.

13

From *Handwriting with Write and See,* Book 1, Teacher's Edition, by B. F. Skinner and Sue-Ann Krakower, p. 25. Copyright 1968 by Lyons and Carnahan, Inc., Educational Division, Meredith Corporation.

> The *Write and See* process requires a special pen and special paper. The pen contains a harmless ink which interacts with the chemically treated paper to produce gray, when the child writes correctly, or yellow, when the child writes incorrectly. The color, in other words, gives him an immediate report on what he has written. This encourages rapid learning. With most traditional methods, the child learns that he has formed a letter correctly only when his teacher tells him so which can be after a considerable length of time (18, p. 1).

Another series—a sample is reproduced on page 243—tries to give meaning to practice by associating it with related pictures. The workbook material shown on page 244 is from still another series which, like this chapter, gives attention to the sound a letter can represent while the children are learning to write it.

The various pages that have been reproduced here are just a few samples from the huge quantity of materials now available. What even these few show is the variety that is possible when writing instruction and practice are the concern. Not equally obvious is that the success of any material still depends upon a teacher who will use it in a way that is best for the children who are her special responsibility.

ONE FINAL WORD

This chapter has given detailed attention to the physical act of writing and, secondly, to the useful connections between writing instruction and initial help with phonics. Not to be forgotten, however, is the communication or composing side of writing; for even young children ought to be given the chance to become authors. At first, when both writing and composing skills are limited, their creative efforts might be as brief as one-word captions for pictures they have drawn. Meanwhile, more extensive material can be group-dictated and in the form of invitations, thank you notes, or simple messages for greeting cards. Later, with both the example and encouragement of a teacher, more and more individuals will be able to write their own versions of what has been seen, done, touched, heard, or felt.

This concern for the composing side of writing leads to the recommendation that children not be switched from manuscript to cursive writing until about third grade. Right now the common practice is to make the change during second; however, classroom observations suggest that when this is the practice, the change comes just when children have gained facility with the physical act of printing and, as a result, are more ready than ever to work at composing. To introduce cursive writing at that point is to impede budding authors.

From *Now We Write,* Worktype Guide 1, by Margaret Rouse and Bobbie Dickson, p. 27. Copyright 1967 by The Economy Company.

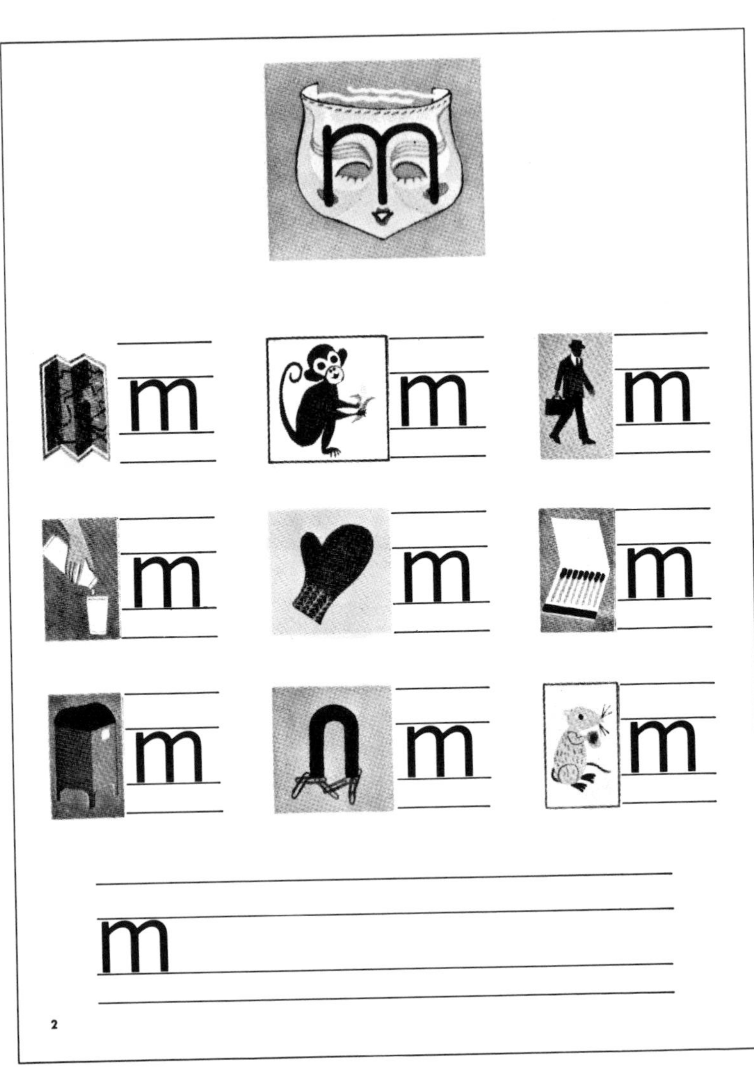

From *We Learn to Listen*, Book A, by Catherine Stern, p. 2. Copyright 1966 by Random House/Singer, School Division.

REFERENCES

1. CARNEGIE, DALE. *How to Win Friends and Influence People.* New York: Simon and Schuster, Inc., 1936.

2. CONNELL, DONNA. "Auditory and Visual Discrimination in Kindergarten," *Elementary English,* XLV (January, 1968), 51–54.

3. DEWEY, JOHN. "The Primary-Education Fetich," *The Forum,* XXV (May, 1898), 315–328.

4. DURKIN, DOLORES. *Children Who Read Early.* New York: Teachers College Press, Columbia University, 1966.

5. ———. "A Language Arts Program for Pre-First Grade Children: Two-Year Achievement Report," *Reading Research Quarterly,* V (Summer, 1970), 534–565.

6. ENSTROM, E. A. "Instructional Goals for Handwriting," *Elementary English,* XLV (January, 1968), 84–88.

7. ———. "But How Soon Can We *Really* Write?" *Elementary English,* XLV (March, 1968), 360–363.

8. ENSTROM, E. A., and ENSTROM, DORIS C. "In Print Handwriting: Preventing and Solving Reversal Problems," *Elementary English,* XLVI (October, 1969), 759–764.

9. FERNALD, GRACE M. *Remedial Techniques in Basic School Subjects.* New York: McGraw-Hill Book Co., Inc., 1943.

10. FREEMAN, FRANK N. "An Evaluation of Manuscript Writing," *Elementary School Journal,* XXXVI (February, 1936), 446–455.

11. ———. "Language: The Development of Ability in Handwriting," *Child Development and the Curriculum,* Chapter XIII. Thirty-Eighth Yearbook of the National Society for the Study of Education, Part I. Bloomington, Ill.: Public School Publishing Co., 1939.

12. GIBSON, ELEANOR J. "Improvement in Perceptual Judgments as a Function of Controlled Practice or Training," *Psychological Bulletin,* L (November, 1953), 401–431.

13. HUEY, EDMUND B. *The Psychology and Pedagogy of Reading.* New York: The Macmillan Co., 1910.

14. KLAPPER, PAUL. *Teaching Children to Read.* New York: D. Appleton and Co., 1915.

15. PATRICK, G. T. W. "Should Children Under Ten Learn to Read and Write?" *Popular Science Monthly,* LIV (February, 1899), 382–392.

16. ROGERS, VINCENT R., ed. *Teaching in the British Primary School.* New York: The Macmillan Co., 1970.

17. SINGER, HARRY. "Research That Should Have Made a Difference," *Elementary English,* XLVII (January, 1970), 27–34.

18. SKINNER, B. F., and KRAKOWER, SUE-ANN. *Handwriting with Write and See* (Teacher's Edition). Chicago: Lyons and Carnahan, Inc., 1968.

19. WEED, KAY, and WATSON, PEARL. "Elect Creative Writing," *Elementary English,* XLVI (March, 1969), 295–299.

9

Teaching Reading: Whole Word Identification

At this point in the book various vocabularies have been considered. Chapter 6 gave attention to listening and speaking vocabularies and thus to the matter of helping children learn the meanings of words. The content of Chapter 7 had ability to write as its focus and so was concerned with writing vocabularies. This present chapter and also the following one deal with reading vocabularies.

FOUR VOCABULARIES

To restress connections among a child's four vocabularies, it might be helpful to list definitions as well as some further comments.

LISTENING VOCABULARY:

Comprised of those words whose meanings are understood when they are used by another.

SPEAKING VOCABULARY:

Comprised of those words which can be pronounced correctly and whose meanings are sufficiently understood by the child that he is able to use them himself. (These two requirements explain why a child's speaking vocabulary is consistently smaller than his listening vocabulary, a trend that continues throughout adulthood.)

WRITING VOCABULARY:

Comprised of those words which a child can spell and write and whose meanings are understood well enough that he can make selections from them when communicating to others. (The level of understanding thus required is comparable to what is demanded in speaking.)

READING VOCABULARY:

Comprised of those words which a child recognizes in their written form. "Recognition" includes meaning, for if a child can pronounce a written word—for instance, *gig*—but has no idea of what a gig might be, it can hardly be said that he is able to read it. Actually, the level of understanding required in reading is like that required in listening. When children and school instruction are the concern, correct pronunciation also enters into the definition of "reading vocabulary"; with adults, however, it is not essential. Foreign words, for example, commonly are read by adults in the sense that they recognize them and understand their meanings sufficiently well that comprehension of written material is not impeded. Ask these same adults to pronounce them, however, and some will be very reluctant to do so. The more honest and secure adults might even admit, "I'd have no idea of how one would say that."

The following classification is more explicit in highlighting some relationships just mentioned:

Receptive Language Arts	Expressive Language Arts
listening	speaking
reading	writing

Regardless of how one might choose to show and discuss relationships among the language arts, the important thing is that teachers recognize them not just in some theoretical way but in their classroom practices as well. Otherwise it is all too likely that a school day will end up being a series of seemingly unconnected activities, which is unrealistic but also inefficient.

Even though this and the next chapter single out the reading vocabulary for special attention, the hope is that you will continue to keep in mind the many ways in which instruction with the other three vocabularies contributes to it.

TEACHING PROCEDURES FOR THE READING VOCABULARY

At the start, the task of teaching children to read is one of helping them learn to recognize, in writing, words they have already learned to recognize and use in oral language. To effect this learning, two teaching procedures are available. One simply identifies words; for example, *baby* is printed on the chalkboard and the children are told, "This says 'baby.'" Or, to take another illustration, a child is outdoors walking with his mother, sees a sign and asks, "What's that word?" In response the mother says, "Stop." In both of these cases whole words were identified; thus whole word identification was the teaching procedure, used first by a teacher and then by a parent.

That telling a child what a word says is a teaching procedure—one commonly used in classrooms, by the way—does not seem to be universally known. I mention this because in the many interviews I have had with parents of children who learned to read before starting school, they commonly expressed the belief that nobody had taught them. For instance, it was not unusual to hear comments like, "He just learned by himself." A few parents even wondered whether reading might not be a natural ability for some children. Yet, when questioned further, these same parents told how they had spent time conversing with their young children, how the children had been so full of questions, and how they themselves had always tried to take the time to answer them. Among the early readers, of course, "What's that word?" was a common query. A common response was its identification. Expectedly, other instances of whole word identification at home often originated from sources like television commercials in which words flashed on the screen were read by a narrator.

There is still another way to develop reading vocabularies. Here I refer to analytical teaching procedures which help a child deal with parts of an unknown word in order to figure out what the whole of it is. If the analysis deals with the sounds its letters record, that would be a phonic analysis; if with larger pieces of a word (root, prefix, suffix, inflectional ending), that would be a structural analysis. Both types come under the heading of analytical procedures, which will be considered in detail in Chapter 10.

This present chapter only concerns itself with whole word identification, a procedure sometimes called "look-say" because of the assumption that its use will enable a child to look at a word and say (think) it without going through any type of analysis. It also is referred to as a "sight method" because, again, the expectation is ability to recognize (read) a word on sight. Regardless of the name assigned to it, the teaching procedure described in this chapter is one that deals with entire words.

SELECTING WORDS

Teaching always involves a series of decisions. When its aim is to develop reading vocabularies by using a whole word approach, one early decision concerns the selection of words. Which ones should be taught initially? Are some words easier than others?

By this point in the book it must surely be clear that the factor of interest ought to play an important role in word selections, and for an obvious reason: A child's interest in a word makes it easier for him to learn to read it. This, of course, is why it is rare to find a child who has difficulty remembering his own name—or, even, the name of his dog. In these cases interest is rooted in the appeal of the referents. At other times, however, it might relate to their specificity, which helps explain why words like *house* and *foot* are easier to remember than *was, there,* or *what.*

With other words appearance can create interest. For example, in response to *puzzle* I have watched as children became excited and made such comments as, "Wow! I've never seen a word that had so many *z*'s in it!" It would be safe to predict that a word like *hippopotamus* would also lead to some excitement. At still other times it is the sound of a word that is the attraction; this could be so for words like *waddle* or, for instance, *tinkle* or *pop* or *nibble.*

Unfortunately—as you might have already noticed—in all of this lies a dilemma; namely, the easiest words to learn often are the least useful, while the more difficult and uninteresting ones are constantly needed. Thus, a child could get along, though unable to read such words as *Christmas* and *bunny.* Take away his ability to read words like *the* and *with,* however, and he soon has problems.

What this suggests is that two criteria must be kept in mind when words are being selected for attention: interest *and* usefulness. There is, however, still another—one dealt with in detail in Chapter 7. This simply recognizes that a child should not be expected to learn to read a word if it has no meaning for him. With this in mind, initial selections for the reading vocabulary ought to be made from a child's listening vocabulary; more ideally, from his speaking vocabulary.

Admittedly, a totally unfamiliar word can sometimes play a role in reading instruction. For instance, I recall being in a room when the word "huge" was used by the teacher. Immediately one child asked, "What does 'huge' mean?" The teacher explained, and also wrote it on the board along with other words the children could read: *tall, big, fat.* As a result of this attention to both the meaning and appearance of "huge," two things could have happened—at least for some of the children. First, "huge" was added to their listening vocabulary and, perhaps, even to their speaking vocabulary. In addition, some might have also added it to their reading vocabulary. In spite of situations like this one, however, the best practice to follow, at least most of the time, is to select words whose meanings are already familiar. At the start, and because initial success is of critical importance to future success, it also is a good practice to concentrate on words that are of special interest. Later, when the children have experienced the genuine joy of their success, then it is time —and even necessary—to start introducing words which might not be very appealing but which are, in fact, basically important. And this leads to the need to mention what is commonly referred to as the *service words.*

"Service words" is the name given to 220 words selected decades ago by Edward Dolch, a reading specialist (8). He chose them as being especially serviceable or useful because of their frequent appearance in written material.* Some examples:

and	come	my	to
are	does	said	very
be	for	the	what
but	from	they	you

The words listed above were selected for attention now because they demonstrate the meaning of "serviceable" and, secondly, because they exemplify a characteristic of our language: The most frequently used words often are irregular in their spelling. Here, "irregular" refers to a discrepancy between the spelling of a word and the way it is pronounced. Some not-so-common words demonstrate irregularity (e.g., *chamois, indict, colonel*) but so, too, do words which children must learn to read fairly quickly because of the frequency with which they occur (e.g., *does, they, you*).

Thus far, three considerations have been mentioned as having relevance when decisions are made about the words that will be taught at the start:

Is the meaning of the word familiar?
Is the word of interest?
Is it useful?

On the basis of many classroom observations of children in the process of learning to read, still another guideline seems important when words are being selected. This stems from the frequency with which

* Because his list was compiled in the mid-1930s, it is likely that some of the 220 words no longer fit the description "most frequently used." Other selections have been proposed but, as yet, nothing has supplanted the Dolch list (12).

beginners confuse words similar in appearance (*was, saw*) or in sound (*park, part*), or in meaning (*look, see*). If children are to experience success in their first efforts to read—and this is most important—then this particular observation lends support to the wisdom of avoiding at the start words that are too much alike in any of the three ways just mentioned: appearance, sound, meaning.*

During the past decade or so, still another selection criterion has been getting attention: spelling patterns. This one has been highlighted by a few linguists who became involved in the development of instructional materials for children (4, 9). They point out that written American English shows frequent use of certain spelling patterns; they claim, therefore, that it is words from these patterns that ought to be selected for the beginning vocabulary. A common one is the *cvc* (consonant, vowel, consonant) pattern. Consequently words like *man, sit,* and *fed* would be considered appropriate choices at the start.

The sample materials reproduced on pages 252 and 253 show the use of spelling patterns in two beginning linguistic readers. Notice, though, how the same materials also demonstrate the almost immediate need to use high-frequency words (*to, the*) whose spellings and pronunciations fail to fit into any pattern.

Those who are currently advocating use of spelling patterns claim it will facilitate learning to read by quickly allowing children to use the patterns to identify words not directly taught. Without this approach, they emphasize, the child fails to see the amount of regularity in our language and thus fails to achieve the independence that is so important for identifying unfamiliar words.

Critics of this approach have something to say too, of course. They quickly point to the irregular spellings of highly important words and, for instance, to the observation that using patterns leads to texts whose content often is uninteresting and, sometimes, sheer nonsense. Some also raise questions about accepting a methodology for teaching beginning reading simply because it has been useful in linguistic study and research.

Actually, until objective evidence is available, not much can now be said about the value—or problems—of using spelling patterns as a selection criterion. Meanwhile, though, you ought to be familiar with the fact that some beginning readers do make use of them, whenever this is possible. Just how the use proceeds is explained in detail in the manuals accompanying these texts.

One further comment about word selection criteria needs to be made, especially for readers of this chapter who feel no need to think

* Once a child is able to deal with letter-sound associations, confusions are reduced.

The Pan

Nat!

Look at the pan.

The pan is on the mat.

Nat ran to the pan.

Nat can bat the pan.

33

From *Merrill Linguistic Readers,* Reader I, by Charles C. Fries, A. C. Fries, R. G. Wilson, and M. K. Rudolph, p. 33. Copyright 1966 Charles E. Merrill Publishing Co.

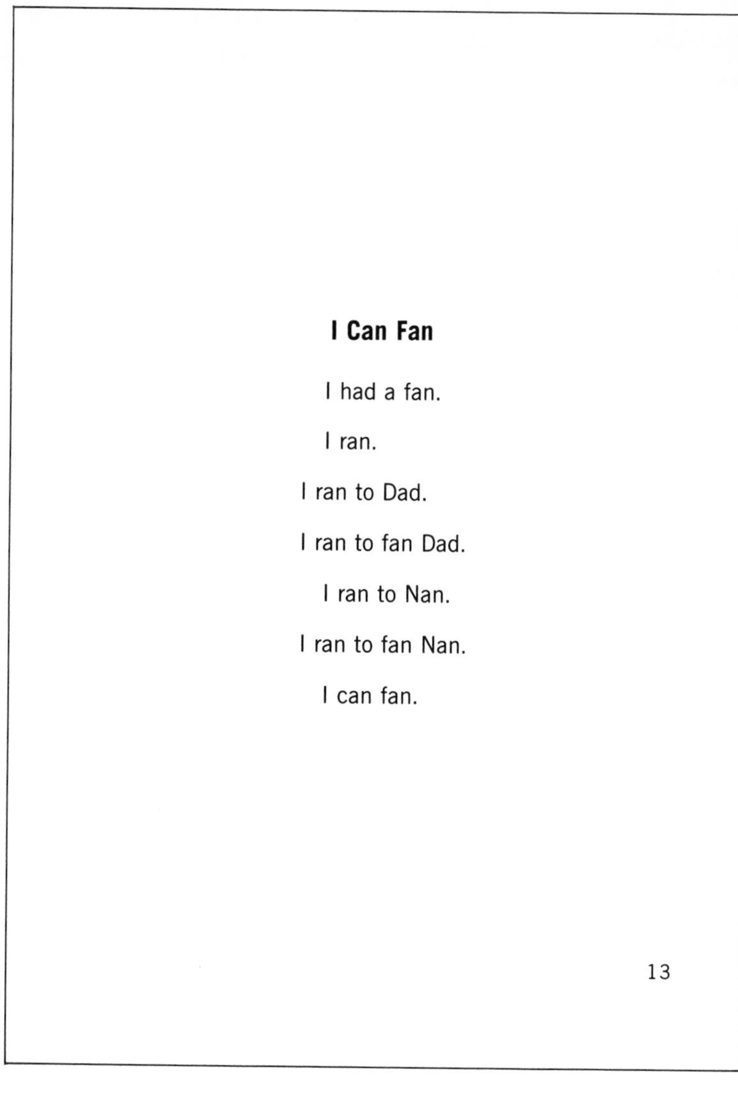

I Can Fan

I had a fan.

I ran.

I ran to Dad.

I ran to fan Dad.

I ran to Nan.

I ran to fan Nan.

I can fan.

13

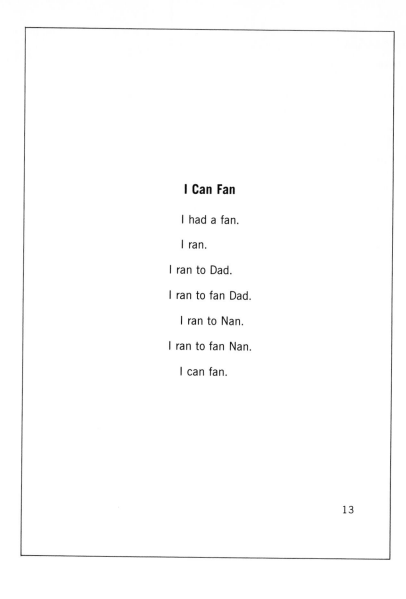

about such matters because they themselves simply teach the words that are in a basal reader. While it always is disappointing to find individuals who have this narrow view of teaching, even they can profit from the criteria that have been discussed. Some (e.g., Is the meaning of the word known?) help explain why certain words in textbooks are difficult for children to remember. Other considerations (e.g., Does the word have an unusual appearance?) offer possible explanations for the ease with which other words are learned. Still another criterion (Does the word deal with something that is of interest?) ought to be a reminder that commercial materials are never sufficient if only because their authors cannot take advantage of the particular interests of a particular group of children. Only their teacher can do that.

WHOLE WORD INSTRUCTION

Were this textbook being written in pre-television years, this section probably would be introduced with a sentence like, "After a decision is made that a certain word is to be taught, the next consideration is for the way it will be introduced." As it is, the sentence must be amended to suggest that the next consideration is to make sure the selected word really is new. I stress this because on so many occasions I have been in kindergartens and first grades in which words thought to be new were not. Once I watched as a teacher wrote *all* on a chalkboard. Before she had time to identify it a boy commented, "That's 'all,' the cold water detergent." In another room the teacher was introducing *my;* it happened that she first wrote it as *My*. Before there was time to write it again with lowercase letters a child said, "I know that. It says 'my.' It's on television in 'My Three Sons.'"

Television, of course, isn't the only productive teacher in the out-of-school lives of young children. In one kindergarten I watched as the teacher wrote *happy* on the board in preparation for making Mother's Day cards. She explained to the children that it was not a word they knew but was a good one for a greeting card. Before she could mention what it said one girl identified it with the explanation, "I can read that because my big sister told me what it says." In still another classroom the new word *hop* was immediately named by a girl who was quick to say she had seen it in the book *Hop on Pop*.

None of the foregoing observations is suggesting, of course, that in each classroom the words being introduced were familiar to all the children. They nonetheless point out that new words are not always new and, as a result, it is a good practice to ask, "Does anyone know what this says?" when calling attention to what is thought to be an unfamiliar word.

When a selected word really is unfamiliar, time needs to be given to a consideration of how it will be introduced. In its skeleton form, whole word methodology requires that it be written and identified. However, learning theory suggests still another basic requirement: *Be sure the children are looking at the word at the time it is being identified.** The message for teachers seems clear; namely, do not begin instruction until you have the children's attention. Without it, efforts to teach are doomed to failure or, at best, minimal success.

A simple way to get children to attend to a word is to have them name, spell, and rename it, once it has been identified. This can be done along with other procedures designed to make the word interesting and thus more likely to win attention. Below are some descriptions of what a few teachers did to make word-learning attractive:

> *see*
> Played game called "I See." (Described an object in the room, after which the children tried to guess its name.) Midway through the game, suggested it would be a good idea to find out what "see" looked like and printed it on the chalkboard. Children read and spelled it. Throughout the rest of the game, periodically called their attention to *see*. At the end had it renamed and spelled.
>
> *blue*
> First called attention to *blue* with a bulletin-board display of blue pictures, each labeled *blue*. The children discussed them and read all the labels. Concluded by naming and spelling *blue*. (Later, a card on which *blue* had been printed was added to a color chart that was gradually evolving. Next to it went a piece of blue construction paper.)
>
> *go, stop*
> Created the need to learn these two words by relating them to the walks we were going to take. Showed the children a sign I had made (attached to a yardstick) which I would hold up when I wanted them either to stop or go. (One side of the sign showed *go;* the other, *stop*.) Explained we could not begin taking walks outdoors until these words were learned. Each was written and identified, then placed on a bulletin board so that they could be named and spelled several times a day. Soon the walks began.

* For a very readable description of the way associative learning theory underscores the essential importance of this, see *The Psychology of Teaching Reading* by Anderson and Dearborn (1).

have

Introduced *have* in connection with a discussion of the children's possessions. Wrote and read "I have ———." (The word *I* was already familiar.) Explained that as each child mentioned something he had, I would print its name in the blank and he could read the whole sentence. Later, at art time, the same unfinished sentence appeared at the bottom of each child's paper. The children's job was to draw a picture of a favorite possession; mine was to print its name. As this was done, each child was asked to read the completed sentence on his paper.

snow

Took advantage of the first snowfall to introduce *snow*. Once it was identified the children renamed it and spelled it; they also counted the number of letters. This was done to find out how many snowballs (white circles) would be required to make the word *snow*. When it was decided there were four, I displayed four round pieces of white paper at the bottom of a bulletin board, printing on each a letter contained in *snow*. Then suggested they might want to make snow (chalk) pictures, which would be labeled with four smaller snowballs. As pictures were being finished each child received four round pieces of paper. After printing *s* on one snowball, *n* on another, *o* on another, and *w* on still another, the four pieces were pasted close together and in correct sequence at the bottom of the pictures. Later, the pictures were displayed on the bulletin board. To make sure labels were correct, those appearing on several were read, spelled, and approved by the children.

me

Distributed dittoed pictures of a clown holding a sign on which *me* was printed. Identified *me* for the children. Suggested the possibility of their making signs with the same label but, first, they would have to practice printing *me* so that it would look as good as the clown's printing. This was done at the bottom of the picture. Following the practice, small rectangular pieces of construction paper were distributed on which the children were directed to print *me*. Straws reinforced with pipe cleaners were passed out next. These were stapled to the rectangles; the result was a sign for every child and, hopefully, a new word for every reading vocabulary.

boy, boys, girl, girls *
Wrote and identified *boy;* then wrote *boys* and identified that:

Talked about the differences in appearance and meaning. Counted the boys in the room and wrote: *11 boys.* Followed the same procedure for *girl* and *girls.* Attention then went to a bulletin-board display of magazine pictures of children. Each was discussed; then the children decided on the label that would be appropriate for each. (Cards showing *boy, boys, girl,* and *girls* had been prepared and were displayed on the chalkboard ledge.) The children took turns making selections from the cards. The others checked their correctness and, when correct, named and spelled the selected label before it was thumbtacked to a picture.

Several important reminders about whole word teaching procedures can be found in these few sample descriptions of instruction. They point out that there are more interesting ways to teach a word than the "raw bones" procedure of writing and identifying it. They also demonstrate the usefulness of letter-name knowledge and, along with that, the close connections among reading, spelling, and writing. What they do not underscore, however, is that even with the most interesting and appealing instruction, a word generally needs to be practiced—that is, repeatedly identified—before it is firmly fixed in a child's sight word vocabulary. This is not always the case, of course. I personally have known children who never seemed to forget a word, once it was identified. However, they are exceptions. And because they are exceptions, the following section gives detailed attention to practice. Before reading it, you might want to examine the reproduced materials on pages 259

* Generally it is best to introduce one word at a time. However in this case the teacher knew she would be using *boys* and *girls* throughout the year as labels for the attendance-taking bulletin board. Thus she felt sure that after a year's exposure the children would be able to read these words and was unconcerned about the possibility that not all would learn them immediately. What is again being demonstrated is that for every rule about teaching (introduce one word at a time) there is at least one exception.

and 260. They show the suggestions of some manuals for introducing new words.

PRACTICE *

The point has been made repeatedly that instruction with new words ought to be maximally interesting. Similarly, the practice for making them a permanent part of a child's reading vocabulary should also be carried out in ways that avoid dullness. In addition, even though repetition is of the very essence of practice, excessive amounts should be avoided. Still other points about reading practice follow.

Use of Contexts

One point can be made in connection with a common query. I refer to the question, "Should new words be practiced alone or as parts of sentences?" Although initial attention goes to the word being introduced, putting it into a context—for instance, a phrase or sentence—also is important because a context reflects how reading is usually done. That is, it is much more customary to read words together rather than isolated from one another. A second and equally important reason to use contexts, both for instruction and practice, has been identified during visits to classrooms. Let me describe that reason now by relating a little of what has been observed.

In one room the teacher wrote *am* on the board—this was a new word—then read it for the group of children she was instructing. It happened that her pronunciation of *am* was very much like the name of the letter *m*, which generated a puzzled expression on one girl's face as well as the comment, "Mrs. ———, that's not just *m*. That's an *a* and *m*." Had this teacher chosen to read *am* and then to say something like, "We use this word all the time. For instance I might say, 'I am a teacher,'" the confusion probably would not have occurred.

The importance of contexts—but also of careful pronunciations—was underscored in another classroom in which *find* was being introduced. In this case, after the teacher had written and identified *find*, she asked for examples of sentences that used it. The one offered first was very revealing. With considerable pride a boy suggested, "It is a fine day."

* Earlier chapters also gave attention to practice. Page 236, for instance, enumerated some of the requirements of productive practice for writing. Because they have equal relevance for reading, you might want to take another look at those requirements now.

Bill will get something for *school.*
He wants *something blue.*
Did Jay get something for school?

Tell the children to read the story silently. Then ask someone to read it aloud. Have volunteers frame the review words as you say them.

Development of New Vocabulary

Context Clues

Present the title of the story, "A Coat for School," by writing it on the chalkboard. Explain that in the story both Bill and Jay have gone to buy something new for school. Call attention to the word *coat* in the title. Have someone read the title aloud.

> *Note:* Hereafter the term *present* will be used to indicate: (1) that the words, phrases, and sentences can be written in manuscript on the chalkboard; and (2) that as the word, phrase, or sentence is displayed, it is also spoken by you.

Present the following story on the chalkboard and have the children read it silently. Then call on someone to read it orally. Later have several children underline the new words as you say them.

A *Coat* for School

Bill went to a *store.*
What did he go for?
He went to get a *coat.*
Bill said, "I *like* that red coat."

Phonic Analysis

Write the words *boat, goat,* and *coat* in a column on the board. Have someone read them. Ask the children how they are alike and how they are different. Have someone underline the parts that are the same in the words. Have the differing initial consonants identified.

> *Note:* When introducing phonic sets words, write the new word under the known word on the chalkboard. Ask the children how the words look alike. Have someone read the words and tell how they sound alike. Discuss how the known word can be changed into the new word.
>
> In many cases, you may also wish to present the words in context.
>
> In introducing phonic sets words, elicit from the children as many words as possible that belong in the set. As they are given, write them under one another, and ask, in each case, "What letter am I going to write first?" (If the children suggest words that rhyme but are spelled differently, write them in a separate list. Ask how they are different from the others. Elicit that although they sound the same, they do not look the same.) Then write one or more sentences using known words, but including (at the end if possible) the new phonic sets word (for example, "Did you get

68 A Coat for School (6–9)

From Teachers' Manual for *Our School,* Sheldon Basic Reading Series, Centennial Edition, by William D. Sheldon, Q. B. Mills, M. C. Austin, R. A. McCracken et al., p. 68. © Copyright 1968 by Allyn and Bacon, Inc. Reproduced by permission of Allyn and Bacon, Inc.

to read both of these short, related stories as one assignment.

Enriching background for story sequence

Use cats as a topic for discussion, showing any available pictures of cats. Bring Velvet, the book children's cat, into the discussion. The pupils will remember Velvet from readiness activities.

2. Presenting Vocabulary

Place the word cards for *Billy, Bolo,* and *Velvet* at the bottom of the Display Stand.

Reviewing former experiences with *Velvet,* the cat

Velvet: Display Introductory Story Card 20. "What is this cat's name?" . . . "The name *Velvet* looks like this." (Indicate the word *Velvet* in the first line with a left-to-right movement.) "Who can read this sentence with the new word in it?" . . . Have the line read and the word *Velvet* underlined or framed.

"Can you find the card for *Velvet* here?" (Indicate the word at the bottom of the Display Stand.) . . . "Choose the card that says *Velvet.*" (Let the pupils find and underline the word *Velvet* in four places on the Introductory Story Card.)

Using sound when language cues do not discriminate

"Whose pet was *Velvet?*" . . . "Did Mary and Mike and Jeff have other pets?" . . . "Find the word *Billy.*" (Indicate the three cards at the bottom of the Display Stand.) . . . "Which card says *Bolo?*" . . . "Now can you read the names of all three of our book friends' pets." (The names *Billy, Bolo,* and *Velvet* are read as each one is indicated.)

Introducing capital and lower-case *v:* seeing the letter and hearing the sound

"Does anyone know the name of the letter with which *Velvet* begins?" . . . "That's right, *V*. We haven't had a word beginning with *V* before.

"Does *Velvet* begin with a big *V* or a little *v?*" . . . "Do you know why it begins with a big *V?*" . . . "Can you find a little *v* in *Velvet?*" . . . "Show it to me." (The small *v* is underlined or framed.)

242

From Teachers' Manual for *Opening Books, A Magic Box, Things You See,* by Albert J. Harris and Mae Knight Clark, p. 242. Copyright 1965 by The Macmillan Company.

Additional classroom illustrations could be given. However just the two already cited probably are enough to point out the significance of contexts and also of a teacher's speech when words are either being introduced or practiced.

When words are being practiced, the sole purpose is to help children remember them forever. Therefore as teachers make plans for practice, it is of basic importance that they understand what does and does not foster both correct and permanent recall. To achieve this understanding, one must first be familiar with what learning theorists call "cues."

Use of Cues

In the case of learning to read individual words, a cue is what is used to help establish an association or connection between a given stimulus (written word) and the correct response to it (what it says). Or, to put it somewhat differently, some aspect (cue) of a written word is selected as a prompt for its identification. If what is selected fixes the correct identification permanently, it would be considered a relevant cue. On the other hand, if it offers only temporary assistance or even leads to confusion and erroneous responses, then it would be irrelevant. With classroom examples, let me first point out some irrelevant cues; later, attention will go to relevant ones.

Not long ago a teacher was providing kindergarteners with practice in reading *red, blue,* and *green.* Thinking it would help, she wrote *red* with red chalk, *blue* with blue, and *green* with green. Predictably the children had no trouble "reading" the three words. Equally predictable, however, is that those children who had difficulty remembering *red, blue,* and *green* prior to this colorful practice session would have equal difficulty when they later found any of the three words in books or, perhaps, written with white chalk or black ink. Why? The teacher used an irrelevant cue (color) to help establish associations between visual stimuli (words) and the correct responses to them.

Examples of other kinds of irrelevant cues have been found in connection with initial instruction, which suggests a reason why subsequent identifications (practice) are required. Once a teacher was heard to say of *look,* "This word is easy to remember. It says 'look' and it has two eyes in the middle of it—just what you use to look." While such a cue might help for a while, use of it leads only to confusion later on; specifically, when words like *took* or maybe *room* have to be learned. "Two eyes," then, is an irrelevant cue because it does not offer the child permanent help in remembering that *look* is the symbol for the familiar word "look."

In another classroom, *monkey* was a new word in a story the children were to read. To help them remember it, the teacher wrote it, said it was the word for "monkey" and, like a monkey, had a tail at the end. Unfortunately, so does *donkey*—and *money* and a long list of other words not one of which says "monkey." Thus, the "tail at the end" is another example of another irrelevant cue.

It wasn't too long ago that commercial materials were encouraging teachers to stress still another type of irrelevant cue; in this case I refer to the use of configuration as an aid in correct word identification. By "configuration" is meant the shape or form of a word. For example:

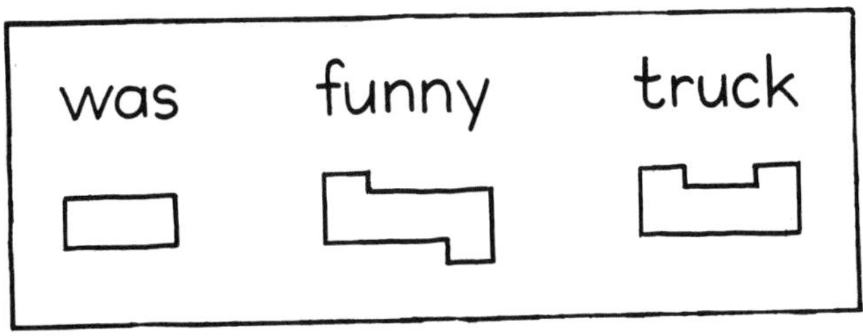

Like the other irrelevant cues that have been mentioned, configuration might offer children temporary assistance; however, so many words in our language have the same shape (*was, are; funny, fancy; truck, brush*) that use of shape for identification soon results in confusion and erroneous responses.

Like teachers and commercial materials, children have also been found using irrelevant cues. I recall one kindergartener who readily volunteered information about her strategy in remembering *Alexander*, the name of a book in the classroom library. She explained, "I always know that word because it has an *x*." In this instance such a cue might serve this child well for a long time because for a long time *Alexander* might be the only long word she will have to learn that has an *x* in it. Nonetheless, noticing one letter in a nine-letter word is to depend upon an irrelevant cue for identification.

This suggests still another type of irrelevant cue selected by children; namely, word length. Its use explains why a word like *something*, often taught early along with much shorter words, is so easily remembered—at least for a while.

Yet another irrelevant cue used by children is pictures—for example, the illustrations in their readers. Because manuals sometimes encourage teachers to encourage children to "look at the picture" when they cannot recall a word, pictures as cues in word identification merits further discussion.

That textbooks for young children are filled with pictures—and some of the newer ones are almost cluttered with them—is obvious to anyone willing to spend even a little time looking through their pages. Why this is so can be explained by a combination of reasons. One is that they add interest to a book. Another is the need for pictures to tell the story when limitations in the children's reading ability make a simple text mandatory.

Some fundamental questions could be raised about both of these reasons (14). For example, even though pictures add interest, might they not be distractions thus impeding progress in learning to read? Too, at a time when children know so few words, should instructional materials attempt to tell stories which depend almost entirely upon pictures? Regardless of important questions like these, the fact is that readers for beginners make generous use of pictures; therefore the question of immediate and practical significance is how they should be used.

How they should *not* be used is demonstrated by the teacher who says to a child having difficulty remembering *toys,* "Look at the picture." In this case the picture on the page shows a child playing with toys so, quickly, the puzzled reader says "toys" not even looking at the symbol *toys.** Predictably, the next time *toys* is encountered, the child will have the same problem remembering it because, in this case, the cue offered by the teacher (picture content) was not only irrelevant but also outside the word itself.

This negative response to an unfortunately common practice is not meant to deny the importance of pictures to instruction. As was noted many times in Chapter 7, pictures can be very valuable in specifying the meanings of words. Too, interesting pictures can often get children to talk—perhaps to tell stories about them. And I have also been in classrooms in which carefully selected pictures were highly successful in motivating children to write imaginative stories. Nonetheless, as cues for word identification they are irrelevant. That they are irrelevant is the reason some of the so-called "linguistic readers" either omit pictures or only include some which are unrelated to the content of the text.

Two other kinds of irrelevant cues, which also are outside the word itself, can be identified through teachers' comments. I refer to one like: "Here (pointing to the word *chair*) is the new word we had yesterday." With this, children do not even have to look at *chair;* all they have to do is recall the word introduced the day before. Still another irrelevant cue is offered by the teacher who, after writing the troublesome word *what* on the board, asks, "Does this say 'that' or 'what'?" in a way that gives such stress to "what" that even the slowest in the group is quick to respond with the correct answer.

With all the attention that has now been given to irrelevant cues,

* The frequency of this is sufficiently great as to warrant repetition of an earlier reminder: Be sure children look at a word *when* it is being identified.

you might be wondering what could possibly be left that might be relevant. One example of a relevant cue for the identification of a word is its letters and their sequence. This is why it is a worthwhile practice to have children name, spell, and rename a word—perhaps write it, too—once it has been identified. Other relevant cues relate to letter-sound associations, which is why the next chapter gives detailed attention to phonics instruction. In fact, what you will learn in the next chapter is that teaching the use of cues is what phonics instruction is all about.

Structural analysis also deals with cues. It takes advantage of the many words in American English that are comprised of roots plus affixes (prefixes and suffixes) and of roots plus inflectional endings (e.g., *s, es, ed, ing*). That such structures provide relevant cues for word identification is the reason for Chapter 10 to include detailed information about teaching structural analysis. Essentially, then, the next chapters will provide an abundance of information about helping children make maximum use of *relevant* cues. Meanwhile, it also is important to know how to make productive use of what has been called the whole word approach because there will be many times in the life of a beginner in reading when, either because of irregular spellings (*was, done, said*) or deficiencies in his analytical skills, words will have to be taught as wholes.

Stressed thus far is that whole words can be introduced in interesting ways, thus winning the children's attention at a time when it is of critical importance. It was also noted that even with the interesting teaching procedures, repeated identifications generally are a requirement. Just how much repetition or practice is necessary varies from word to word and from child to child; consequently no rules exist for the "right" amount. In fact, the only reliable guideline is that *some* practice usually is a necessity.

Samples of Practice

Because a most important part of any reading program is that which deals with practice, let me continue this discussion of whole word methodology by describing some of the interesting and productive kinds seen in classrooms.* The initial descriptions will show how individual words might get repeated attention; the later ones center on groups of words.

A "flashcard technique" (word card is held up and the children say what the word is) hardly is exciting; yet, with the help of a little embellishment, I have watched children enjoy it. This is what a few teachers did to make sure there was enjoyment:

* Other samples were described on pages 85–89.

Made a paper Jack-o'-lantern (two dimensional) with large cut-out eyes. Strip of heavy, narrow paper was fixed so that it could be pulled through them. Words in need of practice were printed on the strip which showed one word at a time as it was moved through the eyes.

Cut out baby ghosts from white construction paper; printed a a word on each. All were placed in a "trick or treat" bag (ordinary grocery bag), then taken out one at a time for the children to identify.

Prepared bingo-like cards on which words were printed. Used for "word bingo."

Each child in a small group received three envelopes labeled: Color Words, Number Words, Size Words. After the labels had been read and discussed, each child was given a number of small, rectangular pieces of construction paper on which words had been printed (e.g., *blue, three, little*). The assigned task was to read each silently and place it in the appropriate envelope. Afterwards, the group read the words in all the envelopes to see whether everyone's decisions had been correct.

From newspaper headlines cut out service words like *the, of,* and *have*. Pasted them on a large sheet of cardboard in random order making a design. Used the sheet for word practice and to encourage the children to make designs from known words found in newspapers and magazines at home. (Stressed the importance of parental permission before the cutting could begin.) Subsequently some of the children brought their own designs to school, which were displayed on a bulletin board. This encouraged still others to be word hunters and to bring in their collections. These allowed for still more practice.

Played a record that tells about seven puppies, each named after a day. As the narrator discussed a puppy (e.g., *Sunday*) I held up a card displaying his name.

When viewed by the children as a means toward a sought-after goal, even an *un*adorned use of flashcards becomes attractive as well as productive. For example, with the help of an explanation for its use, children can come to see straightforward practice as a way to be successful with subsequent activities like these:

Write words in a numbered list on the chalkboard. (All would have been practiced beforehand with flashcards.) Let the children take turns selecting numeral cards from a grab bag (ordinary paper bag). The numeral chosen by a child indicates the word on the board he is to read. If successful he gets to keep the card; if not, it goes back into the bag. (Getting to keep something seems to be of great importance to young children, which turns an ordinary activity like this into something of considerable interest.)

At Christmastime make simple stockings for each child out of inexpensive net-like material. (Depending on the children, these might also be made by them.) Paper cookies can be cut out and on each a word printed. Following flashcard practice with the same words, children get a chance to name a cookie. If successful, the cookie goes into their stocking; if not, into the teacher's. (As these special practice periods come to a close just before Christmas, things can be manipulated in such a way that no child is left with a too-empty stocking. The hope for all the children is that the cookies will be played with and read at home during the Christmas holidays.)

Similar practice sessions can be used just prior to the spring vacation. At that time the children might make paper Easter baskets. Filling them would be accomplished by correctly identifying words, this time printed on paper eggs and paper chicks. (Once again, flashcard practice would precede these special sessions and would be explicitly identified as a means for being successful in getting to keep eggs and chicks. Thus, an interesting activity becomes a reason to work hard at a less appealing one.)

Before moving on to additional illustrations of reading practice, it might now be timely to consider what has been a common, even traditional routine in classrooms occupied by young children. I refer to the labeling of objects. For example, a card on which *door* has been printed is attached to the door; a card showing *pencils* is attached to a box of pencils; or, perhaps, the materials in a table display are identified with labels. What is the value of this?

If, at the start of the year and in the presence of the children, a teacher prints some labels, reads them, and then attaches them to appropriate objects, the children might be learning—presuming this has not already been learned—that the strange looking things we call "words" say things which are quite familiar. Thus, labeling is a way of demonstrating that written language is not as foreign as it might at first appear to be. The important question to be asked about all of this: Are children really in need of such help, especially when television and in particular television commercials are such a constant part of their everyday lives? With most children, such a need is unlikely.

Another purpose which labeling might serve relates to the topic of this chapter. Consequently it is fitting to ask whether there is any hope that children will recognize *door* and *pencils* when they appear in other surroundings—for example, in a book. In this case the answer depends upon the teacher; more specifically upon what else she decides to do with labels in addition to displaying them on appropriate objects. If her decision is to do nothing extra, then it is not likely that the children will be able to read such labels as *door* and *pencils*. I say this because of what is sometimes referred to in learning theory as the "principle of least effort." Applied to labeling the principle suggests that children are more apt to attend to the objects than to the more demanding details of the words that are their names. Also suggested by everyday observation is that labels eventually blend in with the total classroom environment becoming, if not invisible, not eye- or mind-catching either.

In summary, these various comments point out that teachers who want words on labels to become a part of children's reading vocabularies must make plans for them to be practiced when not affixed to the objects they name.

As reading vocabularies grow, whether through labels or something else, an increasing number of opportunities to practice with groups of words becomes available. Even with the groups, however, individual words can still be selected for special attention. Thus, if a word like *it* is causing problems for certain children, something like the following can be typed (primer-size type), duplicated, and distributed:

```
        See It Go
Look, boys and girls.
Come and see it.
It is blue and white.
See it go.
It will go up now.
It is a ___.
```

Reaching the final line is a time for the children to think of a possible referent for *it*. (*Jet* had been selected by the teacher.) If the sound of *j* is familiar, that letter could be proposed as a help. Or, if the children know the sound recorded by *j* and can also read a word like *get*, then initial consonant substitution could be employed to figure out the answer quite independently of any help from a teacher. All she would have to do is to write *jet.**

In one classroom that was visited it happened that the teacher was giving special attention to the word *family;* this was accomplished with sentences but also with the help of an art project. Prior to the project the children's families had been discussed and the word *family* itself written and identified. Then, to provide further practice, the teacher distributed oval frames (paper cut out to look like an oval picture frame) which the children pasted toward the top of large sheets of paper. The number varied according to the makeup of each child's family. (No pets allowed.) Within each frame the children drew pictures of family members, including themselves. After labeling each portrait (*brother, sister, mother, father, me*) copies of the following were distributed, read, and attached to the bottom of the pictures:

```
My name is ___.
This is my family.
My family is here.
See my family.**
```

How art and reading practice go hand in hand also is demonstrated in the reproduced materials shown on pages 269 and 270. In each case the art work was done by a kindergartener. With these younger children, by the way, it has been found helpful to number sentences. This helps them keep their place; it also helps with finding a particular line of text, should that be required. Another common device for helping children keep their place is a paper marker (a rectangular piece of paper). When placed beneath the line being read, markers can cause comprehension problems when sentences are longer than a line. For that reason, when they are used they should be placed just above the line being read.

The use of numbered lines, along with children's art, is illustrated on pages 271 and 272. Page 273 shows a one-page book about "Poor Cat." In this case the cover was drawn by a teacher; however the children could have illustrated their own covers, once they had read of the poor cat's plight.

* These details are added here to remind you that even though separate chapters give attention to whole word identification and to word analysis skills, the two commonly work together in a classroom. How, in fact, they do work together to produce quickly growing vocabularies should be clear by the end of the next chapter.

** One caution about typed, dittoed material: In addition to using the larger primer-size type be sure, too, that all letters are distinct and clear. Too often beginners in reading have difficulty with dittoed material because not all the words are clearly printed. The inevitable result is needless questions and problems.

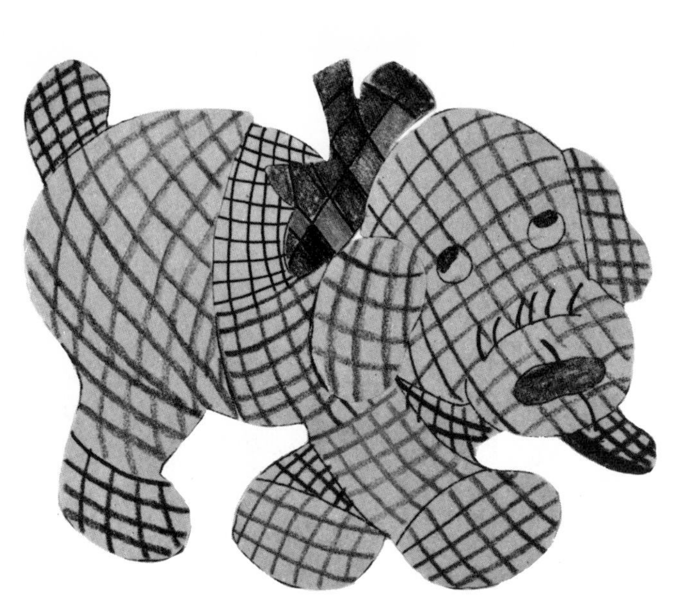

THE TOY DOG

I like the dog.

The dog likes to play.

I like to play.

Come and see the dog.

The dog sat here.

The dog is a toy.

NAME ______________________

IT IS THURSDAY

Today is Thursday.

Come and see all the boys and girls.

The boys and girls like to play.

"I like to jump," said Rita.

"I like to hop," said Becky.

"All the boys and girls like to come to school," Paul said.

I See Something

1. I see something.
2. "It can jump," said Tom.
3. It can jump up and down.
4. The something can go fast.
5. "It likes to play," said Kane.
6. My something is funny.
7. It is my dog.

Come With Me

1. I see something.
2. Look boys and girls.
3. I want to ride.
4. See me ride up and down.
5. See me jump.
6. See me jump fast.
7. "Come ride with me," said Diane.
8. See me ride the funny merry-go-round.
9. It is yelllow, green, red and blue.

1. I like my cat.
2. My cat likes me.
3. My cat is yellow.
4. She likes to eat fish.
5. She likes to drink milk.
6. She likes to go up a tree.
7. She can not come down.
8. Poor cat!

Curriculum areas other than art also offer natural opportunities for reading practice. Instruction in mathematics, for example, might sometimes include exercises like the one below and, in the process, give attention to important words such as *is* and *are:*

2 balls are red.
1 ball is green.
2 and 1 are __.
2 + 1 =

Music is particularly rich with opportunities for reading practice.* Cards like the following, combined with appropriate music, can be a source of enjoyment but also of reading practice:

Hop, boys and girls.

Now jump and jump.

Will you walk now?

Activities selected to extend children's listening-speaking vocabularies also have potential for reading. Using her words, let me describe how one teacher made the most of a trip to a hatchery:

> I began by reading a story called *The Wonderful Egg*. This, I felt, would create interest in the trip and also prepare the children for what they were to see. What they did see gave specific meaning to words like "hatchery," "incubator," and "temperature."
>
> For this trip I took along my polaroid camera. Use of it at the hatchery allowed for an interesting bulletin-board display of photographs, prepared in time for the children to enjoy the next day. After the pictures had been carefully examined ("Where am I?" was the most popular question) I mentioned that a visitor might wonder what the pictures were all about. This led to a group-composed description, which I first printed on the chalkboard:

* Other possibilities in connection with music were described on pages 81–84.

Look and see the baby chickens.
Look and see the boys and girls.
Come and find me.*

On the following day the same three lines of text appeared at the bottom of the bulletin-board display. Later, at art time, each child was given a sheet of white paper folded once so as to allow for a four-page book, the first page being its cover. Printed at the bottom of the three following pages was one line from the descriptive text. Each became a caption for a page. Above each, appropriate drawings were made by the children. The result was little books which they enjoyed taking home to show their parents.

Important Reminders about Practice

What this teacher's account and the other examples of practice have been demonstrating—this point was made earlier (pp. 80–84) but merits repetition—is that reading practice goes on at times other than the period specifically set aside for reading instruction. In fact, it is correct to say that teachers ought to be constantly looking for interesting ways to bring reading and children together. Whether they occur at "reading time" or some other is much less important than that they do occur.

Together, all the foregoing examples either identify or imply other important reminders about practice. Let me make them explicit now.

Work with Small Groups. Some of the practice necessary to achieve permanent recognition of words will be written. That is, instruction will center on a certain word or words, then a written assignment follows for the purpose of helping the children remember them. Other written assignments also will be going on in connection with related skills such as writing and spelling. Even a subject like beginning mathematics has its need for written work.

Times when some children are occupied with written practice or assignments provide opportunities to carry on the most fruitful kind of practice for beginning reading: teacher directed. These sessions should

* A reminder about board work used with beginners: Be sure to leave ample space between words. I have seen children bewildered by words printed much too close together.

occur close to the time when words have first been introduced. They should also be scheduled as often as circumstances allow.*

The examples of practice, both in this and earlier chapters, offered a variety of ideas for what might be done during teacher-supervised sessions. Only indirectly, however, did they point out the importance of carrying them on with small groups rather than, for instance, a whole class. That makes this detail a topic for discussion now.

Generally speaking, small-group practice always is more fruitful than when large numbers are involved; however, with young children the small groups could almost be called mandatory. I say this because of the number of times I have been in classrooms when a potentially good idea for practice deteriorated, simply because too many young children were involved. This is not to suggest that one certain number always is the best. Rather, it is to point out that it is difficult for young children to become involved when a member of a large group. For them, things must be more direct and even personal. The lesson in this? When making plans for teacher-supervised practice, use as small a group as circumstances allow because, generally speaking, the fewer the children the more productive the practice will be.

Just having small numbers, of course, is no guarantee that practice will be personal and of the kind that readily interests young children. This point was underscored recently during a visit to a second grade. In this instance the teacher was working with a group of seven children. However, she was at the board while they sat at a table fairly far from it. The result? Most of the time it seemed as if the teacher was talking to herself. The solution? Bring the table close to the board, creating a more personal and intimate environment.

Let me make the same point with still another classroom illustration, this time from a first grade. Here the teacher was sitting at a small table working with just two boys. They were much slower at learning than all the others in the class; therefore the need to work with them alone was very apparent. But what was happening? One side of the table was next to a wall while the teacher plus the two boys sat together on the opposite side. The result? Anything but a personal, intimate approach as the three faced the wall. The solution? Again there was a simple one. Pull out the table. Have the boys sit on one side with the teacher facing them. Result? Many opportunities for "eyeball-to-eyeball attention," a kind often required with slow or restless children.

* As adults we assume that children like to work with a teacher rather than alone. For that reason, the recent comment of a parent was especially interesting. Her daughter was a first grader and her only complaint about school was having her work interrupted by the need to "go up with the teacher." As she put it, "That reading class sure does mess up my work."

I have been in other classrooms when something else reduced the likelihood of achieving the direct and personal approach that is so significant with the younger ones. Here I refer to what seemed like a teacher's total dependence upon a manual.* In fact, repeatedly I have seen attention to manuals assume greater importance than attention to the children being instructed. One result? A learning situation that was stilted and impersonal, but also one that might just as well have been carried on with the entire class.

Make Decisions in Relation to Needs. Earlier pages gave attention to some possible procedures for word identification practice; however, in a classroom two other concerns come first: (a) *what* to practice, and (b) with *whom*. Generally, answers to these two questions combine into still another reason to work with less than a total class. I refer to the fact that only rarely will all its members have need for the same practice at the same time. Thus, there are pedagogical as well as psychological reasons for small-group work.

Once a teacher is aware—this awareness derives from children's oral and written responses—that certain ones are in need of a certain kind of practice, then she is ready to prepare for it. That is, the goal of the practice has been defined (e.g., ability to distinguish between *was* and *saw*, *look* and *like*, *what* and *that*) and the children selected. The job remaining is to choose an activity (means) that will help these children achieve the ability to read *was, saw, look, like, what, that*. Any means that gets them to this goal is "good"; any that does not should be abandoned—even when it seems "interesting" or "inventive." This latter point is deliberately highlighted, by the way, because classroom observations constantly reveal how easy it is for teachers to become so involved with the means for achieving a goal that the goal itself is forgotten. (Interestingly, this is especially characteristic of conscientious teachers.) This prompts the suggestion that one of the best habits a teacher can adopt is to constantly ask herself, "*Why* am I doing what I'm doing." Honest answers can be extremely productive in improving instruction.

Adopt a Diagnostic Attitude. Having a diagnostic attitude is another way to bring about constantly improving instruction. For teacher-directed practice sessions this means a conscious and continuing effort to learn what children can and cannot do. (Keeping a notebook close at hand is helpful in recalling what was observed.) Knowing what they cannot do is to be able to plan intelligently for future instruction or further practice.

* Teachers' manuals will be discussed at greater length in a subsequent section of this chapter.

What is here being called a "diagnostic attitude" ought to be commonplace and, fortunately, is to be found in most classrooms. However in a few, things like wrong responses or muddled explanations become a reason for chastisement. This is unfortunate not only because it establishes an uncomfortable relationship between child and teacher but also because opportunities are lost for learning about what still needs to be taught, retaught, or practiced.*

A Summary

In theory, a distinction can be made between practice and instruction. During the on-going events of a day in a classroom, however, the two are more alike than different. Consequently this synopsis of what constitutes effective practice for word identification can also serve as a summary description of effective instruction.

With both, effectiveness is rooted in a teacher's awareness of the words that children do not yet know.** One or more are then selected as the focus for initial attention (instruction) and later attention (practice). What usually occurs is that more than one child needs to learn the same words at the same time; as a result, they are grouped. If it happens that a large number has need for the same instruction or practice at the same time, then it was suggested that not all receive it together—in this case not because of pedagogical factors but because of what might be called psychological considerations. I refer here to the very observable fact that young children have difficulty becoming involved and remaining attentive when members of a large group.

Once an appropriate goal has been selected and an instructional group established, the next important consideration is for the way the goal might be reached. The means some teachers selected to reach goals concerned with word recognition were described in earlier sections of the chapter under the headings of "Instruction" and "Practice." Because still other illustrations appeared in prior chapters, the point in need of attention now is the basic importance of not allowing these means to become ends in themselves. Such means-end confusion can be common in classrooms, generally leading to time being wasted on activities that have little educational significance in the sense that they fail to achieve what children need to learn. To maintain a correct perspective, it was suggested that teachers get into the habit of frequently asking, "*Why* am

* For a more detailed discussion of this diagnostic attitude see pages 150–151.

** Word files are one way to keep track of who knows what. With this, each child has a word card box (shoe box) for the words he knows. These collections keep a teacher informed and also help the children learn about alphabetical order. When they are writing, the file can be used for spelling checks.

I doing what I'm doing." Inevitably, honest answers will lead to better reading programs.

COMPREHENSION

Earlier in this chapter, when selection of words for the reading vocabulary was being discussed, the point was made that it is only words whose meanings are familiar that ought to be considered. Such a recommendation was made for two reasons: (a) when a child pronounces written words that have no meaning for him, he is not really reading but only "word calling," and (b) at the beginning, the task of learning to read should not be made unnecessarily difficult by joining the need to learn what a written word says to the need to learn what it means.

Implicit in all of this is the importance to reading of the listening-speaking vocabulary. Also implied is the basic importance of comprehension for reading. Because comprehension is, in fact, of the very essence of reading and, secondly, because it periodically becomes a source of controversy (6), this section of the chapter gives additional and explicit attention to it.

Beginning and Advanced Levels of Reading

What must be immediately stressed about comprehension is that instructional tasks related to it are one thing at the beginning level but something else at more advanced levels. Let me clarify this with illustrations.

When a child is just a beginner in reading, his basic job is to learn to recognize in their written form words he would know were they spoken. Beginning reading, then, is concerned with a shift from spoken language to its written counterpart. More specifically, the beginner must learn to deal with such written words as *Go to the door* or *This is a red toy* just as he would were these same words being spoken. At this early level, therefore, his main job is not one of learning to comprehend or understand something totally unfamiliar but of learning to remember the recorded form of words that are part of an already familiar oral language. What all of this suggests is that beginning instruction is primarily concerned with helping children learn to remember familiar words presented visually. Being suggested, too, is that the child most likely to succeed at this level is one who has a good memory as well as a good command of oral language.*

* The latter prerequisite identifies some of the reasons why children from lower socioeconomic backgrounds have trouble learning to read. Generally their oral language is different from what might be called "book language." In addition, listening-speaking vocabularies are small relative to those of children from more advantaged backgrounds.

What about the more advanced stages? What are the main instructional tasks when children are reading more difficult material? Answers are to be found in the material. What it shows is that reading ability now is very much like thinking ability. That is, even if a child is able to pronounce all the words on a page and is even able to tell the meanings of most or all of them, he still might not be successful in reading the page unless he also is able to think like and with the author.

This very point was made not long ago through a conversation overheard on a bus. A man was speaking to an acquaintance or friend and lamenting, "I'm really getting concerned. I can't even read some of the reports that land on my desk." He went on to explain how, although a physicist, none of his preparation included courses in nuclear physics which now dominated the work in his office.

It could be asked: Does the solution to this worried employee's problem lie in his taking a reading course? Probably not. A more likely source of help would be a course or courses that would enable him to think like a nuclear physicist. Applied to children this might suggest that one of the reasons too many of them never get much beyond beginning levels in reading is that the school continues to teach reading when what it ought to be concentrating on in the middle and upper grades is thinking ability. Unfortunately, too little is still known about thinking while even less is known about how to enhance it in children (17). To know more would be to know much more than we now do about teaching children to comprehend more difficult materials.

Meanwhile, there should at least be more frequent recognition of the dependence of advanced reading upon thinking ability. The following, written by Schneyer after reviewing some research reports, is cited because it is a relatively uncommon observation.

> These studies suggest that underlying mental abilities such as abtract thinking or conceptualization are highly associated with successful reading performance, particularly at upper grade levels, and that one important cause of reading retardation may be lack of development of conceptualizing abilities. It appears possible that, in some cases at least, reading performance may be improved by development of underlying mental abilities even in the absence of reading instruction (15, p. 57).

This emphasis on thinking ability at later levels in reading is not meant to deny its significance for the beginner. At this level, too, thinking is called for but is elicited more often by the question, "What is this word?" than by the concern, "What does all this mean?" In fact, if the latter is a constant concern among beginners, it is possible that instruction should shift away from reading toward concentrated help with oral language. Another possibility is that the material is just too difficult and ought to be replaced with simpler material that deals with familiar things.

To emphasize that meaning or comprehension should be a concern at the beginning levels as well as the later ones, samples of practice dealing with that will now get attention.

Samples of Comprehension Practice

In one way at least, children learning to read are like a beginner studying a foreign language; both are taken up at the start with the job of remembering what individual words say. In the process, it is sometimes difficult to keep track of what the words mean when assembled into phrases, sentences, and paragraphs. This is why comprehension practice ought to start with small groups of words. For example a teacher might say to the children, "Put your hands" and then show cards alternately displaying written directions like:

under your chair

on the table

up to the sky

Watching responses is to check on comprehension.

Assignments done by children working alone might also deal with some brief word groups. For instance a sheet like the following on page 282 could be used. With this, the job for the children is to cut out the words in the first column and paste them in one of the other two. (When initially assigned, it would be wise to first carry on a similar exercise orally to make sure the nature of the task is understood.)

	Where?	When?
in September		
now		
across the street		
in the house		
on the table		
there		
on Friday		

Another type of independent assignment might begin by having the children read something like:

```
This is a toy.
It is orange and yellow.
It can go up and up.
Boys play with it.
Girls can play with it too.
```

In this case the task for the children is to draw a picture of the toy described. (Because assigned tasks ought to affect how children do their reading, they should be announced before the reading begins.)

Something like magazine pictures can also help with comprehension. For instance, cards like these might be prepared:

a white and red ball

the round blue ball

three little white balls

For this comprehension practice, appropriate pictures would be displayed along a chalk ledge. Children would take turns reading a card and placing it with the matching picture. Later, the same procedure might be used with larger groups of words—as large as paragraphs.

Before still other examples of comprehension practice are given, it might be timely and even necessary to point out the distinction between the use of pictures just referred to and the one criticized earlier. Earlier in the chapter, when cues were being discussed, teachers were urged not to use pictures as a prompt for word identification. They were thus discouraged from saying "Look at the picture" when a child was having difficulty recalling a word. That recommendation was made because, for word identification, pictures are irrelevant cues. As a check on comprehension, however, they can be very useful as children match their content with that of written material.

Also useful when comprehension is the concern are the children's names. Just inserting them into sentences like the following can make comprehension practice surprisingly attractive:

Becky, walk to the door and back.

Stand up, David. Then sit down.

Jerry, would you get the book on the table and bring it to me?

Paul, please give something to Anne.

It should be noted here that checks on comprehension like those being described are maximally beneficial only when teachers make sure that all the children involved have the opportunity to see what one among them is both reading and, in the example just cited, doing. More generally, the reminder is to make sure *all* are able to see and thus to read what is being practiced.*

To make practice sessions maximally productive, it also is a good idea to have the material printed on cards or, perhaps, a large sheet of paper *prior to* a session. In fact, to have to take the time to write sentences on the board or to compose them with individual word cards is to waste time. When done while children wait, it can also be a way to lose their attention. With young ones, it should be remembered, instruction that is effective keeps things moving.

Questions and Comprehension

Asking questions about what was read is a very common—perhaps too common—classroom procedure for checking on comprehension. Sometimes, especially at a beginning level when material of necessity is ex-

* The importance of this point warrants another reading of pages 146–147.

tremely simple, it ends up being much-to-do about nothing. After all, do two simple sentences merit ten questions? Usually not. In addition, when asked of every two lines, questions become an unnecessary interruption rather than something that makes reading "meaningful." With this in mind, the first point to be made about questions is: Don't ask them just to be asking questions.

The second point to be made about some of the questions asked of children is that they really do not deal with reading. This is not to say they should never be asked, but it is to point out that teachers ought to relate questions to instructional goals. That is, decisions about goals (e.g., ability to note details) need to be made before others are made about what will be asked (e.g., How many balls did Peter have?). Many of the questions now heard in classrooms probably are serving some purpose but not any directly concerned with reading. Others are so inappropriate in relation to the material being read that they only waste time—time that could be profitably used for the further extension of listening, speaking, and reading vocabularies.

While reading vocabularies are still very small, language comprehension can get attention through questions about oral as well as written material. For example, a teacher might say or read something like:

> It was cold. Ed ran and
> went out the door. He
> played in the snow.

Subsequently she could ask such direct questions as, "What did Ed do?" and such inferential ones as, "Was he wearing a coat?"

Even at the beginning level, questions—again either about written or spoken material—can begin to help children make a distinction between fact and opinion. Paired sentences like the following, for instance, are useful for this:

> The girl's dress is red.
> The girl's dress is pretty.
>
> This book has 100 pages.
> This book is too long.

Riddles suggest other kinds of queries that can help with comprehension. A series of simple, written questions like, "What has legs but cannot run?" would not be too difficult for beginners. (For teachers who run out of ideas, many riddle books are available commercially.)

Still other questions—for instance, "Could you hear this?"—might be posed in relation to brief material like:

A clock telling time
Bugs walking
A fence running around a house

What all these illustrations point out is that interesting comprehension practice can be offered to beginners in forms they can handle. They also demonstrate that it can parallel the tasks of the more advanced reader as he is required to comprehend main ideas and details; note sequence; recognize inferences; distinguish between fact and opinion; and so on. That the bulk of comprehension practice now carried on with beginners continues to be the uninteresting who-said-this and who-said-that type is both unnecessary and unfortunate.

INSTRUCTIONAL MATERIALS

In this present chapter, but also in earlier ones, attention was given to materials that can be used for developing reading vocabularies. What might be called homemade materials generally were highlighted, and this was not unintentional. It was designed to show how homemade things can turn the process of learning to read into something that is very personal and interesting. The attention also should have demonstrated that the widespread use of nothing but commercial materials is unnecessary and, with young children, even questionable.

That commercial materials in the form of basal readers predominate in classrooms throughout the United States is an established fact (3, 6). This makes it important not only to describe them but also to comment about how they might be *profitably* used. First, the description.

Basal Reader Series *

A basal series is comprised of readers and workbooks for the children and manuals for the teacher.

The Readers. Even if you have never taught it is likely that you are at least vaguely familiar with the readers, having used them as a child. I say this because they have been *the* instructional material over several decades and because during the same period of time they have changed relatively little. For instance, they still constitute a series of successively more difficult readers beginning with the short, soft-cover books called *preprimers.* (Prior to the preprimers are the readiness workbooks, dis-

* Every basal series has so many authors that each is customarily identified with a reference to the publisher's name.

cussed in Chapter 3.) These preprimers—usually there are three—still try to tell stories and still depend upon pictures to do this. Most often, in fact, children can "read" a story merely by looking at the pictures.

Following the soft-cover preprimers is the first hard-cover book, the *primer*. After this comes what is usually referred to as the *first reader*. Traditionally, this collection of materials (preprimers, primer, first reader) has been considered a suitable amount of material for the average child to read during first grade. In grade two and grade three it has been customary to have two readers; for grades four to six, one reader each. Some of the basal series also include a reader for grade seven and another for grade eight.*

Achieving successively more difficult material is accomplished, first of all, through a *controlled vocabulary*. This refers to the practice of introducing new words slowly and systematically and of repeating them on subsequent pages and in subsequent readers of the series. In the more difficult books, such control is less than what would prevail in the easier ones. That is, many more new words are introduced and they are repeated less often.

The length and complexity of sentences are other factors that affect difficulty. In the simplest of the basals, short and uncomplicated sentences are used; at the more advanced levels both their length and complexity increase. Content shows comparable changes. In the easier readers it is simple and supposedly related to the interests of younger children. Then, as texts become more difficult and the expected readers older and more able, content changes accordingly. These three variables (vocabulary, sentence structure, content) generally are proposed as the factors that govern *readability*. This term refers to the relative difficulty of written material, whether in basals or something else.**

Descriptions like "first grade reader" or, for that matter, "third grade reader" require some discussion, as do other and related ones—for instance, "first grade reading ability," and "third grade reading ability."

The important point to be made about the book descriptions is that one like "third grade reader" refers not to some very precise and unchanging level of difficulty but only to the placement of that reader

* In some of the newer editions of basals, descriptions like "preprimer" are being replaced by markings referring to levels. In one, for instance, Levels 1 to 10 (ten separate books) are described as its primary program, while Levels 11 to 13 constitute its middle grade program. Because descriptions like "preprimer" have been in use for so long, the newer manuals indicate the meaning of each level in relation to the older descriptions.

** Recent studies are uncovering more sophisticated factors that affect readability (5). What has been cited here, however, can still be considered a general picture of what makes one piece of written material more difficult than another.

in a given series. The practical meaning of this is that a third reader in one series can be easier—or more difficult—than the third in another. That this is so is reflected in the comments of teachers, for example, "I like to use the third reader in this series with my slower children because it's easier."

Descriptions like "first grade reading ability" or "third grade reading ability" also lack a single, unchanging referent. For example, "third grade reading ability" might refer to what is required to be successful with a third grade basal reader. Because what *is* required varies from series to series, so too does a description like "third grade ability." Even when such a description derives from a test score, it still lacks a single referent—and for a similar reason. To be assigned a given ability on the basis of one test might require something quite different from what it would take to be assigned the same ability on another one. Descriptions based on test scores also suffer from another source of variation. Many times, the ability displayed by a child in the process of taking a test is not his everyday ability because tests often bring out what might be called "peak performances." Consequently conclusions derived from them usually overestimate what a child can and will do in the day-by-day work of a classroom.

Criticism of Basal Readers. At the start of this discussion it was said that basal readers have changed relatively little during the many years they have dominated instructional materials. The changes that have been made were responses to criticisms; therefore to mention the critics' complaints is to discuss features of revised basals that make them different from prior editions.

How some series now designate readers is one change. Most still refer to them with labels like "first grade reader" and "third grade reader"; however, a few newer editions now merely number the books in their series. This change relates to the criticism that a label like "third grade reader" encourages third grade teachers to use that book with all her pupils, regardless of their particular abilities. The result, the critics rightly point out, is anything but individualized instruction. Still another reason for the change to numbers is that some kindergartens now teach reading. This creates problems for publishers when the easiest materials in their series have first grade labels.

A second very common criticism leveled at the easier basal readers concerned their use of stories that told of nothing but middle-class Caucasians living in suburbia. In this case, publishers' reactions were both widespread and highly visible during the 1960s. The most usual one was to show multiracial characters in illustrations, and to refer to urban settings in story content as well as in accompanying pictures (7). One of the best known among the series that appeared as a special response to the criticism of narrowness and even prejudice are the Bank Street Readers. A page from one of its books is reproduced on page 290. A less common but still noticeable accommodation to the same complaint has come in the form of animal stories replacing those that dealt with children.

A third but less vocal criticism of basal readers has led to a less pervasive change. This complaint has been coming from linguists and denounces the use of irregularly spelled words in beginning materials. In response, some series are showing more frequent use of spelling patterns. The most obvious examples are found in the readers now called "linguistic"; pages from two of them were reproduced earlier on pages 252 and 253.

Another attempt to deal with the imperfect correspondence in our language between spelling and pronunciation is found in the *i/t/a Readers*. (See page 291.) These use a contrived and augmented alphabet (initial teaching alphabet) that creates consistent correspondence between letters and sounds. Once a child experiences success in reading with this alphabet he shifts to materials employing the regular one, sometimes referred to by i/t/a people as "traditional orthography" or, simply, "t.o."

Value of Changes in Basals. As the various changes in basals were being described, it is possible and even likely that you wondered about their value. Have they resulted in better reading or, perhaps, increased interest? Unfortunately—as is true of so many questions about reading—factual answers are unavailable. What *is* available, and in great quantities, are publishers' advertisements, but such testimonials hardly add up either to reliable evidence or reliable answers. Various short-term studies have also been done but, because of common flaws, just about the same number either support or refute alleged contributions. As a result, all that can be done now is to describe some of the recent changes in basals. What their value is or might be remains unknown.

Teachers' Manuals. Each reader in a basal series is accompanied by a manual. The purpose of manuals is to show how the readers might be used to advance children's abilities. They do this by giving attention both to what to teach and how to teach it.

It is probably true that all the authors of manuals would be quick to say that what they propose are only suggestions; yet the way they make their proposals hardly suggests that. One result—and there are additional reasons for this—is the tendency of teachers to use manuals as if they were following a recipe in a cookbook. Everything is done. Nothing is changed. The consequence is instruction that is stilted and routine, im-

One, Two, Three, Go!

"Let's run to the store," said Ken.
"O.K.," said Max.
"One, two, three, go!"

The boys ran down the street.
They ran fast.

From *Around the City,* Teacher's Edition, by Bank Street College of Education, Bank Street Readers, p. 60. Copyright 1965 by The Macmillan Company.

the baull went up, up, up in the ær.
"lωk at the baull flie!" sed paul.
"lωk at it flie!"

21

From *Early to Read i/t/a Program,* Book 2, p. 21.

personal, and often boring. Still another unfortunate result is instruction that does not always correspond to what children need to learn. When all these things occur year after year, the total result can hardly be called "good education."

That manuals should be viewed only as a source of *possible* things to do is warranted by their flaws and shortcomings (6). For instance—and this is true even of the most recent manuals—they often urge teachers to ask too many questions about nothing, an unfortunate practice mentioned earlier in connection with comprehension. In addition, there is the tendency at beginning levels to give as much or even more attention to pictures than to words. Manuals also continue to encourage teachers to encourage children to use pictures as cues for word identification, a highly questionable practice.

Still another flaw relates to "too little." Here I refer to the fact that too little help is offered for introducing new words. Sometimes, directives like "Introduce new words" or "Provide help with unfamiliar words" or "Call attention to the new words" is all that manuals have to say about a critically important part of reading instruction. This is why the present chapter has given detailed attention to some of the interesting ways in which new words can be introduced and then practiced.

That manuals probably do too much with some things and too little with others is reflected in the various samples reproduced on pages 294–296.

Workbooks. Each reader in a basal series is accompanied by a workbook as well as by the manual.* Of all the pieces and parts of a series, workbooks probably have changed the least over the years. To be sure, the format of current copies looks modern and pictures have been updated. Nonetheless, the content and required tasks continue to be very similar to what they were years ago.

As was true years ago, basal reader workbooks provide material which supplements or extends what was offered children in the corresponding reader. In addition, they also provide for practice both with new words and with the skills taught via readers and the directives of manuals. (Samples of how workbooks provide extra reading material and, secondly, of how they provide for practice are shown on pages 297–298.)

* With the passing of time, basal reader series have grown to include much more than just the readers, manuals, and workbooks. Now, for example, there are such extras as: supplementary readers, word cards, recordings, films and film strips, picture cards, phonics cards, alphabet cards, plastic objects, games, and duplicating master sheets. Some schools order just about everything, while others pick and choose from among all that can be purchased.

Should a Basal Reader Series Be Used?

Answers to this question can only be opinions; consequently you might want to reject mine in favor of another's.

My answer has two parts because I divide the question into two considerations:

1. Should basal readers be used in nursery school and kindergarten?
2. Should they be used at subsequent levels?

At the Nursery School and Kindergarten Level? At the nursery school level, children usually are having their initial experience with school attendance. This makes attention to nonacademic factors extremely important and also very time-consuming. It does not make attention to the language arts, however, either unimportant or inappropriate. In fact, increased facility with oral language should always be one of the most important goals of every nursery school program. Along with that, some attention can also go to written language but always in a way that makes it personal for the children. This makes basals considerably less appropriate than the homemade materials that are described throughout this textbook.

In kindergarten, children are older. Those who have never before been to school typically adjust very quickly. In fact, many have been eagerly waiting to start school. Meanwhile, they have been watching television programs, such as "Sesame Street," making them quite familiar with letters and numerals and written language in general. All these reasons, along with the view of readiness that gets support in this textbook, prompt the recommendation that *all* the language arts receive systematic and frequent attention at the kindergarten level. That such attention can come in the form of instruction and activities which are closely connected with the lives and interests of the children has been verified through the many illustrations appearing throughout this book. What these same illustrations have also been demonstrating is that commercial materials, including texts like basals, are not necessary.

Obviously, commercial materials like basals *are* being used in some kindergartens. However, the most common reason for this often has little to do with appropriateness. I refer to the fact that kindergarten reading has become acceptable and even popular at a time when many kindergarten teachers are unprepared to teach it. (To review the reasons for this see pages 24–25 and pages 29–30.) As a result, there has been the human tendency to want to have the kind of cookbook prescriptions and directions that basal series do offer. One result is the appearance of kindergar-

SEQUENCE 6

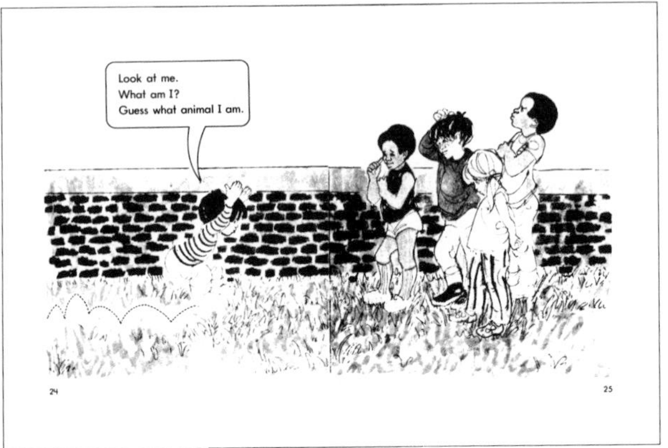

Let's Play pages 24 and 25

■ To guide discussion of pages 27 and 28, say:

Who is pretending now? [Indicate page 27.]

Peggy is telling the others who to look at and what she wants them to do. Who'll read what she says?

Can you guess what animal Barbara and Peggy are?

Let's turn the page and see whether someone in the story guesses.

Did you guess what the girls are pretending to be? Which boy can guess? Who'll read what David says?

■ Use the following comments and questions to guide reading and discussion of pages 29 to 31.

Who is pretending now? [Display page 29.] **Yes, William and David.**

David wants the others to look at them and to guess what they are. Who wants to read what David is saying?

Can you guess what William and David are?

Turn the page and see whether the children in the story can guess.

Do you think Neal can guess? No, he can't. Who'll read what Neal says?

What about Barbara? Who'll read what she says?

Peggy can't guess either. She asks the boys a question.

Read with me what Peggy asks.

■ To help pupils read page 32, say:

Look at the picture on the next page. [Indicate page 32.] **What do you think the boys are pretending to be? Yes, a tree.**

160

Teaching Unit 2, Tigers (9–13)

Page 12

Picture Interpretation

Point to the big picture.

Why couldn't Dan's father see Tiger up in the tree?

Who do you think was probably the first one to see where Tiger was?

Why do you think the truck driver is looking at the boys?

What do you think the boys will do next?

Point to the little pictures beside the text.

How many people said something on this page?

Who spoke first?

Who spoke next?

Silent Reading Assignment

You may not have learned this word yet. **Point to *truck*.** But you know the sounds that *t* and *r* stand for. When these letters come together like this at the beginning of a word, the sounds they stand for come so close together that they almost seem to be just one sound. That's the sound you hear at the beginning of *train* and *tree*. What are the last two letters in this word? . . . When *c* and *k* come together, they stand for the sound that *k* would stand for all by itself. It's the sound you hear at the end of *clock*. If you will think the sounds that *t* and *r* and *k* stand for when you read, you will know what the word is.

The mark after the first word Ben said is called an exclamation mark. **Print an exclamation mark on the board.** It tells you that someone said the word or words before it with great excitement or in a loud voice. Now read these sentences to yourself and find out what the boys wanted. . . .

Oral Reading and Comprehension Checks

Let's see how well you read this page by yourself.

Which boy saw the cat first?

What did Ben want the truck driver to do?

How do you think Ben feels?

Will you read what Dan and Ben said here?

What is this word? **Point to *truck*.**

How did you know it wasn't *trick*? (*no sense*)

How did you know it wasn't *car*? (*wrong sounds*)

Will you read aloud what Dan and Ben said? Make the sentences sound just the way you think Dan and Ben made them sound . . . **Have two or three pupils do this. . . . Make sure pupils read the second sentence with the appropriate inflection.**

What do you think the boys will do if the truck stops?

Let's find out. Turn to page 13. **Show page 13 and point to the numeral 13.**

80

From Manual for *Tigers*, by William K. Durr, Jean M. LePere, and Mary Lou Alsin, p. 80.

"Velvet," pages 25–27

Before beginning oral reading, test the pupils' comprehension during silent reading. Ask: "What did Velvet want?" . . . "Who knew what she wanted?" . . . "What was Mary going to do about it?" . . .

Checking comprehension

Let the discussion about Velvet lead into oral sharing of the story.

2. Guided Oral Reading

PAGE 25. "What is the name of our story?" . . . "The name of a story is its title. Show me the title of this story." . . .

PAGE 26. "What did Mike want Velvet to do?" . . . "Read the words Mike said to Velvet." . . .

"Did Velvet get on the bike with Mike?" . . . "How do you know she didn't? Read the line that tells you." . . .

Recalling story events

"Mike said something to Mary, too. What did he say to her?" . . . "Read the words that tell you that is what he said." . . .

"Look at the picture and see why Mike thought Velvet wanted something."

Noting specific details

PAGE 27. "Read the two lines that tell you Mary knew what Velvet wanted." . . . "What did Mike say to Velvet?" . . . "Read exactly what Mike said." . . .

"What two words tell you that Mary talked? Show them to me." (*Mary said.*) . . . "What two words tell you that Mike talked? Show those words to me." . . .

Reinforcing the use of the word, *said*

"Now let's begin at the beginning of the story (indicate page 25) and read all the things that Mike and Mary said exactly as we think they said them." (Ask one pupil to read the words that tell who was talking. Choose two pupils to read the words that Mary and Mike said, respectively. Ask a fourth pupil to read the places where no one was talking.)

Rereading for a specific purpose: following one specific character through the story

247

From Teachers' Manual for *Opening Books, A Magic Box, Things You See,* by Albert J. Harris and Mae Knight Clark, p. 247. Copyright 1965 by The Macmillan Company.

Something for Surprise

USE: After Yuki's Surprise, p. 29

Yuki ran to call Grandfather.
"Grandfather! Grandfather!"
she called.
"Surprise wants something
to eat.
Please go to the store with me.
I want to get some cat food
for Surprise."

Grandfather and Surprise

Surprise Wants Food

Grandfather and Yuki went
to the store.
Yuki said, "There is a pet store
down this street.
We can get cat food there."

"Good!" said Grandfather.
"Surprise will soon have food."

To the Pet Store for Food

The Pet Down the Street

The pet store man said, "Hello!
Can I help you, little girl?"

"I want some cat food, please,"
said Yuki.

The man gave her the cat food.
Grandfather gave the man
some money for the cat food.
And he and Yuki went home.

Money for Dog Food

At the Pet Store

"Come, Surprise," called Yuki.
"Here is some food for you.
Please come and eat it."

Surprise liked the cat food.
"Look at Surprise eat,"
said Yuki.
Soon he will get big.
"Then he will be a cat."

Surprise Eats Cat Food

The Big Cat

PURPOSE: To give practice in identifying the main idea and selecting appropriate titles.
SUGGESTIONS: Have pupils note title, then read the first part of the story and underline the title which tells about that part of the story. Have them complete page.

12

66

● Read. Draw a line.

It is a box. It goes to school. Lunch is in it. What is it? lunch box   little book
It is big. Boys and girls work in it. So do teachers. What is it? sky   school
All boys have this. All girls have this. All big people have this. What is it? plane   name
You stop your schoolwork. You go to the lunchroom. Then you have it. What is it? your lunch   your boat

Summary of skills. Understanding main idea

Procedure. Direct attention to the sentences in the first box. Explain that this is a riddle. Have the children read the sentences. Call attention to the two answers under the question. "What words tell us what the riddle is about? Draw a line under these words." Have the children complete the page by themselves. ("The New Lunch Boxes")

From Workbook for *Around the City,* Teacher's Edition, by Bank Street College of Education, Bank Street Readers, p. 66. Copyright 1965 by The Macmillan Company.

tens in which whole-class and drill-oriented instruction predominates. Such a development is most unfortunate because kindergarten should be the time when children are learning that school in general, and learning to read in particular, are very enjoyable experiences.

Of course, if it happens that kindergarteners respond positively to the simple readers found in all basal series, then they should be using them. But this use is in striking contrast to the way basals now function in some kindergarten programs.

At the First Grade Level? In first grade much more will be done with reading than at the earlier levels, which is as it ought to be. The children are older and more able, and the school day is longer. In addition, there is the societal expectation that first graders *will* learn to read.

The combination of facts just mentioned leads to the need to have a more intensive instructional program during the first grade year. That there are new expectations for it to succeed is, in my opinion, sufficient reason to recommend that at this level, too, teachers use the personal approach and the homemade materials. Yet, even as I make this recommendation I hear worries and complaints like, "Too much to be done!" "Too much to keep track of!" "Too time consuming!" What must also be recognized along with these reactions is the widely accepted assertion that only a relatively few teachers are prepared to assemble their own reading program at the first grade level.

With all the above in mind, the second recommendation I make to teachers is a compromise: Use some combination of commercial and homemade materials. With such a combination, however, a teacher's initial and continuing concern still has to be for a maximum of individualized instruction. Thus, teaching still begins with questions about what children need to learn. Answers provide goals, and materials help in achieving them.

Since basal reader series are likely to be among the commercial materials selected, let me make some additional comments about them.*

Because manuals have such a major effect upon instruction, they are the most critical part of any series. If teachers would view them merely as a source of suggestions which might be used, altered, supplemented,

* It is difficult to discuss basals in the abstract because how a teacher chooses to use them is of critical importance. I recall one first grade teacher who was using a basal reader story that dealt with a duck and a surprise. Manual suggestions were very ordinary, but what she did was a delight both for the children and the visitor. She began by showing the children a covered box. This created curiosity and also the chance to talk about and write *surprise*. Then, after each child peeked into the box, she wrote, "*It was a little furry duck.*" At this point the stuffed duck was taken out of the box, leading to attention to the word *duck*. After this, the teacher explained that the duck was visiting because he wanted to hear how well everyone was reading. And everyone read very well on that particular morning.

or simply ignored, they could have a positive effect. For instance, they could provide guidelines for the sequence of instruction. (I say "guidelines" because not every child profits equally from a single sequence. The same holds true for a single pace of instruction.) Manuals also offer suggestions—usually not enough—for teaching new words. They can also help with instruction in word analysis skills, although it is in this area that their suggestions quickly develop into an unchanging and therefore monotonous routine.

Clearly, if manuals are to have a positive effect upon instruction, some of their suggestions must be ignored. Often, for example, they recommend activities to go along with a lesson that have little or nothing to do with reading. Typically, they also encourage question-asking that suffers from too much quantity (questions asked about nothing) and too little quality. Worse yet, some manuals go so far as to tell a teacher exactly what to say. It is at this point, it seems to me, that they are clearly assigning to teachers the role of an assistant. And this leads to the need to restress a point made earlier. Materials—no matter how good—should only assist a teacher to reach goals which she has identified as being significant in the sense that they deal with important learnings not yet mastered. Whenever materials—no matter how good—are allowed to dictate both what and how to teach, then teachers become little more than an educational clerk. And such a role hardly becomes a professional person.

What about the readers in basal series? The important consideration about readers has to do with their purpose. One, clearly, is to introduce words for the child's reading vocabulary. Another is to provide the raw material for developing word analysis skills so that a child is eventually able to figure out new words independently.

As now constituted, basal readers at the beginning levels cannot do much more. For instance—and this should not be expected at this level—they do not give a child the chance to read good literature, which is why teachers of the young should be reading to them at least once every day. In addition, their content hardly provides for new comprehension tasks because it is essentially comprised of dialogue with pictures telling the story. One result is that the comprehension questions suggested in manuals often deal with, "Who said this?" "Who said that?" And with such questions there are at least two problems. The conversations often are so trite and uninteresting that a child either forgets who said what, or simply does not care. These reactions could be eliminated if teachers would ask their own questions, but only when the content calls for interrogation.

What about the workbooks? The important point about them can be made briefly. If their tasks deal with what children need to learn, use them. If not, do not. What usually happens in practice—or what ought to happen—is that some children can move through workbooks quickly, skipping pages that are unnecessary for them, while others require supplementary work in the form of teacher-made assignments. Thus, when put into the framework of individualized instruction, basal reader workbooks can be evaluated as follows: They are worthwhile to the extent that they help a teacher match instruction with what children need to learn and practice.

Matching instruction to children also must be the overriding consideration whenever basals are being selected for a particular first grade. For instance, if the children have already begun to read as a result of kindergarten help, they should hardly be given readers designed for beginners. In fact, if first grade instruction does not build on what was learned earlier, then efforts to improve kindergarten programs have little meaning.

What Else Can Be Used?

When development of a child's reading vocabulary is the concern, many materials in addition to what has already been mentioned are available to help. Trade books, for example, offer children the chance to read easy material on their own.* Even though the easiest books in basal series do not provide suitable instructional material for children who started to read in kindergarten, they too can be useful for independent reading. Some of the children's magazines—*Jack and Jill,* for instance—also should be available when children make their own selections for a recreational-type reading.

The distinction being made between instructional material and a recreational type leads to the need to introduce some terms that help teachers put materials into appropriate contexts:

Frustration Level

Materials are at a frustration level for a child when they are so difficult that even with help they would be a source of frustration.

* The term "trade book" usually refers to books that were written for the general bookstore and library market rather than for text use. If you are now of the opinion that not many trade books could be read by beginners, may I suggest you look at a 1969 *Elementary English* article in which twenty pages were needed to list books which beginners could read independently (2). A more recent article in the *Reading Teacher* (13) reflects interest in the open classroom as various centers (Book, Communication, Art, Science, Arithmetic) are described. Each description includes specific information about trade books and other materials that could be read and used independently by young children.

Instructional Level

Materials are at a child's instructional level when they are not so easy that he could learn nothing from them, but not so difficult as to cause frustration.

Independent Level

Materials are at an independent level when the child is able to read them without help.

Just listing definitions points out that frustration level materials always are to be avoided. Instructional level materials, on the other hand, are what teachers should deliberately seek out when they work with children on the achievement of goals still unrealized. Independent level materials are those which children should be given a chance to select and read on their own solely for enjoyment.

There is still another term that figures in discussions of recreational reading for beginners. I refer to the description "high interest-low vocabulary books." (See the sample on page 303.) This is not a label that will be found on covers; rather, it refers to materials that have been written with retarded readers in mind. As a result, authors have tried to select themes which appeal to older children (high interest) but which are treated in a way (low vocabulary) that allows those with limited ability to read these books.

Why include high interest-low vocabulary books—of which there are now literally thousands—in a discussion of free reading for beginners? They are mentioned because they serve well in providing beginners with independent-level material. Because their themes often are masculine, they also accommodate young boys at a time when school programs can be overly feminine.

To use what is called "experience materials" or "experience charts" is another device for sparking the interest of boys. While this will not always be the case, child-composed, group-composed, and teacher-composed material like that referred to on page 275 or shown on page 304 can deal with topics that appeal to the boys. At the start, they can also be helpful in bridging the gap between oral language patterns and those appearing in written commercial materials. (For more detailed attention to experience materials see pages 107–110.)

When "teaching materials" is appropriately viewed as being anything that displays written language, sources like television commercials, labels on packages and cans, menus, and street signs will not be overlooked when reading practice is the concern. Nor will bulletin-board displays. A few that give attention to word identification and practice are described below:

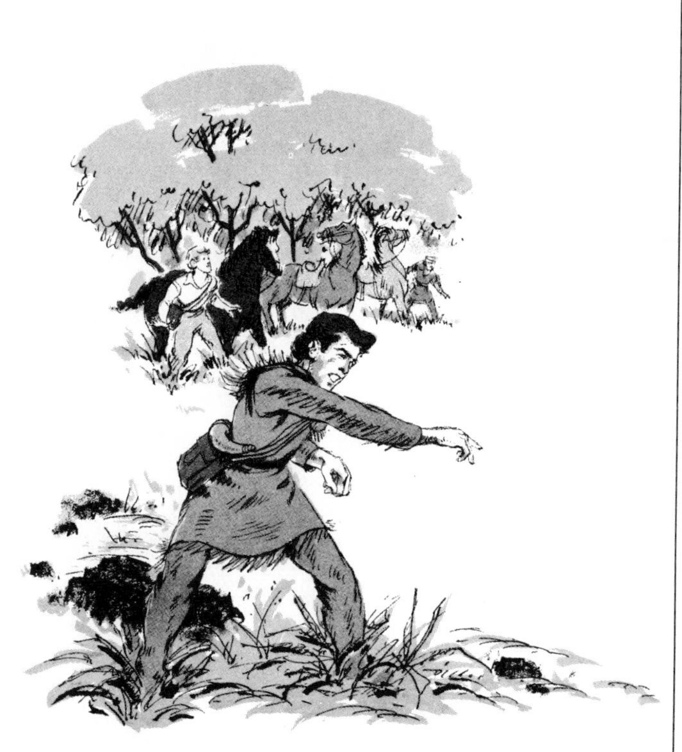

"Help! Help!" called Jimmy.
Dan Frontier was not far away.
Dan's gun was not ready.
But Dan was ready for the bear.

18

From *Don Frontier Goes Hunting*, the Don Frontier Series, p. 18. Copyright 1959 by Benefic Press.

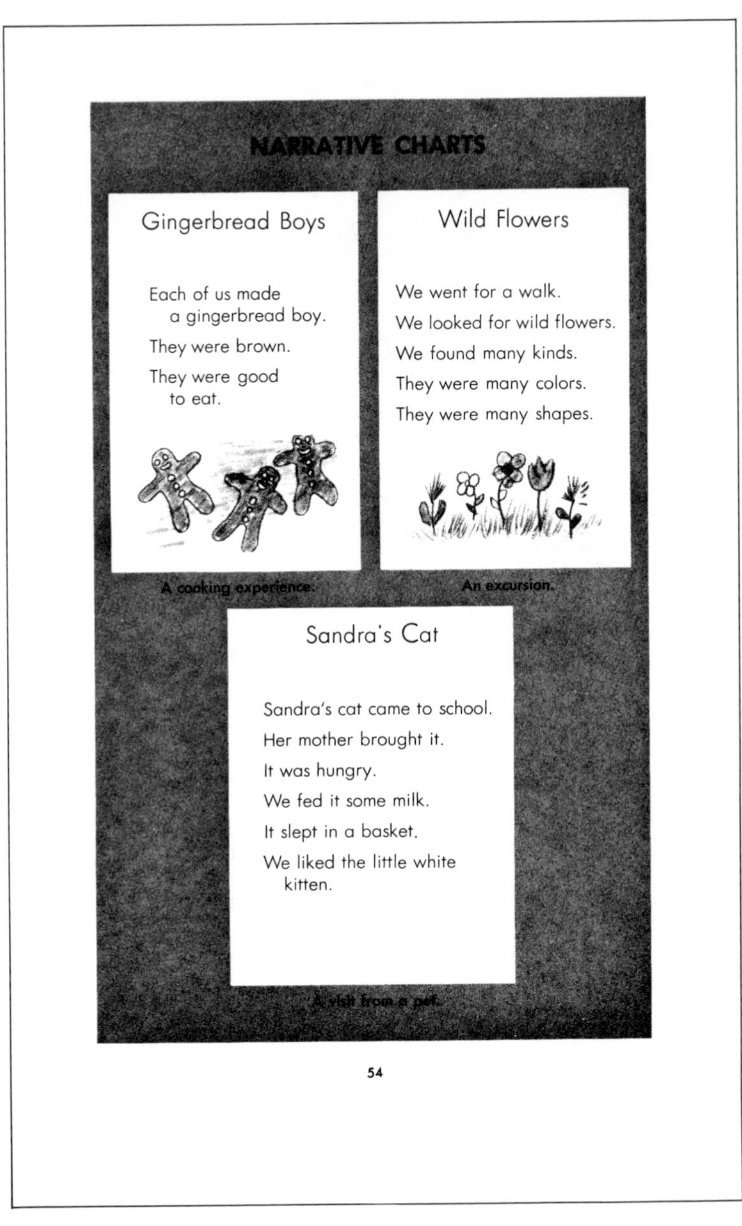

NARRATIVE CHARTS
Gingerbread Boys
Each of us made
a gingerbread boy.
They were brown.
They were good
to eat.
A cooking experience.
Wild Flowers
We went for a walk.
We looked for wild flowers.
We found many kinds.
They were many colors.
They were many shapes.
An excursion.
Sandra's Cat
Sandra's cat came to school.
Her mother brought it.
It was hungry.
We fed it some milk.
It slept in a basket.
We liked the little white
kitten.
A visit from a pet.
54

From *Learning to Read Through Experience,* Second Edition, by Dorris M. Lee and R. V. Allen, p. 54. © Copyright 1963, 1966 by Appleton-Century-Crofts, Educational Division, Meredith Corporation.

A paper apple tree can be thumbtacked to a bulletin board. Apples (round pieces of red construction paper) showing words in need of practice can be either placed on or picked from the tree whenever a child correctly identifies a word. (For variety, leaves might be picked or, in December, a Christmas tree and ornaments can be used to create interest in word practice.)

During April, a bulletin board display might feature umbrellas. A raindrop displaying a word will be added to it each day. On each day, too, the raindrops can be counted and named until, by the end of the month, thirty have accumulated.

One display that was very productive, first under the supervision of the teacher and then with pairs of children taking turns, showed a large paper basket. A backing allowed for an opening at the top. There also was a pocket inside the opening; this held small paper pumpkins on which words had been printed. Children took turns picking pumpkins out of the basket. Those who identified words correctly kept them. Those who did not had to return the pumpkins to the basket. (Possible variations: bowl or cornucopia and fruit; net and fish; mailbox and envelopes; jar and cookies.)

After *Jack and the Beanstalk* had been read to the children, a display showed a tall, thick stalk made by rolling green paper. Long leaves, each with a brief sentence on it, grew along the stalk. Also on the board were figures of Jack and the giant. Children took turns being one or the other; thus, and with the selected figure in hand, they tried to climb the stalk. Misread sentences brought the child crashing to the ground, after which it was someone else's turn to attempt the climb.

Little Bo Peep was the theme for another bulletin-board display. She was shown standing in a field. Children placed her lost sheep on the board by correctly reading brief phrases printed on them.

A SUMMARY

This chapter on whole word methodology has been a long one. But teaching children to be excellent readers is a long process. That this is so is especially important for new teachers to remember because there is the tendency among them either to try to do too much too quickly or to become discouraged by what they see to be an overwhelming responsibility.

The length of the chapter calls for a summary. Like the chapter itself the summary begins with advice about selecting words: Choose those that are meaningful and of interest to the children. In addition, and because of their frequent appearance in all written material, some service words must also be taught. In turn, these allow for early attention to word groups.

Teaching words requires attention to matters other than their selection. Which ones to teach to whom is a basic consideration. How to teach them is another.

Because so many words are unknown at the start, matching goals and children can end up with an instructional group that is too large. This prompted the recommendation that such groups be organized not only on the basis of pedagogical factors but also with psychological considerations in mind. Among the latter, one of the most important is that young children find it difficult to become involved and stay involved when a member of a large group.

Because every child's involvement also is affected by what is going on in his group, the chapter gave a great amount of attention to *interesting* procedures for introducing new words. In no way, however, was this meant to imply that a teaching procedure is commendable merely because it seems interesting. Rather, praise must be reserved for those that reach selected goals. For this chapter, goals were concerned with whole word identification.

To achieve permanently correct identifications, practice is a usual requirement. That was why the chapter also offered detailed help for carrying out interesting and productive practice sessions. For both practice and instruction, some type of materials will be needed; consequently many were described. For the most part, homemade kinds were highlighted because they are the ones most likely to be successful in developing a program closely tied to the interests of particular children.

Some commercial materials also were discussed. With these, most of the attention went to basal reader series simply because they are used in so many classrooms. Never was the attention meant to foster greater use, however. In fact, the recommendation was made that basals *not* be used with nursery school children. At later levels, when reading instruction is longer and more concentrated, they can make helpful contributions but only when used appropriately. Here, "appropriate use" can be defined most quickly with a point made frequently in this and earlier chapters: Materials should assist a teacher to reach goals she has selected as being significant and necessary. When, instead, they are allowed to dictate not only goals but even teaching procedures, the inevitable result is a reading program that is stilted, impersonal, and not always paralleling what individual children need to learn.

Although this particular chapter concentrated on learning that deals with whole word identification, its goal was not meant to overshadow the fact that reading vocabularies also grow as a result of instruction in word analysis skills. And that leads to the next chapter.

REFERENCES

1. ANDERSON, I. H., and DEARBORN, W. F. *The Psychology of Teaching Reading.* New York: The Ronald Press Co., 1952.
2. ARKLEY, ROSE. "Independent Reading for First Grades: A Listing," *Elementary English,* XLVI (April, 1969), 444–465.
3. AUSTIN, MARY C., and MORRISON, COLEMAN. *The First R: The Harvard Report on Reading in the Elementary Schools.* New York: The Macmillan Co., 1963.
4. BLOOMFIELD, L., and BARNHART, C. L. *Let's Read.* Detroit: Wayne State University Press, 1961.
5. BORMUTH, JOHN R. "Readability: A New Approach," *Reading Research Quarterly,* I (Spring, 1966), 79–132.
6. CHALL, JEANNE. *Learning to Read: The Great Debate.* New York: McGraw-Hill Book Co., 1967.
7. COLLIER, MARILYN. "An Evaluation of Multi-Ethnic Basal Readers," *Elementary English,* XLIV (February, 1967), 152–157.
8. DOLCH, EDWARD W. *Problems in Reading.* Champaign, Illinois: The Garrard Press, 1948.
9. FRIES, CHARLES C. *Linguistics and Reading.* New York: Holt, Rinehart and Winston, Inc., 1962.
10. GOODMAN, KENNETH S. "A Linguistic Study of Cues and Miscues in Reading," *Elementary English,* XXXXII (October, 1965), 639–643.
11. GUSZAK, FRANK J. "Dilemmas in Informal Reading Assessments," *Elementary English,* XLVII (May, 1970), 666–670.
12. JOHNSON, DALE D. "The Dolch List Reexamined," *Reading Teacher,* XXIV (February, 1971), 449–457.
13. MILLER, WILMA H. "Organizing a First Grade Classroom for Individualized Reading Instruction," *Reading Teacher,* XXIV (May, 1971), 748–752.
14. SAMUELS, S. JAY. "Effects of Pictures on Learning to Read, Comprehension and Attitudes," *Review of Educational Research,* XL (June, 1970), 397–407.
15. SCHNEYER, J. WESLEY. "Research: Underlying Mental Abilities and Reading," *Reading Teacher,* XXIV (October, 1970), 55–57.
16. SINGER, HARRY. "Research That Should Have Made a Difference," *Elementary English,* XLVII (January, 1970), 27–34.
17. TABA, HILDA. "The Teaching of Thinking," *Elementary English,* LII (May, 1965), 534–542.

10

Teaching Reading: Phonics and Structural Analysis

That some words will be taught as wholes was the assumption of the previous chapter. Assumed in this one is that children should learn how to figure out unfamiliar words as soon as possible. When to identify them, and when to let the children try to do this, will be considered later. For now, attention goes to the kinds of instruction that help children figure out new words.

NATURE OF AMERICAN ENGLISH

That written words *can* be analyzed or figured out reflects two features of American English. First, its words are recorded on the basis of sounds rather than meanings, thus allowing for phonic analyses in which the beginning reader moves from letters to sounds to words. Second, it includes words that combine roots and affixes (*hopeless, untie, repayable*) and roots and inflectional endings (*pays, paying*). This feature allows for structural analyses in which various pieces and parts are assembled into words.

Skill in both phonic and structural analyses makes a child independent in the sense that it enables him to figure out, on his own, words not yet in his reading vocabulary. The obvious importance of such independence assigns equal importance to instruction in word analysis skills which, in turn, accounts for the detailed explanations in this chapter.

The material dealing with phonics is especially extensive. Its length, however, is not meant to suggest that phonics instruction is more important than any other kind. Rather, the detailed attention seems warranted and even necessary for two other reasons. First, phonics is one of the areas of reading instruction about which both teachers and those preparing to teach are least knowledgeable. This is especially true of individuals who were not taught phonics as children; it also characterizes those trained in early childhood education at a time when reading was considered inappropriate for young children. Still another factor accounting for the insufficient knowledge about phonics is that, unlike other phases of reading instruction, it is not something that can be learned quickly. Instead it has to be studied and digested slowly and gradually.

To provide material for such study is the second reason for the detailed attention to phonics. In fact, this chapter might be viewed as a mini-course as, first, it goes over its content and, secondly, how *some* of it can be taught to young children. The security that results from knowing a great deal about phonics should free teachers to select for instruction only what is appropriate, and to teach it in a way that ends up being both an enjoyable as well as a productive experience for children. Thus the purpose of this chapter is not to foster lots of instruction but, rather, *good* instruction.

PHONICS

American English is an alphabetic language in the sense that letters are used to represent the sounds of its words. With our language, however, single and consistent associations between letters and sounds do not exist. The letter *a*, to take one example, is used to record the sound heard at the beginning of *apple* but also the one initially heard in *apron*. And at still other times, as in *all*, *are*, and *apply*, it represents still different sounds.

Such multiple associations create problems for those learning to read; still, they do not make them unimportant. In fact, without a knowledge of letter sounds, a child would be left with the difficult but also unnecessary task of memorizing all the words he was required to read. To avoid this, we teach phonics.

What Is Phonics?

Phonics is comprised of a body of content that specifies letter-sound associations. But, more than that, it is concerned with the use of that content to identify written words. From this it follows that instruction in phonics also has a twofold responsibility. It deals with content and, in addition, with applying it to unknown words. It could also be said, as was done in the previous chapter, that phonics instruction helps children use relevant cues (letters and their sequence) to identify words not yet in their reading vocabulary.

Content of Phonics

The content of phonics consists of statements which deal with observations that have been made about written American English. For instance, it has been observed that the letter *a* often represents the sound heard at the beginning of *at, add,* and *ask.* (This has customarily been referred to in phonics as its "short" sound even though the reference is to a particular sound, not its duration.) It also has been observed that this sound often—not always—occurs when *a* is the only vowel in a syllable and is not its final letter. Both requirements, it should be noted, are found in *at, add,* and *ask.*

Another observation deals with another sound associated with *a.* This one is identical to its name, has customarily been called its "long" sound, and is heard at the beginning of *apron* and *able.* This particular observation points out that when *a* is the only vowel and also the final letter in a syllable (a pron; ba by) it usually—but not always—records its long sound.

From just these few comments about one letter, some of the basic categories of phonics content can be identified. One broad category deals with letter-sound associations; another, with factors that affect them. By implication the comments also show that phonics deals with syllables and, as a result, with the observations that have been made about the syllabication of American English words.

Hopefully, the same comments also made it clear that phonics does not teach "rules," if by this is meant infallible prescriptions that always work. Rather, it teaches generalizations which, like all other generalizations, sometimes apply but sometimes do not. What this underscores is the basic importance, for both teacher and children, of viewing phonic generalizations merely as starting points whenever unknown words are being analyzed.

Possibilities for Teaching the Content

The content of phonics, as the previous section indicated, is comprised of statements about:

1. Letter-sound associations
2. Factors affecting sounds
3. Syllabication

In teaching the content to children, two procedures are possible. One is referred to as inductive and analytical; the other, as deductive and synthetic. Each kind of instruction will be described separately although in the day-by-day work of a classroom, a teacher often uses some combination of both.

Inductive, Analytical Instruction. Dictionaries offer these definitions of "induction":

> Reasoning from particular facts
> to a general conclusion
>
> Reasoning from particular instances
> to a general conclusion

Applied to phonics, induction refers to a reasoning from known words to a conclusion (a) about letter-sound associations; or (b) about factors affecting them; or (c) about syllabication. Thus, with an inductive approach words like those shown below could be analyzed to arrive at a conclusion about a sound that *b* records:

boy
but
bell
bad *

Words like those listed below could be analyzed to arrive at a conclusion about two factors that can affect letter sounds (When a vowel is *the only vowel* in a syllable and is *the final letter,* it usually records its long sound):

me
so
hi

* How to teach phonics will be described in detail later. The goal now is simply to give specific meaning to "inductive, analytical."

With the inductive approach, words like those shown below might be analyzed, in this case to arrive at a conclusion about syllabication (When two consonants are preceded and followed by vowels, a syllabic division often occurs between them):

number
hello
picnic
doctor
rabbit

What is meant by inductive instruction should now be clear. That it depends upon the analysis of words chosen because of a common visual-auditory feature is the reason for describing it as being analytical as well as inductive.

Deductive, Synthetic Instruction. Deductive instruction in phonics is like any other deductive process: It moves from the general to the particular. More specifically, it begins with statements of generalizations about letter sounds (or about factors affecting them or about syllabication) and then applies those generalizations to particular words. For instance, should letter sounds be the concern, a teacher proceeding deductively would begin by identifying the sound recorded by a particular letter. That is, she would start with a generalization about its sound. Once learned, the sound would be combined (synthesized) with others to form syllables and words. This synthetic feature of deductive instruction is portrayed well in the material reproduced on page 310.

PHONICS CONTENT FOR TEACHERS

Before discussing how the content of phonics might be taught it seems desirable—perhaps even necessary—to review it because, after all, one cannot teach what one does not know. In fact, one cannot teach what one does not know *well.* Since the overview is for adults who are at least somewhat familiar with phonics, it will proceed deductively; that is, it will be a telling rather than a reasoning process. In no sense, therefore, should the review be thought of as a model for teaching children.

Because the first step in a phonic analysis of a totally unfamiliar word is to consider its syllables, the initial "telling" will be about syllabication. First, though, there is need to discuss what a syllable is.

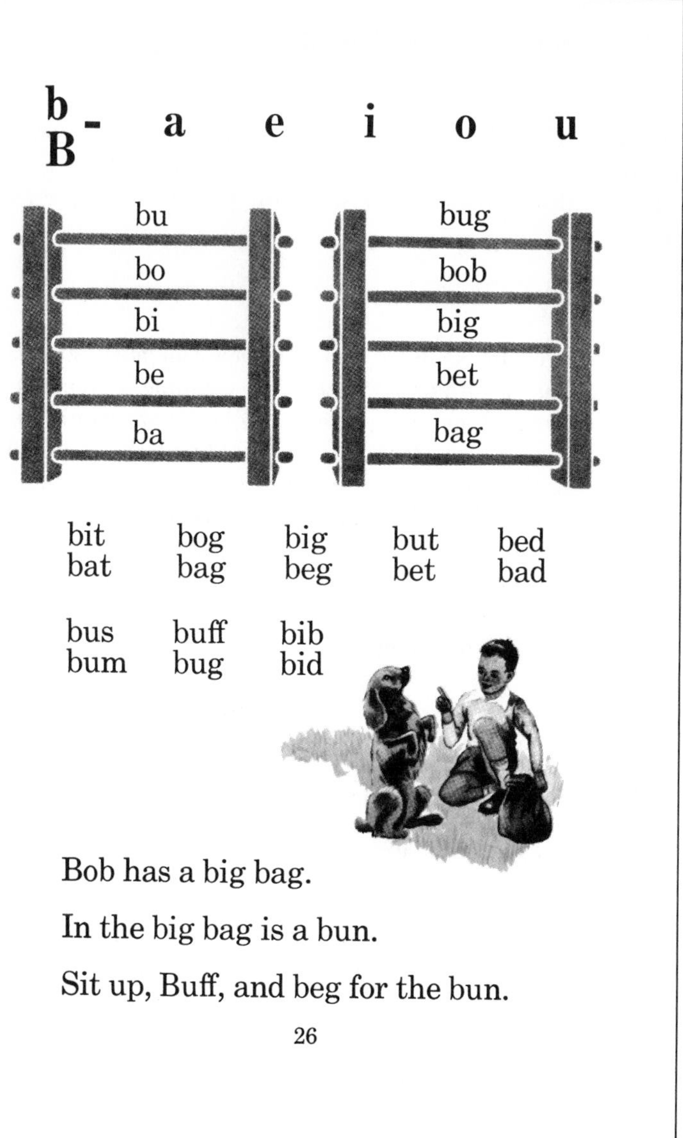

b
B - **a e i o u**

bu	bug
bo	bob
bi	big
be	bet
ba	bag

bit	bog	big	but	bed
bat	bag	beg	bet	bad

bus	buff	bib
bum	bug	bid

Bob has a big bag.

In the big bag is a bun.

Sit up, Buff, and beg for the bun.

26

From *Reading with Phonics,* by Julie Hay and Charles E. Wingo, p. 26. Copyright 1948 by J. B. Lippincott Company.

Syllabication

In American English, a vowel sound is the nucleus of the syllable. In fact, syllables could be defined as vowel sounds which are sometimes combined with consonant sounds. All of the following, for instance, are syllables:

a ac ack tack stack *

What the above also show is that syllables can have sounds in initial, medial, and final positions. With *ac*, for example, *a* records the initial sound while the final one is represented by *c*. There would be no medial position in this case. With *tack*, on the other hand, the sound of *t* is in the initial position, the sound recorded by *a* is in the medial position, while the sound represented by *ck* is in the final position.

Another way of viewing syllables catalogues them as "open" and "closed." Closed syllables end in consonant sounds (*sit, stamp*); open syllables, in vowel sounds (*go, plea*).

What must also be underscored about syllables has been stated well by Wardhaugh:

> Although the number of syllables in an English utterance can be fairly easily determined, the precise point at which one syllable may be said to end and another begin is often impossible to determine. . . . The result is that the syllable divisions recorded in a written text are made according to convention and are essentially arbitrary (17, p. 786).

Even though it is recognized that one syllable flows into another in oral language, this textbook still takes the position that the arbitrary divisions to which Wardhaugh refers are helpful to a child attempting to figure out an unfamiliar written word. These syllabic divisions are the concern now.

In considering syllabication, one very basic point to remember is that:

The syllable is the unit of pronunciation.

At the start, when most of the words children are learning to read are only one syllable, this statement might not seem particularly important. As words increasingly become multisyllabic, however, it is of *basic*

* A word like *oil* also is a syllable even though the diphthong recorded by *oi* is a close blend of two vowel sounds. For purposes of phonics, diphthongs—they will be discussed later in the chapter—function as if they were single vowel sounds.

importance to keep in mind that phonic analyses deal with syllables, not words. Even the generalizations about letter sounds are based on syllables. For instance, a frequently mentioned one is that *w* affects the sound recorded by *a* when it follows it in a word. Actually, this is not correct. The correctly stated generalization is that *w* affects the sound of *a* when it follows it *within the same syllable*. Thus, *w* has an effect on the *a* in *aw ful* but not in *a wake*. With this in mind, you can see why the analysis of a totally unfamiliar word ought to begin by considering syllabication with the help of generalizations that will be cited here.

One source of help is a very fundamental generalization:

> Every syllable must have a sounded vowel.

This statement immediately points out that words like *he, end, bath,* and even *thrust* and *splash* could be no more than one syllable. (Note, by the way, that the generalization does not say that every syllable has one vowel; rather, that every syllable has one sounded vowel. Consequently words like *meet, roam, nine,* and *voice* also are one-syllable words—even though containing more than one vowel—because each has only one sounded vowel. In the case of *voice,* the vowel sound is a diphthong represented by *oi.**)

Because of their fundamental importance, let me repeat the first two generalizations pertaining to syllabication:

> The syllable is the basic unit of pronunciation.
> Every syllable must have a sounded vowel.

While these two are invariably correct and applicable, other generalizations about syllabication should only be considered as starting points in the analysis of a word. One possible starting point is specified below:

> When two consonants are between two vowels, a syllabic division often occurs betwen them. For instance:
>
> num ber bot tom pen cil

That certain details must be included in statements of generalizations is demonstrated by the one just cited. I refer to "are between two vowels." It is this important detail that should keep children from dividing *camp* as *cam p*, or *clock* as *c lock* or *cloc k*. What should also dis-

* Technically, diphthongs as well as the long sounds of *i* and *u* are two closely blended sounds. However, since this chapter is for teachers, not linguists, all these are viewed as being single sounds.

courage incorrect syllabication is a generalization stressed earlier; namely, every syllable must have a sounded vowel.

The following is still another observation about syllabication:

> When a single consonant is between two vowels, the first vowel often is in one syllable while the consonant and the vowel following it are in another. For instance:
>
> be gin   pa per   si lent

Although the next generalization, which deals with an exception to the one just noted, will not have to be used very often by beginners, teachers should still be familiar with it:

> When *x* is preceded and followed by a vowel, the preceding vowel and the *x* are in one syllable while the following vowel is in another. For instance:
>
> ex it   ox en   tax i

Glancing through any dictionary reveals the importance of the next generalization because it would show a large number of words ending with a consonant plus *le*—for instance, *able, purple, trifle, cradle, gargle, article:*

> When a word ends in a consonant followed by *le,* that consonant plus *le* form a syllable. For instance:
>
> i dle   bu gle   thim ble

There is still another generalization to help with syllabication, even though it does not focus on it directly:

> When other vowels are available to record a sound, a final *e* usually is silent.* For instance:
>
> bake   time   mule

How, you might be wondering, does the above generalization help with syllabication? With *bake,* to cite one illustration, the silent *e* leaves only

* Linguists commonly object to such descriptions of letters as "silent" or "has no sound." Admittedly, letters are neither silent nor noisy, nor do they have sounds tucked into them. Actually, to say of a letter that it is "silent" is simply to point out that it is not representing any sound in the word, although it often will be an important cue for the sounds other letters are likely to represent. Certainly this is true of final *e*'s.

one other vowel to record a sound—the *a*. Since, as was emphasized earlier, every syllable must have a sounded vowel, the silent *e* would suggest that *bake* is a one-syllable word because only one vowel (*a*) is available to record the necessary vowel sound. (With a word like *me*, the *e* records a sound because it is the only vowel.)

What all this illustrates is that phonic generalizations—whether about syllables or something else—deal with visual cues that aid in identifying words. As a mature reader you might not at first realize the significance of such help. For example, because you are familiar with *bake* you are able to hear that it is one syllable. However, for the child who cannot yet read it, nothing is heard when he looks at the four letters. Instead, he must find help (cues) not only in those letters but also in their sequence. With *bake*, as was mentioned before, one very relevant cue is the presence of two vowels one of which is a final *e*. With another—*able*, for instance—the *b* followed by *le* offers help with syllabication. Whatever the word, the point to bear in mind is that each offers visual cues (letters and their arrangements) to help identify it. Specifying those cues is what the content of phonics is all about.

Letter Sounds

A great deal of the content of phonics deals with the sounds letters record or, put somewhat differently, with letter-sound associations. In fact, that is the major concern of beginning instruction. Let me initiate this overview of letter sounds by starting with the vowel letters: *a, e, i, o, u*.*

Vowels. As has already been suggested, the five vowels are especially important in American English because every syllable of every word has a vowel sound. As was suggested earlier too, vowels also are the letters that show the greatest variation in the sounds they represent. This characteristic is one of the factors that allows our twenty-six-letter alphabet to represent almost twice that many sounds; however it also is one that influences some publishers, authors, and teachers to temporarily postpone instruction with vowel sounds and, instead, attend first to some of the consonants.

Whatever the decision, there must come a time when children learn about vowel sounds. Those easiest for children to remember, the long sounds, are the names of *a, e, i, o,* and *u*. They are heard at the beginning of:

aim eat ice old use

* Actually, the term "vowel" refers to sounds not letters. Because *a, e, i, o,* and *u* commonly record vowel sounds they often are referred to as vowels, too. Technically, though, both "vowel" and "consonant" are descriptions of sounds.

More difficult for children to distinguish among and remember are the short sounds. These are heard at the beginning of:

am egg if on up

When teaching children to use phonics to figure out words, it has become customary to designate long and short vowel sounds, and "silent" vowels, with diacritical marks:

āge̸ ēa̸ch mēe̸t ĭnch rŭst ăct

Y Functioning as a Vowel. In this discussion of vowel sounds, attention must go to the letter *y* because, though a consonant, it functions as a vowel whenever it appears any place in a syllable other than in initial position. Thus, it records its consonant sound in words like *yes* and *beyond,* but vowel sounds in such words as *myth, carry,* and *dry.*[*]

Some generalizations are helpful when children need to assign a sound to *y* when it appears in an unfamiliar word and is not the first letter in a syllable:

> When *y* is in a closed syllable that has no vowel, it usually records the short *i* sound. For instance:
>
> myth cynic gypsy
>
> When *y* is the final sound in a syllable, it usually records the long *i* sound. For instance:
>
> my python lye
>
> However, when *y* is the final sound in a multisyllabic word, it usually records the long *e* sound. For instance:
>
> heavy carry softly

Schwa Sound. As any dictionary quickly reveals, one of the most common sounds in our language is the schwa sound, symbolized by ə. This can be described as an unstressed short *u* sound which is represented in the following words by the italicized letters:

bi*a*s om*e*n d*i*vide p*o*lite col*u*mn

[*] Linguists consider the sound recorded by *y* in words like *yes* to be a semivowel because of its physiological characteristics.

These words show how the schwa sound is spelled with all five vowels and, secondly, how it occurs in unaccented syllables. For teachers, the same words should also demonstrate the importance of calling attention to the schwa sound in order to avoid artificial and therefore incorrect pronunciations.

The schwa sound is significant in still another way. Earlier, when syllabication was being considered, the following generalization was cited:

> When a word ends in a consonant followed by *le*, that consonant plus *le* form a syllable. For instance:
>
> i dle   bu gle   thim ble

How the schwa sound figures in such words can be seen below:

idle (i dəl)   bugle (bu gəl)   thimble (thim bəl)

Vowel Combinations. When one vowel follows another in a syllable (*meet, oil, caught, food*) the two are sometimes referred to as a vowel digraph. (Literally, *digraph* means "two letters.") However, such combinations fall into separate categories insofar as sounds are concerned. Some of the combinations (*beef, goat, eat, aim*) commonly record the long sound of the first vowel, a fact that will be singled out for attention later. Other combinations (ou, oi, au, oo) are different in that they stand for sounds unlike those associated with either of the two letters comprising them. For instance, the combination *au* commonly records the sound heard at the beginning of *auto*. (The same sound is represented more frequently by *aw*, an observation that shows how the consonant *w* sometimes functions as a vowel.) The vowel combination *oo* records two different sounds. One, which is heard in *room*, is called its long sound while the other, heard in *hood*, is referred to as its short sound. Occasionally there will be an exception, as in the case of *flood*.

Still other vowel combinations (ou, oi) also represent sounds unlike those associated with their individual letters; however these are grouped separately because they record sounds called "diphthongs." (*Diphthong* is a linguistic term referring to a sound that is the close blend of two sounds requiring, as it is made, a change in the mouth position.) The diphthongs associated with *ou* and *oi* are heard at the beginning of *out* and *oil*, respectively. The same sounds frequently are represented by *ow* (*owl*) and *oy* (*boy*) indicating again how consonants—in this case both *w* and *y*—sometimes function as vowels. The consonant *w* also functions as a vowel to stand for still another diphthong; namely, the sound that *ew* represents in *few*.

What has now been said about vowel combinations—some of which include *y* and *w* functioning as vowels—can be summarized by listing the combinations followed by words containing the sounds they commonly record:

Diphthongs Recorded by Vowel Digraphs	Other Sounds Recorded by Vowel Digraphs
oi (oil)	au (auto)
oy (toy)	aw (saw)
ou (out)	oo (room)
ow (owl)	oo (look)
ew (few)	

This attempt to sort out the sounds which combinations of vowels represent is not meant to conceal or even minimize the fact of letter-sound inconsistency in our language. Not being forgotten, for example, is that *i* does not record its long sound in *field,* even though it does in *pie.* Nor are the different sounds recorded by *ow* in *owl* and *low* being overlooked. Rather, the intent here is to help organize some of the content of phonics while, at the same time, it is clearly recognized that flexibility in its use is an absolute necessity if phonics is to be of assistance in identifying unknown words.

Consonants. Compared to the vowels, consonants are much more consistent in what they record. For example, the initial sound in each of the words listed below illustrates a very common one for the initial consonant: *

bat	he	log	put	ten
do **	jam	my	run	very
for	kite	no	see	zoo

Functioning as consonants, *y* and *w* also are stable for they commonly record the sounds heard at the beginning of *yet* and *wet,* respectively.

Two other consonants are not less consistent but each is associated with two sounds. I refer to *c* and *g* which parallel one another in the sense that their two sounds have traditionally been referred to in phonics as "hard" and "soft":

* It is recognized that the sound any letter records is affected by its position in a syllable and by the letters that precede and/or follow it. However, this chapter is for teachers, not linguists; and because of that, the aim is to deal with written language in a way that avoids unnecessary subtleties and distinctions, as well as nonessential nomenclature.

** Sometimes a double consonant records the sound when it occurs at the end of a syllable. For instance: *add,* and also *muff, tell, putt, grass, buzz.*

HARD SOUNDS *	SOFT SOUNDS
car	cent
go	gym

The hard sound of *c* (car), when it is the final sound in a syllable, often is spelled with the combination *ck* (*pick*) but not always (*picnic*). Infrequently, the hard sound is represented by *ch* (*chord, school*).

The hard sound of *g* (*go*), in this case when it occurs at the beginning of a syllable, can also be recorded with two letters. I refer to the combination *gu* appearing in syllables which include vowels other than the *u;* for example, *guess* and *guide*. In such cases the *gu* should be viewed as if it were a single consonant, allowing the other vowels in the words to record the necessary vowel sounds. Thus, *guess* would parallel a word like *less* while *guide* parallels *hide*.

One further note about *c* and *g:* the descriptions "soft" and "hard" probably are impressionistic. That is, the sounds referred to as "hard" (*come, go*) seem harsher than those called "soft" (*cent, gym*). Classroom observations show, however, that children have their own interpretations; commonly, for example, they equate "hard" with "difficult."

Another consonant requiring special attention is *x*. Like *c*, it has no sound that is uniquely its own. (The soft sound of *c*, you will recall, is one that is associated with *s* while its hard sound is like the one that *k* represents.) The three sounds which *x* can record are shown below:

SOUNDS	EXAMPLES
/gz/	exit
/ks/	fix
/z/	xerox

If you have played scrabble, you are aware of one of the characteristics of another consonant. I refer to *q* and to the fact that it is always followed by *u*. For that reason it is the combination *qu* that is dealt with in phonics. In fact, children should be taught to view *qu* as if it were a single consonant that can represent the two sounds shown below:

SOUNDS	EXAMPLES
/kw/	queen
/k/	bouquet

Like the vowels, consonants can be silent. Sometimes this is so for *h:*

* When these different sounds are likely to occur will be discussed in a subsequent section, "Factors Affecting Sounds."

H	GH *	KH	RH
hour	ghost	khaki	rhythm
heir	ghetto	khan	rhubarb

Other consonant clusters in which only one letter records a sound are shown below:

GN	KN	PN
gnaw	knit	pneumonia
sign	know	pneumatic

PS	WR	MN
psalm	wrong	solemn
psychology	write	column

The consonant *b* sometimes is silent:

lamb debt doubt

The consonant *l* can be silent:

talk half balm would

Another consonant that can be silent is *t:*

hasten rustle catch often

Consonant Combinations. Like the vowels, certain consonants commonly follow one another in a syllable. For instance:

shop play with bring

In the illustrations, *sh, pl, th, br,* and *ng* all are consonant combinations; however they are different in one very pertinent way. The combinations *sh, th,* and *ng* record sounds unlike the sound associated with either of the consonants comprising them while the others, *pl* and *br,* record sounds that are a blend of the sounds of each letter in the pair. Because of this difference, it has been customary in phonics to separate frequently occurring consonant combinations into two categories: (a) digraphs and (b) blends.** Let me first discuss the digraphs.

* When *gh* appears at or toward the end of a syllable both the *g* and *h* can be silent, as in *high* and *ought.*

** This is an unfortunate categorization in that "digraph" refers to letters while "blend" refers to sounds. This imprecise use of terms in phonics has received widespread criticism from a few linguists.

Consonant digraphs are similar to the previously discussed vowel digraphs in that they represent a sound which is different from those associated with the individual letters comprising them. The consonant digraphs are listed below and to show the similarity, vowel digraphs are listed too:

CONSONANT DIGRAPHS	VOWEL DIGRAPHS	VOWEL DIGRAPHS REPRESENTING DIPHTHONGS
ch (chap, chef)	au (auto)	ou (out)
ph (phone)	aw (awful)	ow (owl)
gh (rough)	oo (soon)	oi (oil)
sh (shall)	oo (took)	oy (toy)
th (the, thin)		ew (few)
ng (rang)		

Missing from the list of consonant digraphs is one that has been traditionally included. I refer to *wh*. It was not named because—and this is exemplified in *who* and *what*—it records sounds associated with both *w* and *h*. In *who* the sound is /h/ and in *what* it is described as /hw/ by some and simply as /w/ by others.

Additional comments need to be made about some of the consonant digraphs that are listed. For example, you ought to have noticed that *ph* and *gh* can record the same sound, one associated with *f*. The *ph* combination records this sound at both the beginning and end of syllables (*phone, graph*). However, *gh* only records the sound when it is in final position (*laugh, cough*). In contrast, *gh* in initial position is not a special digraph at all, as that term is customarily used in phonics. Rather, as in words like *ghost* and *ghetto*, the *g* records its hard sound while the *h* is silent.

Singling out the special sound of *sh* (*shout, wish*) is not meant to cover up the fact that the same sound is recorded by a great many other letters and letter combinations. It is present in all the following words, for example, even though *sh* is not: *sugar, action, ocean, efficient, mission, mansion, issue, luscious, azure*. The sound of *sh* is also represented by another consonant combination in words borrowed from French. I refer to *ch* and to such borrowings as *chef, champagne,* and *chauffeur*. In many more instances, *ch* records the sound heard at the beginning of *chill*. In final position, this sound is often spelled with *tch* (*pitch, catch*).

When the digraph *th* was listed, two words were used in the illustrations because it records two different sounds. The first, called its "voiced" sound, is heard at the beginning of words like *the* and *that* and at the end of such words as *loathe* and *smooth*. Its "voiceless" sound is heard at the beginning of *thin* and *thumb* and at the end of *math* and *both*. (Voiced and voiceless consonant sounds will be discussed in greater detail in a subsequent section of the chapter.)

The digraph *ng* records a nasal sound. It generally appears at the end of syllables but not always; for instance in a word like *length* it does not. It follows vowels, so its sound can be identified in such combinations as *ing, ang,* and *ung.* This same sound, incidentally, is also represented fairly frequently by the single consonant *n.* This would be so in such words as *ink* (ingk), *thank* (thangk), and *anxiety* (angziety).

That all these consonant digraphs record one rather than two sounds needs to be considered in relation to generalizations cited earlier about syllabication because, in applying them to unfamiliar words, digraphs function as if they were single consonants. Let me illustrate this with examples.

Earlier, the following generalization was presented: When two consonants are preceded and followed by vowels, as in *seldom,* a syllabic division usually occurs between them (*sel dom*). This generalization also is pertinent for a word like *anchor* in which *n* would be considered one of the consonants and *ch* the other. For *anchor,* therefore, the syllabic division would be *an chor* (*ang ker*).

Another generalization cited earlier suggested: When a consonant is preceded and followed by vowels, as in *music,* the first vowel generally is in one syllable while the consonant and the vowel following it are in another (*mu sic*). This particular generalization would be pertinent for a word like *machine,* in which *ch* is treated as if it were a single consonant. Thus, the syllabic division would be *ma chine.*

As was mentioned before, a group of other combinations of consonants occurs frequently in our language; and they have been classified as "blends" because they represent the sound of each letter in the pair, closely blended together. Recently, because of the new influence of linguistics, instructional materials have begun to refer to them as "clusters," a better description because it refers to letters rather than sounds.

Some of the more frequently occurring clusters are listed below:

CONSONANT CLUSTERS

bl	fl	sc	st
br	fr	sk	sw
cl	gl	sl	tr
cr	gr	sm	tw
dr	pl	sn	scr
dw	pr	sp	str

As can be seen in the listing, many of these clusters combine a consonant with *l* or *r.* Others are a combination of *s* and another consonant.

Consonant clusters are dealt with in phonics primarily for efficiency. That is—and this contrasts with the digraphs—each letter could be considered separately because each records a sound. However, unfamiliar words containing clusters are analyzed more quickly if the cluster rather than each letter is considered.

Vowel-Consonant Combinations. Certain vowel-consonant combinations appear frequently in words. Consequently they, too, are considered for reasons of efficiency although some authors also view attention to them as a way of helping beginners in reading deal with the troublesome vowel sounds (19). I refer to combinations like *-ell, -ack, -op, -ight, -ang, -eet,* and to others that are actually words—for instance, *-and, -ill, -ade,* and *-all.* Attention to such vowel-consonant combinations, traditionally called "phonograms" but more recently referred to as "graphemic bases," has been a part only of certain types of phonics instruction. However, as new materials allot more and more space to phonics, phonograms are now getting an amount of attention that has not been customary for several decades.

A Summary

The next section will discuss other phonics content that ought to be familiar to teachers, not because they will necessarily teach it all but because it ought to make them more secure in what they are teaching. It deals with generalizations that are helpful in assigning sounds to single letters and letter-combinations that commonly record more than one. Before starting that section, it is strongly recommended that you systematically review what has already been discussed. The summary on page 326 should help.

Factors Affecting Sounds

Previous pages have been identifying common speech sounds and the letter or letters that record them. In the identification it was shown that the same sounds can be represented by different letters or, to put it the other way, that the same letter or letter combination can represent a variety of sounds. Such variety causes problems for children trying to figure out unfamiliar words. Nonetheless, certain of the observations that have been made about written American English can be of assistance as they attempt to assign sounds to letters. It is these observations, stated as generalizations, that are the concern now.

Vowel Sounds. What follows are some generalizations pretaining to vowel sounds. Each specifies cues which are relevant because they indicate the sound a vowel is likely (*not* inevitably) to record. The first generalization, for instance, specifies two cues (number of vowels; position

SUMMARY

SYLLABLES
- Definition
- Open and closed
- Significance for word analysis
- Generalizations for dividing words into syllables

LETTER SOUNDS
- Single Vowels
  - (1) long sounds
  - (2) short sounds
- Y: Functioning As Vowel
  - (1) long *i* sound
  - (2) short *i* sound
  - (3) long *e* sound
- Schwa Sound
- Vowel Combinations (include *y* and *w*)
  - (1) diphthongs (oi, oy, ou, ow, ew)

LETTER SOUNDS (cont.)
  - (2) digraphs (au, aw, o͞o, o͝o)
- Consonants
  - (1) fairly consistent consonants
  - (2) *c* (hard and soft sounds)
  - (3) *g* (hard and soft sounds)
  - (4) *x* (gz, ks, z)
  - (5) *qu* (kw, k)
  - (6) "silent" consonants
- Consonant Combinations
  - (1) digraphs (ch, ph, gh, sh, th, ng)
  - (2) clusters
- Vowel-Consonant Combinations
  - (1) phonograms

in syllable) that point to the likelihood of a vowel recording its short sound:

> When there is one vowel in a syllable and it is not its final letter, that vowel usually records its short sound. For instance:
>
> act thrust napkin

The same generalization could also be stated in a shorter form: One vowel in a closed syllable usually records its short sound. What the alternative statement suggests, of course, is that there is no such thing as one best way to state a generalization. All pertinent details must be included to be sure. However, the wording itself can take any form that is meaningful to the children.

Like the previous generalization, the next one demonstrates how the number of vowels in a syllable is not a sufficient cue; placement in the syllable must be noticed too:

> When there is one vowel in a syllable and it is the final letter, that vowel usually records its long sound. For instance:
>
> go she silo

This generalization also can be stated in a shorter form: One vowel in an open syllable generally records its long sound.

The next generalization also specifies times when a vowel might record its long sound. When a vowel might be silent is described, too:

> When there are two vowels in a syllable, the first sometimes records its long sound while the second is silent. For instance:
>
> boat five keepsake

In considering the above generalization it is important to remember that the two vowels, if occurring together, might be special digraphs (au, aw, oo, ou, ow, oi, oy, ew) in which case the combinations are likely to record the sounds described earlier in the chapter.

Because so many syllables that have two vowels end with an *e*—for instance, *five*—it is customary to give special attention to that pattern:

> When there are two vowels in a syllable, one of which is a final *e*, the first vowel usually records its long sound while the *e* is silent. For instance:
>
> use strange rye *

Because the final *e* signals the likely sound of another letter, it is referred to as a "marker." How *e* but other letters, too, serve as other kinds of markers will be brought out in subsequent generalizations.

Thus far it has been shown how vowels affect the sounds of other vowels, when they are in the same syllable. Consonants also affect vowel sounds; some generalizations about their effects follow:

> When *r* follows a vowel in a syllable, the vowel plus *r* (ar, er, or, ir, ur) usually record the sounds illustrated below:
>
> art, dollar
> her
> fir
> for, word
> hurt

* Remember: When *y* is not the first letter in a syllable it functions as a vowel. In a word such as *rye*, therefore, the *y* records a vowel sound (long *i*) while the final *e* is silent. In a word such as *ray*, the letter *y* also functions as a vowel but is silent because: When there are two vowels in a syllable, the first usually records its long sound while the second is silent.

From the illustrations it can be seen that all the combinations (ar, er, ir, or, ur) can represent the sound heard in *sir*. Two (ar, or) represent other sounds besides.

The need to call attention to the effect of *r* on the sounds recorded by previous vowels underscores the importance of encouraging children to note not only the number of vowels in a syllable but also the letters that precede and follow them. For instance, a generalization cited earlier (A single vowel in a closed syllable usually records its short sound) suggests that the *e* in *hen* is likely to record its short sound. However, that *r* follows *e* in a word such as *her* indicates something else; namely, that *er* will record the sound heard in words like *first, hurt,* and *word.*

In searching through an unfamiliar word for cues that will help identify it, children must keep in mind not only the effect of *r* on vowels, but also the effect of *re*. This is specified below:

> When a vowel is followed in a syllable by *re,* the vowel plus *re* (are, ere, ire, ore, ure) usually record the sounds illustrated below:
>
> care
> here
> fire
> bore
> sure

The letter *l* is another consonant that affects vowels—in this case just *a*.* The effect is stated below:

> When *ll* follows *a* in a syllable, the *a* often records the sound customarily represented by *au* or *aw*. For instance:
>
> all call enthrall

Other clusters of letters also affect vowel sounds. For instance, it was pointed out earlier that two vowels in a syllable, one of which is a final *e*, generally indicate the first will be long and the *e* silent (*pie, hole*). However, certain clusters suggest the first vowel is more likely to record its short sound:

> When a vowel is followed in a syllable by *nce, nge, dge,* or *ve,* it often records its short sound. For instance:
>
> fence plunge judge give

* Other consonants that affect the sounds of vowels (y, w) were discussed earlier under the headings of "vowel digraphs" and "diphthongs."

Another generalization mentioned before suggested that one vowel in a closed syllable usually indicated a short sound for the vowel (*will, pin*). However, when that vowel is either *i* or *o* and certain consonant clusters follow, they are likely to record their long sounds. These patterns are specified in the next two generalizations:

> When *i* is the only vowel in a syllable and is followed in the syllable by *ld, nd, gn, gh,* or *ght,* it usually records its long sound. For instance:
>
> wild bind sign high light

> When *o* is the only vowel in a syllable and is followed in the syllable by *ld,* it usually records its long sound. For instance:
>
> old bold fold

> Another generalization offering help:

> When a word ends in *ous,* the *ou* records the short *u* sound. For instance:
>
> jealous callous dangerous

Consonant Sounds. The sounds which certain consonants record also are affected by other letters. For example, the soft and hard sounds of *c* and *g* were mentioned and illustrated in a previous section of the chapter. When each tends to record these sounds is described in generalizations that again deal with markers:

> When *c* is followed in a syllable by *e, i,* or *y,* it usually records its soft sound. For instance:
>
> cent cigar cynic
>
> Otherwise, it most likely records the hard sound. For instance:
>
> cat cool cute crib close picnic

Notice that "otherwise" includes times when *c* is the final letter in a syllable, as in *picnic* or *hectic.*

> When *g* is followed in a syllable by *e* or *y,* it usually records its soft sound. For instance:
>
> gem gentle gym gypsy

When *g* is followed by *i*, both the soft and hard sounds are common. For instance:

giant ginger gift giggle

Otherwise, *g* is likely to record its hard sound. For instance:

gas golf gum grow glad wig

The two sounds for both *c* and *g* raise questions about a generalization that sometimes appears in teachers' manuals. I refer to one that deals with multisyllabic words within which are two identical and adjacent consonants; for instance, *carry, allow, pepper.* The generalization suggests that the first of the double consonants is sounded while the second is silent. Actually, this is not always so. More correct observations follow:

When two identical and adjacent consonants (except *c* and *g*) appear within a multisyllabic word, only the one in the accented syllable is sounded. For instance:

dinner	hollow	hello	suppose
din′ n̸er	hol′ l̸ow	hel̸ lo′	sup̸ pose′

When *c* or *g* are doubled within a multisyllabic word, each letter in the pair can record a different sound. For instance:

accent suggest

In *accent* (*ac cent*) the first *c* records its hard sound because it is the final letter in a syllable. The same applies to the first *g* in *suggest* (*sug gest*). On the other hand, the second *c* in *accent,* like the second *g* in *suggest,* records its soft sound because it is followed in a syllable by *e.*

In contrast to the words just mentioned, others include two *c*'s (*accord* and two *g*'s (*wiggle*) and each of the doubled letters technically records the same sound. When this happens the generalization cited initially applies:

accord	wiggle
ac̸ córd	wíg g̸le

In words having two identical and adjacent consonants, the two were never meant to be pronounced—with the exception of words like *accent* and *suggest.* Instead, their presence represents a type of conventional spelling used to signal a short sound for the previous vowel. This can be seen in contrasts like *dinner—diner,* and *comma—coma.*

A Summary

Before attention goes to another concern of phonics—which syllable gets the stress—it is again suggested that you review the content just presented. It described how the presence of certain letters affects the sounds recorded by others, when they appear in the same syllable. To help with the review, a summary outline is presented below.

Stressed Syllables

The correct pronunciation of an unfamiliar multisyllabic word is not achieved until the syllable receiving the primary stress or accent is identified. Actually, such identification can be pertinent even earlier in the sense that it sometimes offers cues about the likely sound of individual

SUMMARY

VOWELS

Generalizations described:

1. When vowels tend to record short sounds
2. When vowels tend to record long sounds
3. When vowels tend to be "silent"

Other generalizations described:

1. Effect of *r* on sound recorded by previous vowel
2. Effect of *re* on sound recorded by previous vowel
3. Effect of *ll* on sound recorded by preceding *a*
4. Effect of *nce, nge, dge,* and *ve* on sound recorded by preceding vowel
5. Effect of *ld, nd, gn, gh,* and *ght* on sound recorded by preceding *i*
6. Effect of *ld* on sound recorded by preceding *o*

CONSONANTS

Generalizations described:

1. When *c* and *g* tend to record soft sounds
2. When *c* and *g* tend to record hard sounds

letters in the word. For instance, it was pointed out earlier that vowel sounds in unaccented syllables often are reduced to the schwa sound; that is, to a sound like a de-emphasized short *u* sound. This is re-illustrated in the words below in which the italicized vowel represents the schwa sound:

pilot	coma	about	offend
pi′ l*o*t	co′ m*a*	*a* bóut	*o*f fénd

Earlier, too, it was pointed out that when a doubled consonant occurs within a word (*hallow, attend*), only the consonant in the stressed syllable is sounded. For example:

hallow	attend
hál l̸ow	at̸ ténd

Although stress can be important even before all the sounds of syllables are figured out, dealing with it often is the final step when an unfamiliar word is being analyzed. Because American English words have been borrowed from a variety of languages, they display no single pattern for stress; consequently, it is fortunate that the conclusions which a child reaches regarding sounds of syllables often are enough to suggest which will be stressed. That is, the sounds of the syllables frequently suggest a word which is known in its spoken form and this, in turn, suggests the accented syllable. Of course, such a succession of events is most likely to happen when the child has a sizeable listening-speaking vocabulary, and when the word being figured out appears in a context—for example, as part of a sentence.

Although American English words do not follow a single, invariable pattern for stress, there are a few generalizations that suggest starting points whenever a child has to decide which syllable in a given word is to get the primary stress:

> When a root word has two syllables, the first usually is stressed. For instance:
>
> cán dy   mó ment   sí lo   pen′ cil

The reason "root word" is used in the statement is that a prefix (e.g., *un* in *untie*) is not given primary stress even though it is the initial syllable in a two-syllable word. A more broadly stated generalization about this follows:

> In derivatives and variants, the accent falls on or within the root.* For instance:
>
> un tíe   re áct   mis cóunt   fore wárn

* Derivatives and variants will be discussed in the section dealing with structural analysis.

What are sometimes called absorbed or inactive prefixes also account for some of the two-syllable words in which it is the second syllable that is stressed (5). I refer to such examples as:

be lów   ad míre   ap próve   a wáy   in strúct

It should be noted, too, that a decision about stress can sometimes be made indirectly; that is, by the process of elimination:

> A final syllable comprised of a consonant plus *le* is not accented. For instance:
>
> gar′ gle   a′ ble   ar′ ti cle

Even when spelled differently, a syllable which records the sound like that represented by the consonant-schwa-consonant pattern is not stressed either. Italicized letters in the words below exemplify this:

í*dol*	bár*rel*	án*gel*	stén*cil*
pú*pil*	scán*dal*	sým*bol*	lógi*cal*

Another time when a stressed syllable might be identified through the process of elimination is described below:

> When *tion* or *ture* are final syllables, they are not stressed. For instance:
>
> státion   excéption   pícture   créature

In any discussion of accented syllables it must be noted that the way a word functions in a sentence can also affect stress. This was nicely illustrated in the motto recently seen on a garbage truck: "We never refuse refuse." Generally, when a word functions as both noun and verb (e.g., *permit, content, rebel, progress, conduct*), the first syllable is stressed when it is a noun and the second when it is used as a verb.

LINGUISTIC INFLUENCE ON PHONICS *

In considering the various features of phonics content, foregoing pages have referred intermittently to the influence of linguistics. Now it is timely to deal with that more directly.

* A much more detailed consideration of linguistics and of its influence on phonics appears in *Phonics and the Teaching of Reading* (7).

To find such influence should not be surprising because anyone interested in reading has to be interested in language. Until the 1960s, reading specialists looked to psychology for help with what they needed to know both about language and language users; but, since then, it is a few individuals in linguistics who have been both vocal and influential. In fact, linguistics turned into something of a bandwagon in the reading field, with most publishers and many authors willing to jump on it.

What is linguistics? Like most academic areas, it has a variety of subdivisions. The one most relevant for this discussion is phonology in which the concern is for oral language, including the identification of the phonemes (sounds) comprising any given language. (This identification is achieved through what is called a method of contrast in which pairs of minimally different words—that is, words differing by only one phoneme—are contrasted.) Such a concern leads to very precise studies of speech sounds. One result is that a person not trained in this field often fails to hear some of the distinctions that eventually are made.

Distinctions that would be obvious to native speakers appear when phonologists are attempting to identify the phonemes that make up their language or dialect. With American English, for example, a phonologist might contrast such minimally different words as *mat* and *fat* and in the process identify two phonemes which an untrained person could hear; namely, /m/ and /f/. [To distinguish language sounds (phonemes) from letters (graphemes), phonologists commonly use slash marks: / /. Thus, the referent for /f/ is a phoneme or sound, while *f* is a letter. Sometimes, as the phonemes just mentioned show, the symbol enclosed in the slash marks or diagonal bars is the same as the letter. At other times, it is not. For example, /æ/ refers to the sound that has been called the short sound of *a*. For a more complete picture of these notations, see the material which is reproduced on page 336 and which shows the great influence of linguistics on some current instructional materials.]

Even this brief and sketchy description calls attention to the way linguistics has influenced the vocabulary of phonics. Some of the newer terms have already been mentioned in earlier sections of the chapter—for instance, graphemic base, cluster, and marker. Others will also be used because they are becoming common in instructional materials. Some of both are listed below, in contrast with the older vocabulary:

Old	New
phonetics	phonics
phonetic analysis	phonic (phonemic) analysis
analyzing words	decoding
sounds	phonemes (phōnēm*e*s)
letters	graphemes (grăphēm*e*s)
short vowel sounds	unglided sounds

OLD	NEW
long vowel sounds	glided sounds
consonant blend	consonant cluster
phonogram	graphemic base
associating letters and sounds	learning grapheme-phoneme correspondences

In addition to the influence on vocabulary, there have been other kinds, too. An obvious one is the amount of phonics now being taught in the very basal readers which not too long ago strongly advocated a whole word approach with beginners. This particular effect is ironic in that linguists interested in reading have been extremely critical of phonics.

Another type of influence is found in methodology. Now, for example, the method of contrast frequently characterizes phonics presentations, accounting for the renewed interest in phonograms and for the use of minimal contrasts like:

fill
pill
bill

Another type of influence stems from the linguist's contention that phonemes have no existence outside words or, put somewhat differently, that they only find their realization in words. Such a contention leads him to conclude that letter sounds must never be isolated from words for the purpose of identification.

The question of isolating sounds will be discussed later when phonics instruction is the concern. For now I would simply like to point out that the goal of that instruction and the goal of phonology are different. For example, phonics is merely a means to an end: independence in figuring out words that are unfamiliar in their written form. It also is pragmatic, which is to say that what is "good" phonics instruction for any given child is what works for him. This means, for instance, that phonics instruction which never isolates sounds might not be good because, without the isolation, he does not "get it." Or, to cite another illustration, it could mean that some of the highly technical distinctions and some of the nomenclature now being introduced into phonics materials might not be good either, even though "linguistically correct." What these various comments point out more generally is the ever present possibility that what is academically respectable can be wrong methodologically—at least for some children.

As with any other development, the best reaction to the appearance of the linguist in the reading field is to maintain an open mind. This

KEY TO THE STANDARD SYSTEM OF PHONEMIC NOTATION USED IN READING 360

VOWEL SOUNDS

Glided		Unglided	
/ey/	bait	/æ/	cat
/iy/	beet	/e/	pet
/ay/	bite	/i/	pin
/ow/	boat	/a/	hot
/uw/	moon	/ə/	nut
/aw/	cow	/u/	put
/ɔy/	boy	/ɔ/	saw

Vowel-Consonant Sequences

/ər/	fur	/yuw/	use
/ar/	car	/yən/	million
/ɔr/	corn		

CONSONANT SOUNDS

/b/	boy	/s/	saw
/č/	child	/š/	shoe
/d/	dog	/t/	tell
/f/	fast	/θ/	thin
/g/	go	/ð/	this
/h/	hat	/v/	valentine
/ǰ/	jump	/w/	we
/k/	cat	/y/	yes
/l/	let	/z/	zoo
/m/	man	/ž/	garage
/n/	no		
/ŋ/	ring	/hw/	when
/p/	pet	/ks/	six
/r/	ran	/kw/	quack

/φ/ (no sound) through

183

would mean avoiding automatic acceptance of whatever a linguist says about reading, merely because he is a specialist in language. But, too, it would mean examining carefully whatever he does say because of the possibility that at least some of it could lead to better reading instruction and thus to more successful children.

PHONICS INSTRUCTION

Reading instruction, as previous chapters indicated, involves much more than phonics instruction. Yet, phonics is an important piece because it is one of the means for helping a child become independent so that, on his own, he can figure out or decode words.

Because of its importance, phonics instruction should get underway as soon as possible. One way to give a little more meaning to "as soon as possible" is to say "when a child is ready." However, because most aspects of getting him ready are the beginning stages of phonics instruction itself, I would prefer to avoid the topic "readiness for phonics" and consider, instead, one like "contributors to success." Whatever the title, the point to remember is that preparing a child for phonics and teaching him phonics are not two entirely separate and different tasks.

Contributors to Success

By this point in the book, the basic importance of the listening-speaking vocabulary to achievement in reading ought to be unquestionably clear. Therefore, it should come as no surprise to learn that the importance continues when phonics is the topic. Exactly how listening-speaking vocabularies and the use of phonics go hand in hand has been effectively described by Roger Brown:

> The usefulness of being able to sound a new word depends on the state of the reader's speaking vocabulary. If the word that is unfamiliar in printed form is also unfamiliar in spoken form the reader who can sound it out will not understand the word any better than the reader who cannot sound it. . . . the real advantage in being able to sound a word that is unfamiliar in print, only appears when the word is familiar in speech. The child's letter-by-letter pronunciation, put together by spelling recipe, will, with the aid of context, call to mind the spoken form. There will be a click of recognition, pronunciation will smooth out, and meaning will transfer to the printed form. The ability to sound out new words is not simply a pronunciation skill; it is a technique for expanding reading comprehension vocabulary to the size of speaking comprehension vocabulary. This is a considerable help since speaking vocabulary is likely to be ten times the size of reading vocabulary for the primary child (1, p. 69).

Highlighting listening-speaking vocabularies as a contributor to success in using phonics is not meant to infer that a teacher ought to work on word pronunciations and meanings first, and only then move to phonics instruction. Rather, the point being emphasized has to do with the dependence of success upon these vocabularies, and with the hope that attention to them will begin early and be continuous. As a previous chapter mentioned, the job of augmenting listening-speaking vocabularies is both important and unending.

Since phonics is concerned with letter sounds, knowing something about letters helps, too. For instance, knowing at least some of their names contributes to success because it facilitates teacher-child communication. After all, it *is* easier to deal with letters by using a name (j) rather than a description (*fish hook*).*

With great detail, the chapter on writing instruction (Chapter 8) discussed a way to teach letter names. Teaching them in connection with writing, however, is not a must. For example, a teacher might choose to give attention to the name of a letter without having the children write it, and then follow that up with attention to its sound. (How to teach sounds will be discussed later.) Others might decide to teach the names of the most commonly used letters, and then single out some for phonics instruction. In other words, there is no one best way to proceed.

While many TV-educated children will arrive in nursery school, or at least kindergarten, already knowing letter names, others might have difficulty learning them. When this happens, it can reflect a visual discrimination weakness, or a poor memory. Here I cannot help but recall one kindergartener who, unlike all the others in his class, could not seem to learn letter names. On the assumption that his might be a visual discrimination problem, I gave him a test dealing with that. Using rows of letters like those shown below, I said: "Would you look at this first letter (pointing to the *B*). Now would you look at all the other letters in this row and show me the ones that look like this first letter." Even with the more difficult discriminations, this child had no problem whatsoever. For him, poor memory was the culprit.**

B	B	T	B	A
o	j	o	o	c
b	g	d	a	b

* As was brought out in the previous chapter, knowing letter names also helps when whole words are being identified. In that case, it allows a child to spell a word which, in turn, fosters attention to its letters and their sequence.

** Poor memory continued to be a problem in subsequent years requiring large amounts of practice for every accomplishment. Because of the key importance of

If it happened that visual discrimination *was* the problem, I would have recommended use of exercises like what was used in the diagnosis —beginning, though, with comparisons of just two letters. What would not have been recommended are some of the commercial materials that have children compare pictures and also geometrical shapes. I stress this because, even though research findings consistently demonstrate the specificity of perception (12, 14), some teachers in some schools are still urged from time to time to use material like that of Frostig (10) in which nonverbal stimuli are the focus of discrimination tasks. Put more simply the point is: If you want to help children deal with letters and words, use letters and words.

As the chapter on writing instruction pointed out, children can be eased into other learnings which contribute to success in phonics and which are, in fact, phonics in its beginning stages. I refer to:

1. Awareness that the writing (spelling) of a word is related to its pronunciation
2. Awareness that letters stand for sounds
3. Understanding of "beginning sound"
4. Ability to recognize similar and dissimilar sounds in words

How these learnings can be accomplished was discussed in the chapter on writing instruction (pp. 229–233) and earlier in the one dealing with reading readiness (pp. 53–54). Nonetheless, some additional comments will be made about the last two.

Knowing exactly what is meant by "beginning sound in a word" is important for success in phonics because beginning sounds often are used to teach letter-sound associations or, as they are now called, grapheme-phoneme correspondences. Later on, beginning sound substitutions (cat ⟶ fat) allow a child to move from a familiar word (*cat*) to the identification of an unfamiliar but related one (*fat*).

Because we, as adults, know the exact meaning of "beginning sound" it is easy to forget how foreign this concept is for most young children.* They know about sounds, of course. They can hear and distinguish among the sounds of music, thunder, a dropped plate, and so on. They also are familiar with the sounds of words but, until phonics comes along, they have no need to deal with anything as precise

---

memory in beginning reading, it is unfortunate that so little is known about memory and ways to improve it.

* At a more elementary level, even descriptions like "same" and "different" might not be fully understood. In fact it has been shown that incorrect answers for discrimination tasks involving closely similar letters (e.g., *b*, *d*) sometimes reflect misunderstanding of "same" and "different" rather than visual perception problems (2).

and sometimes elusive as their beginning sounds. For children, in fact, a word like "ball" probably is thought of as one sound, not the blend of three. What this suggests to teachers is the need to be patient but also to avoid taking for granted that children know exactly what is meant by a question like, "Do 'ball' and 'baby' begin with the same sound?"

In addition to having an understanding of "beginning sound," children also need to have what is usually called "auditory discrimination ability" or "auditory perception." That is, they must know when speech sounds are the same and when they are not. Because perception is specific—this same point was made earlier about visual discrimination—tasks selected to help children with the auditory discrimination required by phonics should focus on words, not on such things as environmental or musical sounds. I feel the need to insert this reminder, by the way, because of what was observed not long ago in a kindergarten. The teacher's schedule called for "Reading Readiness Activities" from 9:30 to 9:50 which was the first disappointment because, as Chapters 3 and 4 indicated, preparing children for reading is not something that ought to be confined to a certain period of time each day. In any case, since I arrived shortly after 9:30, I was surprised to find the children gathered about the piano while the teacher played pairs of high and low notes. After each pair her question was, "Were those two notes the same or different?"

Curious about the omission of what the schedule called "Reading Readiness Activities," I later questioned the teacher. Surprisingly, she explained that what she was doing at the piano was designed to help the children with phonics. Would it?

Playing pairs of similar and dissimilar notes might help teach the meanings of "alike," "unlike" "same" and "different," assuming these words are used in the teacher's questions about the notes. However, that such an activity has anything to do with hearing similar and dissimilar sounds in words is highly questionable. Consequently the point meriting repetition is: If you want to help children learn to discriminate among speech sounds, use words.

Asking questions about words ("Do 'ball' and 'baby' begin with the same sound?" "Do 'table,' 'toy,' and 'door' start with the same sound or a different sound?") is the most obvious way to provide help with auditory discrimination and, at the same time, give specific meaning to "beginning sound." At the start, a teacher might have to answer her own questions, but with the answers she is demonstrating the meaning of those questions. Other procedures for helping children with auditory discrimination were described in Chapters 3 and 8. A few more possibilities follow:

Using pictures of various objects, let individual children in a small group choose one. As each picture is selected, have the child name the object and then another word that starts with the same sound.*

Display a variety of small objects and trinkets on a table (button, pin, bell, envelope, crayon, pen, pencil, mirror, top, car, ball, clip, marble, box, etc.). Name each, or let the children do this. Select one, rename it, and then ask a child to find another object whose name begins with the same sound.

Put small objects into a paper bag, now a "grab bag." Let children in a small group take turns selecting one. As each is selected it is named, and the child then says another word that begins with the same sound. If he can do this, he gets to keep the object (temporarily); otherwise it goes back into the bag.

Periodically at dismissal time, let the children get their coats on the basis of the sounds in their names. For example: "If your first name begins the way 'Tuesday' begins, you can get your coat."

Distribute sets of small, unlabeled pictures of objects. The job for the children is to group them, putting those together whose names begin with the same sound.

Five comments need to be made about these and similar procedures for practice with auditory discrimination. The first pertains to the use of pictures and the need to know the name being assigned them by the children. For example, a picture showing an addressed envelope might be called "envelope" but possibly "letter" or "mail." Not to know what name a child is thinking of is not to know the sound he is considering.

The second point about auditory discrimination also has to do with the use of pictures; specifically with the need to use *un*labeled pictures. With labels, a teacher would never know whether a child was involved with beginning sounds or the beginning letters in the labels.

The third point has to do with questions like, "Can you think of another word that begins the way 'girl' begins?" It is the reminder that it is possible for children to be aware of the beginning sound of "girl," but unable to think of another word that starts the same way. This underscores once more the importance of listening-speaking vocabularies —although a child could have an excellent command of oral language and

* All these procedures can be adapted for practice with medial and final sounds. For instance, should final sounds be the focus, this one would have the children name another word that ends with the same sound.

still not be able to recall appropriate words at the time the request is made. It's like the adult who recalls a very funny and appropriate joke—two days too late. To help the child who has similar problems, riddles can be used. (E.g., "I'm thinking of a word that begins the way 'girl' begins. It's the name of a color." "I'm thinking of a pretty little flower. Its name begins the way 'vase' begins.")

The fourth point meriting attention is that procedures selected to teach auditory discrimination can also help with diagnosis because children's responses tell a teacher what has been learned as well as what still needs to be taught. This assumes, of course, that they have not been elicited by a teacher who gives such special stress to correct answers that even the slowest in a class gives the right one. I refer, for instance, to a teacher who says, "I'm going to say two words. Tell me the one that begins the way 'mother' begins: doll, me." In the process of saying this, such special stress is given to "me" that it would almost be impossible for a child not to know that it is the expected answer.

The last point pertains only to final sounds and is the suggestion that explicit attention to rhyming words might cause problems, even though given with the intention of helping. I say this because I have been in classrooms in which children seemed to have equated "rhyming words" with "words ending with the same sound." (Such a conclusion is logical in that rhyme usually is described in terms of similarity in final sounds.) With the wrong equation in mind these children commonly expressed the belief that words like "bat" and "sat" ended with the same sound, but pairs like "bat" and "sit" did not.

Although I have found no research data to support what I am suggesting as being a source of confusion and, secondly, although I am aware that just about all commercial materials give a great deal of attention to rhyme in their phonics instruction, I would still like to suggest you consider the possibility that such attention might cause children to conclude that only rhyming words have the same final sound.

Now, having discussed what promotes success with beginning phonics, let me summarize by listing each contributor that was mentioned:

1. Substantial listening-speaking vocabulary
2. Knowledge of at least some letter names
3. Awareness that the spelling and pronunciation of a word are related
4. Awareness that letters stand for sounds
5. Understanding of "beginning sound"
6. Ability to recognize similar and dissimilar sounds in words (auditory discrimination)

Teaching the Content of Phonics: Letter Sounds

Once children show progress in what have been called "contributors to success" (especially in auditory discrimination), they are ready to learn to associate particular letters with particular sounds. As they move to this level, memory again becomes an important factor for success. As a result, individuals who might have had no difficulty recognizing similar and dissimilar sounds might encounter some when required to attach a particular sound to a particular letter.

Sequence. Because consonants are the letters which are most consistent in what they record, the recommendation is that instruction begin with some of the consonants. I say "some" because it makes no sense to spend time at the beginning on consonants that only rarely appear in words and, secondly, because vowels are so important that attention to them must come fairly early.

I recognize that many readers of this text will teach consonant sounds in the order in which some commercial material presents them. Even for those individuals, however, knowing about factors that ought to affect sequence is important because they might explain why some children have trouble with some sounds. Two such factors will be discussed.

The first is pertinent because the concern of this text is young children. I refer to the need to be aware of speech sounds that are difficult for some young ones to make; commonly they are the sounds associated with *s*, *r*, *l*, and *z* (11, 13). Although it is true that some young children can recognize sounds which they themselves are unable to articulate, developmental characteristics of speech are still relevant when decisions about the sequence of early phonics instruction are being made. One type of relevance was demonstrated for me in a kindergarten that was visited fairly regularly. In it was a girl who could not make the sounds recorded by *l* and *r*. When phonics instruction dealt with them, she had no problem intellectually. However, she did have some personal difficulties whenever she was asked to name words beginning with *l* or *r* because her efforts were inevitably "rewarded" with the giggles of her peers. Such a reaction turned this child into a very quiet girl when phonics was getting attention.

A second factor worth considering has to do with what linguists call "voiced" and "unvoiced" (voiceless) consonant sounds.* These terms refer to a physiological aspect of certain speech sounds; specifically to

* Linguists use a variety of categories and labels to describe speech sounds. Only those that have relevance for phonics are mentioned in this text.

the state of the vocal cords when they are made. When voiced sounds are produced, the vocal cords are drawn together and they vibrate. With unvoiced sounds, the vocal cords remain open and are "silent."

Of special relevance to phonics instruction is one further classification made by linguists. This pairs certain of the voiced and unvoiced sounds as follows:

Voiced Consonant Sounds	Unvoiced Consonant Sounds
/b/	/p/
/d/	/t/
/g/	/k/
/v/	/f/
/z/	/s/

This list indicates that /p/ is the voiceless counterpart of /b/, that /t/ is the voiceless counterpart of /d/, and so on. What your ear indicates, however, is of greater relevance to this discussion because it points out that the sounds represented by *b* and *p*, by *g* (hard sound) and *k*, and so on, are sufficiently similar to cause confusion for some children, especially when they are just beginning to learn about letter sounds. What the close similarity suggests, therefore, is still another guideline for those who teach beginning phonics: If the sound recorded by *b* is selected for attention, do not follow that up immediately with attention to the sound which *p* represents. Or, to cite another illustration, do not focus on the sound of *t* right after teaching the sound *d* records.

To sum up, the recommendation is to teach some consonant sounds before introducing vowel sounds; to give consideration to speech difficulties when a sequence for instruction is selected; and to avoid teaching too closely together sounds that are similar.*

Inductive and Deductive Instruction. The two possible ways to teach letter-sound relationships (grapheme-phoneme correspondences) were described earlier. With an inductive approach, you will recall, a teacher helps children reason from words having a common visual-auditory feature to the sound a selected letter represents. Thus, by using words as examples she helps them come to understand the difference that a certain letter makes to the pronunciation of words. With an illustration, let me further clarify the meaning of inductive instruction.

Should a teacher decide to teach inductively the sound which *p*

* More advanced instruction in phonics deals with the sounds of letter combinations. At that time, close similarity also is a source of confusion; for instance, with the sounds recorded by *sh* (*shop*) and *ch* (*chop*).

records, she might begin by using pictures of objects whose names begin with *p*. For each picture she would (a) discuss the content; (b) assign the appropriate name to it; and (c) write that name. As a result the chalkboard might show:

Writing these words allows for the first important question about them: "Who sees something that's the same at the beginning of all these words? (They all start with *p*.) Besides starting with *p*, all these words have something else that's the same. You'll hear how they're the same at the beginning if you listen as I say them: *pie, pear, purse, park, pot*. What did you hear that's the same? (No response) Let me say these words again. Watch me when I say them. If you do, you'll see that my mouth is the same when I start to say each one.* That's because all these words start with the same sound. If you listen to the words, maybe you can tell me what that sound is. Listen but also watch me say them: *pie, pear, purse, park, pot*. What did you hear at the beginning of all those words? (puh.) That's right. We can make that sound—that's the sound of *p*—without making any noise. Watch me do that. I'll use my lips but not my voice. . . . Now let's see you make the sound of *p* without making any noise. . . . Good.** Now you'll know, whenever you see a word that begins with *p*, that it might start with the sound you hear at the beginning of *pie, pear, purse, park,* and *pot*. Can you think of some other words that start the way *pie* starts? If you can, I'll write those on the board, too, so that you can see their first letter is *p*. (My name starts with *P*.) Right, a capital *P* because it's your name, but it makes the same sound as the lowercase *p*. Listen. *Paul, pipe, park*. I'll write Paul on the board, too."

* The sound recorded by *p*, and by *b* and *m*, is easily seen on the mouth.
** Detailed attention will be given later to the question of isolating sounds from words.

At the conclusion of this lesson the board showed:

To summarize the lesson, the teacher reread all the words as a way of reinforcing its goal: knowledge of the sound recorded by *p*. On another day the sound would be listened to in final position; that is, in words like *top* and *nap*.

In a different room, another teacher might not introduce this letter-sound association until somewhat later. By then the children would be more accustomed to inducing sounds from words; in addition, their reading vocabulary is likely to include words that start with *p*. In that classroom, therefore, inductive instruction dealing with *p* would be somewhat different and might proceed as follows.

After writing *p* on the chalkboard, this teacher asks the group of children she's instructing: "What's the name of this letter? (P.) That's right. Let me write some words you know that begin with *p*. You can read each one as I write it, but don't say anything until I finish writing because, as you learned yesterday, changing just one letter can change what a word says. OK. Here's the first."

Eventually the board displays:

* This detergent was named by one of the girls as the kind her mother used.

Aware that inductive instruction is most successful when a fairly sizeable number of words is used to illustrate a letter-sound relationship, this teacher had considered two ways to add to the three words listed. She thought about using the names of pictures, as did the previous teacher, but also children's names. She chose the latter because of the interest in names and, secondly, because they would give her the chance to emphasize that lowercase *p* and capital *P* record the same sound. Consequently, she continues the lesson with: "I know some children right in this room who have names that start with *P*. (Immediately Paul, Peter, and Penny raise their hands.) Yes, Penny, Paul, and Peter have names that start with *P*. I'll write them separately because they're names and they start with capital *P*."

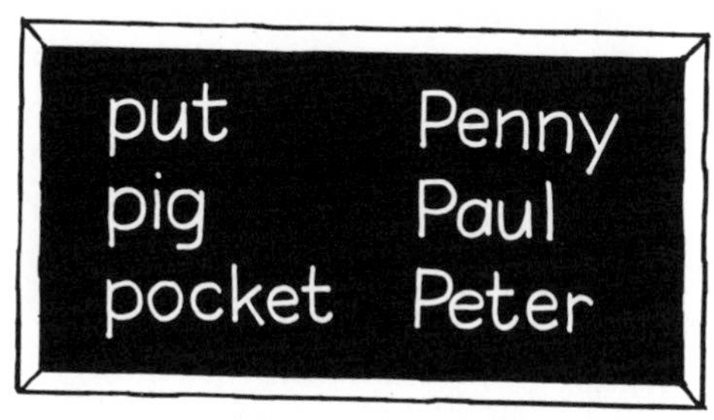

You know all these words. Let's read them together. . . . If you look at these words you'll see something that's the same at the beginning of each. What is it? (They all start with the letter *p*.) Right. And there's something else that's the same, too. In this case it's something you can hear. Say all these words. Then see if you can tell me something about the beginning sound of each. . . . Did you hear something that's the same at the beginning of all these words? (They all start with the same letter.) Letter? We don't hear a letter. We see a letter but we hear a sound. Let's read the words again. As you read them, listen to the sound at the beginning of each one. It's the same sound. Let's see if you'll be able to tell me what that same sound is. . . . Can someone give me the sound that's at the beginning of all these words? (puh.) Right. Let's read the words again and, as we do, listen for the sound. . . . Since we're learning about the sound that *p* stands for, I thought it would be a good idea to put pictures of things that start with that sound on the bulletin board. ("Mrs. J———, 'picture' starts with that sound.") Right. Good for you. I'm going to show you some pictures one at a time. Think of its name. If it starts the way *put*, *pig*, and *pocket* start, raise your hand and then tell me its name. . . ."

Before moving to a description of deductive instruction with letter sounds, let me first make a few comments about the two inductive lessons because they have equal significance for deductive procedures:

1. Whenever possible, words the children can read should be used to illustrate the letter-sound association being taught.
2. Whether they can be identified by the children or not, words that *begin* with the selected letter and sound should be used. (Initial consonant sounds are best for beginning instruction because consonants are more consistent than vowels in what they record and, secondly, because consonants in initial position are more clearly pronounced than either medial or final consonants.) Whenever possible, short words in which the initial consonant is followed by a vowel should be used. (Again, such selections make it easier to hear the sound being highlighted.)
3. Write selected words in columns in order to make the similarity of beginning letters maximally apparent.
4. When it happens that selected words begin with the same two letters (e.g., *Penny, Peter*), try to separate them in the column to divert attention from *Pe* to *P* alone. (See the listing on page 347.)
5. To make sure children recognize the sound being taught, have them name words that start with it.
6. Procedures for teaching vowel sounds or the sounds associated with clusters of letters are the same as what is used when a consonant sound is the concern. To teach about the sounds represented by *st*, for instance, words like *star* and *stay* could be used. With vowel sounds—the short *e* sound, for example—words such as *egg* and *end* would be appropriate.
7. To help children remember a given letter-sound association, stress one picture in particular that shows something whose name begins with that letter and sound.* For example, in the instruction focussing on the sound recorded by *p* the teacher might have noticed the children's enthusiastic response to the colorful picture of a pie. With that in mind she might start the next phonics lesson by showing that picture again. After reviewing the sound of *p* with the help of "pie," she could explain to the children that she is going to hang up its picture to help them in case they forget what the sound of *p* is. Through a little role-playing she might even pretend to be a child and think out loud as she uses the picture to help recall the sound. (This point is stressed because, although most classrooms display a wealth of

* On several occasions I have administered a phonics test to five year olds and learned, because they so often thought out loud, how frequently they recalled the sound of a letter by first recalling a word that began with it. Those experiences account for my encouraging you to use pictures as a source of assistance for children who forget the sound of a letter. Eventually they will be unnecessary but, at the start, they are a help.

potentially helpful pictures, I have never once seen a teacher give explicit demonstrations of how they can be of assistance when sounds are forgotten.)

With the above reminders in the background, let me now move to an example of deductive instruction. Again the goal is to teach the sound of *p*.

As an earlier section of the chapter mentioned, deductive instruction is a telling process. Applied to teaching letter sounds, it begins by telling the children the sound a certain letter represents. For instance when *p* is the focus, a teacher might talk about the way letters stand for sounds and then say something like: "This is the letter *p* (writes it on the board), and it has the sound of *puh*. Listen to that sound when I say some words that begin with *p: pay, pin, put, pond, pee*k. I think I'll write those words so that you'll be able to see that they all begin with *p*. (All are renamed and written in a column.) As I point to each of these words, I'll tell you again what they say. As I say them, listen to the sound with which all of them begin. . . . Can you think of some other words that begin with the same sound as *pay, pin, put, pond,* and *peek?* If you can, I'll write them on the board, too." Responses come in the following order: *pants, pumpkin, penny, nickel, play*. Thus the board shows:

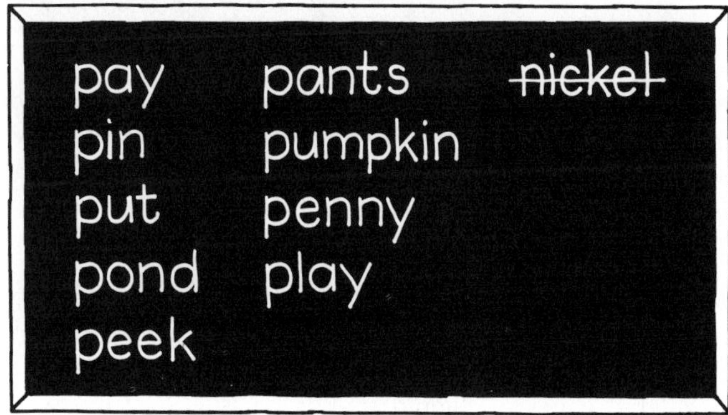

To further emphasize the sound of *p*, this teacher next moves to some contrasts; for example, "I'm going to say two words. Listen, and then tell me which starts with the letter *p*. *Paste, glue*. . . . *Blanket, pillow*. . . . *Pig, parrot*. . . ."

For variety and still more practice, the teacher continues with: "I'm going to read some sentences, but I'm not going to tell you what the last word is. It will begin with the letter *p*, so that should help you. Here's the first one. Tell me what the last word might be. The name of a color is —— (purple). Right. But I know another color that starts with *p*. Do you? (Pink?) Right. Good. Here's another sentence. Tell me what the last word is. We call a dog's foot a —— (paw). Right again. . . ."

Because this teacher keeps in mind that reading is visual and, therefore, that children should be seeing what they are hearing, she remembers to write at least some of the responses. Thus the board now displays:

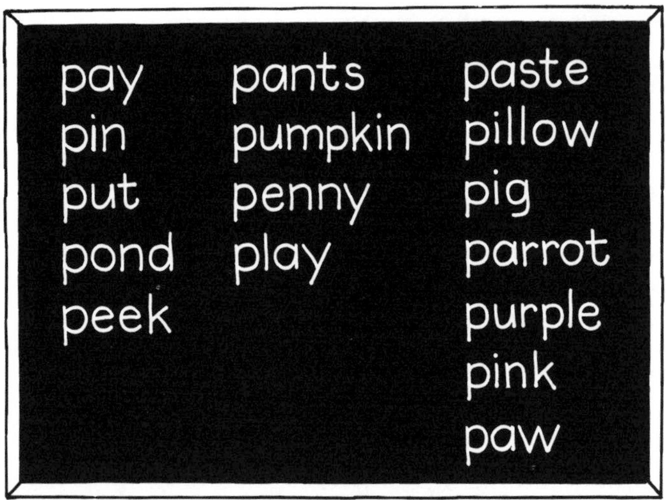

Recognizing the importance of ending instruction with some type of summary, she concludes this attention to the sound of *p* by reading all the words, encouraging the children to listen to beginning sounds and to join in whenever she points to a word they can read.

Isolating Letter Sounds. Examples of inductive and deductive procedures for teaching letter sounds have been presented. Which to use, therefore, is a timely question. Before proposing an answer, let me first discuss a related concern: Should sounds be isolated from words?

In answering this important question it must first be noted that special training is not required to know that the sound "puh" is not heard in a word like *pan*. It is heard in *pun*—and *puff* and *pumpkin* and *puddle*—but in all those words is represented by *pu*, not *p*. Educators with responsibility for teaching reading have always been aware of what has been called the "impurity" of consonant sounds when they are pronounced apart from words. However, from the time a few linguists became involved with instructional materials in the 1960s, isolating any sound has become almost sinful. How these linguists view sounds (phonemes) can be explained quickly with a quote from one linguist, Charles Fries:

> These phonemes are not separate *sounds*, but *bundles* of sound contrasts that are phonetically actualized differently in various environments.* One cannot pronounce the English phoneme /t/. He can pronounce the phonetic realization of this phoneme as it occurs initially in the word *top,* or as it occurs finally in the word *pot,* or as it occurs in the initial cluster of the word *stop.* And these three pronunciations would all be different (9, p. 159).

What Fries and other linguists are saying is that phonemes are not separate sounds; in fact, they do not even exist apart from words. Therefore they can hardly be pronounced. Because I am not a linguist I am not in a position to comment on this. However I am in a position to say that, to my untrained ear, the following observation makes sense:

> It is part of the very essence of language that sounds are uttered in very rapid sequences which become words. Each sound has such a fleeting existence that it is not truly reproducible outside the context of a word. Wresting it out of its natural place makes it something different, altering its length and the amount of breath put into it, and sometimes making it into a syllable by the addition of another sound (15, p. 11).

What is the meaning of this for teaching letter sounds? The goal of such teaching, it must be remembered, is to help children figure out words that are unknown in their written form. Although words do flow from one to another, that flow stops whenever an unfamiliar one is encountered in written material. At that time, at least if the word is critical to comprehension, the reader must stop—even an adult reader—and "wrest it out of its natural place." The reason for this chapter is that once it has been "wrested" a way to deal with it is to consider its letters, their sequence, and their sounds. After the word has been identified and becomes familiar, its pronunciation will change in the sense that the reader will have no further need to slow down to decode it. Instead, it now is a part of that flowing language in which sounds are "uttered in very rapid sequences."

With all this in mind, I can accept the idea that "each sound has such a fleeting existence that it is not truly reproducible outside the context of a word," but still be aware of the need with *some* children to isolate sounds. That is, it has been my experience to observe that some

* "Various environments" refers to different positions in a word. For example *p* is in three different environments in *pin, nap,* and *spun.* According to linguists, it would also represent three different sounds. This leads to subclasses of phonemes, referred to as "allophones."

children cannot induce letter-sound associations from examples. For instance, no matter how many questions a teacher might ask about words like *pond, put,* and *pen,* they are not able to arrive at a conclusion regarding the sound that *p* stands for. They seem to require at least one explicit identification. This can be made carefully so as to minimize the addition of the short *u* sound. Such care, by the way, is especially necessary for what linguists call "stop sounds"; these are the sounds associated with *b, k, d, p, t,* and *g* (hard sound). Special care is required because stop sounds cannot be produced apart from words without the addition of the short *u* sound.

To take the position that some children will require isolation of sounds is not to condone what has been heard in some classrooms. Here I refer to day-by-day drills with *puh, puh, puh,* even after children have demonstrated their awareness of the sound of *p*. And I also refer to the times I have heard teachers pronounce (mispronounce) the sound recorded by *r* as *"er,"* by *dr* as *"der,"* and by *cl* as *"cul."*

Inductive or Deductive Instruction? As the teaching illustrations indicated earlier, the key difference between deductive and inductive instruction applied to letter sounds is that the former begins with their identification while with the latter they are induced from words containing them. However, as was also mentioned earlier, if a child is unable to induce a sound from the examples, it will have to be identified for him. In such instances there is less of a difference between deductive and inductive instruction than might otherwise be the case. Even when this happens, it is important to note, there still is a sufficiently important difference between the two procedures as to require an answer to, "Which to use?"

The difference is that inductive instruction, whether applied to sounds, factors affecting them, or syllabication, gives children an opportunity to arrive at an understanding of the nature of written language. (This point was the underlying theme of the chapter on writing instruction.) Too, inductive instruction gives children a strategy for learning which, in turn, allows some to discover many letter-sound relationships on their own. Further, it makes the idea of "letters standing for sounds" more meaningful because letters and sounds are dealt with through the vehicle of words, much more familiar to all. In contrast, deductive instruction tends to plunge children into sounds immediately, probably leaving at least a few in a state of bewilderment about all the hissing and puffing and blowing that suddenly surrounds them.

With these differences in mind, the recommendation of this textbook is to introduce phonics with inductive instruction. Once children seem to understand what is going on, then a combination of inductive and deductive methods can be used. When to use which? Advice recently spoken by a teacher provides an answer: "If you look at a child and his eyes tell you he doesn't know what in the world you're talking about, have enough sense to try something else."

Teaching the Content of Phonics: Factors Affecting Sounds

As you will recall from the earlier overview, phonics content deals not only with letter sounds but also with features of a syllable (cues) that suggest the sounds which certain letters are likely to record. These features are described with such statements as: "When there is one vowel in a syllable and it comes at the end (*go, he*), it usually records its long sound. Obviously, such content lacks relevance until a child is aware that letters can represent different sounds. With the generalization just cited, he would not be ready to learn about a time when a vowel is likely to record its long sound until he knows the long sounds, but the short ones as well. This offers a guideline for the sequence of phonics instruction: Teach letter sounds (not necessarily them all) before you deal with factors that affect them.

Teaching a child about these factors is important because such knowledge increases noticeably his ability to figure out words independently. And that, after all, is what phonics is all about. Still, nothing can be done until the different sounds of a letter are dealt with. For example, the summary of content presented in one basal series at the first grade level (see page 354) suggests a generous amount; yet, you will notice, only one sound for each letter has been considered. Other possibilities, of course, would be to teach less of what is shown, thus allowing time for attention to such things as both the long and short vowel sounds and, perhaps, the soft and hard sounds for *c* and *g*.

Theoretically, early attention to variety makes sense in that it should foster flexibility in the use of phonics—an absolute "must" with our language. A specific application of this would be to teach the short and long sounds of the vowels in close proximity, thus demonstrating early to children that sounds sometimes have to be "tried out" to see what makes sense. On the other hand, it could also be argued that the challenge of diversity is too much challenge too soon; that it should be introduced only after children have experienced success in using the more stable letter-sound relationships.

Actually, such questions are among the many in reading which have no well-substantiated and inevitably correct answer. But, this might be further proof of what teachers witness year after year: What is helpful for one child turns into a problem for another.

In any case, at some point children do have to learn about and deal

WORD SERVICE PROGRAM FOR GRADE ONE

I. Phonology

CONSONANT SOUNDS

Single Consonant Letters	Reading Skills Book
/s/ as in *Sandy*	One
/b/ as in *Bing*	One
/w/ as in *was*	One
/g/ as in *good*	One
/m/ as in *morning*	One
/r/ as in *ran*	One
/l/ as in *little*	One
/h/ as in *hid*	One
/d/ as in *down*	One
/p/ as in *pond*	One
/t/ as in *turtle*	One
/k/ as in *Kevin*	Two
/j/ as in *Jan*	Two
/n/ as in *not*	Two
/f/ as in *fast*	Two
/v/ as in *very*	Two
/k/ as in *can*	Two
/y/ as in *yes*	Two
/ks/ as in *mix*	Four
/z/ as in *has*	Four
/kw/ as in *quack*	Four
/j/ as in *cage*	Four
/s/ as in *city*	Four
Double Consonant Letters	
/l/ as in *tell*	Two
/s/ as in *grass*	Two
/k/ as in *duck*	Two
/z/ as in *buzz*	Three
Consonant Digraphs	
/sh/ as in *shadow*	Two
/th/ as in *that*	Two
/ch/ as in *chair*	Two
/ng/ as in *sing*	Two
/nk/ as in *thank*	Four
Consonant Clusters	
/st/ as in *star*	Three
/sk/ as in *sky*	Three
/sl/ as in *sleep*	Three
/wh/ as in *when*	Three
/gr/ as in *grass*	Three
/br/ as in *bright*	Three
/pl/ as in *plane*	Three
/fl/ as in *flower*	Three

Consonant Clusters (cont'd)	Reading Skills Book
/bl/ as in *black*	Three
/sp/ as in *spin*	Three
/dr/ as in *drink*	Three
/tr/ as in *truck*	Three
/str/ as in *street*	Three
/fr/ as in *frog*	Four
/nd/ as in *band*	Four
/nt/ as in *sent*	Four
/kr/ as in *cried*	Four
/kl/ as in *clay*	Four
/sn/ as in *sniff*	Four
/sm/ as in *small*	Four
/ld/ as in *held*	Four

VOWEL SOUNDS

/a/ as in *hat*	Three
/i/ as in *spin*	Three
/u/ as in *bug*	Three
/e/ as in *bed*	Four
/o/ as in *hop*	Four

II. Morphology

SUFFIXES		Reading Skills Book
–s	as in *bugs*	One
–ed	as in *looked*	Two
–s	as in *plays*	Three
–d	as in *danced*	Three
–ing	as in *looking*	Three
–es	as in *boxes*	Three
–s	as in *houses*	Three
double consonant –ed	as in *hopped*	Four
double consonant –ing	as in *hopping*	Four

III. Word Study

		Reading Skills Book
Possessives	as in *Kevin's*	Two
Abbreviations	as in *Mr.*	Two
Contractions	as in *can't*	Two
Compound words	as in *moonlight*	Three
Homophones	as in *be-bee*	Four

Teaching Reading in Grade One 11

From *Sun Up and Reading Skills One,* Teacher's Edition, The Bookmark Reading Program, p. 11. Copyright 1970 by Harcourt, Brace & World, Inc.

with variety; this might come through attention to the hard and soft sounds for *c* and *g*, or the short and long sounds for the vowels. For illustrative purposes, let us say a group of children has learned about long and short vowel sounds. On many occasions they have demonstrated their knowledge of both, and so are now ready to learn when each is likely to occur in a word.* Let us say, either because of the materials being used or a teacher's own decision, the plan is to teach about a time when vowels probably will represent their long sounds. More specifically, the selected goal is to help children understand the following generalization: *When there is one vowel in a syllable and it comes at the end, it usually records its long sound.* How might such a goal be realized? Let me answer with illustrations.

Whatever instructional procedure is selected, it should begin with a review of the long and short sounds, which I would not hesitate to isolate from words. I say this because I have never known a child who developed problems because of questions like, "What is the short sound of *o*?" However, I have known many who had problems because sounds were not reviewed sufficiently, especially the difficult short vowel sounds.

Once a teacher feels sure the children she's instructing know the long and short sounds, she would probably write some known words on the board, especially if she had decided to proceed inductively:

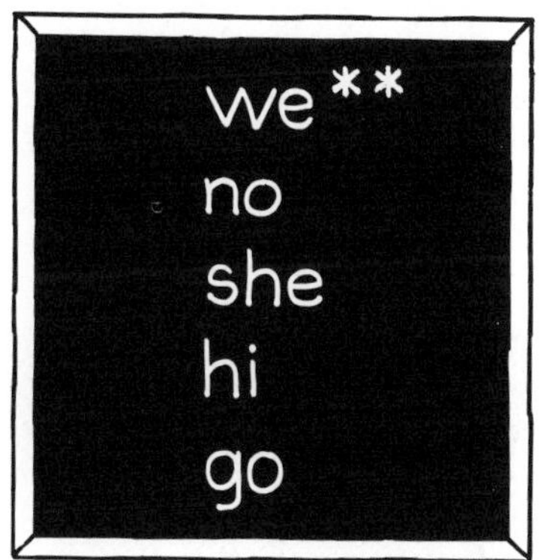

With these words as the focus, instruction would begin by having the children read them. Then, to bring out the visual and auditory features that are relevant, question-asking begins: "Would you look at each of

* With relative beginners in phonics, one-syllable words would be used in order to simplify instruction as much as possible. This makes it unnecessary *at this time* to differentiate between a syllable and a word in applying generalizations.

** A list of words containing all five vowels would be preferable. However, suitable one-syllable words ending with *a* and *u* are nonexistent.

these words? How many vowels does each have? (One) What sound does the *e* makes in *we*? (*ē*) Well, yes, it says its own name, but what do we call that sound? (The long sound.) Fine. Good. Let's look at *no*. You said there's one vowel in *no*—an *o*. What sound does *o* make in the word *no*? (The long sound) Right again. What about the *e* in *she*? What sound does that make? (The long sound) Yes. You can really hear that 'e' sound in *she*, can't you? What about *hi*? There's only one vowel in *hi*—an *i*. What sound does the *i* make in *hi*? (*ī*) Yes, it says its own name. It has the long sound. What about the last word? What sound does *o* make in *go*? (The long sound) Well, you've told me lots of things that are the same about these words. You said they all have just one vowel. And then you said that each of those vowels stands for its long sound. Can you tell me one more thing that's the same about all these words? (They all have two letters.*) Do they? What about *she*? How many letters in *she*? Let's count. (One-two-three) Yes, *she* has three letters. No, there's something else that's the same about all these words, about the vowel in each one. (I know. They come at the end.) Right, in each word the vowel is at the end. Now you've told me three things that are the same about all these words. You told me they all have one vowel, the vowel is at the end, and the vowel stands for its long sound. Knowing all those things will help you figure out new words. Now, whenever you come across a new word that has one vowel and it's at the end, you'll know that it will have the long sound—or, at least most of the time it will have the long sound. Remember. When a word has one vowel and it's at the end, the vowel usually has the long sound. Let's get all those things on the board to help us remember."

As the teacher writes, she reads:

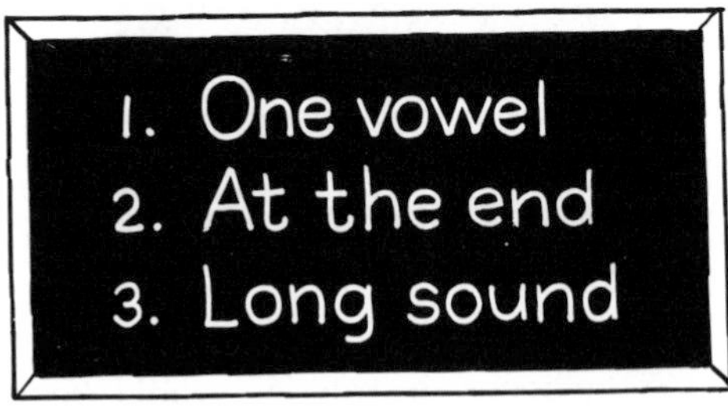

Pointing to each, she helps the children get through a statement of the generalization. (How the children would be taught to use it to decode unknown words will be considered in a subsequent section of the chapter.)

* This response demonstrates the importance of having something other than two-letter words because, in this case, the number of letters is irrelevant.

Sometime later, to prepare for another generalization but also to reinforce the meaning and usefulness of the present one, this same teacher chooses to pair and ask questions about words like:

no not
he hen
hi him
go got
be bed

As before, questions would call the children's attention to visual cues; in this case, not only the number of vowels but also their placement in the syllable. Through contrast (*no–not, he–hen*) the children can begin to see the relevance of both for the way a word is pronounced.

While words like *not, hen,* and *bed* are preparing children for another generalization (When a word has one vowel that is not at the end, it usually stands for its short sound) use of these kinds of words (consonant-vowel-consonant pattern) could lead them to think that it is only when a single vowel is in the middle of a syllable that it records its short sound. To discourage that erroneous conclusion, a list like the following is useful:

got
end
up
fat
ask
in

Teaching Use of Phonics Content

Thus far, the chapter has reviewed the content of phonics, has illustrated how letter sounds can be taught and, just now, has shown how children can learn generalizations dealing with features of a syllable that offer cues about the sounds certain letters are likely to represent.

Teaching this content is important; still, there is more to phonics instruction than that. In fact, to teach only the content alters the role of phonics. Instead of being a helpful means for identifying words, it becomes an end in itself. To maintain its correct role, therefore, just as much attention must go to the *use* of phonics content as to the content itself.

Remembering that phonics is merely a means to an end becomes increasingly important because, currently, more and more phonics is being taught earlier and earlier. Whenever this happens there always is the possibility that teachers will begin to view phonics content as an end in itself, forgetting that instruction merits the description "successful" only when children demonstrate ability to use what has been taught to figure out unknown words. In fact, how well they use phonics with new words is the only meaningful criterion for evaluating any type of instruction.

When phonics is correctly viewed as a means to an end, a successful program also is one that gives children freedom to use it in their own way—assuming their way is efficient and productive. This second criterion is mentioned because from time to time individual children will be found who are able to manipulate letter sounds in their own unique, somewhat unorthodox way and come out with right answers. Ask these same individuals to verbalize the more usual content and generalizations and they might be much less successful. Of this kind of child, Wardhaugh has written:

> He may not be able to verbalize the rule any more than he could tell you how he ties his shoe laces; but just as he can demonstrate that he knows the rules for tying shoe laces by tying shoe laces, so he can demonstrate his knowledge of the rules for pronouncing *c* by reading *city* and *cat* correctly. His knowledge of the rules is demonstrated by his performance and it is unnecessary for him to learn to verbalize a statement about what he has learned, that is, about what he knows (18, p. 136).

Because the vast majority of children will not develop their own system and "rules," instruction both in the content of phonics and in how it can be used is essential.

Separating, as this chapter does, the topics of "Teaching Content" and "Teaching Its Use" is not intended to suggest that instruction dealing with use begins only after all the content has been taught. Rather, the recommendation is to teach some content (for example, some consonant sounds), then how it can be used to decode words, then more content, then how that can be used, and so on. In between, of course, there would be reviews, attempts to find out what children have actually been learning and, when necessary, some reteaching.

Teaching Use of Letter Sounds. Because consonant sounds generally are taught first, this discussion of use of content will begin with them.

And it will begin with the reminder that use is as much caught as it is taught. This means that if teachers do not display use of phonics in their own behavior, they must not expect children to do differently. This point is underscored because classroom observations uncover many instances in which opportunities to demonstrate use are not taken advantage of. I refer, for instance, to times when children misread a word and the teacher's only reaction is to supply the correct response. Because many word identification errors could be explained through failure to make use of what had been taught in phonics, reactions should be different. To be even more specific, I have recently heard errors like the following, and the teacher's only reaction was to offer correct responses.

Word	Read as
waited	wanted
her	she
left	felt
soon	on
beside	below
neighbor	neighborhood

Admittedly, there *are* times when circumstances allow for nothing more than a correction; however, there are many other occasions when a teacher could—and should—explain erroneous responses by calling the child's attention to relevant cues that he failed to use.* With *waited* and *wanted*, for instance, she might write:

Depending on what the child knows about letter sounds, his teacher might only be able to remind him that the sound of *n* could not be heard in *wait* because it has no *n*. Thus, *wait* could not be *want*. If he knows more phonics, she could remind him of the two vowels in *wait* and then ask questions about their significance. (When there are two vowels, the first often records its long sound and the second is silent.)

* In this discussion it is recognized that *constant* corrections cause problems in that they undermine a child's self-confidence. This always is to be avoided because a child must be willing to take a chance at being wrong, when he is learning to read. The point to be stressed, therefore, is that if constant corrections *are* necessary, they indicate the child is being asked to read too-difficult material, which should never be the case.

Probably one reason why teachers have gotten into the habit of supplying a correct answer rather than an explanation of the wrong one is that basal readers traditionally used a fairly large number of irregularly spelled words in beginning materials. A consequence is that not much could be done to explain some of the wrong responses because they were just as logical as the correct ones. Now that basals are changing to early and more frequent use of regularly spelled words, teachers will have many more opportunities to display in their own behavior appropriate use of phonics.

Some of the ways children need to learn to use what they know is shown below. As this summary indicates, use in these cases combines use of a known word and a letter sound.

SUBSTITUTIONS: INITIAL SOUNDS

Known word:	cat	in	top
Known sound:	/f/	/ă/ *	/ch/
Decoded word:	fat	an	chop

SUBSTITUTIONS: FINAL SOUNDS

Known word:	feel	he	cat
Known sound:	/d/	/ī/	/sh/
Decoded word:	feed	hi	cash

SUBSTITUTIONS: MEDIAL SOUNDS

Known word:	act	man	bell
Known sound:	/n/	/ĕ/	/ĭ/
Decoded word:	ant	men	bill

ADDITIONS: INITIAL SOUNDS

Known word:	all	and	in
Known sound:	/b/	/st/	/th/
Decoded word:	ball	stand	thin

ADDITIONS: FINAL SOUNDS

Known word:	star	in	fir
Known sound:	/t/	/ch/	/st/
Decoded word:	start	inch	first

Classroom observations would suggest that of the various phonic substitutions and additions that are possible, final additions (car ⟶ card) generally are the easiest because they start with a familiar sound to which a final one is appended. However they are not as frequently available as initial substitutions (car ⟶ far). That is, many more words can be identified through initial substitutions than final additions. For

* In this summary, phonic [/ă/] rather than linguistic [/æ/] symbols are used to indicate the phoneme.

that reason most instructional materials introduce use of letter sounds with substitutions; more specifically, with initial consonant substitutions (ball ⟶ tall). With them, a sequence for instruction would be determined by (a) the words children can read, and (b) the sounds they know. For instance, if it happened that they could read *ball*, and also knew the sounds which *t*, *f*, and *w* represent, they would be ready to learn how to use initial consonant substitutions as one way to figure out unfamiliar words:

ball
tall
fall
wall

In initiating instruction, it is a good practice to write the familiar word (*ball*) and the unfamiliar ones (*tall, fall, wall*) in a column to stress both identical and different parts.* Prior to this, however, *ball* should be reviewed—that is, named by the children—along with the sounds that *t*, *f*, and *w* record. In fact, whenever instruction is to focus on the use of something, that something should always be reviewed at the start. With this lesson, the next step is to point out (or ask) how the listed words are the same and how they are different visually. Once that is done, a variety of procedures is possible for introducing the sound-substitution process. One teacher might choose to write sentences like the following on the chalkboard:

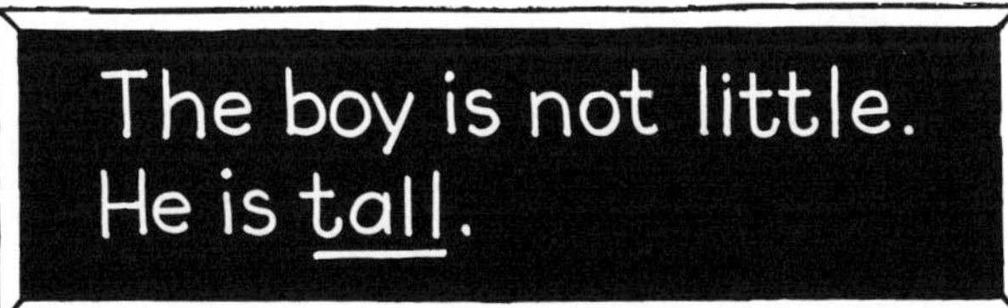

The boy is not little.
He is tall.

In this case a context helps with the substitution, and such help is important initially. Should it happen that it is not enough and the children are unable to identify *tall*, the teacher could tell them what it says

* If any of the so-called unfamiliar words are in fact known to the children, different ones should be selected. Otherwise, the lesson will be one of word review rather than instruction in use of substitutions. I mention this because I have been in classrooms in which words to be "worked on" were being mumbled (correctly) by the children, but still the teacher persisted with her lesson plan. Having done this, she would not be able to know whether the children were merely reading words they knew or, on the other hand, were actually learning something about sound substitutions.

and then say together *ball* and *tall* to stress the connection. Next, other sentences might be written:

I do not want to fall off my chair.

If *fall* causes problems, the teacher might name *ball*, review the sound of *f*, and then read *fall*. (Actually, self-answered questions are frequently necessary in the beginning because the children are just starting to know what the substitution process is all about.) If it should turn out that they are quite successful in employing substitutions and readily read *tall*, *fall* and *wall*, other practice could be provided—for instance with a word like *mall* since the sound of *m* is familiar. (I deliberately introduce *mall* into this discussion because its meaning is not likely to be known by all the children. It thus provides an opportunity to respond to the question, "Should words unknown in their meaning be used?" In response, the answer can only be, "It depends." For instance, if children are having no problems with—in this case—initial consonant substitutions, a word like *mall* might be used for practice and, in addition, to provide the opportunity to discuss its meaning. When, to the contrary, children have problems with substitutions, then it makes much more sense to select only those words that are likely to be in their listening-speaking vocabulary.)

There is still another point to be made about processes like substitution. I refer to the fact that even when children have no difficulty moving from *ball* to words like *tall*, *fall*, and *wall*, it cannot be assumed they will automatically employ similar substitutions on their own. More specifically, if some or all need to read a sentence like *He is fat*, it cannot be assumed they will be able to decode *fat* just because they know *bat* and the sound of *f*. I say this because identifying *fat* on their own requires that they themselves recall both *bat* and the sound of *f*. In the instruction described earlier, you will remember, the teacher recalled the relevant material for them. What successful transfer requires, therefore, is instruction and practice which focus on sentences containing words that could be figured out on the basis of what children know, presuming they are able to recall what they know that is of relevance. As with other new learnings, children will need help at the start but, with practice, they can learn to be quite successful in recalling the known in order to decode the unknown. (A sample of such practice is described on page 374.)

That sentences are helpful in getting children to make use of what they know has just been demonstrated. Another of their contributions is related to the need to get children to be flexible in that use. Although with words like *ball, tall, fall,* and *wall*—or *bat* and *fat*—flexibility is unnecessary, with many others it is an absolute requirement. Not to employ it, for instance, in moving from the known word *cow* to an unknown one like *low* is to create rather than to solve a problem. In such cases, a context (e.g., The plane was flying low) coupled with the always important question, "Does such-and-such a pronunciation make sense?" is absolutely essential. Essential, too, is encouragement for the children to try out a variety of sounds—especially for vowels and vowel combinations—whenever a pronunciation does not make sense. Thus, once it is decided that *low* does not follow the pronunciation of *cow,* children should be given help and encouragement to mentally run through all the possible vowel sounds on the assumption that *ow* could record any one of them. (Detailed attention to this appears on pages 370–371.) Once the correctness of a pronunciation is verified with the help of the context (The plane was flying low) other words in which *ow* represents the long *o* sound could be written and identified; for instance *grow* and *own.*

To sum up, then, important ways for using letter sounds to decode words are substitutions and additions. When these processes first get attention, words isolated from contexts might be used in order to emphasize relevant relationships between the known (*ball*) and the unknown (*fall, tall, wall*). For the most part, however, words being decoded with the help of substitutions and additions ought to be placed in sentences. This allows for realistic reading in the sense that good readers use not only letter-sound cues for word identification but also the help that comes from a context. In fact, contexts allow for the question that must always be asked when words are being decoded: Does such-and-such a pronunciation *make sense?*

Teaching Use of Generalizations about Factors Affecting Sounds. With beginners, phonics instruction dealing with use might go no further than substitutions and additions. Still, teachers need to be ready to go further in case individual children are ready for more. With that in mind, this section deals with some of the ways children can be taught to use generalizations describing factors which affect sounds—for example: When there is one vowel in a syllable and it is not at the end, it generally records its short sound. Earlier, ways for teaching this particular generalization were described (p. 357). Now the question is: How can children be taught to use it to decode unknown words?

It should first be noted that some words to which this generalization applies ought to be figured out with the help of familiar words plus additions or substitutions. For example, it applies to a word like *man;*

yet, if a child can read *an* and knows the sound of *m*, a phonic addition should be employed to identify *man* because that is an efficient procedure. Still other words to which the same generalization applies (*ant, pan, in*) could be figured out efficiently in such ways as these:

Known Word	Unknown Word	Decoding Procedure
an	man	initial consonant addition
an	ant	final consonant addition
an	in	initial vowel substitution

While the above decoding procedures are more efficient than a detailed letter-by-letter analysis, they are not always possible because words that could be used (e.g., *an*) might not be known. For that reason, children need to learn the significance of a generalization like: When there is one vowel and it is not at the end, it usually stands for its short sound.

To illustrate how its significance might be taught, let us say the teacher who introduced the generalization in the way described on page 360 decides to demonstrate its usefulness with the unknown word *fast*. (The assumption is that related words like *last* and *past* are not known either. Otherwise, consonant substitution would be employed.) As was suggested earlier, she would begin with a review, in this case of the sounds of *f, s,* and *t* (or the cluster *st,* if that had been taught). She would also review the generalization itself; in fact, she might even choose to go over very quickly the way it was first taught. Following the review, attention to application begins.

It would probably begin by writing *fast* on the chalkboard—not as part of a sentence because, in this case, the goal of the instruction is to demonstrate how a generalization, not a context, can help with decoding. Then questions about *fast* would be posed by the teacher; for instance: "How many vowels are in this new word? . . . Is that vowel at the end of the word? . . . What do you know about the sound a vowel usually stands for when it is the only vowel and is not at the end of a word? . . . What is the short sound of *a*? . . . Can anyone tell me what this word is?"

Let's assume that nobody can; this probably would be so in an actual classroom and, in addition, it provides an opportunity to describe sound-by-sound blending. With *fast,* such blending would be guided by a sequence of questions like:

1. What is the sound of short *a*? (ă)
2. Let's put the sound of *f* in front of that. What is the sound of *fa*? (fă)
3. Let's add the sound of *s* to the end of "fă." (făs)
4. Say that again but add the sound of *t* to the end. (făst)

As these questions are being asked and answered, the teacher is writing the following to add the visual dimension:

Had the children been taught to deal with clusters (st), one less question would be asked and one less step would be shown:

In either case, notice that the first step in the blending dealt with the vowel sound, even though the first letter in the word was *f*. This was done to avoid isolating the sound of *f* and, in turn, to avoid an "answer" that might sound something like *fu-ast.* Had the unknown word been one that started with a vowel—*end,* for instance—the blending sequence would simply follow the left-to-right sequence of the letters:

To sum up, the blending of sounds to form syllables proceeds in a left-to-right progression, except when a consonant is the initial letter. In those cases the first vowel sound is made, the initial consonant sound is then affixed and, afterwards, a left-to-right sequence is followed. More illustrations of this recommended procedure, and the use of other generalizations, are shown below:

Unknown Word	Blending Sequence
hot	ŏ ⟶ hŏ ⟶ hŏt
stop	ŏ ⟶ stŏ ⟶ stŏp
champ	ă ⟶ chă ⟶ chăm ⟶ chămp
wait	āi̸ ⟶ wāi̸ ⟶ wāi̸t
owl	ow ⟶ owl
ade	ā ⟶ āde̸

At more advanced levels of reading, when some multisyllabic words have to be analyzed in a letter-by-letter, sound-by-sound fashion, the same procedures would be followed—once the word is divided into syllables with the help of generalizations cited earlier (pp. 315–317). With these, each syllable is considered separately and is treated as if it were a word. Whether the unknown word has one or more than one syllable, however, blending is used only when a child cannot identify it with other and quicker procedures. With *fast,* for example, blending would not have been used had the children been able to decode it immediately through their knowledge of the sounds of *f, s,* and *t,* and the short sound of *a,* or because they knew words like *last* or *past.* Actually, to use blending when it is unnecessary is to turn it into an end in itself. And that, as with any other aspect of phonics, can never be defended.

Providing for Practice

No matter how good instruction in phonics might be, provisions for practice always are necessary. When scheduled soon after a new learning has been presented, practice activities give children a chance to use and apply what they have learned. Simultaneously, they give a teacher the chance to diagnose; that is, to learn what the children have or have not been learning. Scheduled later, practice allows for review and is a way to help children maintain what they have learned.

Using Unexpected Opportunities for Practice. While most practice ought to be preplanned and thus carefully matched to what children need to learn, use, review, or whatever, opportunities for it do appear unexpectedly. These can be productive—sometimes more productive than the prearranged type. Consequently teachers should learn to take advantage of the unexpected.

Let me describe a few examples of times when teachers did *not* use unexpected opportunities for phonics practice. With the same descriptions, what is meant by "opportunities" should become clearer.

> A teacher chose to read a story called *Mike Mulligan.* Just a week earlier the children had been learning about the sound that *m* usually represents; yet the teacher never commented about the *M*'s in the title—it wasn't even shown to the children —nor did she ask anything like, "Could someone tell me the first letter in Mike's two names?"
>
> In this same room—again soon after instruction with the *m* sound had been initiated—the children were reading a story about a mirror. It happened that the mirror was shown in illustrations, but the word for it never appeared in the story. Again, however, the teacher did not ask what the first letter in *mirror* would be, nor did she ever write it on the board.
>
> In another classroom the children developed the habit of shouting out a word's identity before the teacher finished writing it. To discourage this, and to demonstrate the importance of every letter to every word, she could have deliberately started out to write a predictable word—e.g., *big*—and then change it by writing *d* or *n* in the place of the predicted *g*.
>
> A phonics assignment given a group of children dealt with a seeing-eye dog. It had no name, but one of the children said it should have one and suggested Rin Tin Tin. This group had been learning about the likelihood of short vowel sounds, when there is one vowel in a word and it is not at the end. As a result, a question like, "Can someone spell the three words in that name?" would have been timely. Or, the teacher might have chosen to write the name, after which she could refer to the generalization and the way it helped her know how to spell Rin Tin Tin. Instead, nothing was done.
>
> In a discussion of community helpers, a child said he knew one but could not remember his name. He explained, "He pulls teeth." The teacher might have said something like, "I'll give you a hint. His name begins with *d.* Think of the sound *d* stands for and maybe you'll be able to think of that helper's name." Instead she commented, "Oh, you mean the dentist."

Other opportunities to display the usefulness of phonics have been bypassed in connection with basal reader lessons. With these, it was as if the teacher had a plan (e.g., Review vocabulary. Read story.) and nothing—not even misread words—was going to get in the way of that plan. Repeatedly, for example, I have been in classrooms in which children read words incorrectly; yet nothing was ever done except to tell them what the responses should have been. More specifically, I have been in rooms when such errors as the following were heard:

Word	Read as
play	baby
see	look
house	barn

In spite of such errors and in spite of the fact that all these children knew about initial consonant sounds—and much more—the teacher did nothing except to offer the correct response. Such "telling" not only fails to demonstrate the reason why something like letter sounds is taught but, in addition, fails to give children maximum help for learning correct responses to words like *play*, *see*, and *house*. In such instances, therefore, telling is not teaching.

Some Reminders about Planned Practice. Before presenting samples of planned phonics practice, let me first make a few general comments about it in the form of reminders.

The first is that phonics practice can often be carried on in conjunction with whole word identification. As the previous chapter indicated, some whole word instruction always is necessary with beginners because they have not yet learned the skills necessary for decoding. In spite of that, however, whole word instruction and the use of phonics are not either-or procedures. In fact, initial use of the earliest phonic learnings can go hand in hand with word identification. Thus, instead of merely saying to children, "This word is a new one. It says 'day,'" a teacher might list the following on the board, all unknown to the children being instructed:

Focussing on such words as these, the teacher would begin by reviewing the sounds represented by *g*, *l*, and *d*. Next her comment might be: "One of these words is in our story for this morning. It's the word 'day.' One of these words says 'day.' Which one?" Responses tell whether their knowledge of sounds has real meaning for the children.

A more advanced level of the same type of procedure might start with a review of the sounds of *l*, *t*, *p*, and *d*, and with a list of unknown words such as these:

In this case an appropriate question calling for use of phonics along with whole word identification would be, "Which of these words says 'lap'?" Once identified, of course, *lap* would have to be repeatedly identified by the children before it could be expected to become part of their sight word vocabulary.

The same holds true for words identified with nothing but the help of phonics. And this constitutes the second reminder: Once words are identified through substitutions, additions, or sound-by-sound blending, they have to be practiced before children will recognize them "on sight." To be more specific, if children are able to figure out a word like *fall* because they know *ball*, the sound of *f*, and how to substitute sounds, one cannot assume that *fall* automatically becomes one of those words they recognize immediately. In fact, to avoid their having to analyze *fall* each time they come across it in written material, it must be included in practice sessions designed to extend sight word vocabularies. (For ideas about word identification practice, see pages 264–266.) With their knowledge of letter-sound relationships, less practice will be required than might otherwise be the case.

The third general reminder about phonics practice has to do with the need to make it realistic. And realistically, children use phonics on unfamiliar words which appear in sentences, paragraphs, pages, and books. In other words, they get help and find cues not only in a word itself but also in such relevant factors as what is being communicated with other words that happen to be known. Even though, as previous pages explained, there will be times when unfamiliar words ought to be isolated from a context and placed in columns, there will be many more occasions when words to be decoded ought to be placed within the context of a sentence or even more.

To make some headway with this realistic type of practice even before children are able to do much reading or know much about phonics, the contexts of *spoken* language can be used. For instance, after the sound of *t* is reviewed (or any other that had been taught), a teacher might say: "I'm going to read some sentences, but I'll stop just before I get to the last word. It will begin with *t*. See if you can think of a word that starts with the sound of *t* and that makes sense. Here's the first sentence. 'When we cry, our eyes get wet from our ———.'" (Since reading is visual, responses should be written on the chalkboard, not with the expectation that the children will learn to read the words immediately but in order to show them what they said.)

When children are reading, the combination of a context and a beginning sound such as /t/ will not always be enough for the correct identification of a word; and that can be demonstrated orally, too. On another day, unfinished spoken sentences might go something like, "All of us have ——— in our mouths." Hopefully, some children will suggest "tongues"; others, "teeth." This gives the teacher the chance to explain, as she writes *tongues* and *teeth,* the importance of looking at more than just the first letter in a word. If it happened that the children had learned about the sounds for *th,* the teacher could point to *teeth,* explain that it was the word in the sentence, and then ask, "Does this say 'tongues' or 'teeth'?" Naturally the next question would be, "Why do you think so?"

The need to put unknown words into a context gets further reinforcement from the next and final reminder: Provide children with practice in applying what they know *with flexibility.* Because vowels are notorious for their variability, let me use them to illustrate once more the meaning of "flexibility."

As prior sections of the chapter indicated, children need to learn to deal with the sounds which single vowels and pairs of vowels represent. These sounds were discussed earlier in the overview of phonics content, and are represented in the words shown below by the underlined letter or letters:

Vowel Phonemes *

at	age	oil
end	eat	out
if	ice	auto
on	old	room
up	use	book

* It is recognized that this is an oversimplified treatment of these phonemes. For example, the sound represented by *u* in *use* is described by some linguists as /yu/;

If each of these fifteen vowel sounds were always recorded by the same letter or letters, there would be few problems in using them to decode unknown words. The fact is, however, that vowels represent different sounds at different times. For that reason the sounds being represented by the underlined letters in the list can be viewed as an inventory of sounds from which a child can make selections whenever he thinks a vowel sound might be impeding the correct identification of a word. (This suggestion assumes, of course, that the child has already learned all the sounds represented in the list. Thus, the flexibility now being discussed pertains to phonics work beyond the beginning stage.) An example will help clarify this way to achieve flexibility and also show the relevance of a context for that goal.

Let us assume that *shoe* is not known in its written form. If a child was asked to decode it apart from a context, he might end up and be satisfied with a pronunciation that follows the pattern of *toe* (toe ⟶ shoe). He might even conclude it is the word we spell s-h-o-w. However, had *shoe* been in a context (e.g., He was only wearing one shoe) and, secondly, had the child been taught to end every analysis by asking "Does this make sense?" he would not—or should not—have been satisfied with the sound "shō." Knowing about the different sounds that vowels and vowel combinations can represent, he should begin to consider other possibilities for *oe* by trying out the vowel sounds heard in the fifteen words listed earlier. As it turns out, the sound that makes sense is the one in *room.**

What all this suggests—again—is the necessity of teaching flexibility and, secondly, of putting unknown words into contexts *if* that flexibility is to flourish.

Before citing examples of phonics practice, which is the next topic in this chapter, let me summarize these reminders for it.

1. At the beginning, practice in using phonics can be carried on in conjunction with whole word instruction. For instance, instead of immediately identifying *day*, a teacher might write *day* plus another unknown word (e.g., *rag*) and then ask, "Which of these could be the word for 'day'? . . . Why?"

---

by others, as /yuw/. In either case, the description indicates it is a vowel-semivowel combination. While linguists have to be concerned with these precisely accurate descriptions, the teacher of reading does not. Her responsibility is to teach about sounds in the simplest way possible for, in phonics, knowledge of them is merely a means to an end: ability to decode unfamiliar words. With that in mind, acting like a linguist is unnecessary. In fact, it can lead to unnecessary complications for the children.

* In this case, of course, knowledge of the sound recorded by *sh*, plus use of the context, might have been enough to decode *shoe* correctly.

2. If a word which is figured out through letter sounds is to become part of a child's sight word vocabulary, it must be practiced. That is, opportunities to read it more than once must be provided. This suggests that practice is essential whether a word was originally identified by the teacher or through a knowledge of phonics. With that knowledge, less practice will be required because relevant cues are now available to act as prompts.
3. Phonics practice should deal with words that are part of a context—for example, a sentence. This insures realistic practice in that words which have to be decoded generally appear in a context. Contexts also allow for the question, "Does this make sense?" once a tentative conclusion about the identification of a word is reached. They also are essential if children are to learn to use what they know about phonics with flexibility and, as a result, with success.

Samples of Practice. A great many samples of phonics practice appeared in previous chapters. As a start, therefore, you might want to reread: pages 81, 85–89 (Chapter 4); page 144 (Chapter 6); and pages 230–233 (Chapter 8). It should be pointed out, too, that recommendations made for word identification practice (Chapter 9) can be adapted for phonics work. For instance, one teacher of young children did this for word practice:

> Cut out baby ghosts from white construction paper and printed a word on each. All were placed in a "trick or treat" bag (ordinary grocery bag), then taken out one at a time for the children to identify.

To adapt the above for phonics, a single letter or letter combination could be printed on the ghost, and the task for the children would be to think of its sound and name a word that starts (or ends) with it. (Adaptation, whether of this type or some other, is important for teaching because it expands one useful idea into many.) Following are some more ideas for phonics practice. Others will be mentioned when bulletin-board displays and commercial materials are discussed.

To strengthen letter-sound associations, once they have been taught, phonic leaders can be drawn on a chalkboard as at the top of page 373. To climb a rung of the ladder successfully, children must think of the letter, then its sound (short sound in this case), then say a word that starts with it. For variation, letters can be printed around the edge of a paper plate, now a race track. (Switching from a ladder to the race track is another example of adaptation.)

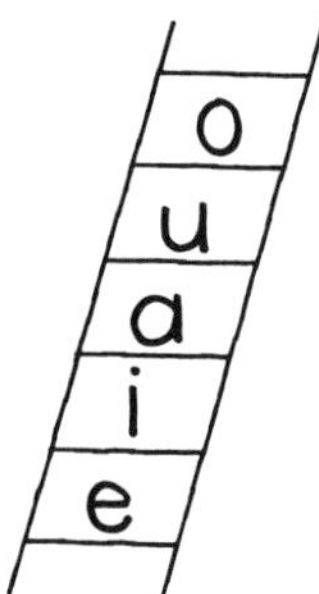

Simple drawings made by the children also help a teacher learn what is being remembered about letter sounds. For instance, a group can be directed to fold sheets of paper so that they have eight rectangles, and to print specified letters in each:

s	st
sl	sh
sn	sw
sp	sm

This practice assignment requires the children to draw in each rectangle a picture of something whose name begins with the letter(s) printed there.

The teacher who has collections of trinkets or small pictures can use them to provide still more practice in associating particular letters with particular sounds. With the help of boxes that have been assigned a letter, she could direct children to think of the name of each trinket (picture) and to put it into the box marked with the letter that stands for its beginning (final) sound.

Thus far, only initial and final sounds have been mentioned. But medial sounds must figure in practice sessions, too. To include them, a teacher might have children divide or fold sheets of paper into three sections as at the top of page 374.

Each child would receive cutout letters whose sounds, to be heard in various parts of a syllable, have been selected for review. For this, one of the letters would be named and its sound recalled. Then the teacher would say a three-letter word containing that sound. The job for each

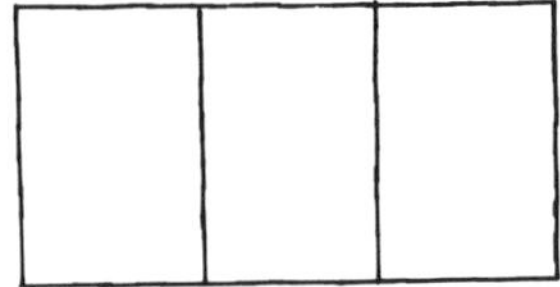

child is to place that letter in the first section of his paper if the sound was a beginning sound in the word; in the middle section if a medial sound; and in the last section if a final sound. More specifically, if the selected letter was *n* and the word spoken by the teacher was "ant," the children should place their *n*'s in the middle section of their papers. Had it been "ten," all the *n*'s would go in the last one.

Another way to learn whether children can hear but also make use of medial sounds—in this case, medial short vowel sounds—is to have them write unfamiliar words on the chalkboard. With about seven or eight at the board, a teacher might begin by asking them to write *cat*. (If they are unable to spell it, she could tell them.) Then the short sound of *a* would be reviewed, followed by the short sounds of the other four vowels. Next the teacher would ask them to write, on their own, related words like *cut* and *cot*. Other word groups would also be written; for instance, *big* (*bag, bug*), *fun* (*fan, fin*), *pen* (*pan, pin*). Word groups like these also provide a natural opportunity to review a generalization about some relevant cues: When there is one vowel in a word and it is not the last letter, it usually stands for its short sound.

Thus far the samples of practice have dealt with attempts to reinforce letter-sound associations and to help children hear and use sounds in various positions in words. If children show a weakness with such matters, these kinds of practice would be suitable. On the other hand, if what they need is more work in using the sounds they know to decode words, then other procedures would have to be used.

For example, once the process of initial substitution has been introduced, a teacher would want to give children the chance to practice using it. Consequently she might ditto a series of sentences like this:

1. I am going to ________________ my ball.
   (ride) (h)

With this assignment the children are given the help of a word (*ride*) and sound /h/ they know to fill in the missing word (*hide*). The context is a source of help too, of course. Later, less assistance would be provided:

1. A little __________ ran under the car.
   (house)

Still later, unfamiliar words might simply be underlined. Again, the children would be directed to think of known words and sounds to figure them out. In this way they are gradually led to deal with more realistic reading situations in which no explicit help is offered and the children themselves must decide what it is they know that is relevant for dealing with unfamiliar words. And so it can be seen that practice, like instruction itself, gradually builds up to more difficult and challenging tasks.

Bulletin-Board Displays and Practice. At the start, phonics instruction is primarily concerned with letter sounds. One consequence is that much of the phonics practice that goes on at that time is designed to help children remember the sounds that particular letters represent. Offering much potential for this goal are bulletin-board displays. Their special contribution is their ability to highlight a selected letter-sound association and to offer children something specific to help them remember it.

Often, the outline of an object whose name begins with the selected letter and sound can serve as the background for a display. I readily recall one example used to highlight the sound of *m*. In this case a very large paper mitten (about 4 by 7 feet) was thumbtacked to a board; affixed to it were pictures of objects whose names begin with *m*. The display was used to review its sound on the day after it had first been taught. Fortunately, the teacher remembered to stress the connection between the mitten and the pictures and the sound. She also remembered to place at the top of the display a capital *M* and a lowercase *m*. This last detail with important because the display was not being used merely for auditory discrimination practice; rather, its goal was to help strengthen an association between a particular letter and a particular sound. (Teachers who neglect to ask themselves, "*Why* am I doing this?" could easily neglect this detail.)

Not content to use only the bulletin-board display, this same teacher had the children make a pair of paper mittens for themselves during the art period. The pair was later tied together with knitting yarn which, at home time, went around the children's necks. And so it was that they ran home with two mittens, one with a capital *M* printed on it; the other, with *m* displayed. The next day—it happened to be a Thursday—this same class made muffins, to which margarine and marmalade were added when they ate them. Everyone was quite happy, with the exception of a girl. She complained because she felt they should have waited until Monday to make the muffins because that is the only day of the week which begins with *M*.

While teachers will not always be able to get a sound into the stomachs as well as the heads of children, they *can* prepare attractive bulletin boards to dramatize and review letter-sound associations. A few are described below:

To review the short sound of *u*, the outline of a large umbrella was featured. Again the board displayed a cutout *U* and *u*. The word *umbrella* also appeared under the outline. Because of the lack of pictures of appropriate objects, the teacher used words the children could read (*us, up, under, upon*); these were printed on small, umbrella-shaped cards which also appeared on the board. The prefix *un* had been taught, so that was printed on a card, too. Later, the children made their own umbrella outlines. An added attraction was the chance to select "fabric" from an old book of wallpaper samples, obtained from a paint dealer.

A bulletin board in another classroom displayed the title, "Oscar the Octopus." This, of course, was to highlight the short sound of *o*. In this case the children had been working on medial short sounds; consequently the pictures arranged on the board showed objects like: clock, doll, pot, mop.

"Helping Hands" was the title on another board in another room. For this, large outlines of two paper hands formed the background. Attached to one were pictures of objects whose names begin with *h*. Attached to the other were cards showing familiar words, also beginning with *h*. Both the pictures and the words were used to reinforce the connection between *h* and its sound. The children's interest in their own telephone numbers suggested the theme for still another phonics display. Because there were twenty-three children in this room, twenty-three small outlines of a telephone appeared in rows. On each, a child had carefully printed his name and number. At the top of the board the word "telephone" appeared in large letters. At the bottom, capital *T* and lowercase *t* were displayed.

All the bulletin boards described thus far gave attention only to one letter and sound. However, they can be used to review more. The following, for instance, have been seen:

A large colorful picture of a farm (commercially prepared) hung on one bulletin board. Cutout letters whose sounds had been introduced were thumbtacked beneath it. To provide a review, individual children were directed to name a letter, think of its sound, then name something in the picture whose name began (ended) with it. (The picture was especially appropriate because, in addition to showing a house, barn, farmer, and so on, it included a great variety of animals.)

Another board showed rows of cutout flowers, each with a different letter printed on its center. Two paper bees appeared at the top, next to which was printed:

The bees want to fly. You can play with them.

This board was used under the direction of the teacher but, later, by pairs of children at free-choice time. In either case, a child could become a bee by holding a paper bee and would fly from flower to flower naming words that started with the letter printed on it. (Each flower could be picked up like a flap. When this was done, lists of familiar words beginning with its letter could be found and read.)

Another board provided practice with phonograms. Called, "Iceberg Hop," it showed icebergs at the bottom on which phonograms (e.g., *-ake, -ell, -all*) had been printed. With this, children were turned into penguins. Again, they held a paper penguin and hopped from iceberg to iceberg by naming a word that combined the letter held by the teacher and the phonogram shown on an iceberg. For instance, if the teacher held up *b*, a "penguin" would hope from one iceberg to another by saying "bake," "bell," "ball," and so on.

Phonograms figured in another display that featured a paper clown who was holding balloons (circular paper of different colors) attached to the end of string. On each of the four balloons a letter appeared: *d, f, n, l*. In this case, the teacher displayed phonogram cards and the job for the children was to name words comprised of the letters followed by the phonogram. For instance, if the teacher held up [-ine] a child would say: *dine, fine, nine, line*. Each time this was done, the teacher wrote the group of words on a nearby chalkboard so that what had been said could be seen.

Commercial Materials and Practice. With the current move toward more and more phonics instruction, one does not have to look either long or hard to find commercial materials for phonics practice because they are available in an unbelievable quantity (8). As a result, the current and more difficult job is to distinguish between good material and that which has less educational potential, or which might contain meaningless activities or even erroneous content.

As you should be able to predict by this time, what *is* "good" depends first of all on what children need to practice. If what they need is dealt with in certain materials, then using them might make good educational sense, at least for that particular group of children. How they are used—here the focus shifts to the teacher—will affect their value but so, too, will the nature of the materials themselves. Because, with beginning phonics, commercial materials are characterized by a generous use of pictures, let me discuss them first.

Typically, names of pictured objects are used to help with auditory discrimination (see page 379) and, later, with letter-sound associations (see page 381). In either case, and this point was made before, it is important for teachers to know the name a child has assigned a picture; otherwise it is possible that he will be thinking of one thing while they think of something else. Lacking a meeting of minds, practice sessions are very apt to result in confusion and even mislearnings.

Often, it should be noted, the combination of pictures and phonics leads to "incorrect" responses which, under any other circumstances, would be "correct." For example, a child might say an illustration is picturing a chicken; yet, in that instance it has to be called "turkey" because the lesson is dealing with the sound of *t*. When this happens—and it happens frequently—an explanation should be given as to why it must be called "turkey" even though resembling a chicken. Such explanations are important for psychological as well as pedagogical reasons.

Other kinds of connections also should be clarified. For instance, if a workbook page dealing with the sound of *p* is headed by an attractive sketch of a puppy, connections between that, the letter *p*, and its sound ought to be explained either through questions asked of the children or statements made by the teacher. In fact, without some type of explicit explanation, certain children would never see the connections and so end up having an interesting activity, but not phonics practice.

One example of a connection that was never made comes from a visit to a first grade. In this case a group of children was reviewing the sound that *b* records. To help, workbook pictures of objects whose names begin with *b* were being named. Then, under each, the children were directed by the teacher to print a lowercase *b*. Because explanations during this lesson had been unusually skimpy, I quietly asked one of the children why she was printing *b*'s under the pictures. A totally blank expression was her answer.

Also found during classroom visits is an unusually generous use of ditto sheets. In fact it seems correct to say that, when it comes time for

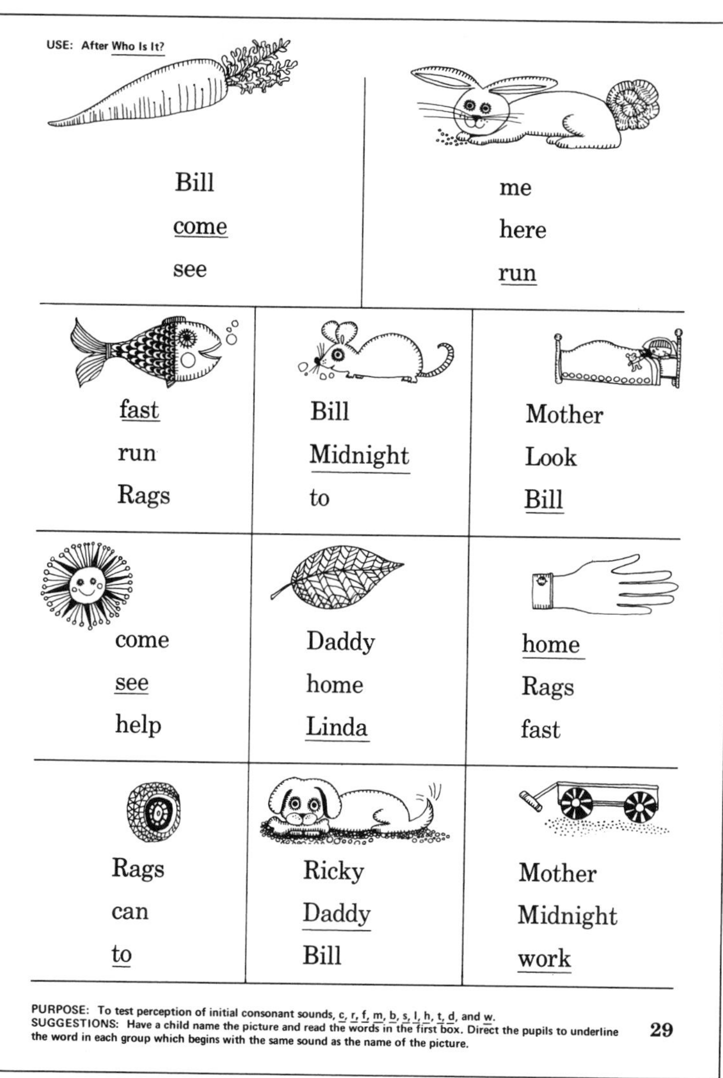

USE: After Who Is It?

Bill
come
see

me
here
run

fast
run
Rags

Bill
Midnight
to

Mother
Look
Bill

come
see
help

Daddy
home
Linda

home
Rags
fast

Rags
can
to

Ricky
Daddy
Bill

Mother
Midnight
work

PURPOSE: To test perception of initial consonant sounds, c, r, f, m, b, s, l, h, t, d, and w.
SUGGESTIONS: Have a child name the picture and read the words in the first box. Direct the pupils to underline the word in each group which begins with the same sound as the name of the picture.

29

phonics practice, teachers really grind them out. Assuming that what these sheets deal with is what children need to learn or review, no excuse is required for using them. However, there are times when classroom visits cause one to wonder. I recall visiting three third grades in one school and, much to my surprise, found all three teachers using the very same ditto sheet with everyone in their class. That this could be justified educationally hardly seems possible.

Like phonics workbooks (see page 382), ditto sheets also make generous use of pictures. Because they are less expensive and produced more hastily, their pictures tend to cause more problems than the others. For instance, some are a little old-fashioned. To use a picture of a hairpin for the sound of *h*—to cite one illustration—is to cause some puzzlement and wild guesses as to what it might be. Other pictures are simply poorly drawn. I remember one used in connection with the sound of *h*, but all that I could think it might be was a scrubbing brush. In fact, it was a very good picture of a scrubbing brush. The problem was that it had to be called "hedge." Another time a man was pictured standing behind some vaguely sketched object. That day the phonics lesson dealt with the hard sound of *c* but I, for one, did not know what to name the picture. In this case, the answer turned out to be "cashier."

Even among the more expensive and, presumably, more carefully prepared practice materials, flaws can be found. I recall one basal reader workbook page in which the children were directed to read all the words listed, and to draw a line under the vowel in each that recorded a short sound. Surprisingly, each of the thirty-five words contained only one vowel. As a result, any child who knew that *a, e, i, o,* and *u* are vowels could complete the page correctly and, in the process, be mistakenly credited with knowing all about short vowel sounds even though they were never considered in doing the page.

Still other questionable material dealing with vowel sounds appears when words like *rule* or *suit* or *tune* or *dew* are used, supposedly to illustrate the long sound for *u*. Once, after observing a teacher who seemed content with such examples, I asked, "Do you really hear the long *u* sound in words like *rule* and *tune?*" Surprisingly her answer was "no." Disappointingly her explanation was, "The book has them, so I use them."

Similar explanations have been given for examples that were inappropriate because of dialect differences. In some areas of the United States, words like *ostrich* and *frog* do contain the short *o* sound; however in many others they have the sound heard at the beginning of *auto*. It was in one of the latter regions that I first heard a teacher using *ostrich* and *frog* for the short *o* sound and so it was there that I again asked, "Why?" In essence, the answer was the same. For that reason it seems

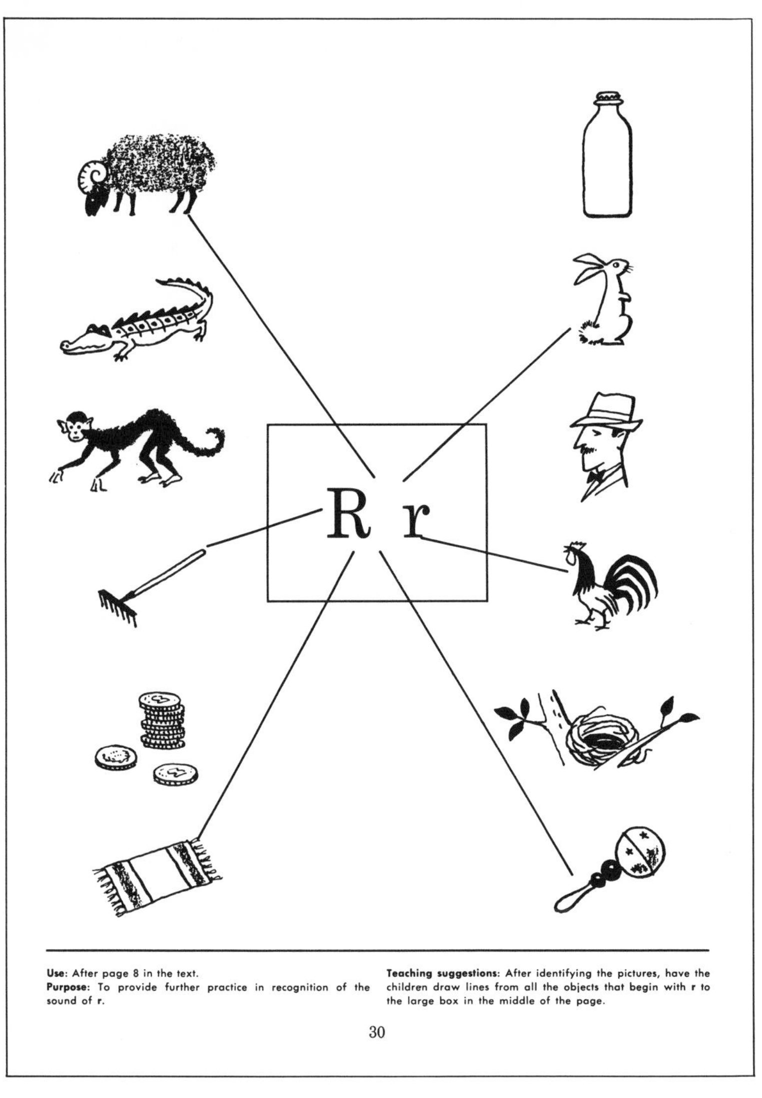

R r

Use: After page 8 in the text.
Purpose: To provide further practice in recognition of the sound of r.

Teaching suggestions: After identifying the pictures, have the children draw lines from all the objects that begin with r to the large box in the middle of the page.

30

From *Pre-Primer Workbook,* Teacher's Edition, by G. McCracken and C. G. Walcutt, p. 30. Copyright 1963 by J. B. Lippincott Company.

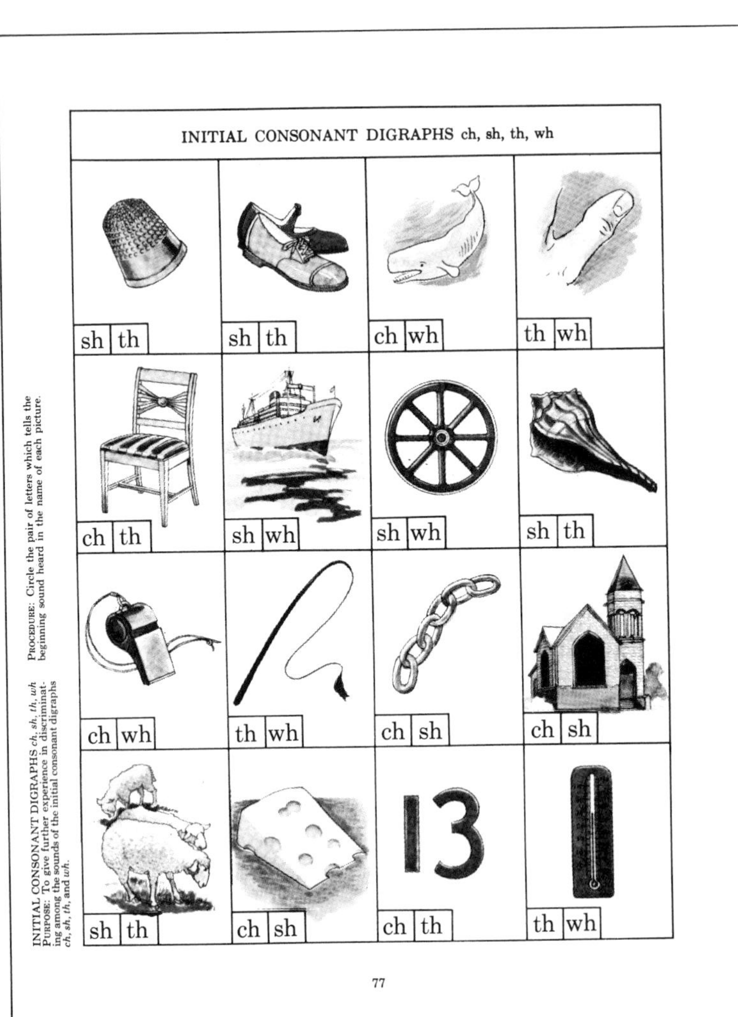
INITIAL CONSONANT DIGRAPHS ch, sh, th, wh

sh th	sh th	ch wh	th wh
ch th	sh wh	sh wh	sh th
ch wh	th wh	ch sh	ch sh
sh th	ch sh	ch th	th wh

INITIAL CONSONANT DIGRAPHS *ch, sh, th, wh*
PURPOSE: To give further experience in discriminating among the sounds of the initial consonant digraphs *ch, sh, th,* and *wh.*

PROCEDURE: Circle the pair of letters which tells the beginning sound heard in the name of each picture.

77

From *Phonics We Use*, Book B, by Mabel Halvorsen, Mary Meigham, and Marjorie Pratt, p. 77. Copyright 1966 by Lyons and Carnahan, Inc., Educational Division, Meredith Corporation.

best to conclude this discussion of workbook and dittoed materials with a plea that has appeared many times before in this textbook: Do not allow materials to dictate either what or how you will teach. If they have errors, point them out to the children; and, if they have meaningless pages, skip them.

Materials other than the workbook-type must be considered when phonics practice is the topic. For instance, if a goal is practice in using what has been taught, many of the so-called "linguistic readers" can be very helpful because of their use of spelling patterns to select vocabulary (see pages 252 and 253). The same could be said of some trade books, notably those by Dr. Seuss.

Alphabet books also can be helpful—depending upon their particular make-up and, too, upon what the children know. One that presents *A* and also a generous collection of pictures showing an apple but also an apron, airplane, automobile, and arm might confuse rather than help children who are just beginning to learn one of the sounds for *a*. Consequently, at this point it should not be used. Or, if the children have recently been learning the sound which *k* records, an alphabet book that shows *C* coupled with pictures depicting a candle and a clock might also be a source of problems and so should not be used—at least not yet. What this all underscores once more is the importance of selecting instructional goals *before* decisions are made about materials. And the principle holds, whether the materials are for instruction or for practice.

STRUCTURAL ANALYSIS

In all the words that were used to show how phonics helps with decoding, only roots (e.g., *act*) appeared. The selection was deliberate because derived words (*react*) and inflected words (*acting*) are dealt with through a combination of phonic *and* structural analyses. In fact, when an unknown word is encountered, consideration of its structure comes prior to a consideration of its letters and the sounds they are likely to represent. If unclear now, this point will be clarified a little later with some illustrations. For now, let me interject into this discussion some terms and definitions that are important for structural analysis.

Of immediate importance is the term "root." * A root is the smallest unit in which related words can exist. For instance, *untie* is not a root word because it can be reduced to *tie*. *Tie*, however, is a root because it cannot be further divided. Or, to cite another illustration, *teacher* is not a root word because it can be reduced to *teach*. *Teach*, on the other hand,

* Some materials use "stem" or "base" as synonymous terms, although there are differences. Technically, for instance, a word like *bluebird* is a stem because an affix can be added to it. However, it is two roots: *blue* and *bird*.

is a root because it cannot be further reduced and still maintain a relationship of meaning to the word family: *teach, teacher, teaching, reteach, teachable,* and so on.*

Other terms with relevance for structural analysis are: derivative, inflected word (also called "variant"), prefix, suffix, affix, and inflectional ending. Let me first define "prefix."

"Prefix" refers to a letter (*a*) or group of letters (*fore*) which are added or affixed to the beginning of roots (*moral, warn*). The new combination (*amoral, forewarn*) is called a "derivative." Derivatives also are comprised of roots (*spot, care*) plus suffixes (*less, ful*). Thus, *spotless* and *careful* are derivatives, too. A more encompassing term, "affix," also is relevant because it refers to a prefix or suffix or both. For that reason, derivatives can be described as combinations of roots and affixes and would be illustrated by words like *reteach, teachable,* and *reteachable.***

The term "inflected word" also enters into discussions of structural analysis, for it refers to the combination of a root and an inflectional ending. Inflectional endings (e.g., *s, es, ing, ly*) relate to grammatical usage. Specifically, an inflection can indicate number, case, or gender, if the root is a noun; tense, voice, or mood, if the root is a verb; and comparison, if it is an adjective or adverb. Admittedly, some inflected words —*men* and *mice,* for instance—do not reflect this description. However, they can be considered exceptions in the sense that they do not follow the type of structural patterns which are characteristic of American English.

In perusing current instructional materials, you might find slight differences in the definitions offered for the terms just discussed. At least in part, this reflects the new linguistic influence. To show this, let me list below some of the definitions given by one linguist, Ronald Wardhaugh, in the Glossary for his book, *Reading: A Linguistic Perspective* (18). Presenting definitions that pertain to structural analysis will allow for an explanation of some of the new language now appearing in recent instructional materials.

> *root*
> A morpheme that can occur with various other morphemes to form different words but always retains its meaning: *joy* in *joys, joyful,* and *enjoy.*

* Two points mentioned might require further explanations. Some of you might have thought about reducing *teach* to *each.* This is possible, but it would be a phonic rather than a structural reduction. The second point has to do with the term "word family." Traditionally, most phonics materials referred to groups of words like *hit, pit,* and *kit,* as a "family." However, that was a misuse of the term. Word families (*act, actor, react, acting,* and so on) are groups of words which are related in origin and meaning.

** For a listing of some common affixes, see page 202.

prefix
An affix placed before the morpheme or morphemes to which it is attached: *in*tolerant, *dis*honor, and *re*flect.

inflection
An affix (in English, usually a suffix) that changes the form of a word without changing its form class or basic meaning: *cat* and *man* may be inflected for "plural" (*cats, men*) or possessive (*cat's, man's*) or both (*cats', men's*).

derivation
A process by which noninflectional affixes are added to bases to form words, as in govern*ment*, hope*ful*, *dis*trust*ful*.

suffix
A morpheme placed at the end of the morpheme or morphemes to which it is attached. The *s* in *cats* is an inflectional suffix, whereas the *ment* in *judgment* is a derivational one.

The term "morpheme," which appears in almost all the definitions cited, comes from linguistics. It is defined most simply as a minimal unit of meaning; more technically, as "a significant meaning-bearing unit" (18, p. 32). In American English, roots are examples of morphemes, which is what you would expect; but so too is an inflection like *s* because in such words as *tops* and *mats* it signals meaning pertaining to number. For that reason linguists would say that *tops* and *mats* are each comprised of two morphemes and so, too, are words like *planted* (*ed* signals tense), *unhappy* (*un* signals the negative) and *actor* (*or* signals doer).

Although this discussion of terminology might make structural analysis seem complicated—perhaps too complicated for young children—it has relevance for their reading almost from the very beginning. This is so because even beginners must deal with more than just singular nouns and, for instance, present-tense verbs. More specifically, the child who recognizes words like *duck* and *top* is ready to learn to read *ducks* and *tops*. And the child who is able to read *look* and *play* is ready for *looked* and *played*. More generally, these beginners are ready for structural analysis. How might it be introduced?

Inflections

As with all other phases of reading instruction, there is no one best way to deal with word structure. Knowing that a certain group of children can read *the, is, top,* and *green,* one teacher might choose to introduce it by writing a sentence:

After the children read the sentence, their attention is called to a picture of three green tops. Once they have discussed and, in particular, counted the tops, the teacher might choose to say: "Would you read the sentence on the board again? . . . How many tops does it tell us about? . . . It doesn't tell us about this picture then, does it? . . . What would I have to write so that it would tell us about the picture? . . . That's right. Let me write that:

The top is green.
The tops are green.

Following this, the teacher would go on to explain how the addition of *s* to a word indicates more than one. Using singular nouns the children can read, she might write and talk about such contrasts as:

girl boy hat car
girls boys hats cars

Subsequently, dittoed sentences like the following could be distributed for a reading-writing assignment:

1. The____________are going fast.
car cars

2. The girl has a blue____________.
hat hats

Combined, all these procedures serve to introduce children to word structure and, with the final one, to another use of contextual help.

Before presenting still another lesson, let me point out a few of the important details about the procedures just described. Probably the most important one relates to the dependence of success upon oral language, which identifies still another reason why children who have deficiencies in that also have problems learning to read. In the lesson dealing with the formation of plurals through the addition of *s*, the teacher evoked oral language with a picture. That is, she asked the children, "What would I have to write so that it would tell us about the picture?" In response the children said, "The tops are green." Thus, to introduce a new learning in reading, the teacher made a natural shift from spoken to written language.

Use of spoken language entered the scene again, though covertly, when the children moved from a plural like *tops* to one like *girls*. In this case it allowed them, and quite unconsciously, to assign /z/ to the *s* in *girls*, even though they had assigned /s/ to the *s* in *tops*. Of course, what also would keep them from assigning /s/ to both *s*'s is the pronunciation difficulties and awkwardness that would result. (Try, for instance, assigning /s/ to the *s* in *girls*, and /z/ to the *s* in *tops*.) Initially, nothing needs to be done to specify when *s* stands for /s/ and when it records /z/ because, in this case, doing what comes naturally is to be correct. Later on, what is done "without thinking" can (but need not) be brought to the conscious level by teaching a generalization:

> When the last spoken sound in the singular form is one associated with *p*, *t*, *k*, or *f*, the *s* records /s/. Otherwise it stands for /z/. For example:

tops	cats	tacks	puffs	coughs
days	toys	dads	rags	bells

The same generalization applies to the pronunciation of a verb inflection; for instance, *s* stands for /s/ in verbs like *stops*, *wants*, *picks*, and *coughs*, but for /z/ in such words as *plays*, *runs*, and *tells*.

The goal of the next lesson to be described also deals with verb inflections; specifically, with the tense marker *ed*. Once again the teacher makes use of oral language plus words the children can read. This time familiar words might be combined as:

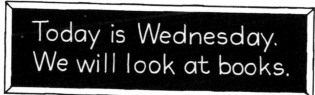

Today is Wednesday.
We will look at books.

What is described by the two sentences is a daily practice in this classroom. Consequently, after they are read a teacher might comment: "If today is Wednesday, what day was yesterday? . . . Let me write Tuesday to see what we can say about that:

Today is Wednesday.
We will look at books.
On Tuesday we

If we want to tell about looking at books yesterday, on Tuesday, what would we have to say? . . . Yes, we'd have to say, 'On Tuesday we looked at books.' Let me write that:

Today is Wednesday.
We will look at books.
On Tuesday we looked at books too.

Would someone read all three sentences for us? . . . Let's take a close look at what I did to the word *look* to make it say 'looked':

Notice how I added *ed* to the end of *look* to make it say 'looked.' When we do that to words, they can tell us what happened not today, but yesterday or maybe last week or even last year. Let me show you how that works with other words you know. . . ." At the end, the board displays:

jump call laugh show
jumped called laughed showed

talk walk work play
talked walked worked played

With pairs of words like those shown above, other unconscious behavior will again be observed. Automatically, children will shift from assigning /t/ to *ed* (*looked, jumped*) to assigning /d/ (*called, showed, played*). Later on—although this is not essential—attention might be called to a generalization which describes when *ed* stands for /d/ and when it records /t/:

> When the sound preceding *ed* is one associated with *p, k, f,* or *s,* the *ed* records /t/. Otherwise it stands for /d/. For example:
>
> topped asked puffed passed
> tagged flowed stayed peeled

Often, and certainly with beginners, to call attention to generalizations like the one above is to complicate matters at a time when everything should be done to simplify the various tasks they face in learning to cope with written language. For that reason, teaching it immediately is not only unnecessary but even questionable.

What *is* necessary, however, is a generalization specifying when the tense marker *ed* is a separate syllable:

> When the inflection *ed* is added to a verb ending with *t* or *d,* it forms a separate syllable. Otherwise it does not. For example:
>
> want ed paint ed need ed land ed
> played asked wished helped

As a separate syllable, *ed* records the sound "əd."

With these past-tense verbs, the close connection between oral and written language is very apparent. Specifically, some young children will still be learning to cope with the syllabication of *ed* in oral language and, as a result, can be heard saying things like "pla-dud" for *played*. When this happens, similar pronunciations appear in their reading but with time and practice they drop out, first from their speech and then from their reading.

Affixes

In the discussion of structural analysis thus far, only inflections have been singled out for attention. (Samples of how workbook pages provide practice in using them are shown on pages 391 and 392.) With children, inflections also are dealt with before affixes, and for several reasons. One practical reason is that written material includes inflected words almost from the start. A second factor accounting for the sequence is that inflections appear early in the child's spoken language, which allows for a natural and meaningful shift to its written counterpart. Still another reason is that the root in inflected words, which is what the children already know, is what comes first. For instance, in an inflected word like *played* the familiar part (*play*) is what comes first and is what the child is likely to see first. On the other hand, with a derivative like *replay* it is the new feature (*re*) that appears initially with the familiar one (*play*) being a little less apparent.

Because noticing the familiar part of a word first can be a help, it might seem logical to introduce derivatives that are comprised of a root and a suffix (*playable*) before doing anything with derivatives comprised of a root and a prefix (*replay*). Actually, in this case it is not the better of the two sequences for a reason that has to do with meaning. As the list of prefixes and suffixes on page 202 pointed out earlier, many of the suffixes denote abstractions (e.g., soft*ness*, child*hood*), which are difficult for children to comprehend. For that reason the recommendation is to teach some inflectional endings, then some prefixes, and then some suffixes. For now let me describe how a prefix (*un*) could be taught.

With *un* as the focus, a teacher might proceed by engaging the children in a conversation about safety. (This teacher knows they can read *safe* and so are ready to learn the pronunciation and meaning of *unsafe*.) Together they talk about the need to stay away from dangerous things: buildings still under construction, traffic, hot stoves, matches, and

"At the Farm"

1. Mary ___ after the goat. run <u>runs</u>	2. Daddy will ___ at the farm. <u>stop</u> stops
3. Mike can ___ what it is. <u>tell</u> tells	4. Jeff ___ the farmer. know <u>knows</u>
5. Mike ___ the ball. <u>bounces</u> bounce	6. Mother ___ Mike to stop. ask <u>asks</u>
7. Jeff can ___ the picnic. <u>take</u> takes	8. Mike ___ a ball to Mother. <u>shows</u> show
9. The little goat ___ down. jump <u>jumps</u>	10. Daddy ___ Mary to come. tell <u>tells</u>

• Read the sentence. Draw a line under the run-away word.

STOP 23

From Discovery Book to accompany *Worlds of Wonder*, Teacher's Edition, by Educational Development Corp., p. 23. Copyright 1966 by The Macmillan Company.

USE: After The Egg Game

help helps helped	worked work works	wanted wants want	jump jumped jumps
play played plays	paint paints painted	showed show shows	worked works work
laugh laughs laughed	plays play played	looked looks look	worked works work
wants wanted want	painted paints paint	jumped jump jumps	ask asks asked

PURPOSE: To give practice recognizing inflectional variants formed by adding s or ed.
SUGGESTIONS: Read a sentence using one of the words in the first box, repeat the word, and direct the class to underline it. Continue in the same manner for all the boxes.

83

so on. Summarizing, the teacher says: "There's a word that describes all these things. It means 'dangerous.' It means 'not safe,' and yet the word 'safe' is part of it. Does anyone know the word I'm thinking of? (Scary?) No. Remember, I said that this word has the word 'safe' in it, yet it means 'not safe.' I think I'll tell you. The word I'm thinking of is 'unsafe.' Have you ever heard that word before? (No.) Well, now you know a new word. What is it? (Unsafe.) Let me write it:

See how the new word looks exactly like *safe,* except for the *u* and the *n.* They say 'ŭn.' When we put *u* and *n* in front of a word like *safe,* it means 'not'; in this case 'not safe.' Let me put some other words you know on the board, and I'll put *un* in front of each one. What does the *u* and *n* say? (Ŭn.) What does it mean? (Not.) Good. First I'll write a word you can read, and then I'll put *u* and *n* in front of it. . . ." Soon the board shows:

safe happy kind
unsafe unhappy unkind

In calling the children's attention to each of the three derivatives, the teacher emphasizes its spelling, pronunciation, and the effect the prefix has on the meaning of the familiar root. Later on, when more root words are in their reading vocabulary, she will teach another meaning for *un* (to do the opposite) through derivatives like: *undo, undress, unpin, unlock, untie, unpack, uncover.* What all this is preparing the children to deal with are more complex words like *unwanted, unwilling, unlawful, unspoken,* and *unpaved.* Thus, by putting prefixes, suffixes, inflections, and roots into various combinations, attention to structural analysis eventually leads not only to sizeable reading vocabularies but also enlarged listening-speaking vocabularies.

Structural Analysis Combined with Phonics

At the beginning of this discussion of structural analysis, the following point was made: When an unknown word is encountered by a reader, a consideration of its structure ought to come prior to a consideration of its letters and the sounds they are likely to represent. By citing a generalization, let me show what this means.

Structure is considered first because:

> Affixes and inflections usually form separate syllables. For instance:
>
> | | | | |
> |---|---|---|---|
> | un tie | dis trust | spot less | teach er |
> | do ing | safe ly | want ed | small er |

How this generalization figures in decoding can be explained through a derivative like *unhurt*. Let us assume a child finds it in something he's reading; specifically in the sentence, "The boy fell off the horse but was unhurt." Let us also assume it is totally unfamiliar—that is, the root isn't even known. For that reason the child's first thought should be, "Might the *un* be a prefix?" Assuming it is, he mentally lays that aside for he has been taught that: (a) it will be a separate syllable; (b) it is pronounced "ŭn"; and (c) it will mean either "not" or "to do the opposite." Having made at least a tentative decision about *un,* the child is now ready to decode *hurt,* which he assumes is a root. Sequentially, his thoughts might go something like this:

SYLLABLES

Hurt could only be one syllable because every syllable must have a sounded vowel, and hurt has only one vowel.

SOUNDS

h: *probably sounds as it does in words like home and house.*

ur: *these two letters go together because when r follows a vowel in a syllable, those letters have a special sound. Ur probably sounds like "er."*

t: *probably has its usual sound, like in top or fat.*

BLENDING

I'll start with the ur because this word starts with a consonant. So the blending would be: ur ⟶ hur ⟶ hurt. Oh sure, I know that word—unhurt. The boy didn't get hurt when he fell off the horse.

Sometimes, children have to decide which syllable in a decoded word is to get the stress. (In this case—and this is what usually happens

—the blended sounds suggested a word the child was familiar with in oral language; consequently its stressed syllable was no problem.) When necessary, the following generalization is available to help:

> In derived and inflected words, the accent falls on or within the root. For instance:
>
> miscóunt disobéy cárefully sínging

Admittedly, the kind of decoding just described for dealing with *unhurt* will not be common in classrooms occupied by beginners in reading because what they know about phonics and structural analysis usually is not enough to make it possible. For instance, to decode *unhurt* the child needed to know about prefixes including the fact that they form separate syllables. More specifically, he needed to have learned about *un* and its effect on the meaning of roots to which it is affixed. The child also had to be familiar with the sounds for *h, ur,* and *t,* as well as how to blend them into a syllable. But, even before that, he had to know that every syllable must have a sounded vowel because that suggested *hurt* could be no more than one syllable.

While, with effective instruction, such learnings as these accumulate surprisingly quickly, most young children still are not ready for the decoding like that described for *unhurt.* In spite of that, however, their teachers should know about it because it provides them with a picture of what they are readying children to do. As a result, their day-by-day efforts take on a more meaningful perspective.

Structural Analysis: A Summary

As the discussion has pointed out, close connections exist between structural analysis and oral language. Routinely, teaching about inflections depends directly upon the children's spoken language. ("If we want to talk about more than one top, what do we say?") Dealing with affixes, on the other hand, often is a way to add to it.

Whether the focus happens to be a prefix, a suffix, or an inflectional ending, instruction concerned with structural analysis should always result in three learnings. With the prefix *un*—to cite one illustration—children should learn about (a) its syllabication, (b) its pronunciation, and (c) its effect on the meaning of a root. When these learnings are achieved, children should be helped to apply them—either simply, as in moving from a known word like *book* to the unfamiliar *books* or in a more complicated fashion, as was demonstrated with the decoding of *unhurt.*

What and how much to teach about structural analysis are important considerations. Yet, as the descriptions of sample lessons indicated, answers depend upon the children being instructed; in particular upon what they already know. Generally, some inflectional endings are taught first. These would include plurals for nouns and the past tense for verbs because such inflections appear in written material almost immediately. Later, some prefixes can be taught and, still later, some suffixes. Once any inflection, prefix, or suffix has received attention, children should be helped to use it both for decoding words and figuring out their meanings. Thus, like phonics, structural analysis is a means to an end—in this case the twofold end of helping with both pronunciation and meaning. As with phonics, instruction can be considered successful only to the extent that what is being taught is being used successfully by the children.

HOW TO TEACH NEW WORDS

This as well as the previous chapter has had a great deal to say about teaching new words. Chapter 9 concentrated on whole word methodology; with that, entire words are simply identified. This present chapter went on to discuss two other possibilities for dealing with unknown words: phonic analysis and structural analysis. Now it seems timely to try to put together all three possibilities by considering the question: *How* should new words be taught? More specifically, when should they be identified? When should the children be expected to decode them through their knowledge of sounds? And, when does structural analysis enter the picture?

In responding to these important questions, I would first like to point out that words ought to be identified for children only when circumstances allow for nothing else. Here, appropriate circumstances would include times when it simply makes good sense to quickly identify a word rather than to take time for children to decode it. This might occur occasionally when a child is reading something aloud and comes to a word he doesn't know. Rather than have him analyze it, a teacher might wisely decide to tell him what it is, perhaps make a mental or written note of the fact that it was unknown, and then move on with the oral reading.*

Other of these circumstances relate to a child's ability in decoding. If figuring out a particular word requires some learnings he has not yet achieved, then the word has to be identified for him—even when there is a close correspondence between its spelling and pronunciation. For

* Oral versus silent reading are some of the topics to be discussed in the next chapter.

instance, if it was something like *lake,* decoding could be accomplished through an initial consonant substitution (e.g., make ⟶ lake) or, if words like *make* or *take* are not known, through other learnings and abilities:

GENERALIZATIONS

1. When there are two vowels, one of which is a final *e,* the first usually records its long sound and the *e* is silent.
2. Every syllable must have a sounded vowel.

SOUNDS

l, a (long), k

BLENDING

ā ⟶ lā ⟶ lāk~~e~~

If either related words or the prerequisite learnings and abilities are not available to help, then a word like *lake*—though regularly spelled —would have to be identified. Other times for whole word methodology occur when a new word is so irregularly spelled (e.g., *one, eye, colonel*) that attempts to decode would only meet with failure. Once irregular words *are* identified, however, some (e.g., *would*) are then useful in decoding others (e.g., *could, should*).

In this discussion of whole word methodology, at least an indirect answer has been given regarding the role of phonics. As has been suggested, new words should be decoded by the children themselves whenever this is possible. In fact, it is only when spellings are sufficiently irregular or when the children's ability in decoding is sufficiently meager that new words ought to be directly identified. To use any other guideline is to deprive children of the chance to develop maximum ability in dealing with them both successfully *and* independently.

What about structural analysis? It plays a role only when a new word is inflected or is a derivative. (It also plays a less significant role with compound words—for instance, *into* and *armchair*—and contractions.) With these, it offers help not only with their pronunciation but also with their meaning. Consequently, when a new word is inflected or includes a prefix or a suffix or both, children should use their knowledge of structural analysis along with phonic learnings. Together, the two allow for quick advancement in sight word vocabularies.

What is likely to lead to problems rather than advancement is a practice sometimes encouraged by teachers. I refer to the very questionable procedure of "looking for little words in big words" as a way of figuring out the latter. To see *in* in *rain,* for example, or to recognize the familiar word *on* in *pony* is hardly going to help with either *rain* or *pony.*

These illustrations, along with many others that could be cited, exemplify the two reasons why "looking for little words" so often leads to problems. First, it neglects the fact that unfamiliar words should be divided into syllables—if their spelling suggests more than one—*before* sounds are considered. If the syllabication of *pony* had been dealt with initially, the division *po ny* would have resulted. (A single consonant preceded and followed by vowels suggests a syllabic division after the vowel which precedes it.) With such a division, the *o* and the *n* end up in different syllables. The same point explains why finding *dig* in *digest, rot* in *rotate, on* in *bonus,* and so on, can only lead to difficulties for decoders.

Even with one-syllable words, it should be noted, looking for smaller words is still a questionable strategy—as is shown when a child finds *in* in *pain, it* in *write, he* in *them* or, for instance, *my* in *myth.* What has been overlooked in these cases is another important guideline for decoding; namely, that the whole of a syllable should be examined before individual letters are considered. Thus, seeing *in* in *pain* neglects to note that with two adjacent vowels which do not represent diphthongs, it is common for the first to record its long sound while the second is silent. To see *it* in *write* is to overlook the final *e* which so often signals silence for itself and a long sound for the previous vowel. Finding *he* in *them* obviously overlooks the digraph *th,* while reading *my* in *myth* neglects the fact that when *y* appears in a *closed* syllable which contains no vowels it records the short *i* sound. Clearly, "looking for little words in big words" should *not* be encouraged.

In all this discussion and in the bulk of this and the previous chapter, word identification and the development of sight word vocabularies have been the central concern. This might lead some to wonder whether the perceptual side of reading has been highlighted almost to the point of neglecting its conceptual side. For that reason, concluding comments probably should deal with the latter.

That successful reading always involves "getting meaning" has been explicitly recognized throughout this textbook. That this often begins with getting the meaning of individual words was the reason for including a chapter (Chapter 7) that gave very detailed attention to the many ways in which children's listening-speaking vocabularies can be extended. Because "getting meaning" also involves the comprehension of more than individual words, various sections of various chapters also dealt with the comprehension of sentences and more. Too, using contexts—which involves comprehension—was recommended for practice assignments concerned with whole word identification and the use of phonics and structural analysis.

Admittedly, these various kinds of attention to comprehension took up less space than was allotted to the development of reading vocabularies. That was intentional and reflects the philosophy of this textbook regarding beginning instruction in reading. As viewed here, the essential though not exclusive responsibility of teachers working with beginners is to develop sizeable sight word vocabularies as quickly as possible. One very important assumption is that selections for these vocabularies will be made from the very large number of words in the children's listening-speaking vocabularies. Such selections, combined with the short and simple sentences read by beginners, should result in very few comprehension problems—certainly far fewer than are suggested by unfortunate practices like asking ten questions about every line of text.

When problems with comprehension do exist among beginners, two factors generally explain them. The first is exemplified in the child who has to ponder over the identification of so many individual words that what they mean when put together is lost. This problem is the reason for a two-pronged theme which has characterized so much of this book: Beginners should be given much practice for developing sight word vocabularies and, secondly, with a little imagination on the part of their teachers, this can be not only productive but also interesting and even enjoyable.

The other factor which accounts for comprehension difficulties among beginners was mentioned in an earlier part of the book when it was said that "The reading comprehension problems of many children are really symptoms of more basic deficiencies in language comprehension." This observation was made at that point to help explain why a language arts approach makes sense—even when reading ability is the primary goal—in that it should encourage teachers to recognize the dependent relationships existing between spoken and written language.

What these language arts programs might look like is considered in Chapter 11.

REFERENCES

1. Brown, Roger. *Words and Things.* New York: The Free Press, 1958.
2. Caldwell, E. C., and Hall, V. C. "The Influence of Concept Training on Letter Discrimination," *Child Development,* XL (March, 1969), 63–71.
3. Cordts, Anna D. *Phonics for the Reading Teacher.* New York: Holt, Rinehart and Winston, Inc., 1965.
4. Dawson, Mildred A., compiler. *Teaching Word Recognition Skills.* Newark, Delaware: International Reading Association, 1971.
5. Deighton, Lee C. *Vocabulary Development in the Classroom.* New York: Teachers College Press, Columbia University, 1959.
6. Durkin, Dolores. "Linguistics and the Teaching of Reading," *Reading Teacher,* XVI (March, 1963), 342–346.

7. Durkin, Dolores. *Phonics and the Teaching of Reading*. New York: Teachers College Press, Columbia University, 1965.
8. ———. "Phonics Materials: A Big Seller," *Reading Teacher*, XX (April, 1967), 610–614.
9. Fries, Charles C. *Linguistics and Reading*. New York: Holt, Rinehart and Winston, Inc., 1963.
10. Frostig, Marianne; Lefever, D. W.; and Whittlesey, J. R. B. *Marianne Frostig Developmental Test of Visual Perception*. Palo Alto, Calif.: Consulting Psychologists Press, 1964.
11. Huckleberry, Alan W., and Strother, Edward S. *Speech Education for the Elementary Teacher*. Boston: Allyn and Bacon, 1966.
12. Leibert, Robert E., and Sherk, John K. "Three Frostig Visual Percepton Sub-tests and Specific Reading Tasks for Kindergarten, First, and Second Grade Children," *Reading Teacher*, XXIV (November, 1970), 130–137.
13. Poole, Irene. "Genetic Development of Articulation of Consonant Sounds in Speech," *Elementary English Review*, XI (June, 1934), 159–161.
14. Singer, Harry. "Research That Should Have Made a Difference," *Elementary English*, XLVII (January, 1970), 27–34.
15. Stott, D. H. Manual for "Programmed Reading Kits 1 and 2." Toronto, Canada: Gage Educational Publishing Limited, 1970.
16. Venezky, Richard L. "Reading: Grapheme-Phoneme Relationships," *Education*, LXXXVII (May, 1967), 519–524.
17. Wardhaugh, Ronald. "Syl-lab-i-ca-tion." *Elementary English*, XLIII (November, 1966), 785–788.
18. ———. *Reading: A Linguistic Perspective*. New York: Harcourt, Brace and World, Inc., 1969.
19. Wylie, Richard E., and Durrell, Donald D. "Teaching Words Through Phonograms," *Elementary English*, XLVII (October, 1970), 787–791.

11

Language Arts Programs

In the earlier description of a language arts approach for teaching reading (Chapter 4), the focus was more on possibilities for nursery school and kindergarten than first grade. Consequently this chapter discusses language arts programs as they might be carried out beyond the kindergarten level.* Whatever the level, certain characteristics ought to prevail. Those discussed in Chapter 4 are summarized below; others will get attention throughout this present chapter.

1. Language arts programs to teach reading are built on certain assumptions. One basic one is that success with written language depends upon a child's abilities in oral language. Because of the dependency, a continuous goal is the development of listening-speaking vocabularies. Some programs will also have to allot special time for help with more basic things like encourag-

* A good preparation for this chapter would be a rereading of Chapter 4. Together, the two chapters draw a bigger and more detailed picture of language arts programs for teaching reading.

ing children to talk and, eventually, to talk in ways that approach standard American English (11).

2. The goals of each language arts program should match what the children are ready to learn. Consequently no arbitrary achievement expectations should be established. Whenever they are, either boredom or frustration are inevitable consequences.
3. Because goals should be selected in relation to readiness, teachers need to know what the achievement possibilities are for all the language arts. Thus—to cite one illustration—a kindergarten teacher needs to know much more about the content of reading instruction than she is ever likely to teach. The "extra" allows her to make appropriate choices and, too, to see connections between what she is doing and what will be taught in subsequent years.
4. When goals are selected on the basis of what children are ready to learn, small-group instruction becomes a necessity. Without teaching assistants, this is difficult to achieve but worth the effort it takes.
5. With young children, language arts goals pervade the whole of a school program. In addition to the special periods of time allotted for them, other areas of the curriculum—art and music, for instance—are viewed as means for achieving them, too.
6. The best instructional materials include some of the "homemade" variety. These allow for a close match between children and instruction. They can also take advantage of the children's favorite topic: themselves.

With this review of basic guidelines in the background, attention will now go to some of the practical considerations for programs beyond the kindergarten level. For instance, what about a daily schedule? Assuming that other curriculum areas will be tapped for their contributions, what time should be specifically allotted to the language arts?

DAILY SCHEDULES

To promote integration of all the language arts, some subscribe to one large block of time referred to in a schedule as "Language Arts." The length of such a period would be affected by what else has to be accomplished and, too, by the requirements of each school system. Some teachers work well within the broad focus; nonetheless it is probably accurate to say that most feel more secure and do a better job when prescribed periods of time are set aside for areas like reading, spelling, writing, and so on.

When separate periods are used, do they invariably lead to a separation of what in fact are closely related concerns? Not at all. Actually, when disconnected instruction does take place, it generally is the result not of separate periods but of a teacher who has separated the language arts in her own thinking. Consequently the separation that makes a difference is not what appears on paper or in a plan book but what characterizes the teacher's outlook.

With separate periods, assurance that connections among the language arts will be taken advantage of can be built in. For example, one teacher might label a certain period "Writing" and, during that time, carry on a combination of writing and phonics instruction much like that described in Chapter 8. Another might teach in a school requiring use of a spelling workbook which happens to give much attention to letter sounds and spelling patterns. For that reason she extends the period called "Spelling" in order to deal with that but also with phonics. In turn, both of these enter the period set aside for instruction in manuscript writing in the sense that choices for letters to be practiced are partially based on what is getting attention during the spelling-phonics period. Also entering into the writing period are the words taught during "Reading," for they are the ones the children practice writing.

In still another school another teacher might decide against using an optional language workbook in which capitalization and punctuation are introduced. Instead, she uses simple material composed by the children (with her help) to teach about both and also to bridge the gap between spoken and written language. And so the variations go. Characterizing them all is a teacher who began with goals for all the language arts and then combined them into a meaningful whole.

CLASSROOM ORGANIZATION *

Getting a classroom organized for instruction has at least two things in common with putting together a daily schedule: (a) both require attention at the beginning of a school year, and (b) decisions about them are always tentative in the sense that the changes which occur during the course of a year often create the need for adjustments in both.

With classroom organization—as with so many other facets of teaching—the first point meriting attention is that there is no such thing as one best kind for all teachers and all children. This is not to say that all kinds are equally good. In fact, because the reason for any organization is to permit individualized instruction, only those which are in-

* A much more detailed discussion of this topic constitutes Chapter 7 in *Teaching Them to Read* (6).

strumental in achieving that goal merit the description "good." To those of you who are now teaching and thus make use of some type of organization, this offers a criterion for judging its quality: To what degree does it facilitate instruction that is a match for all the children?

If it happened that all the children in a classroom were identical in such relevant factors as family background, prior learnings, interests, abilities, and personality, classroom organization could be listed among the easier matters to deal with. As it is, differences rather than similarities are characteristic. Because they are, organization—or, if you will, the logistics of instruction—is a topic of both great and immediate importance.

General Achievement Differences

Because organization is a means for dealing with differences, the kinds likely to exist within a classroom become the bases for organizational decisions. With reading, the most apparent difference relates to general achievement. Put into the framework of graded materials like the basal readers, this same point could be made by saying that some children in a classroom might be able to read preprimers, others will be able to handle a primer, while still others might read well enough for a first reader. Or it could happen that one group is just ready to start the first preprimer, while in the same room other individuals are sufficiently advanced that they are ready for second grade material. The point of all this is that in every classroom, children will be reading at a variety of general achievement levels. Because these are the easiest to identify when a school year is just underway, classroom organization usually starts with decisions for establishing several small instructional groups, often called "subgroups," each comprised of children reading at approximately the same general level.

Identifying General Achievement Levels

Various procedures are possible for identifying the general achievement level of each child; what is actually used often depends upon the practices of a particular school. In one it might be that kindergarteners are given continuous opportunities to begin to read. As a result, most do. Consequently another practice is for kindergarten teachers to pass on information about the children's accomplishments including, for example, the fact that some completed two preprimers (or their equivalent) while others went through three and are ready to start at a primer level. Still other information might deal with the letters and sounds they know and whether or not time was given to writing instruction. If it did get attention, samples of the children's printing might also be passed along.

In another school it could happen that first grade teachers receive no information. They know their kindergartens do nothing with reading—not even simple work with letters. They also are aware that the family background of the children hardly suggests that an activity like reading would be either prized or emphasized at home. For those two reasons, first grade teachers in this school assume the children cannot read—although they always look out for individuals who might have begun—and so they start the year by organizing instructional groups simply on the basis of numbers. For instance in each room three groups might be formed, all comprised of about eight children. Because teachers are expected to use a certain basal reader series, each group starts with its beginning materials. Not many weeks pass, however, before different children are making different progress. Therefore new subgroups, now based on achievement, are organized.

In still another school, much is done in kindergarten with all the language arts. However no written records are kept. One consequence is that first grade teachers have only lunchroom comments to go by. They are enough to suggest that some kindergarteners learned everything that was ever taught, while others retained very little. This is why these first grade teachers use the beginning weeks of the school year to carry on what are usually called "informal basal reader tests." Whatever the label and whatever materials are used, the purpose is to learn about each child's general achievement level by having him read brief selections from materials of increasing difficulty. Once he begins to make errors and have problems, it is assumed his instructional level has been reached. (To review the meaning of "instructional level" and related terms, see pages 301–302.) In the framework of classroom organization, his general achievement level has been identified. Having this information for each child allows these first grade teachers to make intelligent—but still tentative—decisions about general achievement subgroups. It also enables them to select appropriate materials.

Special Needs Differences

What becomes apparent next, as a teacher works with subgroups, is that children who are fairly alike in general achievement are not always alike in particular needs. And that is to be expected, for what contributes or adds up to the same general achievement can be different for different children. One might have reached what we will call a primer level because of his wonderful memory. Tell him a word once, and he never forgets it. Phonic skills, on the other hand, do not come so easily. What he needs, therefore, is some special help with decoding to insure continuous progress and maximum independence. Another child—she is in the same general achievement subgroup—has considerably more trouble remembering words; however, what got her to the primer level is her skill in analyzing unknown words. What she seems to need, therefore, is much, much practice with words that are important but whose spellings are irregular.

Other kinds of special needs are likely to be identified, too. Perhaps a teacher might begin to notice that certain children in two different general achievement subgroups read everything so quickly they rarely give correct answers to comprehension questions. It might also be observed that some of the children in the highest achievement group do everything they are asked to do, and correctly, but show little interest in reading books on their own. What they need, therefore, is someone—or something—to spark their interest in independent reading.

Once needs like these are identified, a classroom organization has to begin to incorporate some combination of general-achievement and special-needs groupings. How might this be done? Differently by different teachers. Let us see what one chose to do.

In this teacher's classroom the period scheduled for reading combines use of basal readers and supplementary phonics materials. At the start of the year this instructional time was divided among three general achievement subgroups. For each, goals pertained to the extension of reading vocabularies, the teaching of phonics, and simple comprehension skills.

Although the time set aside for manuscript writing involved working with the entire class, differences in ability were still recognized and accommodated. When letters were practiced, different ones were often selected for different children. The same was true for words.

It happened that required spelling instruction did not begin until second grade. However, for use with an unusually able and mature group of six children—they were immediately successful with every phase of learning to read—this teacher was able to obtain spelling workbooks that gave considerable attention to spelling patterns and thus to phonics. With a little help each day, the six were able to complete the book themselves. Meanwhile, their teacher was free to give the remaining children additional help—sometimes review—with phonics or structural analysis or, perhaps, the difficult but important service words.

On the surface it would appear that this particular teacher only employed general achievement subgroups. Actually, however, she was using them plus special needs groupings plus special assignments. As so often is the case, special needs in this room included both extra help *and* extra challenge.

In another room the organization looked quite different—though still aiming for a maximum of individualized instruction. Here, after the first month of school, the teacher scheduled general achievement subgroupings for three days a week, while frequently changing special-needs groups met on the other two. As a result, Wednesday—one of the days set aside for special needs instruction—might find this teacher abandoning commercial materials to work on quick recognition of a selected group of service words with some children; on simple comprehension tasks with others; and on creating interest in the library corner and in independent reading with still another group. By Friday, another time set aside for special needs instruction, she might still be working on service words with some children; on the ways in which punctuation helps with comprehension with another group; and on structural analysis and word meanings with still other children. The next week brings still more help with special needs, although by then both the groups and the needs might be different.

What these two illustrations of classroom practices are able to demonstrate is that there is no single best way to deal with the differences invariably found among children assigned to the same grade and same classroom. Such factors as earlier learnings, available materials, number of children, and the ability of the teacher enter into decisions and result in different details. Nonetheless, in every case decisions should eventually add up to an organization that allows a teacher to carry on instruction that matches what the children need and are ready to learn. Without that, the inevitable result can only be the not-so-sweet combination of both bored and frustrated children.

A SAMPLE LESSON

The variety of procedures that can constitute a "lesson" has been dealt with in the chapters on writing, whole word identification, and phonics and structural analysis. This section deals with lessons again, this time within the framework of classroom organization.

To put the discussion into that framework, let me begin by showing on page 408 how one teacher scheduled time for the language arts. (Expectedly, there would be changes as both the school year and the children's abilities progressed. For instance, the future would show less time allotted for manuscript writing and more for creative writing done by the children. Another predictable change would be less attention to whole word identification and, subsequently, closer ties between the reading and phonics periods. Not reflected in the schedule, either, is this teacher's generous use of homemade materials. Nor does it show how she sometimes eliminates writing in order to extend the reading period, es-

Period	Frequency	Usual Materials	Usual Concerns
Reading	Daily	Basal readers, workbooks, teacher-made assignments	1. Developing reading vocabularies through whole word identification, phonics, and structural analysis 2. Simple comprehension tasks 3. Extending listening-speaking vocabularies
Phonics	Daily	Phonics-writing workbook, commercial ditto sheets, teacher-prepared sheets	1. Letter sounds 2. Phonic substitutions 3. Writing letters, words, and brief sentences
Writing	Mon., Wed., Fri.	Manuscript paper, pencils	1. Skill in manuscript writing 2. Review and use of letter sounds
Free Choice *	Tues, Thurs.	Books, small chalkboards, manuscript paper and pencils, games, dot-to-dot pictures, reading-coloring pages, bulletin-board displays, etc.	1. Practice through self-selected activities 2. Free time for teacher to work with individual children
Storytime	Daily	Storybooks; sometimes alphabet or numeral books	1. Enjoyment 2. Stimulating children's interest in learning to read 3. Extending listening-speaking vocabularies

* What is made available for free choice generally is something that was first used under the supervision of the teacher. This is to insure correct use when the children work alone.

pecially when subgroups are brought together to work on special needs. Essentially, then, what a schedule-on-paper never communicates is the flexibility that is essential for productive teaching. To be noted, too, is that a schedule which is right for one classroom might be entirely wrong for another because of differences in teacher, children, and materials.)

Assumed in this description of a sample lesson is that this particular teacher is required to use basal readers; however she is wise and secure enough to view their manuals not as a source of prescriptions but, rather, of suggestions which can be followed, ignored, supplemented, or adapted. Also assumed is that the lesson takes place during the reading period and is carried on with a general achievement group of eight children.

Because a basal reader and its workbook are to be used, the children carry their copies of both to a kidney-shaped table. (The table replaces the customary small chairs, thus eliminating the need for children to hold materials in their laps.) Automatically, both readers and workbooks are placed under the chairs. The children then seat themselves around the table, all in a position to see the chalkboard behind it. (A lesson usually does not begin with either the reader or workbook; for that reason they are put under chairs as a way of minimizing distractions. If there is a need for pencils, the teacher will distribute them when they are to be used—no sooner.)

Once the teacher gets all the children to look at the board, she writes three letters:

Guided by the teacher's questions, the children name them and recall their sounds. Next, three unfamiliar words are written as on page 410. The teacher tells the children that the story they will be reading is about a puppy, and that one of the three words on the board says "puppy." She reminds them to think of its beginning sound so that they will know which one it is. Quickly, they tell her it is the last one. The teacher identifies the other two words, then erases them so that all the attention can go to *puppy,* which is named, spelled, and renamed. One child comments about all the *p*'s in *puppy*. A few others tell about puppies they have owned.

Next the teacher writes a familiar word:

Once *get* is identified by the children, the teacher writes *p* and has them recall its sound again. Then she shows:

She comments about *pet* being a new word, and that it is different from *get* only in the first letter. Asking, "Can someone tell me the new word?" she quickly hears "pet" from all. The question, "Do you know what a 'pet' is?" leads to more discussion about pets at home—some a little unusual and probably imaginary.

The teacher then tells the children that the story they will be reading is about a puppy who wished to be a pet, but nobody wanted him because he had—and then the following is written:

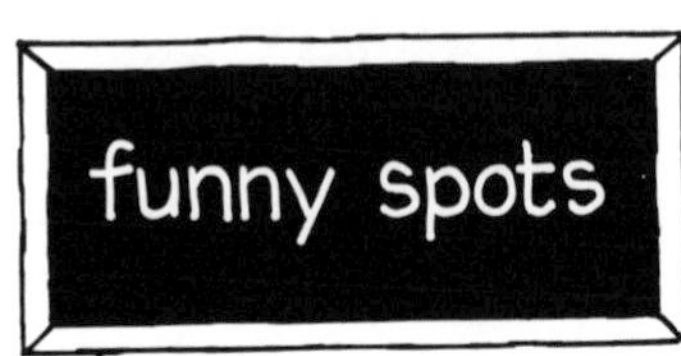

The familiar word *funny* is quickly identified, but *spots* brings silence. Consequently the teacher writes another familiar word:

Moving from the known word (*got*) to the new one (*spots*) is accomplished through a series of questions about:

Once identified, spelled, and discussed, *spots* is left on the board while the other words are erased. Then, to review the new words, the teacher writes and the children reidentify:

* In reviewing words like this, it generally is best to present them in a sequence that is different from the one used when they were originally introduced. This is to discourage children from using sequence rather than the words themselves as a prompt for their responses.

To provide practice with the new words in context, the teacher has prepared cards displaying sentences like:

The puppy is little.

A puppy can have spots.

This puppy has brown spots.

With each card, the children are directed to think of the sentence and then one is asked to read it aloud. (Generally, silent reading precedes oral reading.)

Having introduced the new words and reviewed others, the teacher asks that readers be opened to page 47. Knowing the children will look at the illustrations, she allows time for that. While they discuss them among themselves, she distributes dittoed copies of the sheet shown on page 413. As the children look at the assignment sheet, they are reminded to read the questions before they start the story. (The nature of the questions should affect the kind of reading that ought to be done. Therefore, questions are read first.) To be sure all of them can be read, she has the group go over each one silently; then individuals read them aloud. The children also are told that the story at the bottom of the dittoed page is about still another puppy whose picture is to be drawn on the other side of the assignment sheet. Next, pages 15 and 16 in the workbooks are examined with attention going to the directions for doing them. Finally, the sequence for completing the assigned work is reviewed: Read questions. Read story silently. Think about answers to questions. Do page 15 and 16 in workbook. Read story about another puppy. Draw his picture on back of paper.

With that, the group leaves the table to begin the silent reading and independent assignments. Later, both the questions and the drawings will be discussed. Meanwhile, another general achievement subgroup sits around the reading table in preparation for its lesson.

It is possible that the one just described raised questions about independent assignments and about oral and silent reading. How the teacher arrived at certain decisions might be still another question. Let

①

1. Why is the puppy unhappy?
2. How many boys and girls say they do not want him?
3. Who gets the puppy?
4. Why does he take this puppy?

②

Workbook: 15,16

③

A Puppy

This puppy is a pet. He is little and he is running. He has funny spots. Some are brown. Some are black. Some spots are very little, but some are big.

me deal with that first, beginning with decisions about the new vocabulary.

NEW VOCABULARY

The basal reader manual indicated three new words (*puppy, pet, spots*) appeared in the story, "The Funny Puppy," and suggested they be identified for the children. However, because these children had received more phonics instruction than yet appeared in this basal series, they were able to decode both *pet* and *spots* through consonant substitutions and additions. Although not sufficiently skilled to figure out *puppy,* knowledge of the sound of *p* was nonetheless put to use. Thus, contrary to manual suggestions, only one of the three new words was identified directly and even with that there was a reference to the sound recorded by its initial letter.

PRACTICE WITH NEW WORDS

In addition to naming, spelling, and discussing the new words, the children identified them in sentences printed beforehand on cards. Actually, the manual had suggested that sentences be written on the chalkboard or assembled in the word-card pocket holder. However, this teacher had learned from previous experiences that preparing them before a lesson began resulted in additional time for practice. Further opportunities to identify the new words would come when the children read the story silently and when they completed the two workbook pages. They also appeared in that part of their assignment which described another puppy.

COMPREHENSION PRACTICE

Even though the manual suggested asking questions about every page of text, this teacher asked only four for the entire story. She felt the reduction was justified because of the uncomplicated plot. She also had learned that asking too many questions impedes rather than promotes comprehension. Further, other comprehension tasks would be dealt with in one of the workbook pages, and again when the children read the description of the second puppy in order to draw his picture.

ILLUSTRATIONS

That much of the story was told through illustrations was still another reason for asking fewer questions than the manual proposed.

Knowing that the children would look at them—whether or not they were supposed to—was the reason why time was allotted for examining and discussing all the pictures that went with the story. On the assumption that the children could "read" pictures as well as herself, the teacher did not turn looking-at-pictures into a big production, which is what manuals sometimes come close to doing.

WORKBOOK ASSIGNMENT

As the manual suggested, two workbook pages were assigned because they provided the children with practice in both word identification and comprehension.

INDEPENDENT ASSIGNMENTS

In this chapter's discussion of classroom organization but more explicitly in its description of a sample lesson, the need for children to work independently some of the time became apparent. That such work should always be "meaningful," "interesting," "productive," etc., is easy to say and equally easy to accept. What is difficult is to come up daily with independent assignments ("seat work") that do in fact have these laudatory characteristics. While the activities which have been suggested throughout this textbook should help, there is no pretense about their offering all the ideas a teacher will ever need for assignments. Yet, combined with still other suggestions that might come from magazines and journals as well as other teachers, they should at least be a start. Some additional comments now should provide still further help in thinking about them.

The first is the reminder that most subject matter areas have something to do with reading; even beginning mathematics, for instance, requires some. Consequently independent assignments can relate to subjects like mathematics as well as to the language arts per se.

Another reminder pertains to the availability—and helpfulness—of long-term assignments. For example, one on-going concern for all in a class might be the development of phonics scrapbooks in which both magazine and child-made pictures are used to illustrate sounds. Scrapbooks also can help when listening-speaking vocabularies are the concern. At another time a long-term project might be the preparation of alphabet books like those commercially available. And then there always is the hope that another persistent "project" will be free reading. An obvious advantage of all long-term projects is the way they can keep children profitably occupied for more than one reading period. Combined with shorter assignments, they also provide a variety that makes independent work more pleasant.

Still other variety should come from the content of assignments. For example, knowing that one requires a fair amount of writing, a teacher might deliberately couple that assignment with another which has the children color, cut, and paste.

Whenever more than one assignment is given—and that generally is the best procedure—care must be taken to see to it that children have reminders of their various responsibilities. In the sample lesson, the typed dittoed sheet offered help with what was to be done as well as the order for doing it. Without another lesson, help might come from a simple listing like:

1. Reader: pages 53–60
2. Questions
3. Workbook: page 23
4. *st* paper

Such a list could be written on a chalkboard or, better yet, on chart paper placed in an easel located close to the group of children who will be using it.

How these independent assignments are combined with teacher-directed instruction can be illustrated by using the sample lesson ("The Funny Puppy") which was carried on with a general achievement sub-group while the rest of the class worked alone. "Doing what?" you are probably wondering.

The lesson was for the first group to work with the teacher. Earlier, she had shown the whole class several commercial alphabet books in order to suggest ideas for the ones they were now making. (This is the current long-term project.) For every letter whose sound has been taught, each child prints a page of lowercase and capital letters and then draws a page of pictures whose names start with it. The letter for this particular day is *n*. Along with showing the alphabet books, therefore, the teacher reviews its sound as well as how its lowercase and capital forms are made. (Both had been practiced several weeks earlier during the writing period.)

While members of the first instructional group get themselves organized at the reading table and the second starts printing rows of *n*'s, the third group is given a structural-analysis assignment sheet (singular-plural nouns) along with directions for doing it. In this classroom, therefore, the reading period on this particular morning divides as is shown at the top of the next page.

Instructional Group I	Instructional Group II	Instructional Group III
1. Works with teacher.	1. Works on alphabet book.	1. Completes structural-analysis assignment.
2. Completes assignments related to basal reader.	2. Works with teacher.	2. Works on alphabet book.
3. Works on alphabet book, if time allows.	3. Completes assignments related to basal reader.	3. Works with teacher.

When this reading period ends, the third instructional group has assignments which follow from its work with the teacher. Completing them allows more opportunities for special needs instruction during the next period (Phonics) because only Instructional Groups I and II will be involved, at least at the start.

On subsequent days this teacher will use a different sequence for meeting with general achievement groups. And, of course, other teachers in other classrooms will be found working in still different ways. In each, however, individualized instruction ought to prevail because of (a) the way the classroom is organized; (b) the kinds of materials that are selected; and (c) the kinds of assignments that are given.

ORAL AND SILENT READING *

The sample lesson described earlier is useful for dealing with another important question: When should reading be silent and when should it be oral?

Predictably, if readers of this textbook were to think back to the time when they themselves were learning to read, they would visualize lessons in which one child read aloud while the others were told to follow the same material silently. This oral-silent reading routine can still be found but, fortunately, with a little less frequency than was once the case. Why it should not be found at all will be explained through comments about two major differences between oral and silent reading.

Differences between Oral and Silent Reading

The most obvious difference has to do with vocalization. The second is less apparent, for it concerns eye movements. Because these two differences have implications for teaching, both will be discussed.

* For a much more detailed consideration of oral and silent reading, see Chapter 8 in *Teaching Them to Read* (6).

Vocalization. Obviously, to read orally is to vocalize. In contrast, the best silent reading is devoid even of subvocalization. What is subvocalization?

It refers to that inner, mental pronunciation of words which, though unobservable, is very real to the person doing the subvocalizing. Probably we all do it some of the time; thus we all are personally aware not only of its existence but also of the way it impedes the rate of our silent reading.* An assumption of this textbook is that one reason why all or almost all of us do subvocalize is that all or almost all of us spent many days in classrooms in which the oral-silent reading combination referred to earlier was *the* routine for teaching reading. Just how that routine and subvocalization might be connected will be dealt with later. For now let me introduce into this discussion the second major difference between oral and silent reading.

Eye Movements. Because reading is visual, eyes are busy whether one is reading aloud or silently. Prior to the existence of highly sensitive cameras, it was commonly believed that the eyes move steadily across each line of print during the reading process. Subsequent information from eye-movement films, however, changed all that (1, 5). Today it is recognized that a reader's eyes stop intermittently, a phenomenon referred to as a "fixation." These fixations or pauses are so brief they have to be measured in milliseconds (1/1000 sec.). In spite of their brevity, it is during fixations that all the seeing required by reading is done.

Another fact uncovered with the help of sophisticated cameras is that a reader's eyes sometimes move backwards—that is, in a right-to-left direction. This is called a "regression." Other but different backward movements are "return sweeps," caused by the need to go from right-to-left to begin each new line of text.

As a summary of what has been said thus far about eye movements, the following list of basic terms should be helpful:

Eye Fixation. Pause in eye movements when words are seen. Duration of a fixation is so brief it is measured in milliseconds.

Recognition Span. Number of words seen during fixation.

Eye Regression. Backward or right-to-left movement caused

* With extremely difficult material it is likely that some subvocalizing aids comprehension. With the more usual kinds of material, however, it should approach nonexistence. One further comment. The subvocalization being discussed is different from the very observable mumbling commonly done by beginners as they supposedly read "silently." Young children often think out loud. Therefore it is natural for them to read out loud, even when doing "silent reading." With increased skill, this disappears.

by such things as missed words and the multiple pronunciations of identically spelled words.

Return Sweep. The necessary right-to-left movement required by the start of each line of text.

Typically, as a child gains skill in silent reading, both fixations and regressions decrease in number. Improvement also is accompanied by shorter fixations (4). Thus, one way to describe mature silent reading is to say it is characterized by a minimal number of fixations and regressions and by fixations that are very brief.

What about oral reading? As with silent reading, eye movements of the oral reader show both fixations and regressions. But, they are different. How they differ can be explained with a reference to eye and voice spans.

During any instance of oral reading, both the voice and the eye are busy. Essentially they are busy with the same thing—words—but each is able to deal with them at different rates. The discrepancy causes something of a conflict, which is resolved as the eye yields unconsciously to the slower pace of the voice. With the accommodation, however, the eye is still active. For example, while it "waits" it also wanders and regresses. In fact, regressions in oral reading "operate to reduce the separation between the eyes and the voice" (1, p. 125). The eye also fixates longer than would be the case were the material being read silently.

With these facts in mind, eye-movement differences can be summarized by saying that if a person were to read the same material both orally and silently, his oral reading would inevitably show more regressions and, too, fixations that were greater in number and longer in duration.

Implications of Differences

For teachers, the obvious implication of these eye-movement differences is the need to avoid for silent readers whatever might inflict upon them the less efficient eye-movement pattern required in oral reading. That such a need is disregarded when children are habitually expected to follow silently what another is reading orally seems too obvious to warrant an explanation.

The difference related to vocalization also has relevance for instruction. Again it has to do with avoidance; this time of situations that encourage silent readers to pronounce words much like the oral reader must do. For still a second reason, therefore, the oral-silent reading combination found in so many classrooms must be questioned in that it could be fostering exactly what is not wanted: subvocalization during silent reading.

Surprisingly, the connections and problems just mentioned have almost been completely bypassed by researchers as topics for investigation. One study by Gilbert has suggested the correctness of what was said about eye movements (8). However, one piece of research is hardly enough to establish facts. Without them, I can only suggest that the oral-silent reading combination still characterizing so much of our instruction in reading is likely to result in flaws in silent reading in the form of unnecessary subvocalization and inefficient eye movements. That it makes little sense for the oral reader can be shown by underscoring the various functions oral reading serves.

FUNCTIONS OF ORAL READING

In the everyday life of an adult, oral reading is relatively uncommon. In fact, it seems safe to predict that readers of this textbook would find it difficult to recall the last time they had to read something aloud. Perhaps it was a weather report or a newspaper headline or, maybe, a phone number. In any case, the material probably was brief and the reading was done to share its content with someone else.

In school, sharing is one of the reasons to have oral reading. It is done so that the reader has a chance to communicate to others—one or more others—what he has learned or found or simply enjoyed. Such a purpose immediately establishes some important guidelines for teachers to keep in mind: (a) The oral reader should have read and comprehended the material silently before he reads it to others; and (b) the oral reader should have an audience—again one or more listeners—that is unfamiliar with what is being read.

Still another reason to have oral reading in school has to do with materials. Here I refer to the fact that the nature of certain kinds requires it. For example, the part of a play found on page 421 exemplifies a kind that calls for a group of children, now characters in a story, to take turns reading aloud. With more advanced material, certain poems will be found that were written as much for their sound as their sense and thus are only fully appreciated and enjoyed when read aloud. Often, something like choral reading (also referred to as "group reading," "choral speaking," and "verse choir") enhances this kind of material and, at the same time, improves oral reading ability.*

A third reason for oral reading has to do with the need for verifi-

* For those interested, two items in the list of references at the end of this chapter (2, 3) offer teachers specific help with choral reading.

THE STORY OF THE THREE BEARS

ACT ONE: In the bears' house

Storyteller: Once a long time ago there were three bears. They lived in the big woods. They liked to eat porridge for their breakfast.

Mother: Come, Father Bear and Baby. The porridge is ready.

Baby: I am bringing my wee chair to sit in. Come, Father Bear.

Father: Coming, Baby Bear, coming. I must get my shoes on.

Mother: Bring your big chair when you come.

43

From *Happy Sounds,* by Mildred A. Dawson and Georgiana Newman, p. 43. Copyright 1969 by Benefic Press.

cation. An example of this occurred in the sample lesson ("The Funny Puppy") described earlier. You will recall that the teacher had individual children read questions aloud in order to verify that they could be read so that eventually they could be answered. Another type of verification might be necessary after a group has read something silently—for instance, a basal reader story. It could happen that several children offer different and even conflicting answers for the same question. As a result, each might be asked to read aloud that part of the story which prompted his particular response.

The final reason for having oral reading in school is essentially different from all the others. In turn, this establishes different guidelines for it. This last reason relates to the fact that oral reading can be a means for learning about a child's specific abilities and, in particular, his specific problems in learning to read. Thus, it can begin to provide answers to questions like: What does this reader do when he gets to an unfamiliar word? Does he use what he knows about phonics and structural analysis? Is he overly dependent upon contextual help? Does he use or ignore punctuation? Is he willing to substitute one word for another? Does he tend to omit words—even important ones?

Within this framework, the reason for oral reading is diagnosis. That is, not being clairvoyants, teachers sometimes need to use oral reading to learn about a child's silent reading. Such instances of diagnosis do not occur in classrooms as often as they should, because of the lack of time and opportunities. In reading clinics, where there are more teachers and fewer students, they are the rule rather than the exception.

The reproduced material shown on page 423 illustrates how a teacher might record various kinds of errors, when oral reading is being used for diagnostic purposes. The summary sheet on page 424 also indicates what can be learned about silent reading by listening carefully to a child who is reading orally.*

Although hardly a daily occurrence, oral reading done for diagnosis has requirements that teachers need to keep in mind. Essentially they are two. First, the material should be unfamiliar to the child because the purpose is to learn what he is able to do without a "rehearsal." Second, this oral reading should be carried on as privately as circumstances permit to avoid possible embarrassment.

To emphasize the different requirements for oral reading done for

* Earlier (page 405) the use of oral reading to learn about general achievement levels was mentioned. When that is the goal the focus is less detailed and the diagnostic period is shorter. That type of diagnosis, you will recall, is often referred to as an "informal basal reader test" because basal readers are commonly used for the graded material it requires. The more detailed diagnosis being discussed now is usually referred to as a "reading inventory."

The following symbols will enable the teacher to quickly record the type of word recognition errors made during the oral reading:

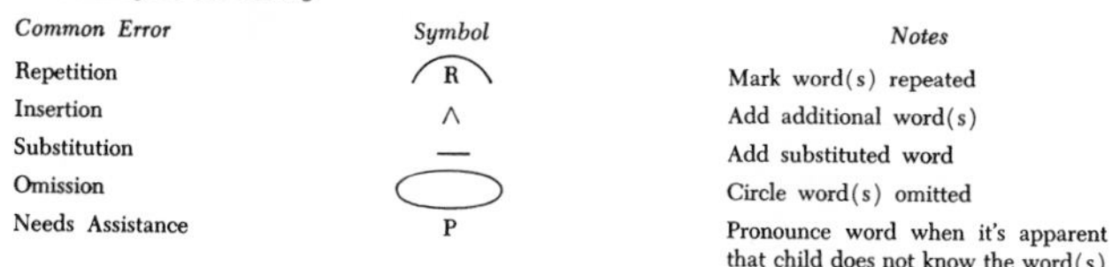

Common Error	*Symbol*	*Notes*
Repetition	⁀R⁀	Mark word(s) repeated
Insertion	^	Add additional word(s)
Substitution	—	Add substituted word
Omission	⬭	Circle word(s) omitted
Needs Assistance	P	Pronounce word when it's apparent that child does not know the word(s)

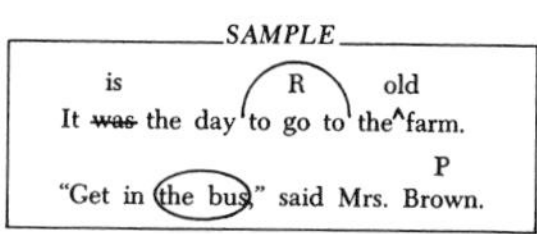

SAMPLE
is R old
It ~~was~~ the day to go to the^farm.
P
"Get in the bus," said Mrs. Brown.

Observe the child's general reaction while reading. If frustrated, he is likely to manifest excessive head movement and pointing, tension, a slow-labored rate of reading, or a soft whispered voice. It is recommended that the oral reading be stopped at or before the child reaches this point.

COMPREHENSION

After each oral selection the child is asked to answer five questions about what he has just read. The questions deal with the facts, inferences and vocabulary contained in each selection. The questions for each selection are in the separate Inventory Record and labeled; F (fact), I (inference) and V (vocabulary). Answers provided for each question are merely guides or probable answers to the question. Therefore, the teacher must judge the adequacy of each response made by the child.

Partial credit (½, ¼, etc.) is allowed for responses to questions. In some cases it is helpful to record the child's responses.

SCORING

WR (Word Recognition) COMP (Comprehension)

A scoring guide accompanies each oral selection. Each guide indicates the number of WR and COMP errors permitted within the limits of IND (independent), INST (instructional) and FRUST (frustration) levels of reading performance. Note (sample): each guide lists the number of errors permitted at each reading level. Therefore, the teacher must select the appropriate reading levels i.e., IND, INST, FRUST, based on the child's *actual errors* and the *suggested error limits* for each reading level.

SAMPLE

Scoring Guide: Second

WR Errors		COMP Errors	
IND	0	IND	0-1
INST	2-3	INST	1½-2
FRUST	5+	FRUST	2½+

xv

CHECKLIST OF READING DIFFICULTIES

A. Sight-Word Vocabulary

______Limited	______Slow, fumbling
______Adequate	______Adequate for Instructional Level
______Good	______Dependent upon context

B. Word Analysis Techniques

______Adequate	Uses phonics:
______Dependent upon spelling	______letter-by-letter
______Substitutes for meaning	______in larger units
	______slowly, laboriously
Weak in:	______easily, quickly
______consonant sounds	Guesses:
______consonant blends	______by general shape
______vowel sounds	______by first letters
______common syllables	______indiscriminately
______blending	

C. Oral Reading

General:	Excessive errors in:
______head movements	______additions
______loses place easily	______omissions
______ill at ease, tense	______repetitions
______points to words	______substitutions
______indifference or dislike toward reading	______words aided
______holds booklet incorrectly	______self-correction

27

diagnosis and for communication, the following contrast should be helpful:

ORAL READING

Communication	*Diagnosis*
1. Material should be pre-read silently.	1. Material should be unfamiliar.
2. Oral reader should have a genuine audience.	2. Reading should be done as privately as possible.

Keeping in mind the difference between oral and silent reading (vocalization and eye movements) and the two quite different functions of oral reading (communication and diagnosis) should allow for an even better understanding of why the oral-silent reading routine referred to earlier is a highly questionable practice when carried on day after day and year after year, which is the case in some schools.

Traditionally, this routine has been suggested in basal reader manuals as they presented a sequence for a lesson. Abbreviated it might look like this:

1. Readiness for story (motivation, new vocabulary)
2. Silent reading and questions
3. Oral reading of same material (One child reads aloud; others are expected to be reading the material silently)
4. Follow-up activities

Because of the foregoing discussion, all the possible flaws in Step 3 should now be apparent. Looked at from the point of view of all the silent readers, it probably is encouraging them to subvocalize and to adopt the less efficient eye-movement pattern of the oral reader. Neither consequence is desirable.

Looked at from the point of view of the child reading aloud, the procedure is somewhat puzzling and, in a sense, doubly questionable. That is, if his oral reading is for communication, the obvious flaw is the lack of a genuine audience because the other children have already read what he is now reading aloud. If, to the contrary, the oral reading is for diagnosis, then other problems exist. First, the material has been rehearsed and, second, the situation is not as private as diagnosis requires.

Do all these comments suggest that oral reading in classrooms should be completely outlawed? Not really. Although it ought to be much less common than is typically the case, there *are* times when beginners will and should be reading aloud. For instance, much instructional time at this level goes to the development of reading vocabularies. As a result, children commonly read and decode words aloud.

In addition, there will be times when the need for verification requires oral reading. In the sample lesson, silently read questions were later read aloud by individuals as a way of making sure that all could manage them. If it happened, in the same lesson, that one child drew a picture of a puppy who had brown spots or, perhaps, no spots at all, he might be asked to read aloud the three sentences which suggested something else. This would help to find out whether his problem is inadequate vocabulary or careless reading.

Sometimes, but not often at the beginning level, the nature of material will also call for oral reading. The part of a play reproduced earlier on page 421 exemplifies this. Another page from the same book (see page 427) shows riddles which, again, could be read aloud by individual children. (This reproduced page is taken from the teacher's edition in order to show how it correctly reminds teachers to have the riddles read silently before individuals read them orally. Fortunately, it does *not* suggest that the children follow each riddle silently while it is being read aloud by one of them.)

You will recall that another reason for oral reading has to do with sharing. Among beginners, this should be fairly *un*common because few have enough skill to share effectively. Whenever oral reading is done for this purpose, what is read ought to be brief. Beforehand, it should have been read and comprehended silently. In fact, even among more advanced readers, oral reading done to share is not really the time for comprehending but, rather, for communicating to others what has already been comprehended.* At these more advanced stages, communication is facilitated by the correct pronunciation and careful enunciation of words, and by a suitable kind and amount of expression. I would like to suggest that all of this is as much caught as it is taught, making the oral reading teachers do especially important because it serves as a model which, for better or worse, is likely to be copied. One further reminder is that personality enters into oral reading as a very significant factor, which leads to the conclusion that not all children—no matter how well they read silently—will turn out to be magnificent oral readers. But, considering the small role played by oral reading in our everyday lives, this should not be of great concern to anyone. Yet it appears to be of considerable concern to some teachers and textbook authors.

* What happened when one boy was asked to summarize in his own words what he had just finished reading aloud with great gusto is relevant here. Unable to respond he explained, "I forgot to listen!" Now, as some linguists are suggesting that appropriate expression reflects successful comprehension (7), it is important to keep such an incident in mind to serve as a reminder about not taking every "linguistic proposal" too seriously.

RIDDLES riddles

Have silent reading first. Let each child choose which riddle to read.

Read one of the riddles out loud. See if the other children can guess the answer.

Advanced children may write out other riddles for classmates to read.

1. What has a head, but no eye?

2. What has an eye, but no head?

3. What has four legs but can't run?

4. What has a head but can't think?

5. What has a face but can't eat?

6. I am gray and brown. I live up in a tree. My ears are short. My tail is long and curls up over my back. I like nuts to eat.

Check on d, t, and k endings. 53

From *Happy Sounds,* by Mildred A. Dawson and Georgiana Newman, p. 53. Copyright 1969 by Benefic Press.

THE CLASSROOM ENVIRONMENT

From the huge amount of school visiting I have done, I would say that classrooms occupied by young children are generally very attractive and alive, which is exactly what they ought to be. Perhaps a few are a little too feminine. If so, that can be remedied or at least improved with bulletin boards devoted to themes like sports, machinery, cars and trucks, and moon explorers. Trade books dealing with topics of interest to boys also help and should be a part of every classroom collection of materials for free reading.

For both boys and girls, such a collection can be made a little more enticing when teachers take the time to arrange books attractively and in a way that helps children make appropriate choices. In some rooms, teachers add something like a question box from which slips can be drawn by the children. On each, clues are written about a particular book—these suggest which one it is. Following the descriptive clues are two or three questions that can be answered by reading the book.

Such a procedure could be combined with others. For example, time might be allotted—perhaps once a week or once every two weeks—for children to read to partners who, in turn, also read something from a book they selected earlier in the week. Still another way to promote free reading is to "advertise" certain books as they are added to a classroom's collection. This might be done by showing some of their illustrations or, perhaps, by reading just enough from them to create interest and curiosity. Whatever the device, every classroom should have collections of books and magazines from which children make their own selections.

In addition to these collections, there should be materials designed to help children remember what they have been learning. A large chart, for example, might display a series of rectangular pieces of construction paper of different colors. Beside each, the appropriate color word would be printed. Or, to help children remember the short vowel sounds, something like that at the top of page 429 might be displayed. How to make such self-help material maximally useful was explained earlier when teachers were reminded to demonstrate—by role-playing, for example—when and how it can be useful. How to make the same material maximally meaningful can be explained through a description of the practices of one second grade teacher.

Besides teaching school she was the mother of two children, one a four and the other a five year old. It was her practice to use large quantities of what this textbook has called "homemade" materials. For instance on one occasion she might collect interesting magazine pic-

Short Vowel Sounds		
A ă		apple
E ĕ		engine
I ĭ		Indian
O ŏ		octopus
U ŭ		umbrella

tures, each done in one dominant color. After pasting them on heavy chart paper, she would print the appropriate color words beside or under them. To be specially emphasized is that charts like this one commonly were made with the assistance of her own two children. They helped find pictures, reacted to various placements on the paper, and so on.

The next day the finished chart would be brought to school, but the children there were never as interested because, of course, they had *not* been involved in its production. The point of all this is that children tend to be more interested in materials which have been gradually assembled over time, in their presence and, perhaps, with their help. This explains why some very sophisticated commercial materials are quickly forgotten, even while less attractive homemade things maintain interest. It also underscores the need for teachers to make a distinction between preparations that have educational significance for children and those which do not. Without such distinctions it is possible to have some of the more valuable work go on in a teacher's home or before or after school.

While the children's lack of involvement in preparing materials can be one reason why they are soon forgotten and overlooked, there are other reasons for the waning interest, too. A common one is that they are displayed for too long. After awhile, and this also is true for adults, what is displayed is no longer seen by the children. It is as if it has blended in with the rest of the environment and no longer exists as something separate and apart. Every so often I have been in classrooms at the start of a school year and again at the end and have been both surprised and disappointed to find everything pretty much the same. This hardly reflects what a classroom ought to be: a lively, attractive environment that changes as the lives and learnings of the children change.

EXPECTATIONS FOR LANGUAGE ARTS PROGRAMS

What learnings can be expected from language arts programs? As with any program, a combination of factors will affect accomplishments. While the children themselves always are a key factor, I believe the teacher is even more critical in the sense that what they learn is so dependent upon what she does or does not do. That I have seen the behavior and responses of whole groups of children change—sometimes radically—as they move from one classroom to another is still a second reason for my placing great stress on the importance of the teacher.

Some of the many factors about a teacher that can affect young children's behavior and accomplishments were discussed in detail in Chapter 6. Meriting repetition is her need to be knowledgeable about the content of instruction. With instruction in reading, for instance, knowing much more than she is ever likely to teach places what she does teach in perspective and, in addition, allows her to make choices that provide the best of her pupils with appropriate challenge.

Still another important factor is the teacher's optimistic but not naive faith in the learning abilities of young children. My various contacts with teachers would suggest that those whose professional preparation came at a time when social and emotional needs received an almost exclusive attention probably need to work a little at expanding their expectations for academic accomplishments. After all, to expect little is to get little. Also in need of change are attitudes like the one reflected in a first grade teacher's comment, heard in early October: "I'd predict those two children will fail." Better to have heard something like, "I think both Bobby and Carol are going to have a hard time learning, but if I watch the pace of my instruction with them and also take advantage of their special interests, I'll probably be pleasantly surprised at all they know by the end of the year."

In addition to the teacher variable, other factors accounting for differences in accomplishments will lie with the children themselves. From my work with young ones engaged in the process of learning to read, I would say that the children most likely to succeed are those (a) whose parents are interested but *not too interested* in academic achievement; (b) who attend school regularly; and (c) whose long-term memory is good. On many occasions I have also been impressed with all that young children learn at home from older sisters who like to play school. Still one other very critical factor is what might be called, for a lack of a more descriptive name, "maturity." Here I refer indirectly to the fact that in just about every classroom there seems to be at least one child who learns very little because of what appears to be an inability to work alone and independently. These are the individuals who, instead of getting down to work, twist, turn, and wander. Presumably their restlessness and hyperactivity is caused by a variety of factors, few of which could be dealt with by a teacher. For that very reason, I have often wondered why their omnipresence has not prompted schools to hire assistants to supervise their independent work. Even one assistant for several teachers would make a considerable difference, especially if she had the privacy of a room to which restless children could be sent, not to be policed but to get the help, reminders, praise, and encouragement which they seem to require when working on assignments. When one thinks of the way money is spent in much less helpful ways, it does seem unfortunate that some very creative and conscientious teachers are denied the chance to develop maximally productive programs because of the unavailability of another adult. Hopefully there will come a time when this is no longer so.

In addition to teachers and the children themselves, still another factor affecting accomplishments is materials. This is especially true when instructional decisions are based on them rather than on what children are ready to learn. Here the comments of two teachers are worth repeating.

In the first instance I had been visiting a first grade and had the privilege of observing excellent instruction. During this relatively brief visit the teacher was working with a subgroup on consonant sounds. They were first reviewed, then used with great success by the children. Later, while complimenting the teacher, I commented, "I imagine you'll soon introduce those children to vowel sounds." Surprisingly her response was, "Oh no. Vowels are introduced in the second grade reader."

The other comment is a more recent one. In this case it was made by a first grade teacher who worked in a school which had recently switched from one set of basal readers to another. The second taught more and taught it earlier. After using the second series for several months this teacher commented, "The children know so much more!" What was unexpected was not the observation but, rather, the teacher's surprise that they did know more. What she seemed to have forgotten is what teachers should always remember: Children learn what they have the opportunity to learn.

REFERENCES

1. Anderson, I. H., and Dearborn, W. F. *The Psychology of Teaching Reading.* New York: The Ronald Press, 1952.
2. Arbuthnot, May Hill. *Children and Books.* Chicago: Scott, Foresman and Company, 1964.
3. ———, and Root, S. L. *Time for Poetry.* Glenview, Ill.: Scott Foresman and Company, 1968.
4. Buswell, G. T. *Fundamental Reading Habits: A Study of Their Development.* Supplementary Educational Monographs, No. 21. Chicago: University of Chicago Press, 1922.
5. Dodge, R., and Cline, T. S. "The Angle Velocity of Eye Movements, *Psychological Review,* VIII (March, 1901), 145–157.
6. Durkin, Dolores. *Teaching Them to Read.* Boston: Allyn and Bacon, Inc., 1970.
7. Fries, Charles C. *Linguistics and Reading.* New York: Holt, Rinehart and Winston, Inc., 1962.
8. Gilbert, L. C. "Effect on Silent Reading of Attempting to Follow Oral Reading," *Elementary School Journal,* XL (April, 1940), 614–621.
9. Guszak, Frank J. "Dilemmas in Informal Reading Assessments," *Elementary English,* XLVII (May, 1970), 666–670.
10. Lynn, R. "Reading Readiness and the Perceptual Abilities of Young Children," *Educational Research,* VI (November, 1963), 10–15.
11. Yonemura, Margaret. *Developing Language Programs for Young Disadvantaged Children.* New York: Teachers College Press, Columbia University, 1969.

IV

Parents

12

Parents and Reading

Anyone who has the chance to get to know young children in school learns very quickly that they are reflections of life at home. In fact, to know their families is to understand why certain children behave—and learn—as they do (6, 7, 8). Occasionally, of course, there are the surprises and the mysteries. Yet, on the whole, to know a family is to understand a young child better.

It is because of the special influence of the family upon young children that those responsible for their schooling need to be concerned about life at home. Admittedly, schools cannot do a great deal to change it. In addition, there are those who would say that the schools are already trying to do too much. However, even if both observations are accurate, they still are not a denial of the fact that helping parents is one of the best ways to help teachers do a better job in the classroom. With that goal in mind, it is strongly recommended that schools have procedures that make a contribution to parent education.

The special importance of the early years means that the best procedures will include home contacts when children are still *pre*schoolers. Under most circumstances these would amount to no more than a few group meetings. Still, a few good ones can be very helpful. Or, to put it somewhat differently, something is better than nothing.

Because the focus of this textbook is on what might be called the "academics," this chapter will deal in particular with topics for meetings which are concerned with that. However, at least in passing, the influence of parent behavior on child behavior will also be considered.

PARENTAL INFLUENCE ON CHILD BEHAVIOR

In many ways, parents are like teachers. I say this because what is involved in being a good parent becomes clear most quickly as questionable behavior is observed. For that reason, this section will focus on what is viewed to be undesirable behavior on the part of parents. Indirectly, then, it will outline some of the kinds of topics that merit serious discussion when parents and teachers get together at parent education programs or meetings. Like this chapter, such meetings cannot deal with everything that is important. Thus, only a little of what affects children's behavior in school will be discussed here.

What has a very visible effect relates to physical needs like sufficient rest and adequate meals. With children from poverty areas, too little sleep and poor nutrition might be expected. Yet, calling immediate attention to physical needs is the result of knowing far too many young children *from all socioeconomic levels* who habitually came to school either tired or hungry or both. Most explanations for the fatigue were identified quickly. All one had to do was listen to the children's conversations because inevitably they included comments about television programs shown the night before at a time when people their age should have been in bed and asleep. Reasons for a skimpy breakfast, or simply no breakfast, varied. Often, however, parents who got up too late to prepare a meal was the explanation.*

At first, spending time with parents discussing the connection between unmet physical needs and less-than-satisfactory behavior in school might seem like a waste of time. That is, it might seem that common sense is sufficient to understand how one is linked with the other. If this happens to be your thought at the moment, I can only say that common sense is not nearly as common as the name suggests. This is why the topic "Physical Needs and School Behavior" is recommended as one that ought to be at the top of parent meeting agendas.

* Why some young children are always late for school has the same explanation. This means they should be warmly welcomed by teachers, not chastised.

Equally basic but more difficult to communicate is the causal relationship between unmet emotional needs and undesirable behavior in school (15). Seemingly, what is not understood by many parents is that when a child's emotional needs are not satisfied by his family, he commonly uses the classroom situation to satisfy them rather than to learn what a curriculum offers. Often, the result is discipline problems.

While it is recognized that the reasons for insufficient affection and love at home are often both complex and obscure, some discussion with parents of the basic importance of "tender, loving care" might help, at least a little. Other discussions about the importance of acceptance and, in contrast, the problems related to such things as unfavorable sibling comparisons also are appropriate.

With some parent groups, attention to the method of discipline used at home might be called for because that is another factor that determines what a child is and becomes when he gets to school. Some homes, for example, have systems of bribery, not discipline. (I refer here to the practice of offering gifts and even money in return for "good" behavior.) As would be expected, these youngsters have something of a problem when they get to school, where rewards are not nearly so lucrative. Problems also await the child who lives in a home where expectations for behavior are inconsistent or where he has learned that parents can be manipulated. It is with these children that "testing the limits" becomes a way of life, taking up much of their energy and attention during the early weeks of a school year.

Clearly, many of the problems and shortcomings connected with "life at home" are complex. This points out that not even the best of parent education programs will be able to offer easy or quick solutions. Still, they can at least open up communication between the school and the home and, in the process, help teachers understand better the children who are their responsibility.

HOME–SCHOOL COMMUNICATION ABOUT THE ACADEMICS

Helping parents understand what is happening in school is still another important function of parent education programs. But, even before children enter its doors, certain topics can be discussed. These will be mentioned under the heading "At Home." Topics assuming importance once children start school will be considered later.

At Home

With any parent group that reads and believes newspapers as well as magazines like *Ladies' Home Journal* and *McCall's*, one topic deserving early discussion has to do with the influence of the environment on a child's eventual intelligence. As Chapter 2 pointed out, we have just recently passed through an era characterized by unprecedented excitement about the unique importance of the preschool years, in particular, about the need for them to be intellectually stimulating. Even though the psychology texts that promoted this were based simply on reinterpretations of old research (3, 10) and, in addition, even though their authors were careful to say the new interpretations were only hypotheses, what appeared subsequently in the popular press was anything but cautious. There, theories suddenly became facts as parents were encouraged to believe that something like genius is more the result of just the right early environment than of genetic endowment. Headlines and titles like "How Smart Do You Want Your Child to Be?" "How to Raise a Brighter Child," and, of course, "How to Teach Your Baby to Read" became commonplace (2, 5, 13). What also became common were overly anxious parents who, with all of the hullabaloo about the critical importance of early stimulation, turned their homes into schools.

When parent groups include individuals like this, there is a great need to help them understand the difference between theories and facts and, at the practical level, the difference between a home that is intellectually stimulating and one that goes overboard and becomes, in the process, intellectually suffocating.

This is not to suggest, by the way, that schools ought to return to their former practice of making parents feel guilty if they offered children any assistance with the academics before they started school. The position getting support in this textbook is that parents ought to be taught how they can help preschoolers in ways that are productive but also enjoyable, both for themselves and the children (7). Who else will do this, if the schools don't?

One of the things schools can do is to help parents understand how a child's success with reading is very much related to his prior—that is, his *pre*school experiences with books. Here I refer in particular to the importance of encouraging parents of young children to read to them in ways that are pleasurable for both child and adult. Specific help can come in the form of demonstrations which show how children should be read to, and how a book's illustrations might be used (12). A tour of the local library could help parents feel more at home there but, too, it can be a time to teach them about the kinds of stories that appeal to young children (1, 9). Learning about the location of suitable books and, if available, about the library's storytelling program would be still other outcomes of such tours.

Additional topics for discussion might again be considered common sense; still, reminders about them never hurt. In this case I refer to such matters as the significance of a child's listening-speaking vocabulary for reading and, therefore, of the importance of parents' talking with their children, answering their questions, and providing them with experiences which result in new vocabulary.* That language is as much caught as it is taught is something parents should be made aware of. In turn, this might encourage them to use it in a way that merits imitation.

The point of all these topics is that parents need not become school teachers. Rather, their greatest contribution is to give of themselves in the form of time spent with a child. Within such a framework, conversations, storytelling, and some special excursions now and again add up to the kinds of experiences that ready children for school and, in some instances, even begin to teach them to read.

What can also begin to teach a child is his own interest in learning to print (7). It is the possibility of such an interest, rather than the possibility of it leading to reading ability, that is the reason schools should teach parents how to print. One group lesson usually is enough, especially if they also are given a copy of the way letters will be taught, once the children get to school. This can be a one-page sheet showing all the letters, capital and lowercase, as well as the sequence for making each one. (See pages 220 and 221 for examples.) The thinking behind this recommendation is uncomplicated: (a) Some preschoolers are interested in learning to print; and (b) as with any other interest, parents should respond with correct help—in this instance, help that conforms to the way letters will be taught in school.

In School

By the time children are attending school, topics for parent meetings can deal more directly with reading. For instance, because parents are far removed in time from their own experiences with learning to read, they can profit first of all from a few reminders about some of the difficulties in becoming a reader. One very effective way to communicate about them is exemplified in a publication entitled, *Back to the First Grade Again!* (11). Written by Paul McKee, this is a preprimer for

* The need to help parents see the connection between ability in spoken language and ability in reading became especially apparent through the many phone calls which came from parents at the time my studies of preschool readers were being publicized (7). Inevitably they said they had very bright children—usually about three years old—and they wanted to know how they should go about teaching them to read. In my efforts to point out that the research pertained to children who had been interested in learning to read, not to parents who were interested in teaching them, I always tried to explain that teaching a young child the meaning of a word is just as significant as teaching him to read it. Although this appeared to fall on deaf ears, we need to continue efforts to make such connections clear to parents.

“V‡‡⊐, ⊥+⚲. V‡‡⊐ +Λ Λ⊏⊗ ⊔⊸X⊐. Ƨ‡⊸ ⊶+ΛX⊏ ⚲⊗ ⊥⊏‡‡Λ ⊏⊔⚲.”

⊥+⚲ ⊶+ΛX⊏⊗⊔ ⊔+⊔⊔Ƨ ⊥⊏‡‡Λ Λ⊏⊗ ⊔⊸X⊐. ⊏⊗ ⊶+ΛX⊏⊗⊔ Λ⊏⊗ ⊔⊸X⊐ Δ+VV.

“Ƨ‡⊸ ⊔⊔⊔ ⚲‡Λ ⊏+⊶⊗ Λ‡ ⊥⊏‡‡Λ,” V+⊸⋒⊏⊗⊔ ⊥+⚲. “Λ⊏⊗ Δ+VV ⊶‡⊸V⊔ ⊏+⊶⊗ ⊐⊔VV⊗⊔ ⊏⊔⚲.”

16

From *Back to the First Grade Again!* by Paul McKee. Copyright 1948 by Houghton Mifflin Company.

parents, page 16 of which is reproduced on page 440. In attempting to learn to read with its new and different alphabet, parents experience some of the problems children have. As a result, this should help them to be more patient and accepting at a time when both patience and acceptance are of considerable importance.

Still another topic to be dealt with at this point in time has to do with the details of a school's reading program. Presumably, each school does certain things in certain ways for certain reasons. In turn, at least some of these details ought to be explained to parents. It is their children and, after all, their tax money that supports the school. For both reasons, parents *have the right* to know:

What methods are used to teach reading, and why
What materials have been chosen, and why
What grouping procedures are used, and why

More generally, parents should know what the school is trying to accomplish and, secondly, how its staff has chosen to reach these selected goals. Other important matters pertain to the reporting system and to the role parents are to play in assisting their children at home.

Presumably, all such details about reading will be different for different schools. In addition, parents themselves will vary from one community to another. This can only mean that parent education programs will also be different. What should never vary, however, are school efforts to communicate with parents about reading. In fact, it is only when there is this communication that parents and teachers have the chance to be genuine partners in a most important endeavor: helping young children learn to read.

REFERENCES

1. Arbuthnot, May Hill. *Children's Reading in the Home*. Glenview, Illinois: Scott, Foresman and Company, 1969.
2. Beck, Joan. *How to Raise a Brighter Child*. New York: Trident Press, 1967.
3. Bloom, Benjamin S. *Stability and Change in Human Characteristics*. New York: John Wiley & Sons, 1964.
4. Davis, S. Elizabeth. "Parents and School Should Share," *Reading Teacher*, XXIII (May, 1970), 707–710.
5. Doman, Glenn. *How to Teach Your Baby to Read*. New York: Random House, 1964.
6. Durkin, Dolores. "A Case-Study Approach Toward an Identification of Factors Associated with Success and Failure in Learning to Read," *California Journal of Educational Research*, XI (January, 1960), 26–33.

7. Durkin, Dolores. *Children Who Read Early.* New York: Teachers College Press, Columbia University, 1966.

8. ———. "A Language Arts Program for Pre-First Grade Children: Two-Year Achievement Report," *Reading Research Quarterly,* V (Summer, 1970), 534–565.

9. Englehardt, Elizabeth. "A Pre-Reading Program," *Reading Teacher,* XXIII (March, 1970), 535–538.

10. Hunt, J. McVicker. *Intelligence and Experience.* New York: The Ronald Press Co., 1961.

11. McKee, Paul. *Back to the First Grade Again!* Boston: Houghton Mifflin Co., 1948.

12. Swift, Marshall S. "Training Poverty Mothers in Communication Skills," *Reading Teacher,* XXIII (January, 1970), 360–367.

13. Tunney, John V. "How Smart Do You Want Your Child to Be?" *McCall's* XCVIII (October, 1970), 62–64.

14. Wartenberg, Herbert. "Parents in the Reading Program," *Reading Teacher,* XXIII (May, 1970), 717–721.

15. Zigler, Edward. "The Environmental Mystique," *Childhood Education,* XXXXVI (May, 1970), 402–412.

Index